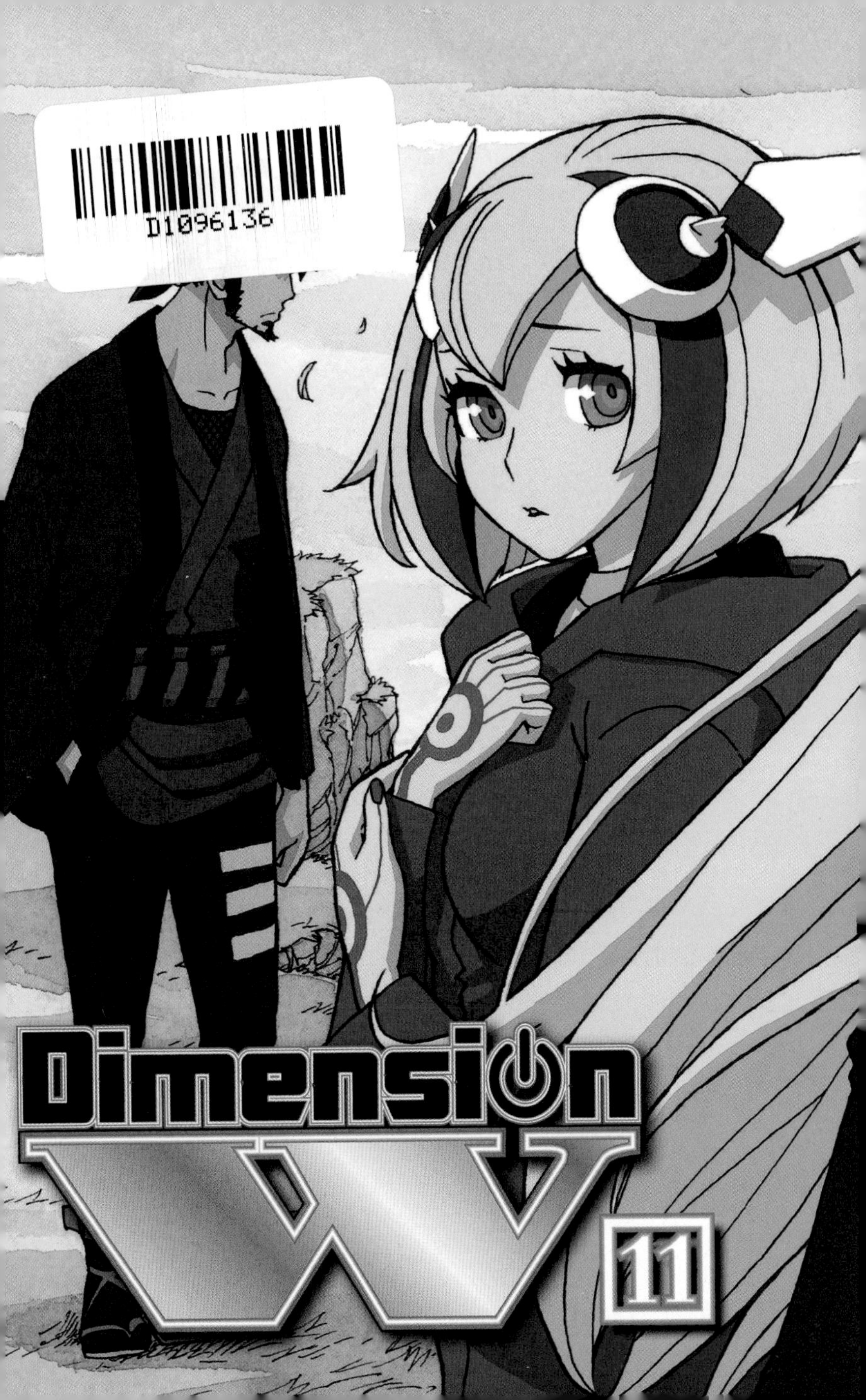
Dimension
W
11

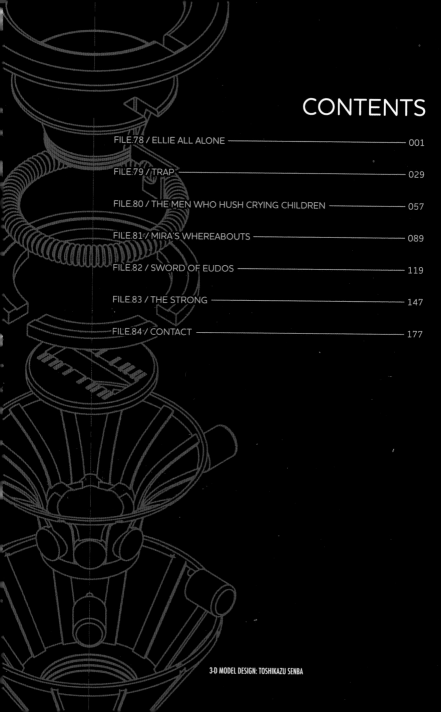

CONTENTS

3-D MODEL DESIGN: TOSHIKAZU SENBA

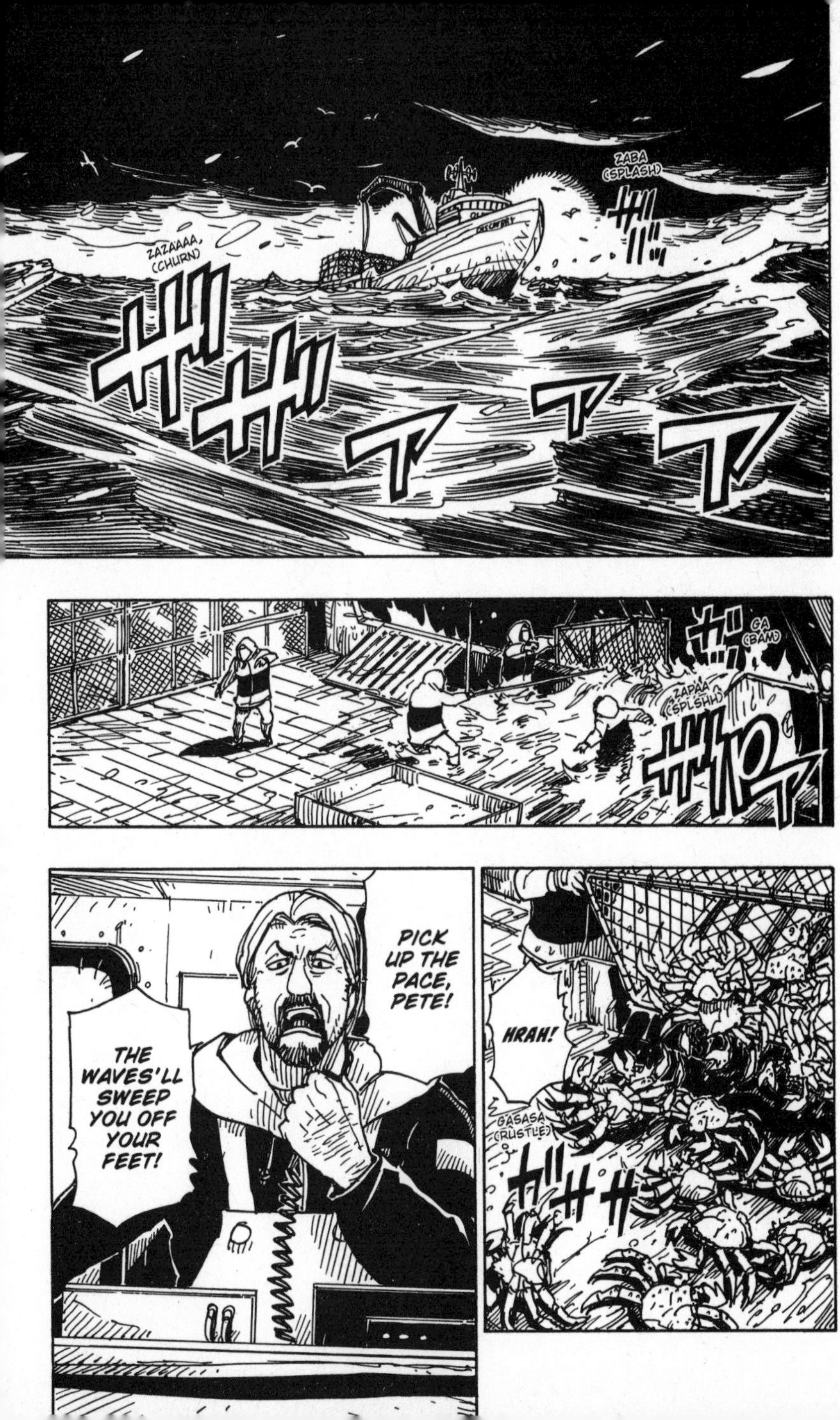
ZABA (SPLASH)
ZAZAAAA, (CHURN)
GA (BAM)
ZAPAA (SPLSHH)
HRAH!
GASASA (RUSTLE)
PICK UP THE PACE, PETE!
THE WAVES'LL SWEEP YOU OFF YOUR FEET!

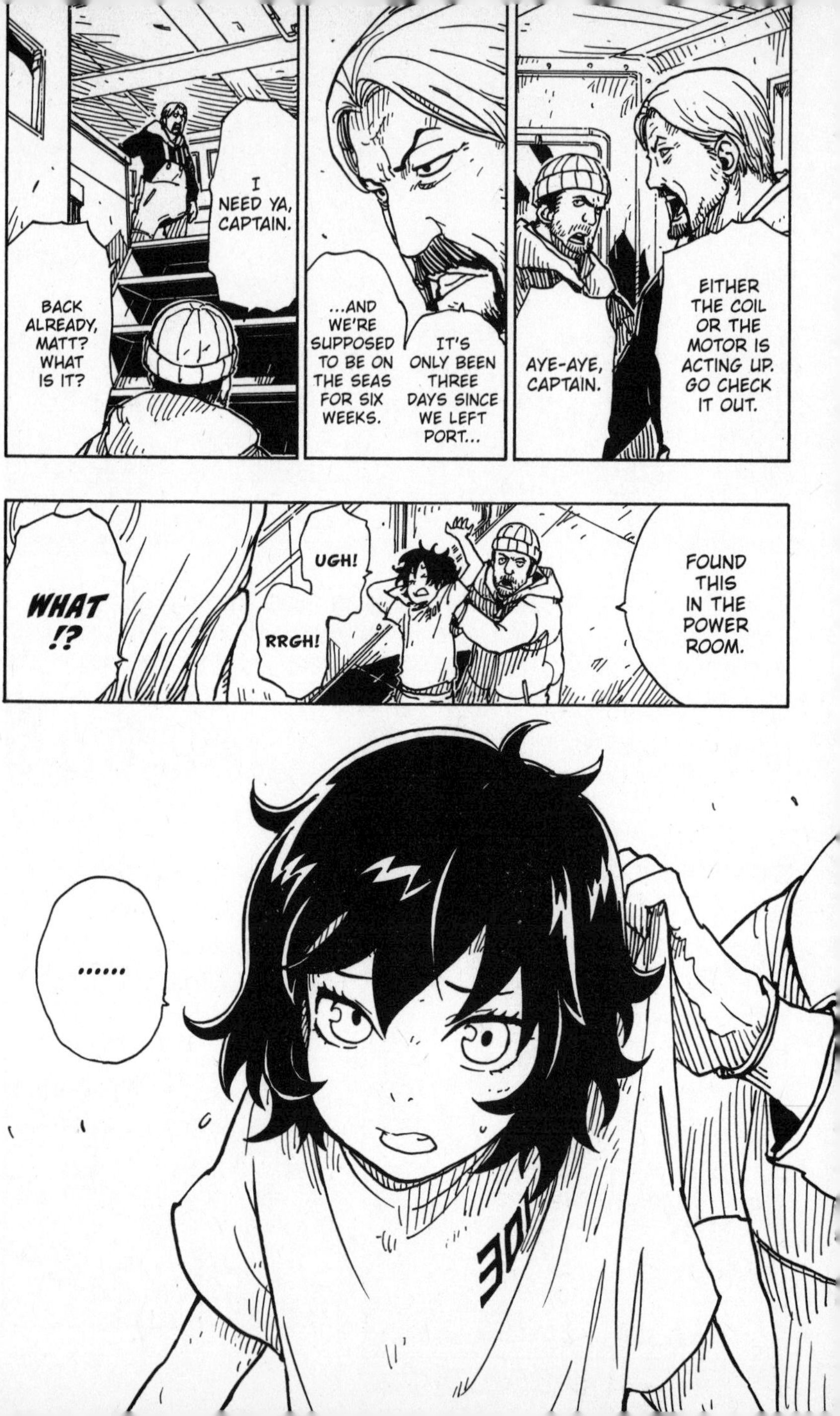

EITHER THE COIL OR THE MOTOR IS ACTING UP. GO CHECK IT OUT.
AYE-AYE, CAPTAIN.
IT'S ONLY BEEN THREE DAYS SINCE WE LEFT PORT...
...AND WE'RE SUPPOSED TO BE ON THE SEAS FOR SIX WEEKS.
I NEED YA, CAPTAIN.
BACK ALREADY, MATT? WHAT IS IT?
FOUND THIS IN THE POWER ROOM.
UGH!
RRGH!
WHAT!?
......

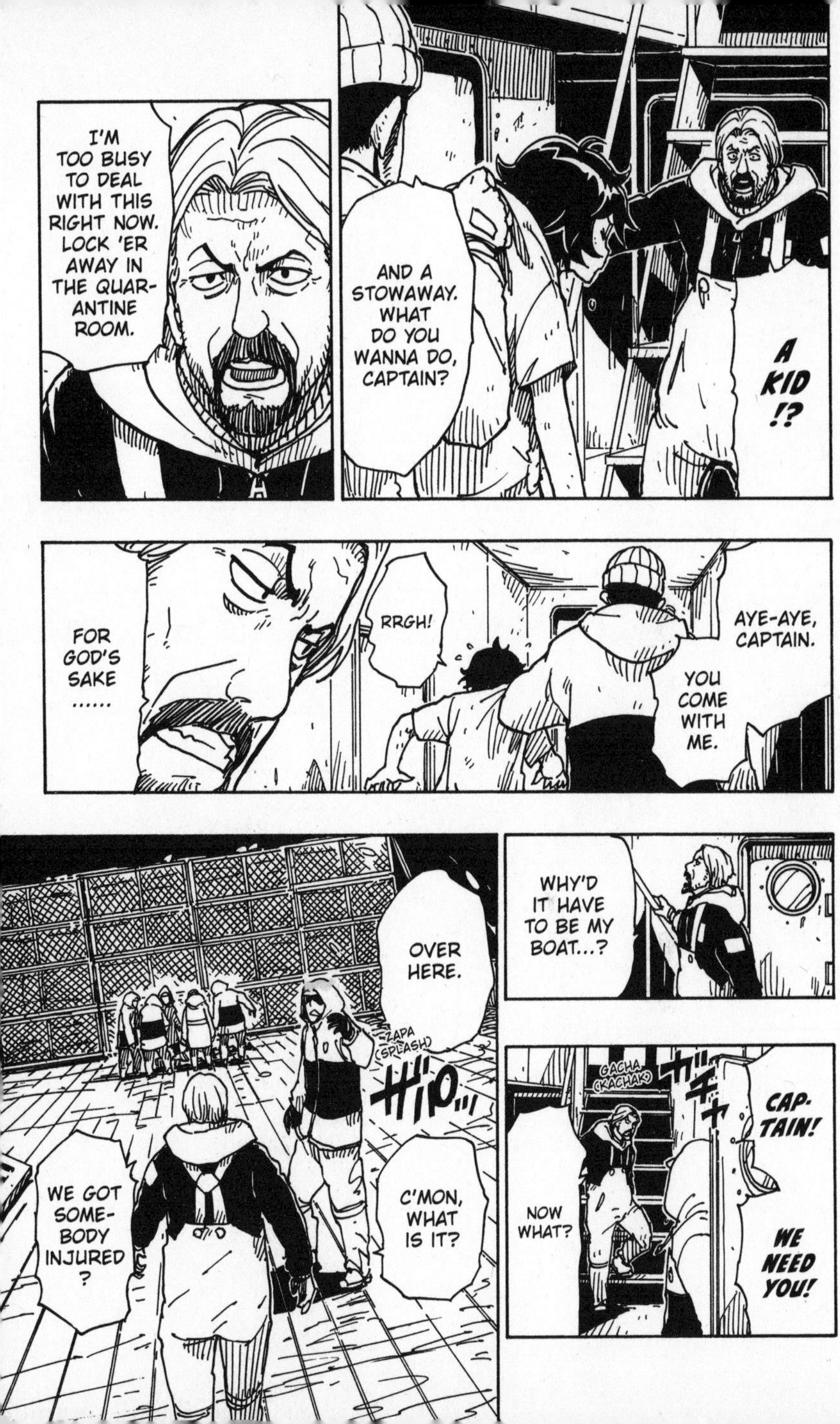
A KID!?
AND A STOWAWAY. WHAT DO YOU WANNA DO, CAPTAIN?
I'M TOO BUSY TO DEAL WITH THIS RIGHT NOW. LOCK 'ER AWAY IN THE QUAR-ANTINE ROOM.
AYE-AYE, CAPTAIN.
YOU COME WITH ME.
RRGH!
FOR GOD'S SAKE......
WHY'D IT HAVE TO BE MY BOAT...?
CAP-TAIN!
GACHA (KACHAK)
NOW WHAT?
WE NEED YOU!
OVER HERE.
ZAPA (SPLASH)
C'MON, WHAT IS IT?
WE GOT SOME-BODY INJURED?

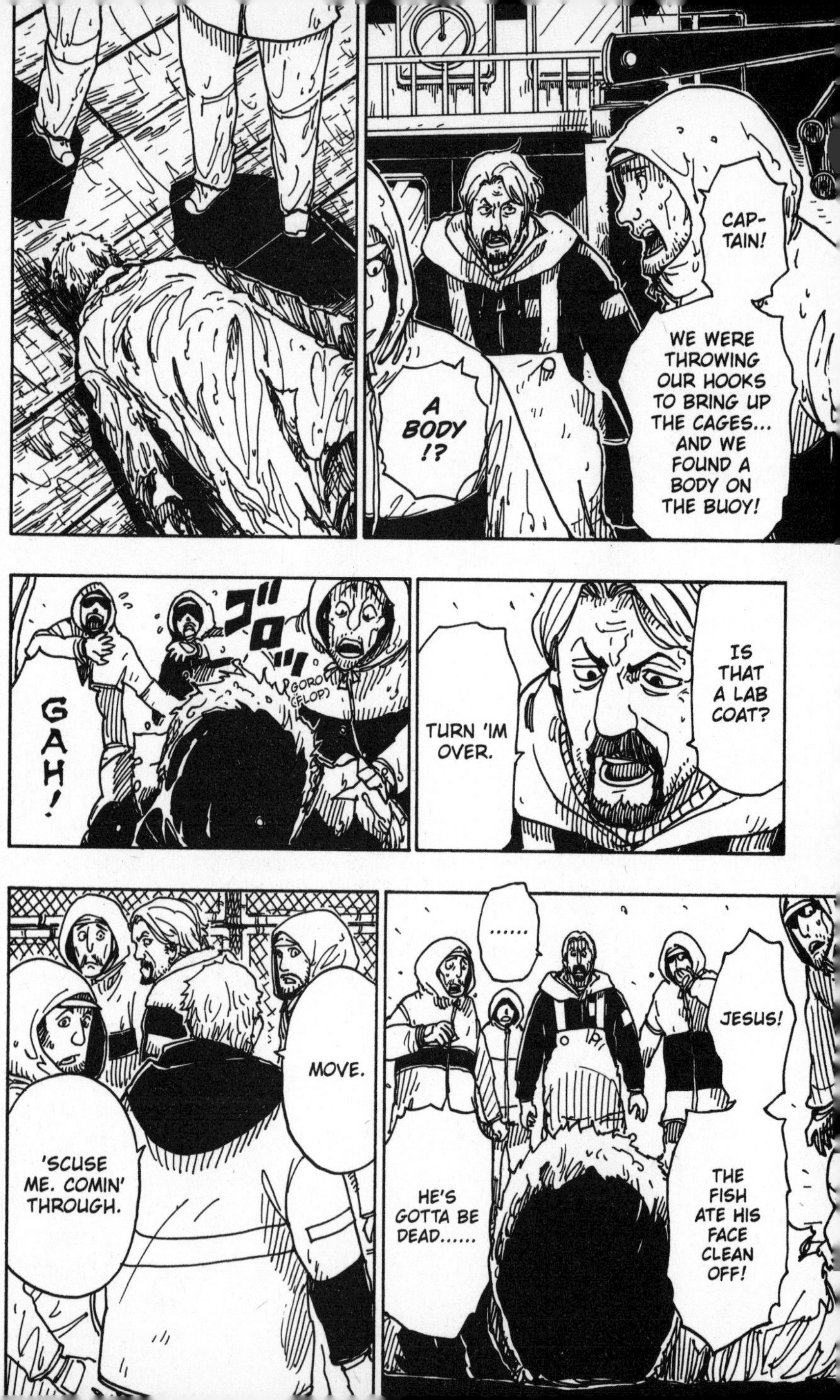
CAP-TAIN!
WE WERE THROWING OUR HOOKS TO BRING UP THE CAGES... AND WE FOUND A BODY ON THE BUOY!
A BODY !?
IS THAT A LAB COAT?
TURN 'IM OVER.
GORO (FLOP)
GAH!
JESUS!
......
THE FISH ATE HIS FACE CLEAN OFF!
HE'S GOTTA BE DEAD......
MOVE.
'SCUSE ME. COMIN' THROUGH.

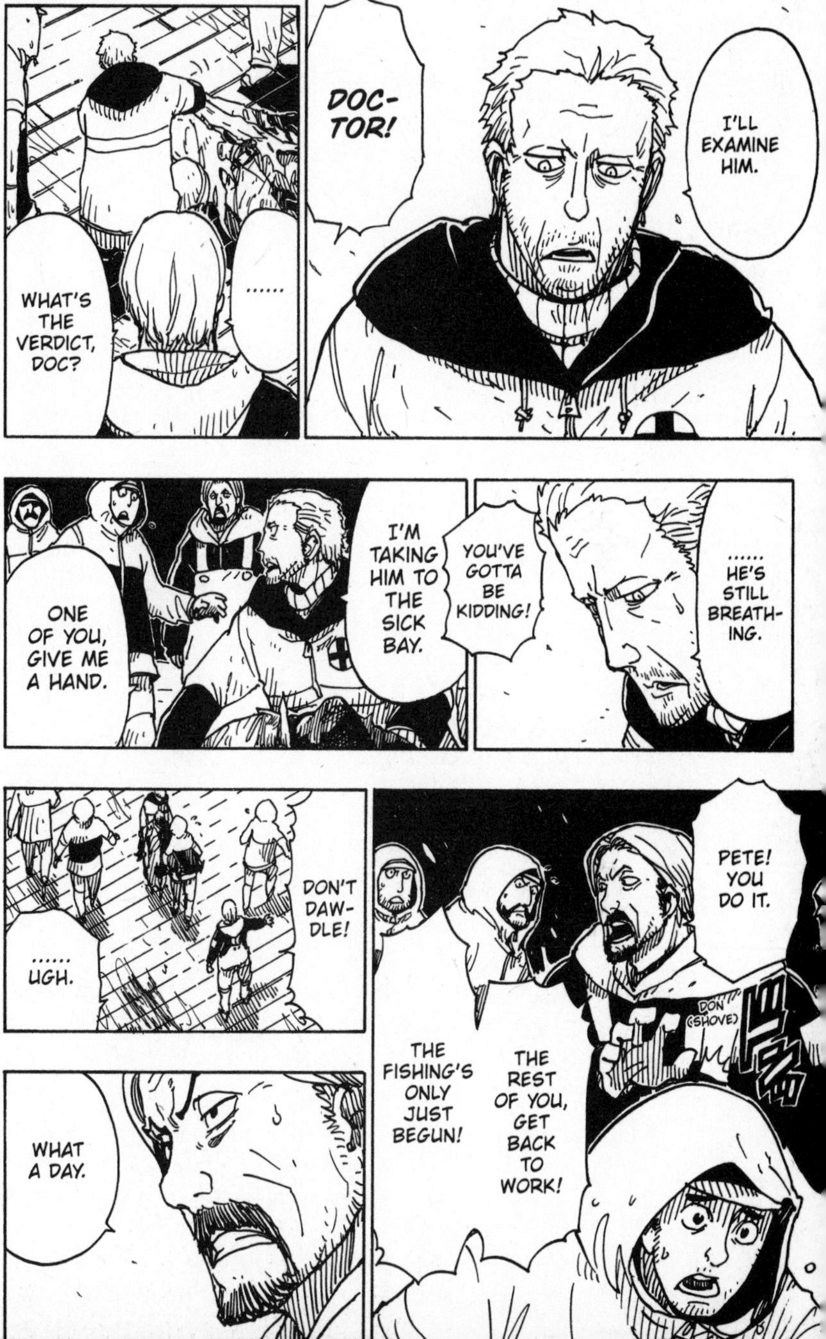
I'LL EXAMINE HIM.
DOC-TOR!
......
WHAT'S THE VERDICT, DOC?
...... HE'S STILL BREATH-ING.
YOU'VE GOTTA BE KIDDING!
I'M TAKING HIM TO THE SICK BAY.
ONE OF YOU, GIVE ME A HAND.
PETE! YOU DO IT.
DON (SHOVE)
THE REST OF YOU, GET BACK TO WORK!
THE FISHING'S ONLY JUST BEGUN!
DON'T DAWDLE!
...... UGH.
WHAT A DAY.

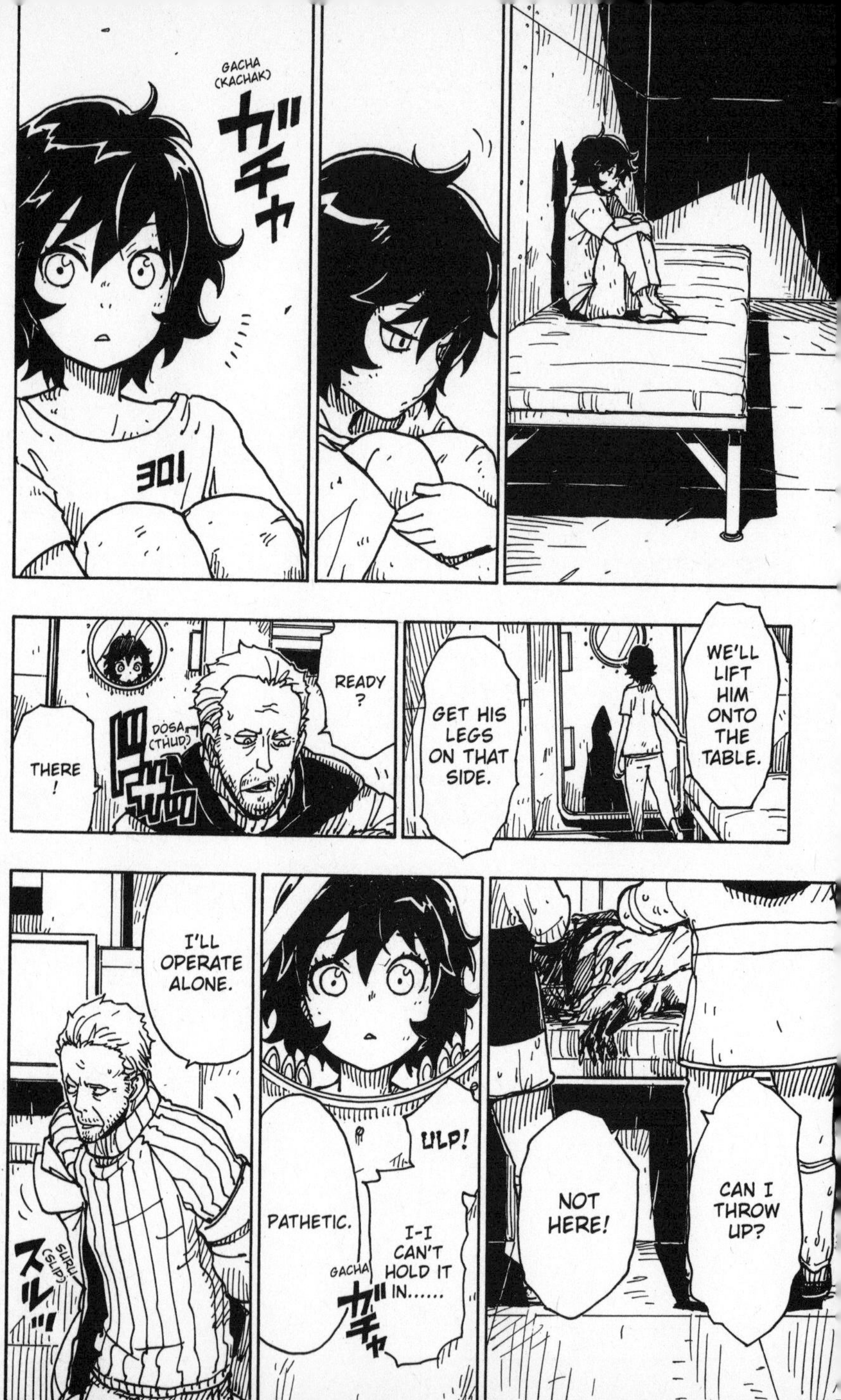
GACHA (KACHAK)
ガチャ
WE'LL LIFT HIM ONTO THE TABLE.
GET HIS LEGS ON THAT SIDE.
READY?
DOSA (THUD)
THERE!
CAN I THROW UP?
NOT HERE!
ULP!
I-I CAN'T HOLD IT IN......
GACHA
ガチャ
PATHETIC.
I'LL OPERATE ALONE.
SURU (SLIP)

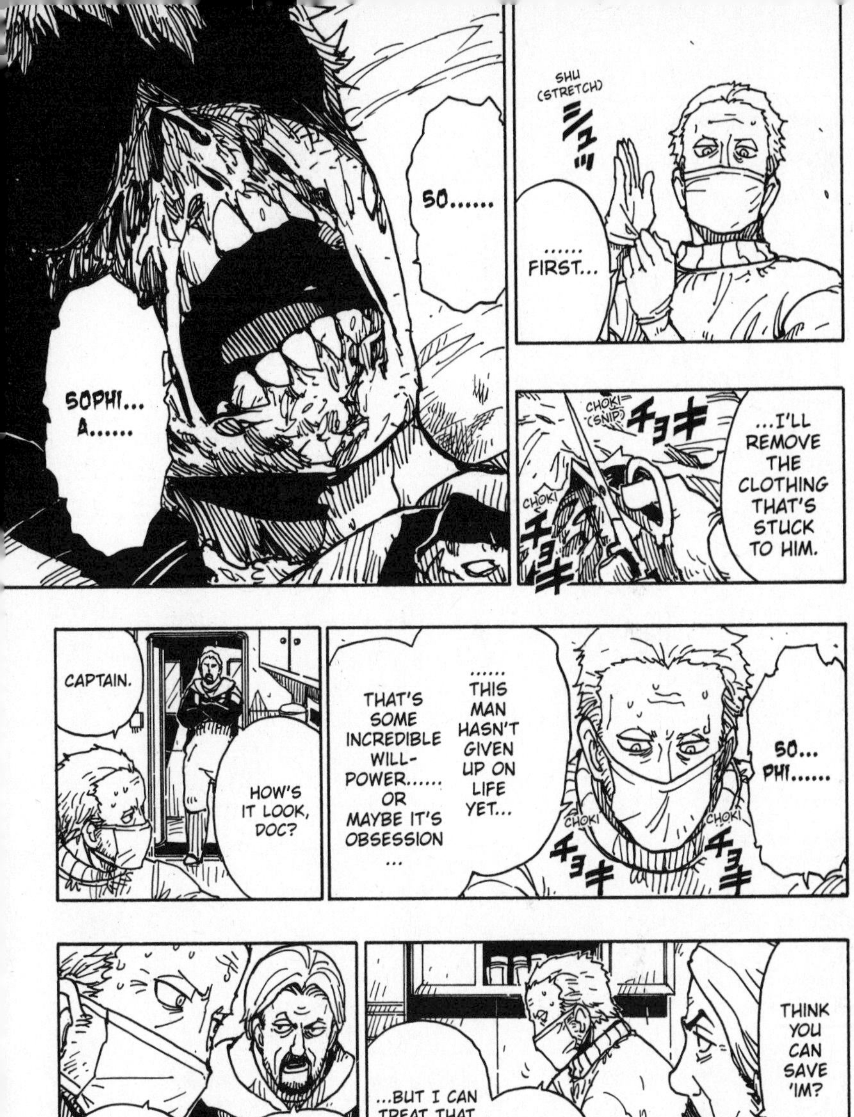
SHU (STRETCH)
シュッ
......
FIRST...
CHOKI (SNIP)
チョキ
...I'LL REMOVE THE CLOTHING THAT'S STUCK TO HIM.
CHOKI
チョキ
SO......
SOPHI... A......
SO... PHI......
......THIS MAN HASN'T GIVEN UP ON LIFE YET...
THAT'S SOME INCREDIBLE WILL-POWER...... OR MAYBE IT'S OBSESSION ...
CHOKI
チョキ
CHOKI
チョキ
CAPTAIN.
HOW'S IT LOOK, DOC?
THINK YOU CAN SAVE 'IM?
THE GANGRENE IS SPREAD-ING. I'LL HAVE TO AMPUTATE.
...BUT I CAN TREAT THAT AS WELL WITH THE TEMPORARY PROS-THETICS WE HAVE ON BOARD.
SHOULDN'T WE CALL FOR A HELICOPTER? HAVE HIM TAKEN TO A HOSPITAL?
IT WOULDN'T MAKE IT IN TIME. GOTTA DO IT NOW, OR HE'LL DIE.

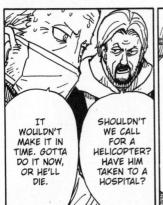

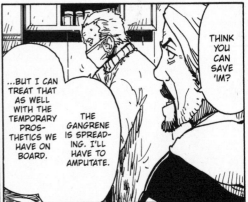

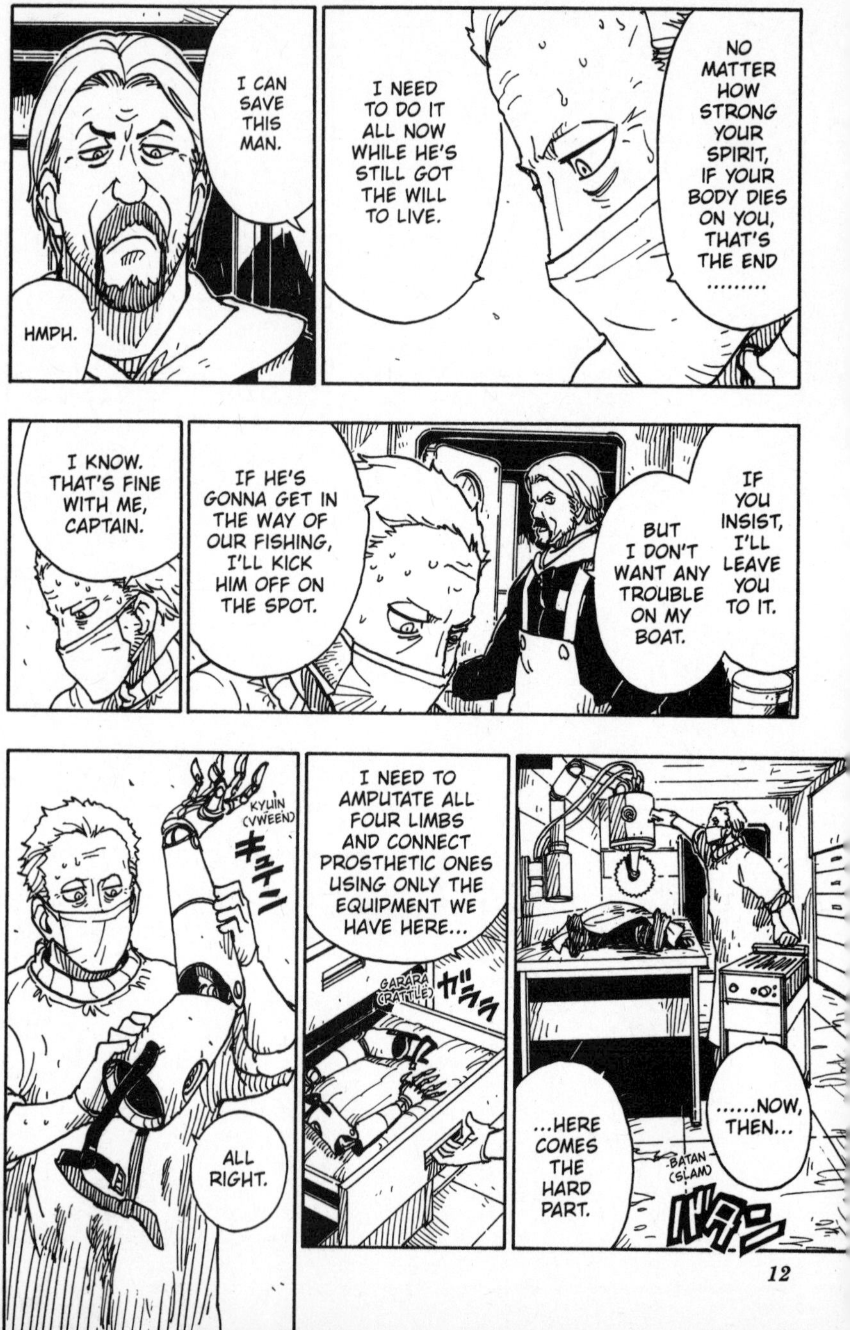
NO MATTER HOW STRONG YOUR SPIRIT, IF YOUR BODY DIES ON YOU, THAT'S THE END ....
I NEED TO DO IT ALL NOW WHILE HE'S STILL GOT THE WILL TO LIVE.
I CAN SAVE THIS MAN.
HMPH.
IF YOU INSIST, I'LL LEAVE YOU TO IT.
BUT I DON'T WANT ANY TROUBLE ON MY BOAT.
IF HE'S GONNA GET IN THE WAY OF OUR FISHING, I'LL KICK HIM OFF ON THE SPOT.
I KNOW. THAT'S FINE WITH ME, CAPTAIN.
......NOW, THEN...
BATAN (SLAM)
...HERE COMES THE HARD PART.
I NEED TO AMPUTATE ALL FOUR LIMBS AND CONNECT PROSTHETIC ONES USING ONLY THE EQUIPMENT WE HAVE HERE...
GARARA (RATTLE)
KYUIN (VWEEN)
ALL RIGHT.

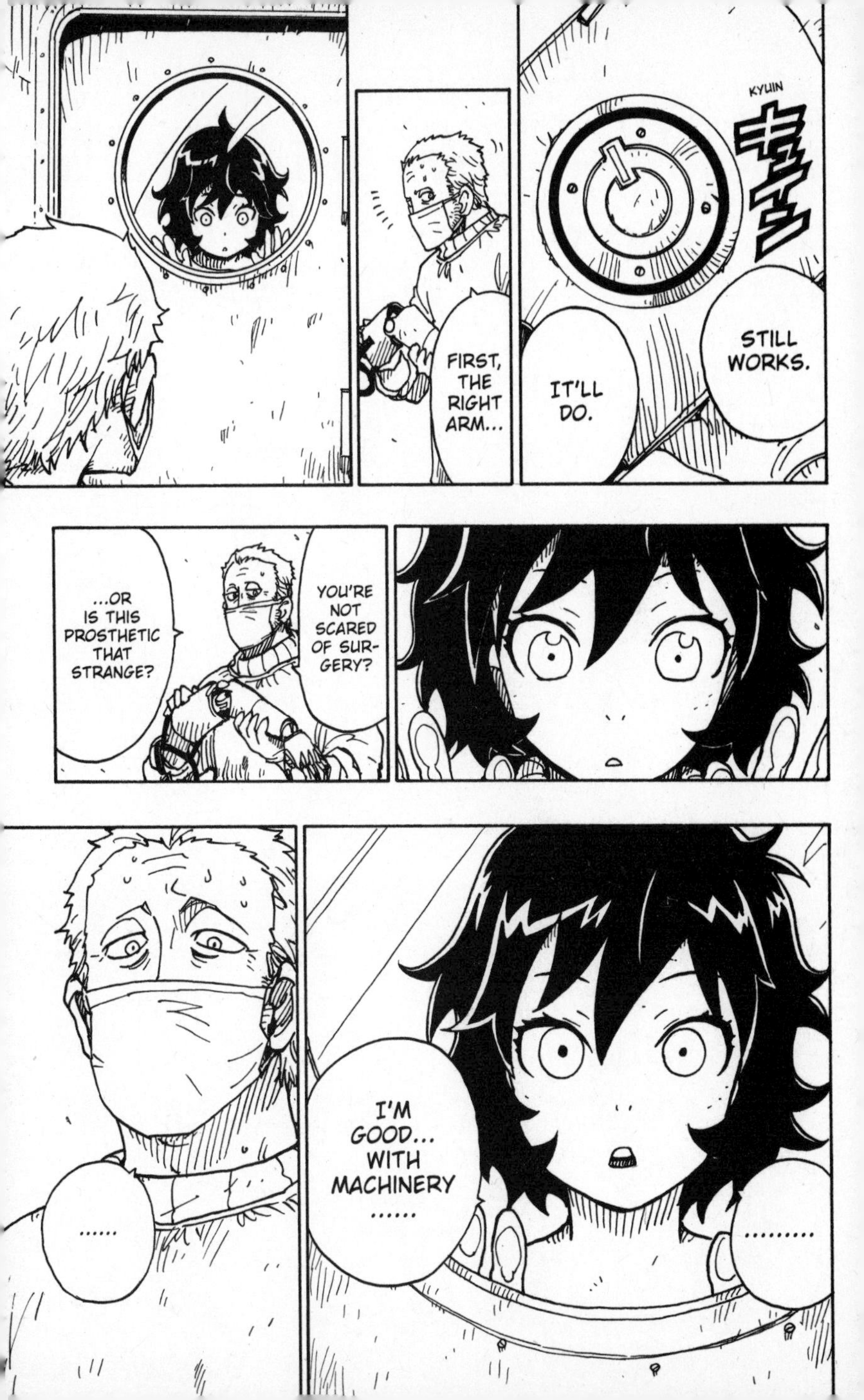
KYUIN
キュイン
STILL WORKS.
IT'LL DO.
FIRST, THE RIGHT ARM...
YOU'RE NOT SCARED OF SUR-GERY?
...OR IS THIS PROSTHETIC THAT STRANGE?
....
I'M GOOD... WITH MACHINERY ......
......

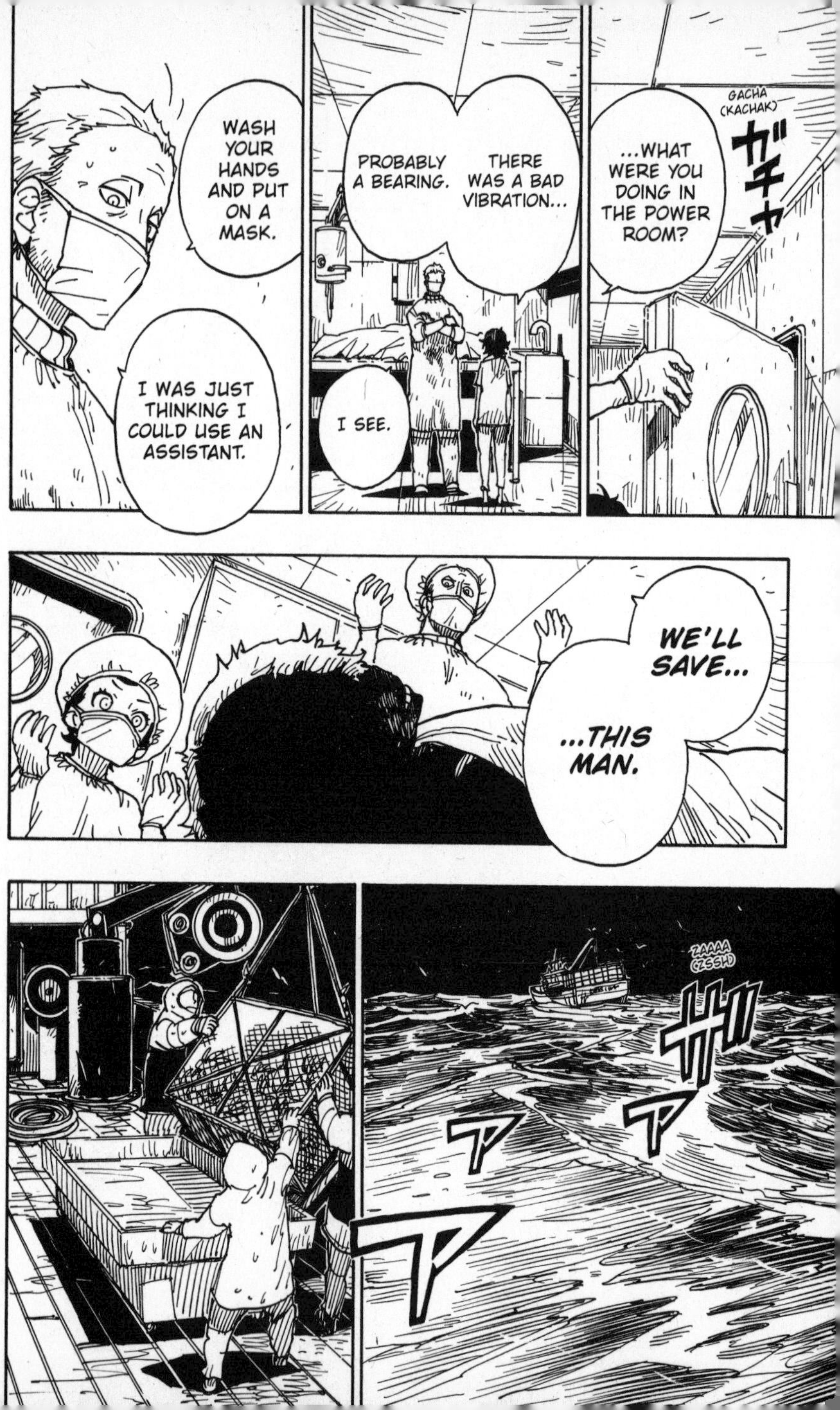
GACHA (KACHAK)
ガチャ
...WHAT WERE YOU DOING IN THE POWER ROOM?
THERE WAS A BAD VIBRATION...
PROBABLY A BEARING.
I SEE.
WASH YOUR HANDS AND PUT ON A MASK.
I WAS JUST THINKING I COULD USE AN ASSISTANT.
WE'LL SAVE...
...THIS MAN.
ZAAAA (ZSSSH)
ザァァァ

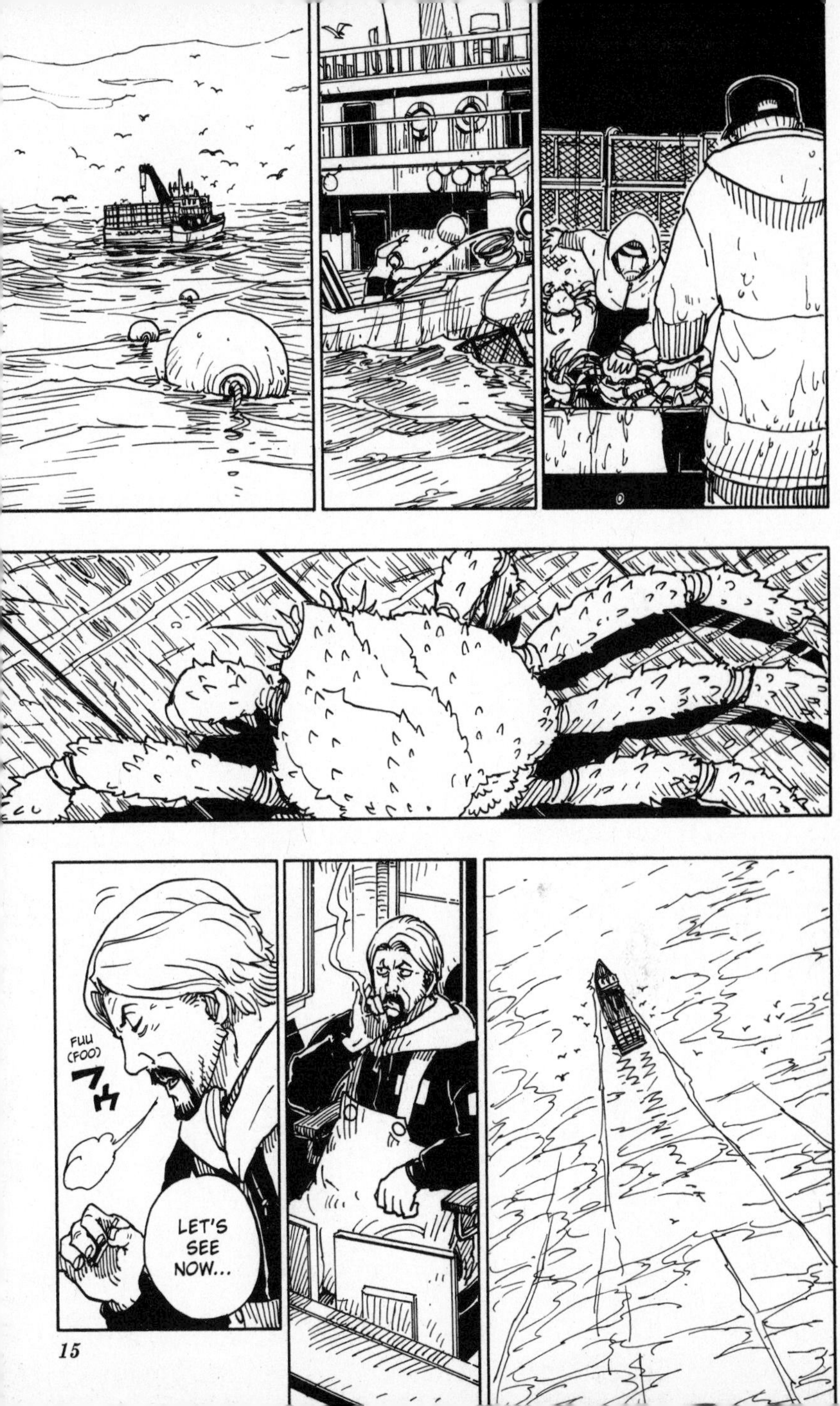

FUU (FOO)
フゥ
LET'S SEE NOW...

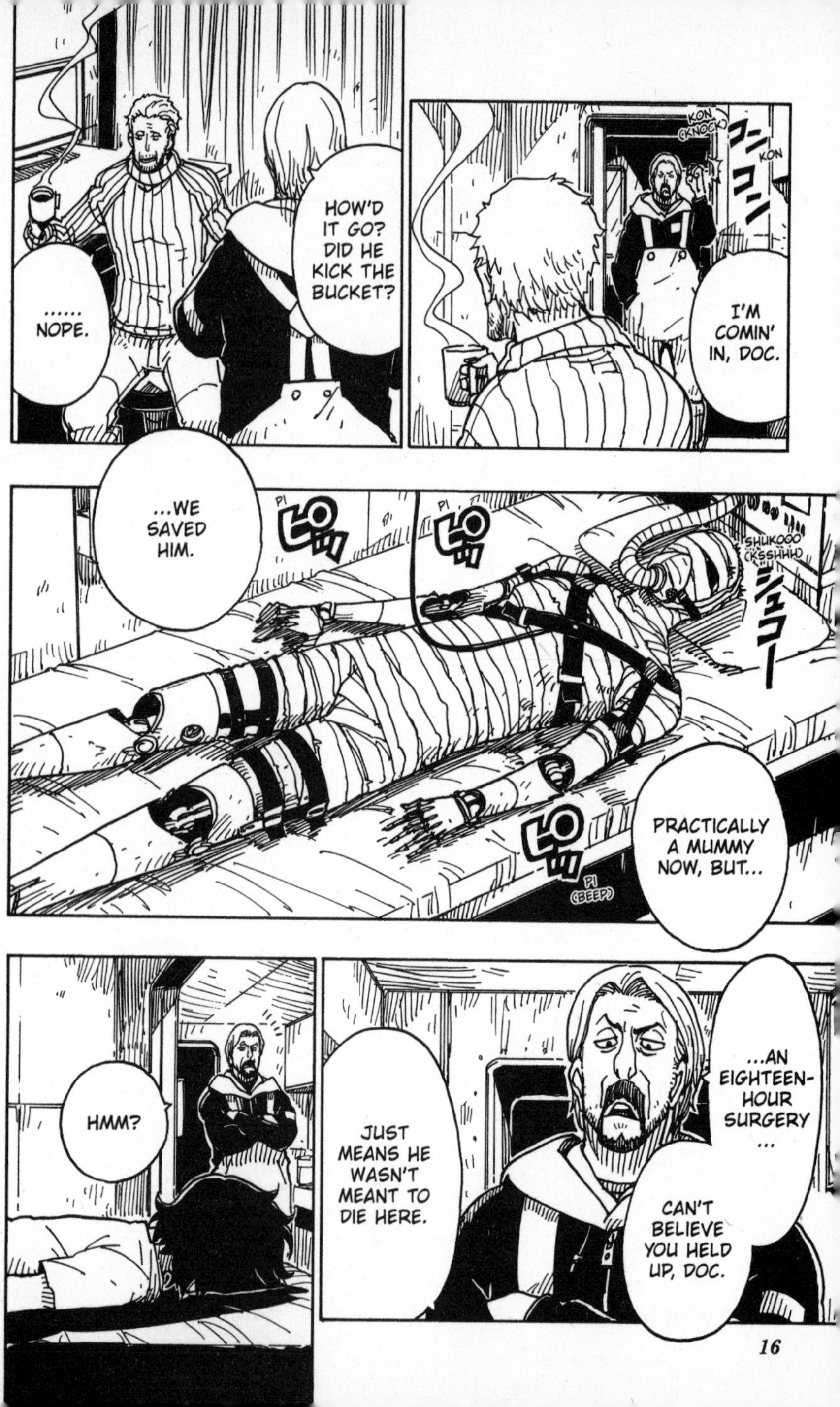
KON (KNOCK)
KON
I'M COMIN' IN, DOC.
HOW'D IT GO? DID HE KICK THE BUCKET?
...... NOPE.
SHUKOOO (KSSHHH)
PI
PI
...WE SAVED HIM.
PRACTICALLY A MUMMY NOW, BUT...
PI (BEEP)
...AN EIGHTEEN-HOUR SURGERY ...
CAN'T BELIEVE YOU HELD UP, DOC.
JUST MEANS HE WASN'T MEANT TO DIE HERE.
HMM?

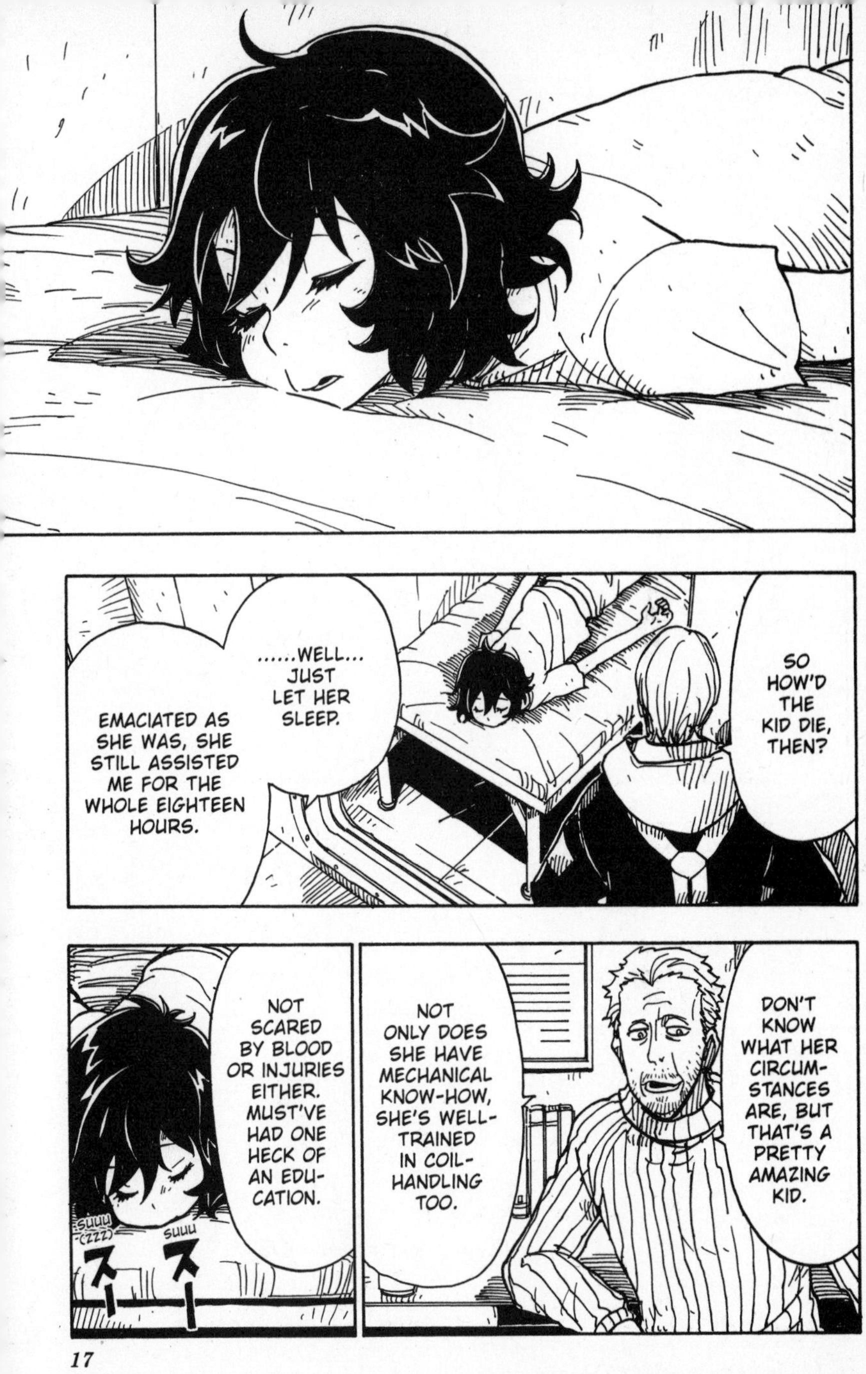
SO HOW'D THE KID DIE, THEN?
......WELL... JUST LET HER SLEEP.
EMACIATED AS SHE WAS, SHE STILL ASSISTED ME FOR THE WHOLE EIGHTEEN HOURS.
DON'T KNOW WHAT HER CIRCUM-STANCES ARE, BUT THAT'S A PRETTY AMAZING KID.
NOT ONLY DOES SHE HAVE MECHANICAL KNOW-HOW, SHE'S WELL-TRAINED IN COIL-HANDLING TOO.
NOT SCARED BY BLOOD OR INJURIES EITHER. MUST'VE HAD ONE HECK OF AN EDU-CATION.
SUUU
スー
SUUU (ZZZ)
スー

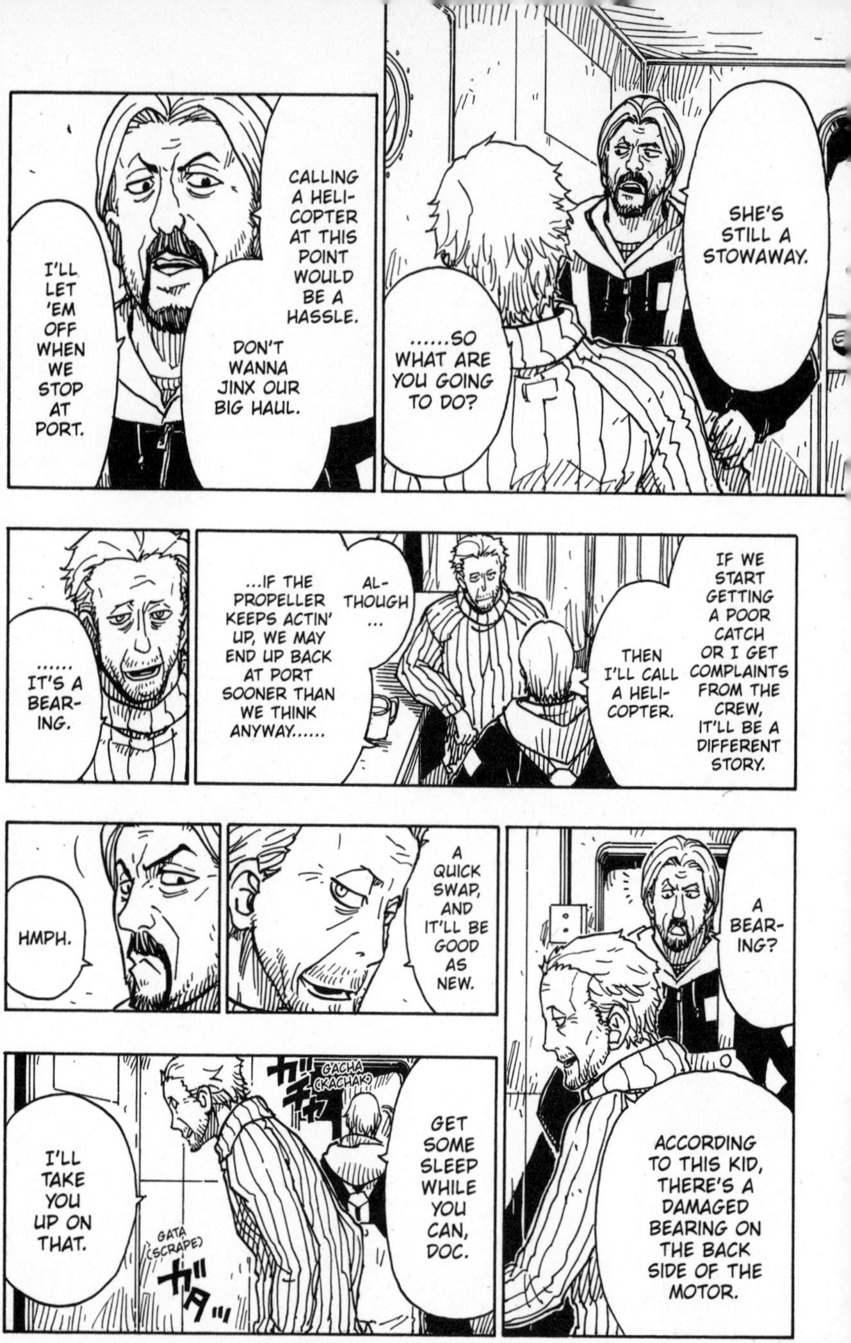
SHE'S STILL A STOWAWAY.
......SO WHAT ARE YOU GOING TO DO?
CALLING A HELI-COPTER AT THIS POINT WOULD BE A HASSLE.
DON'T WANNA JINX OUR BIG HAUL.
I'LL LET 'EM OFF WHEN WE STOP AT PORT.
IF WE START GETTING A POOR CATCH OR I GET COMPLAINTS FROM THE CREW, IT'LL BE A DIFFERENT STORY.
THEN I'LL CALL A HELI-COPTER.
AL-THOUGH ...
...IF THE PROPELLER KEEPS ACTIN' UP, WE MAY END UP BACK AT PORT SOONER THAN WE THINK ANYWAY......
...... IT'S A BEAR-ING.
A BEAR-ING?
ACCORDING TO THIS KID, THERE'S A DAMAGED BEARING ON THE BACK SIDE OF THE MOTOR.
A QUICK SWAP, AND IT'LL BE GOOD AS NEW.
HMPH.
GET SOME SLEEP WHILE YOU CAN, DOC.
ガチャ
GACHA (KACHAK)
I'LL TAKE YOU UP ON THAT.
GATA (SCRAPE)
ガタッ

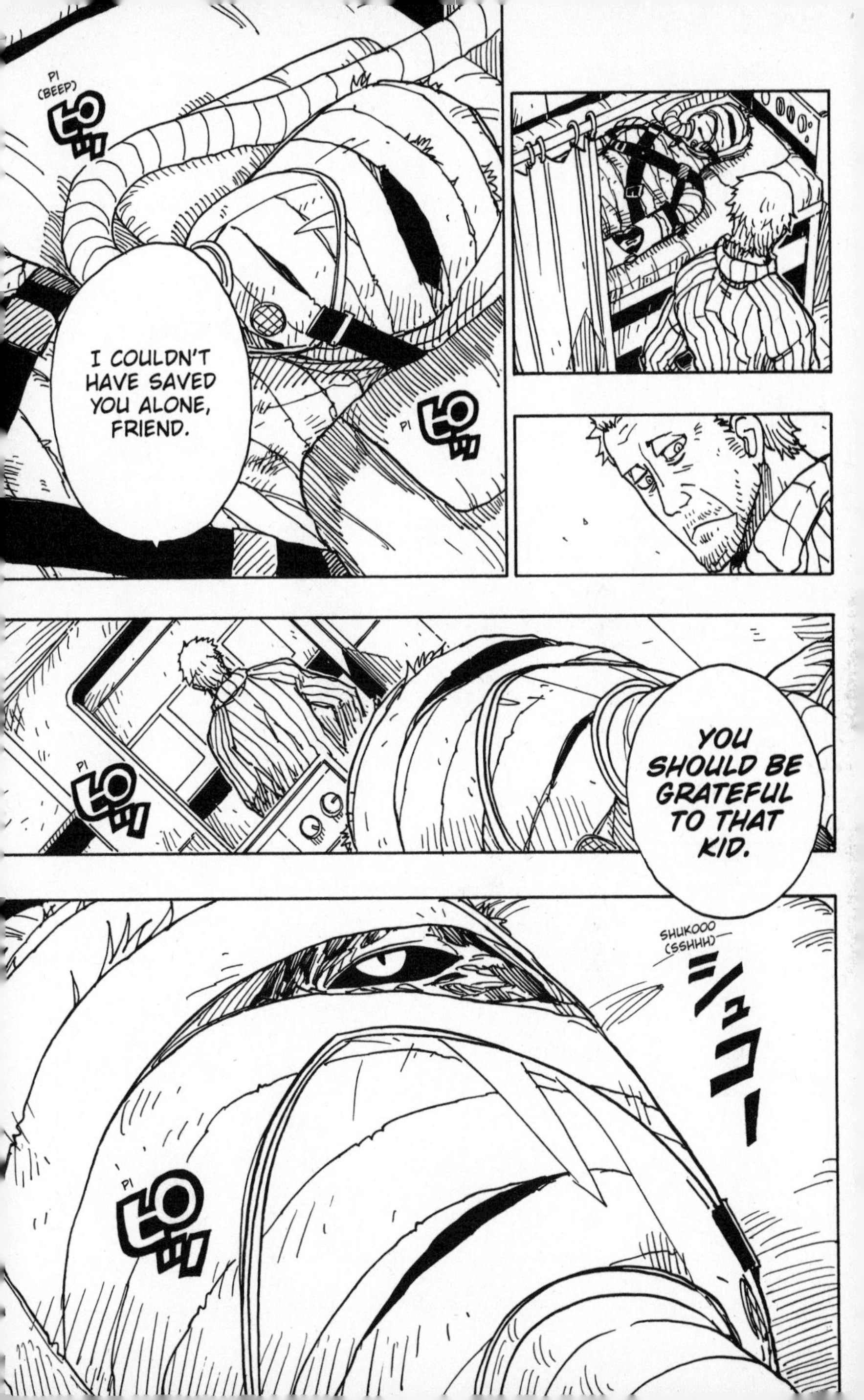
PI (BEEP)
I COULDN'T HAVE SAVED YOU ALONE, FRIEND.
PI
YOU SHOULD BE GRATEFUL TO THAT KID.
PI
SHUKOOO (SSHHH)
PI

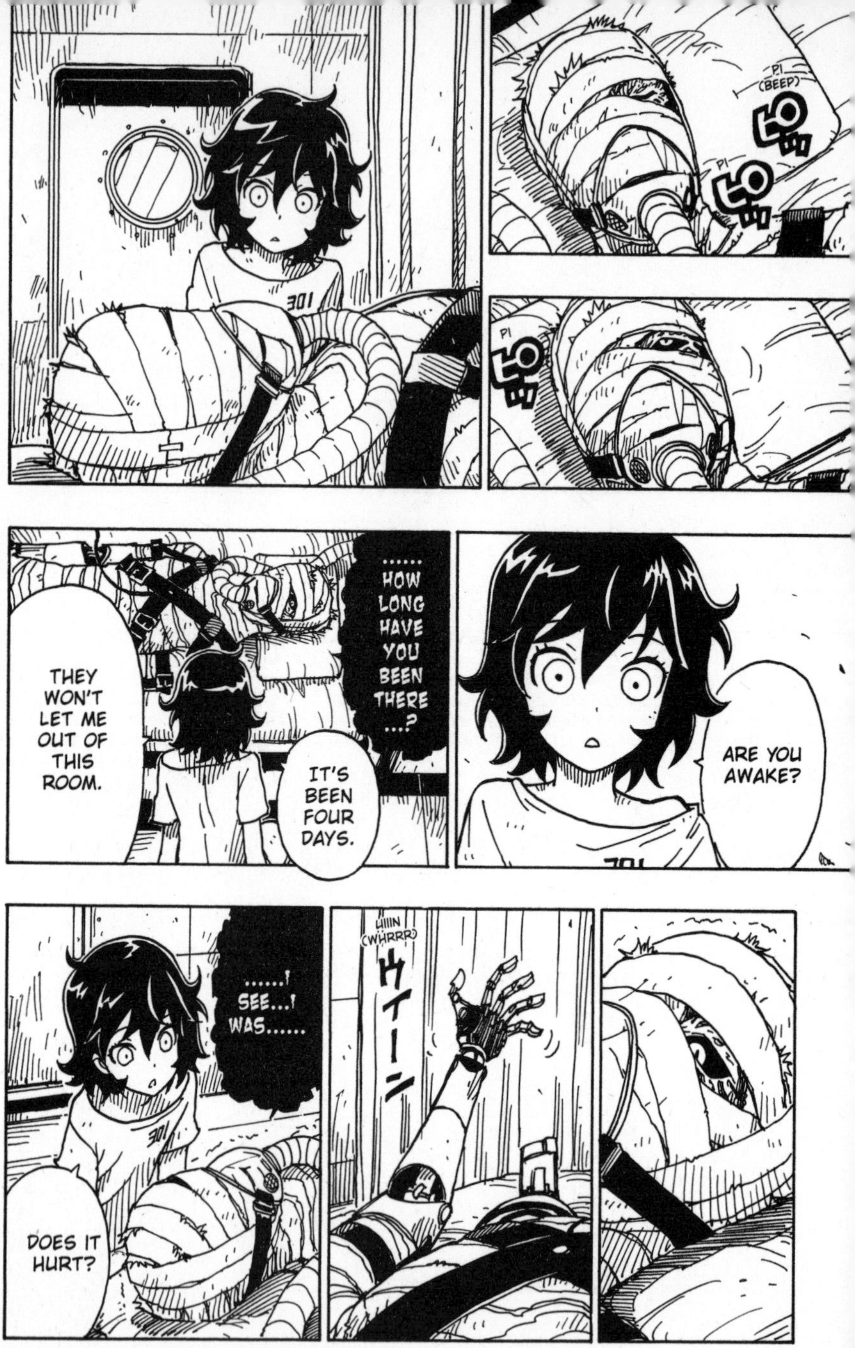
PI (BEEP)
PI
PI
ARE YOU AWAKE?
......HOW LONG HAVE YOU BEEN THERE ....?
IT'S BEEN FOUR DAYS.
THEY WON'T LET ME OUT OF THIS ROOM.
UIIIN (WHRRR)
......I SEE...I WAS......
DOES IT HURT?

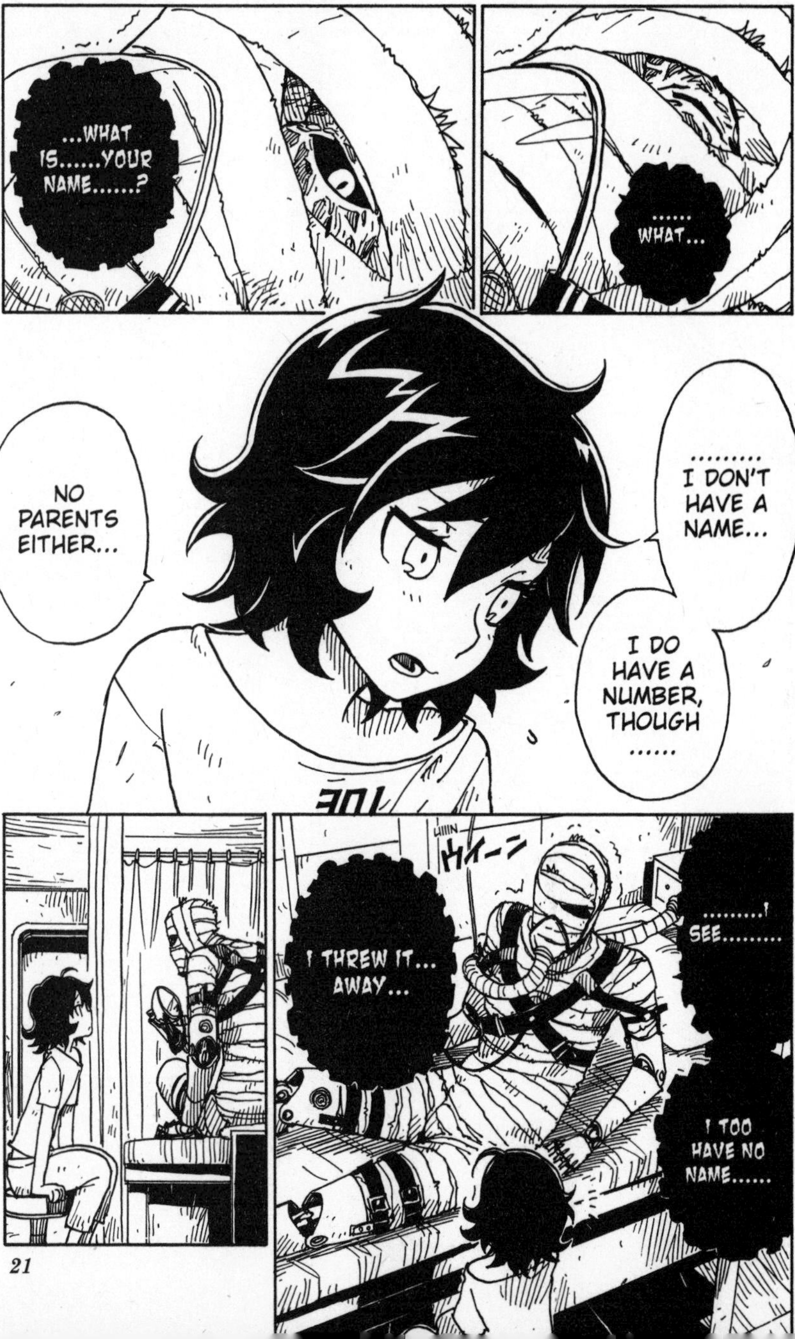
......WHAT...
...WHAT IS......YOUR NAME.......?
.... I DON'T HAVE A NAME...
I DO HAVE A NUMBER, THOUGH ......
NO PARENTS EITHER...
UIIIN
ウィーン
.........I SEE.........
I TOO HAVE NO NAME......
I THREW IT... AWAY...

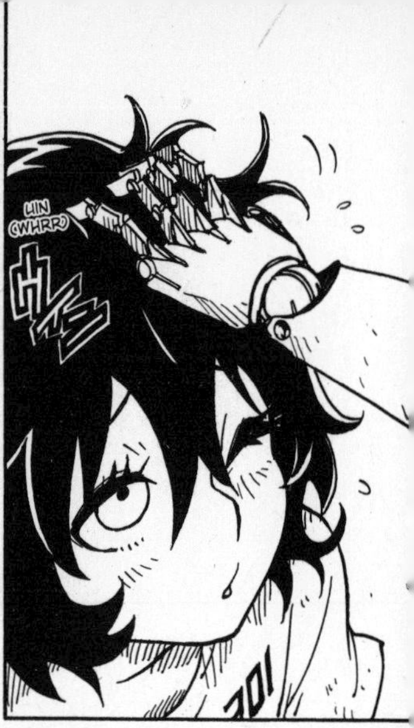
UIN (WHRR)

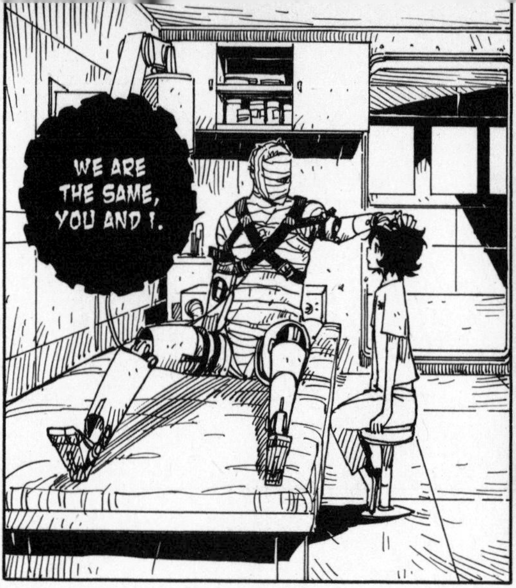
WE ARE THE SAME, YOU AND I.

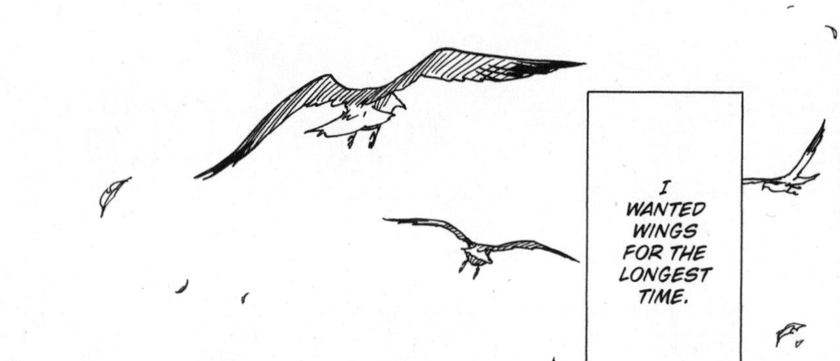
I WANTED WINGS FOR THE LONGEST TIME.

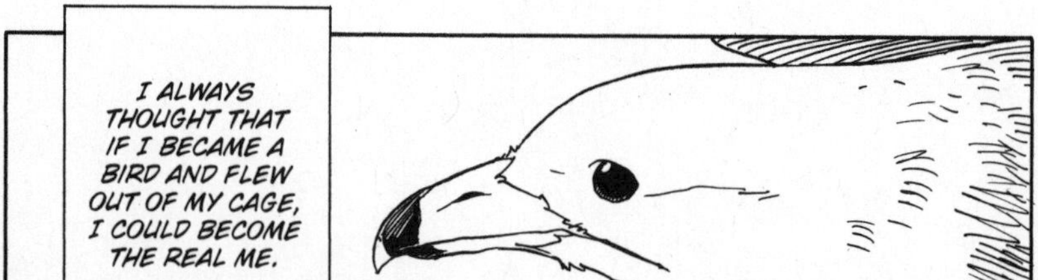
I ALWAYS THOUGHT THAT IF I BECAME A BIRD AND FLEW OUT OF MY CAGE, I COULD BECOME THE REAL ME.

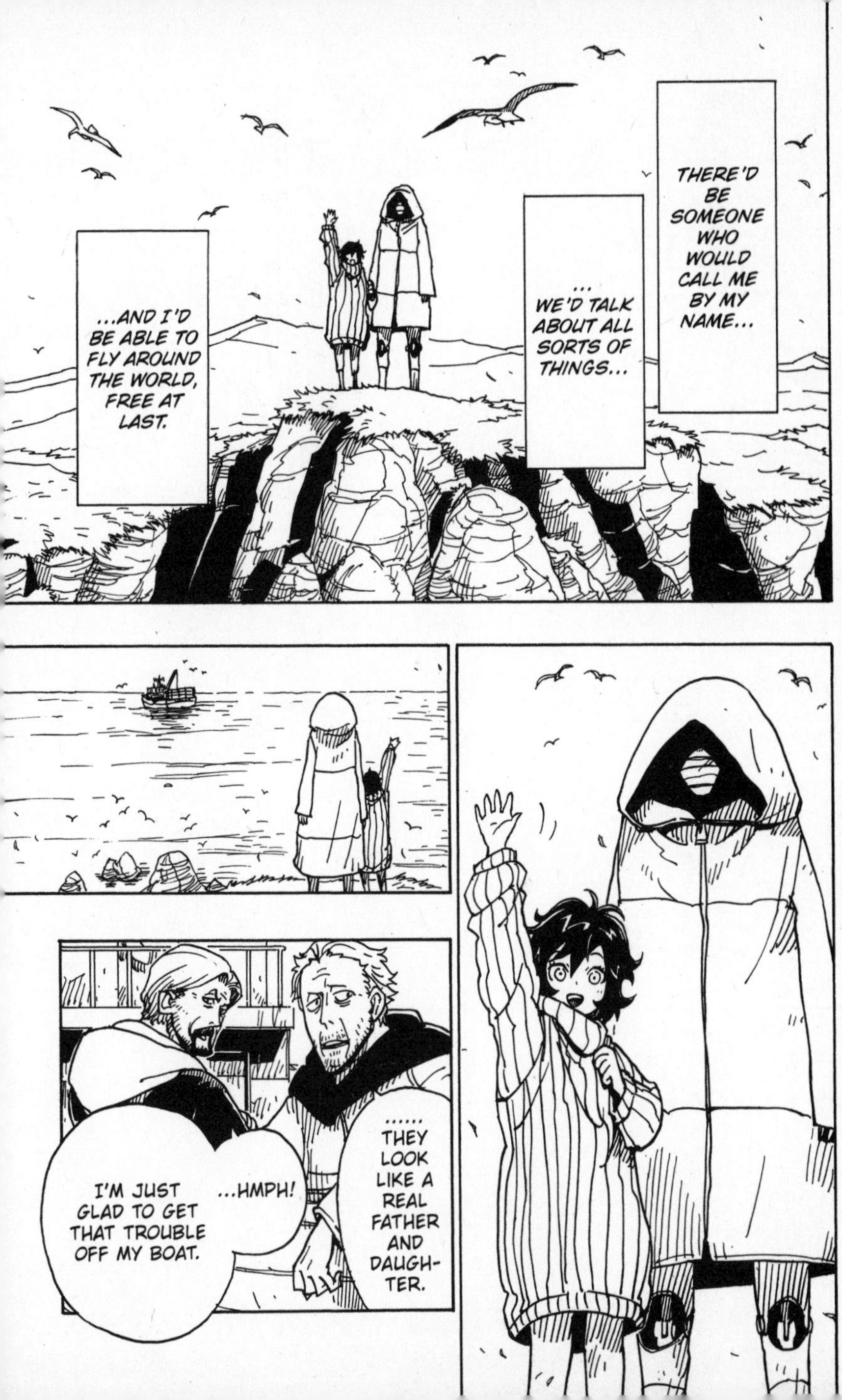
THERE'D BE SOMEONE WHO WOULD CALL ME BY MY NAME...
...WE'D TALK ABOUT ALL SORTS OF THINGS...
...AND I'D BE ABLE TO FLY AROUND THE WORLD, FREE AT LAST.
...... THEY LOOK LIKE A REAL FATHER AND DAUGH-TER.
...HMPH!
I'M JUST GLAD TO GET THAT TROUBLE OFF MY BOAT.

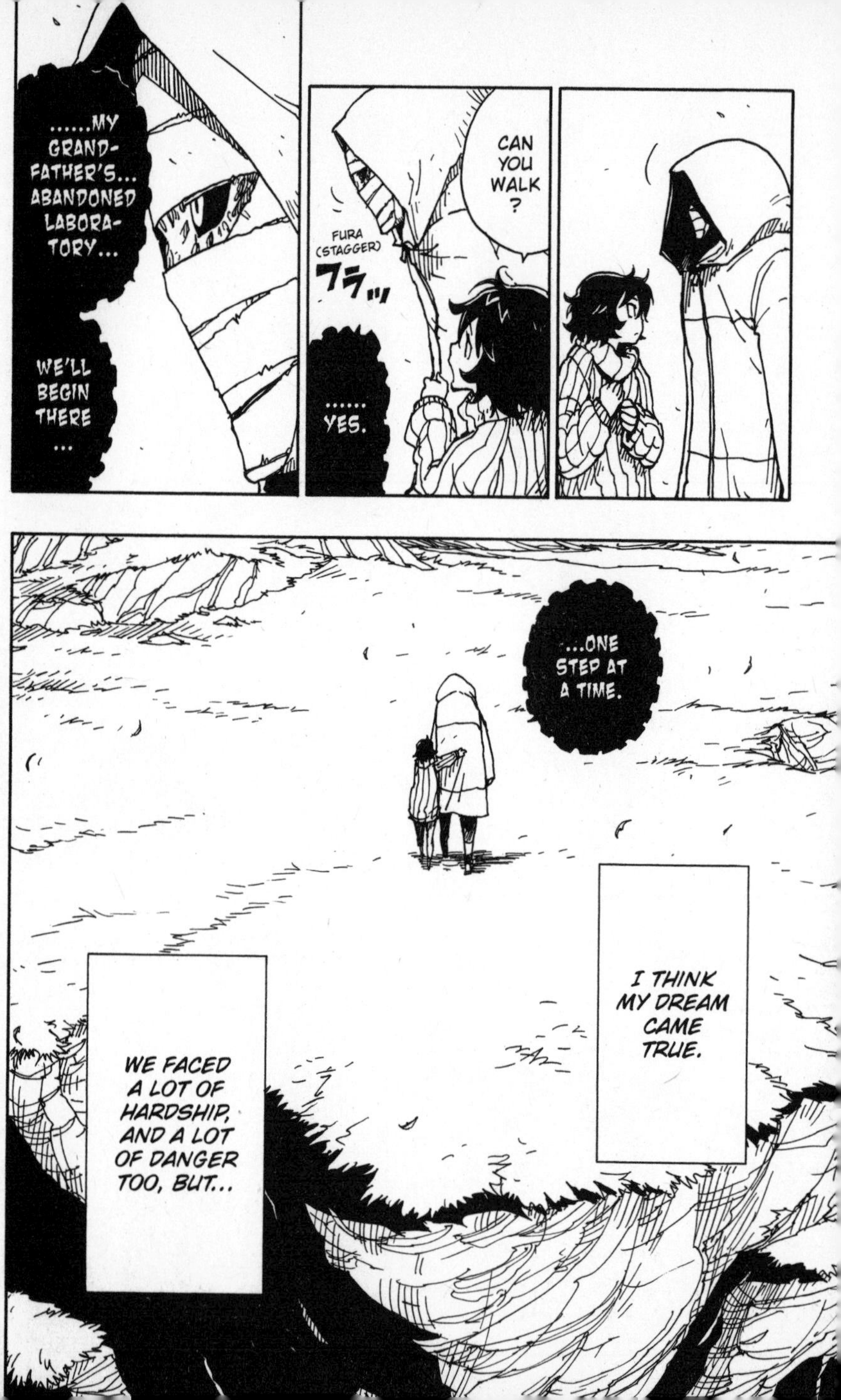
CAN YOU WALK?
FURA (STAGGER)
フラッ
......YES.
......MY GRANDFATHER'S... ABANDONED LABORATORY...
WE'LL BEGIN THERE...
...ONE STEP AT A TIME.
I THINK MY DREAM CAME TRUE.
WE FACED A LOT OF HARDSHIP, AND A LOT OF DANGER TOO, BUT...

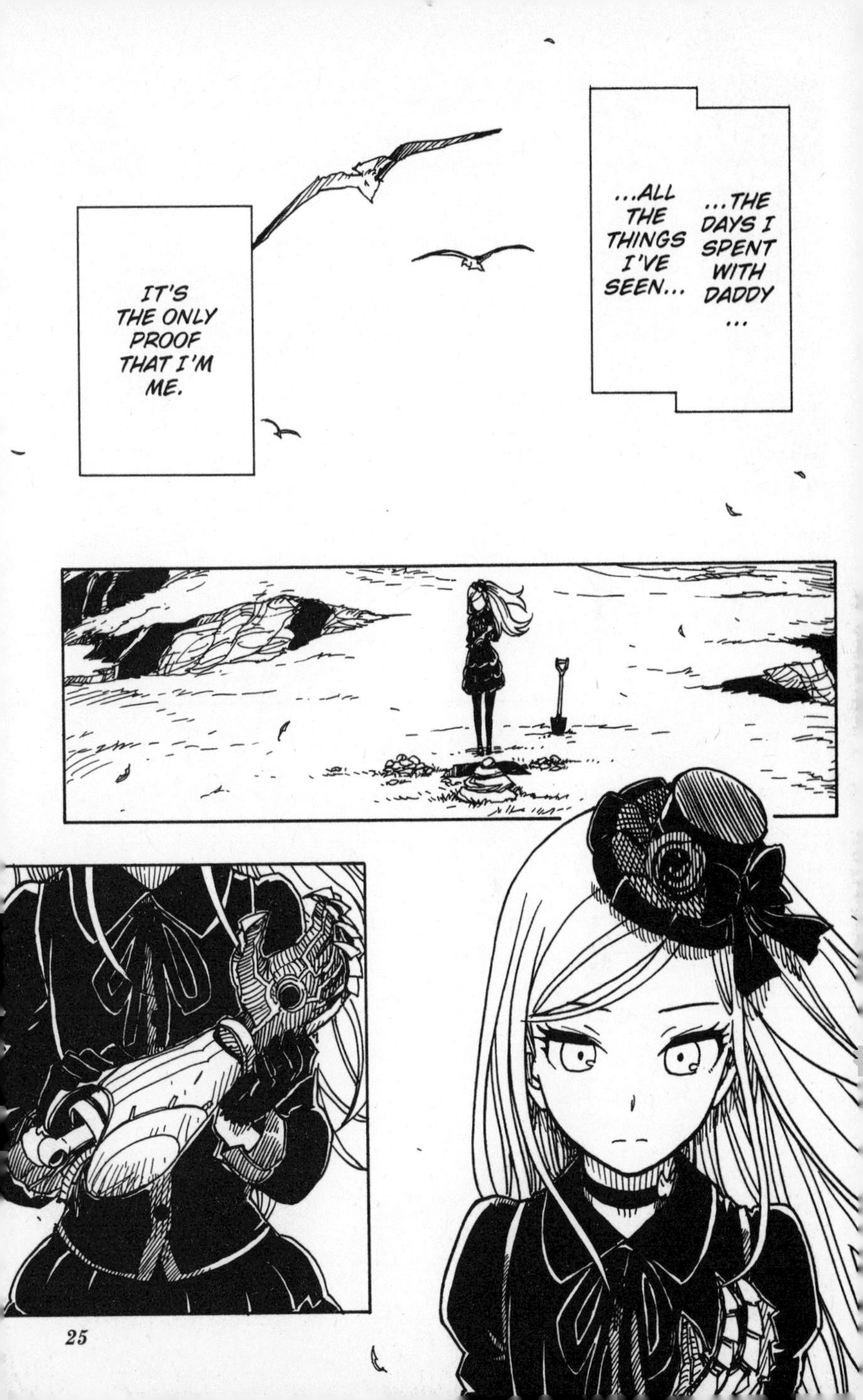
...THE DAYS I SPENT WITH DADDY...
...ALL THE THINGS I'VE SEEN...
IT'S THE ONLY PROOF THAT I'M ME.

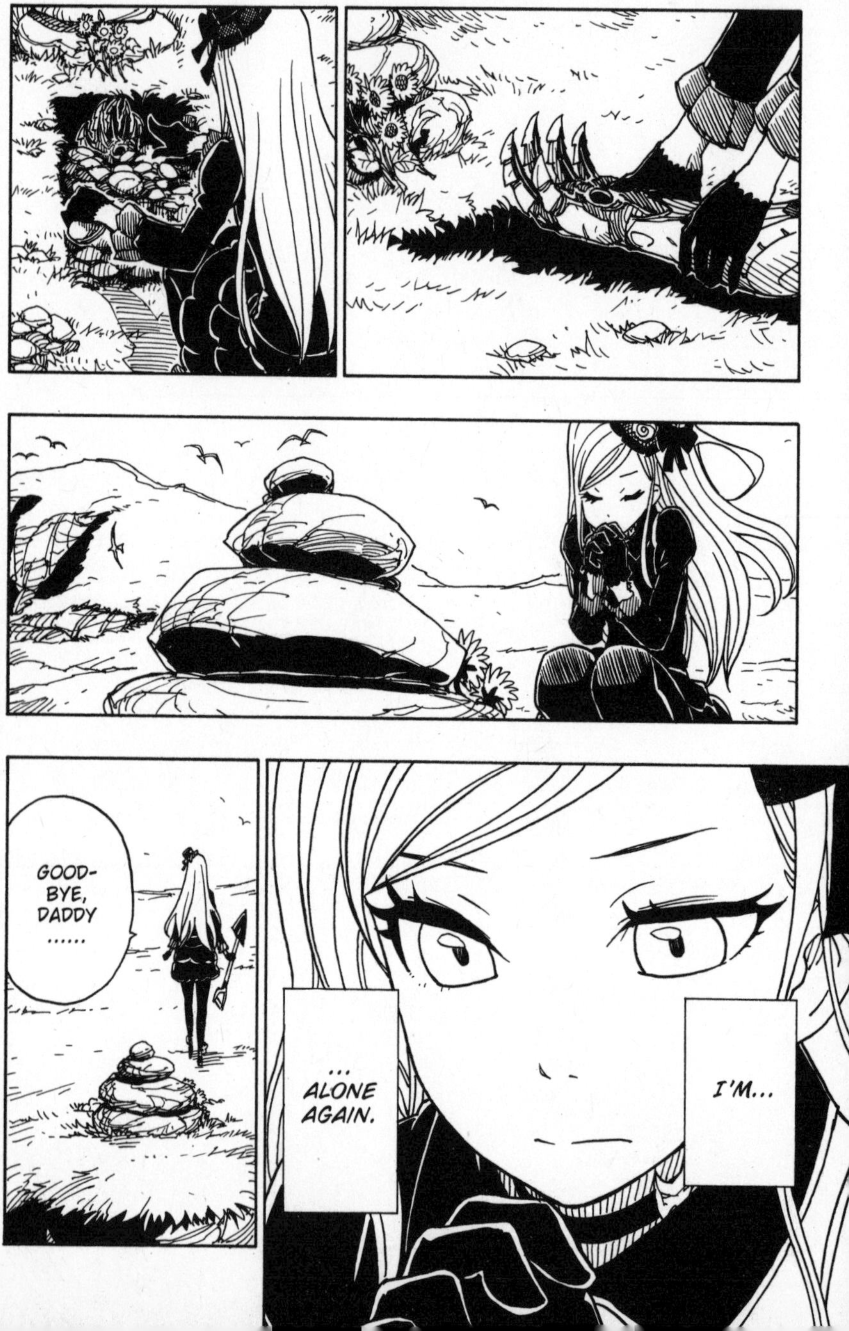
I'M...
... ALONE AGAIN.
GOOD-BYE, DADDY ......

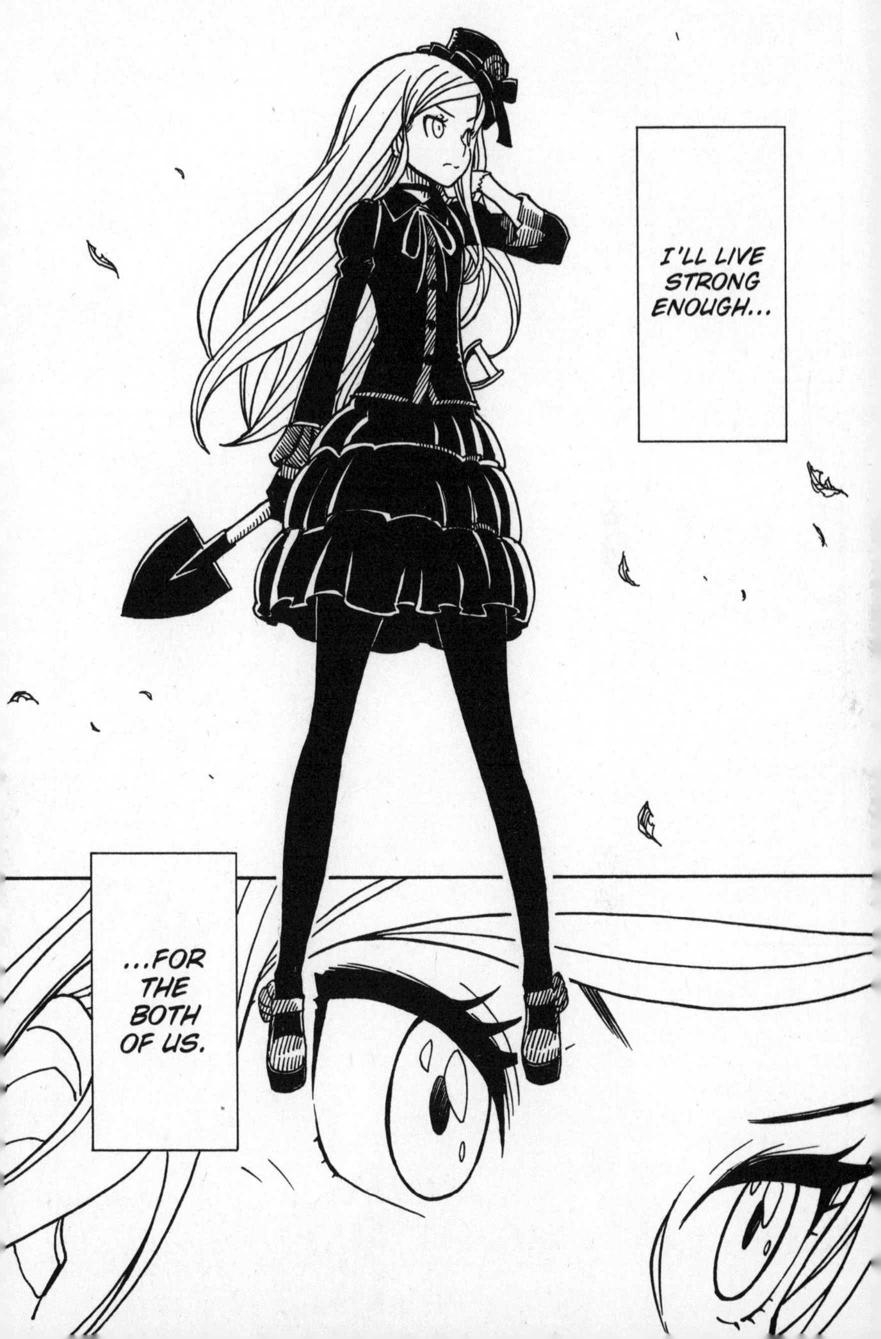
I'LL LIVE STRONG ENOUGH...
...FOR THE BOTH OF US.

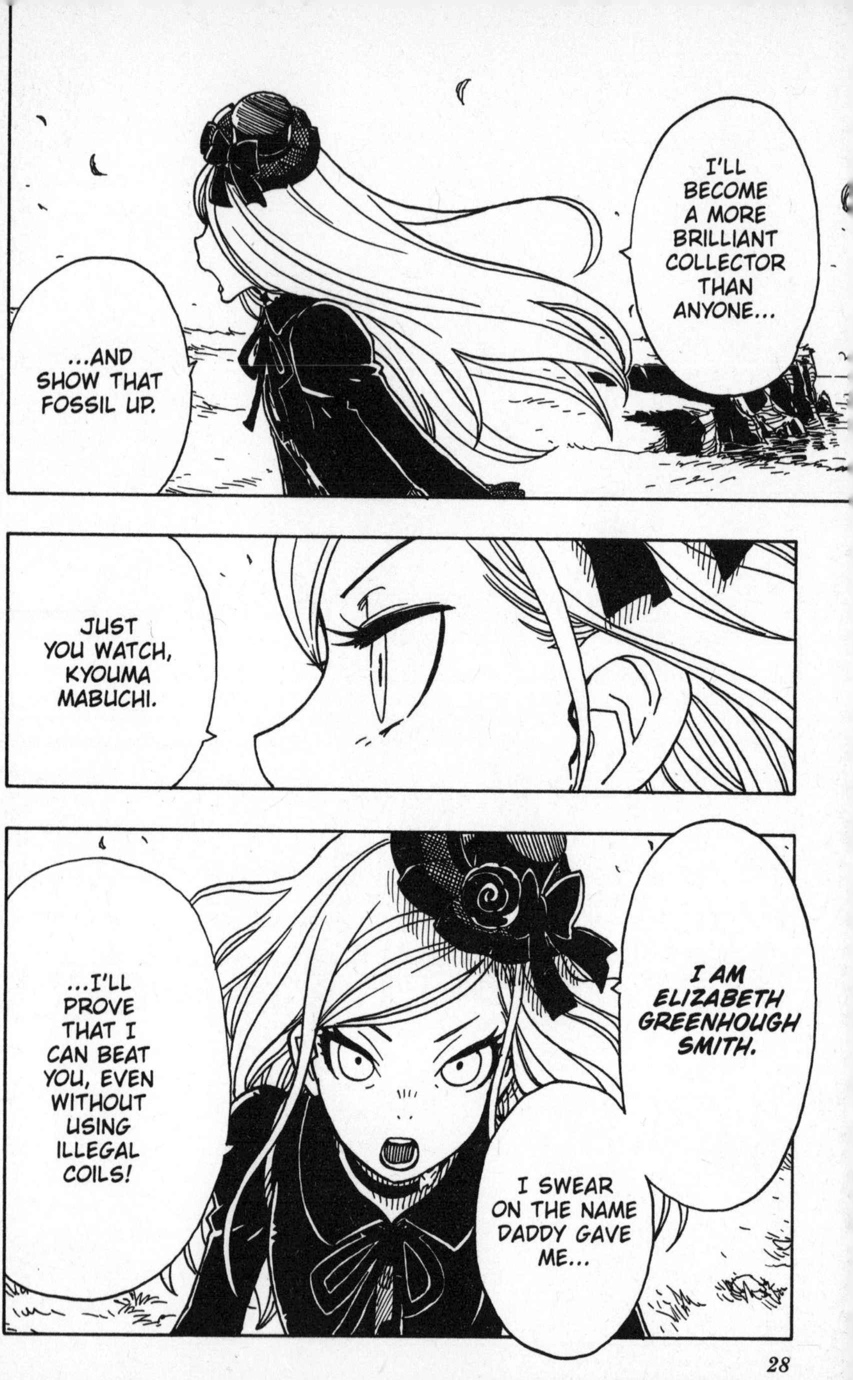
I'LL BECOME A MORE BRILLIANT COLLECTOR THAN ANYONE...
...AND SHOW THAT FOSSIL UP.
JUST YOU WATCH, KYOUMA MABUCHI.
I AM ELIZABETH GREENHOUGH SMITH.
I SWEAR ON THE NAME DADDY GAVE ME...
...I'LL PROVE THAT I CAN BEAT YOU, EVEN WITHOUT USING ILLEGAL COILS!

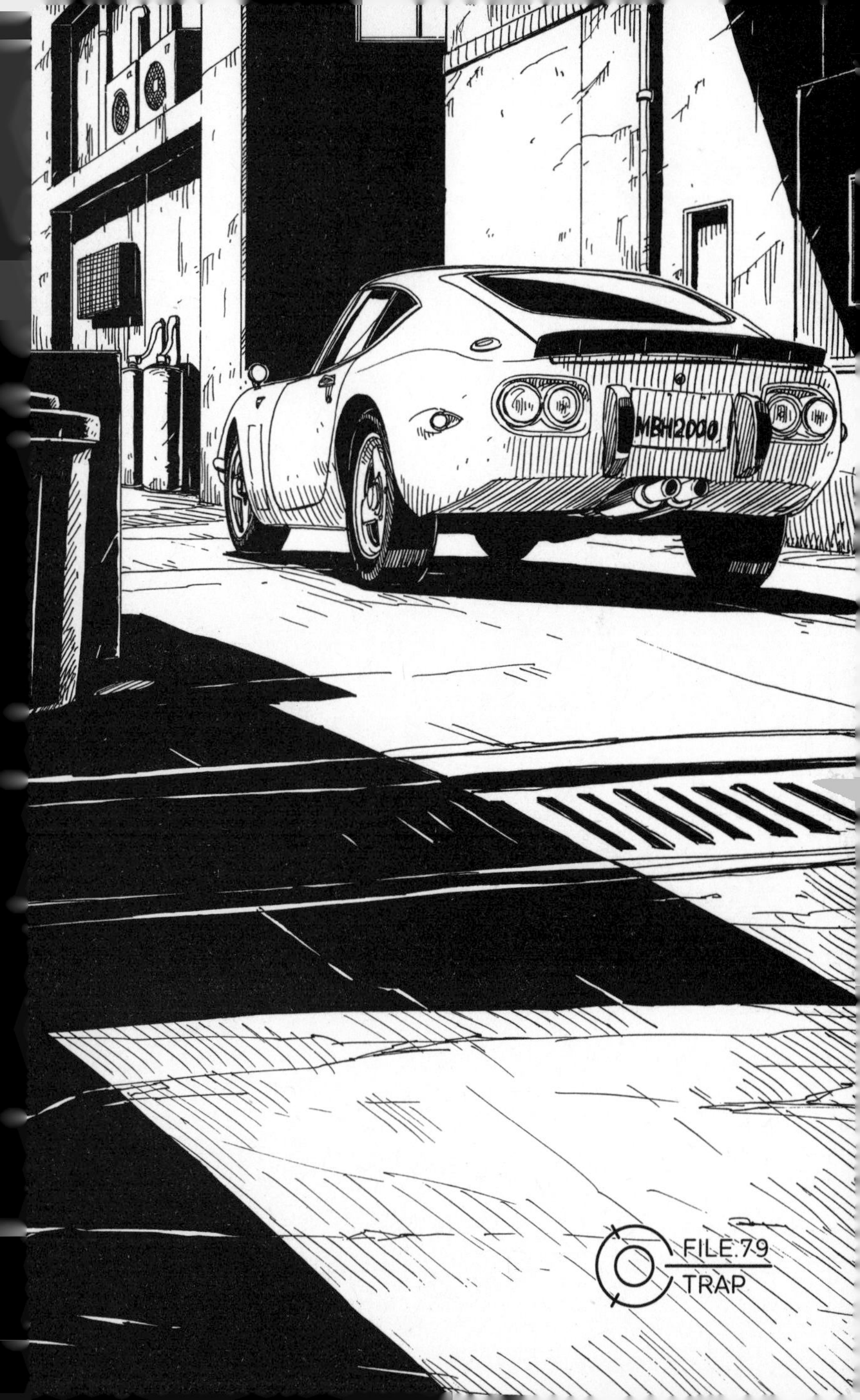
MBH2000
FILE.79
TRAP

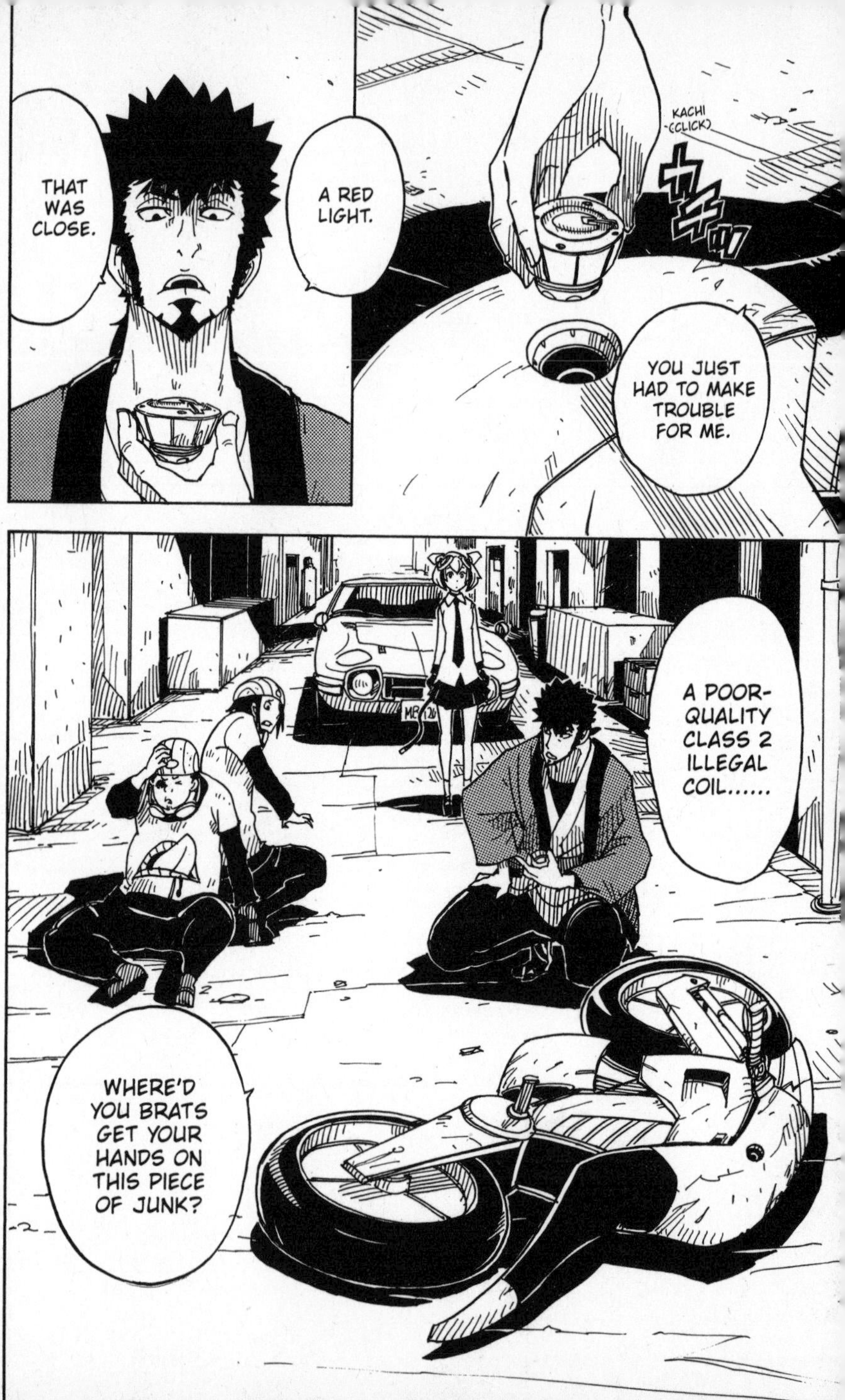
KACHI (CLICK)
YOU JUST HAD TO MAKE TROUBLE FOR ME.
A RED LIGHT.
THAT WAS CLOSE.
A POOR-QUALITY CLASS 2 ILLEGAL COIL......
WHERE'D YOU BRATS GET YOUR HANDS ON THIS PIECE OF JUNK?

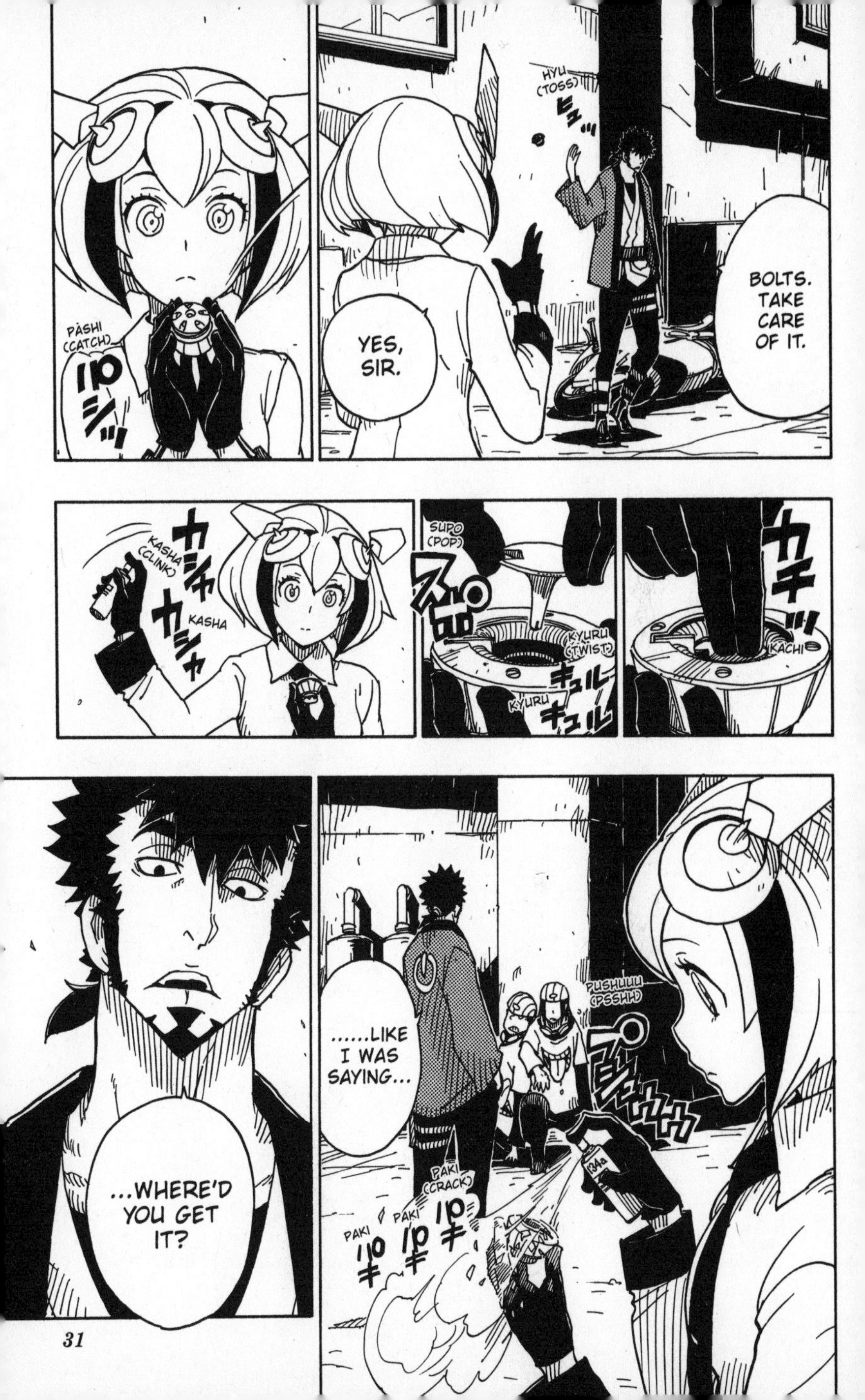
HYU (TOSS)
ヒュッ
BOLTS. TAKE CARE OF IT.
YES, SIR.
PASHI (CATCH)
パシッ
KACHI
カチッ
SUPO (POP)
スポ
KYURU (TWIST)
キュル
KYURU
キュル
KASHA (CLINK)
カシャ
KASHA
カシャ
......LIKE I WAS SAYING...
PUSHUUU (PSSHH)
PAKI (CRACK)
パキ
PAKI
パキ
PAKI
パキ
134a
...WHERE'D YOU GET IT?

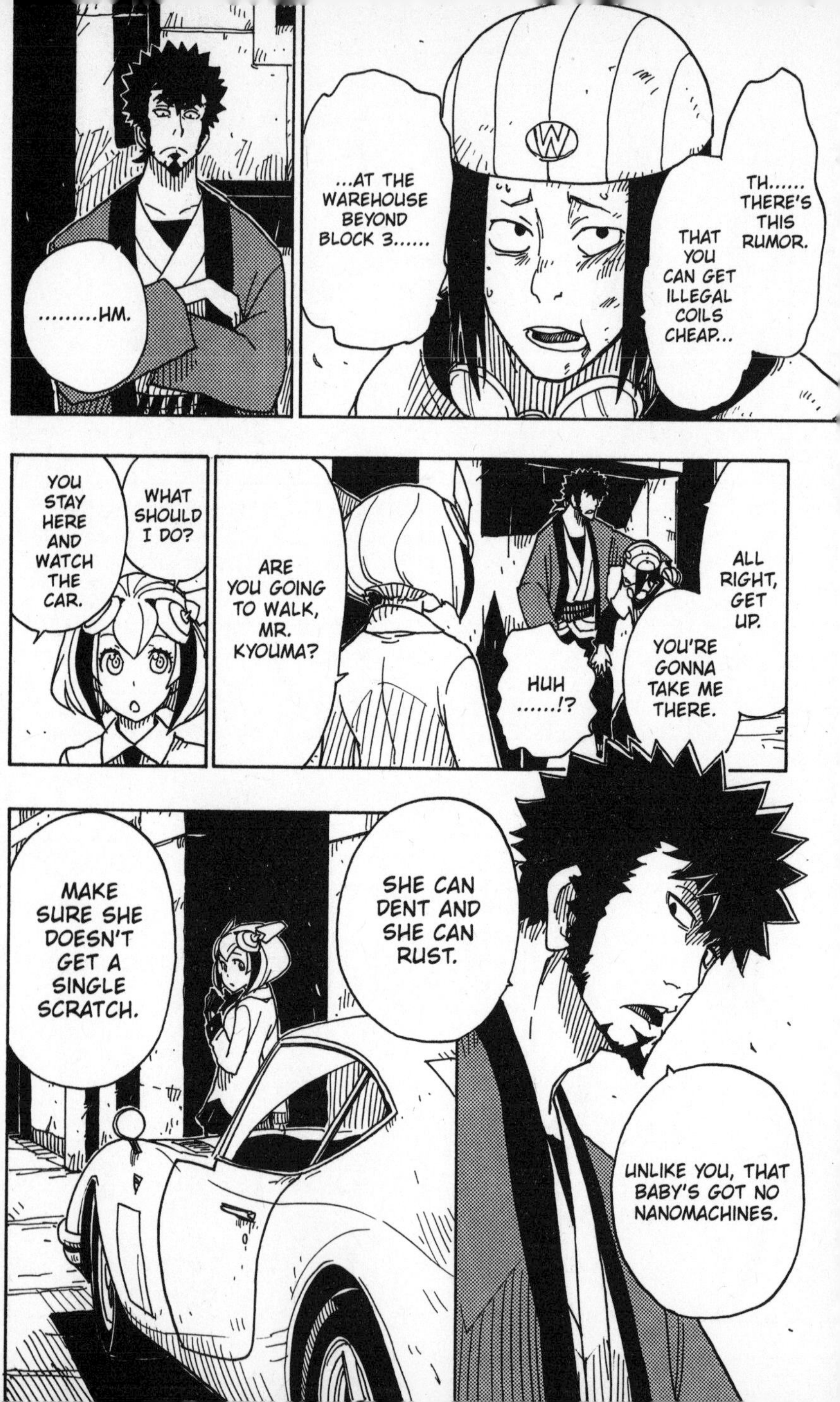
TH...... THERE'S THIS RUMOR.
THAT YOU CAN GET ILLEGAL COILS CHEAP...
...AT THE WAREHOUSE BEYOND BLOCK 3......
.........HM.
ALL RIGHT, GET UP.
YOU'RE GONNA TAKE ME THERE.
HUH ......!?
ARE YOU GOING TO WALK, MR. KYOUMA?
WHAT SHOULD I DO?
YOU STAY HERE AND WATCH THE CAR.
SHE CAN DENT AND SHE CAN RUST.
MAKE SURE SHE DOESN'T GET A SINGLE SCRATCH.
UNLIKE YOU, THAT BABY'S GOT NO NANOMACHINES.

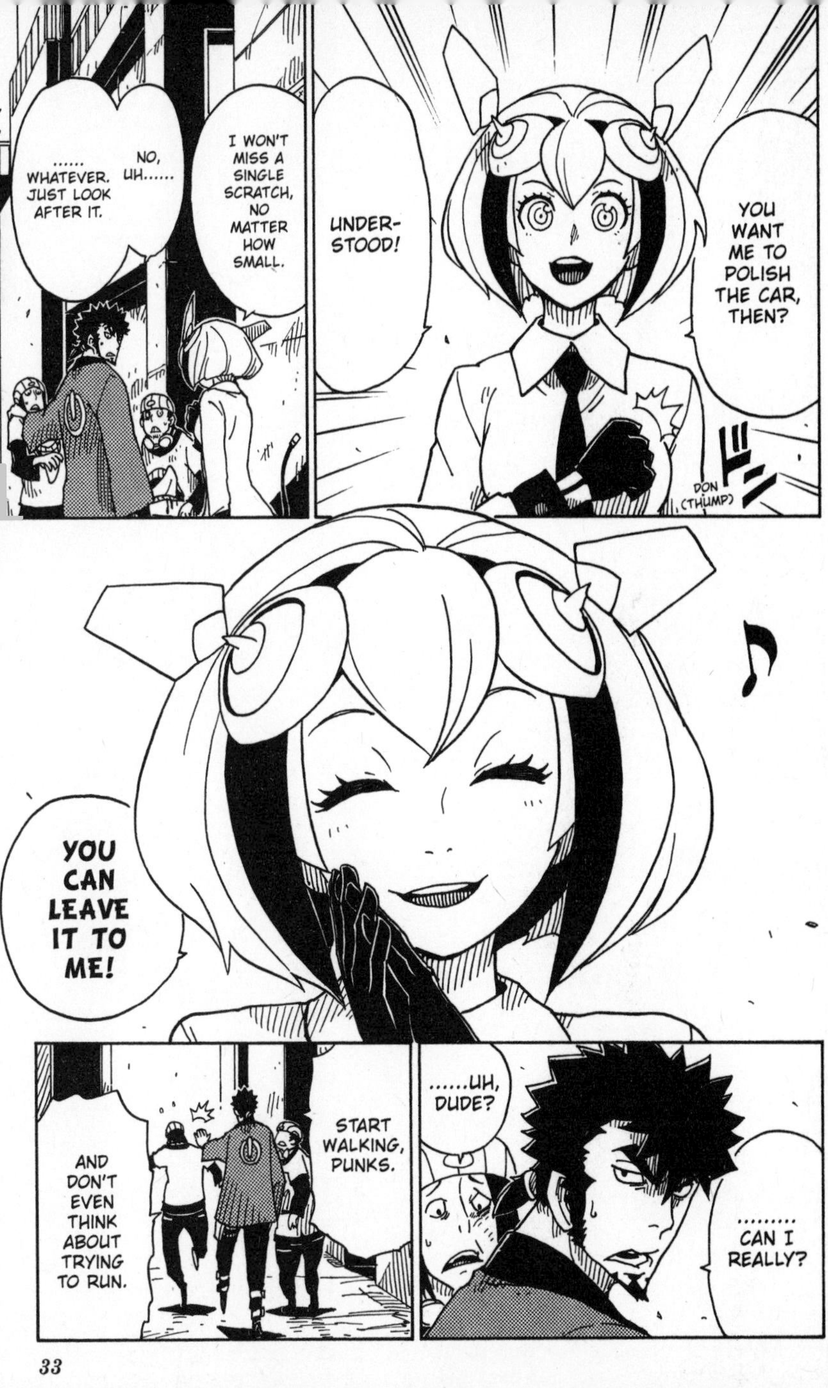
YOU WANT ME TO POLISH THE CAR, THEN?
DON (THUMP)
UNDER-STOOD!
I WON'T MISS A SINGLE SCRATCH, NO MATTER HOW SMALL.
NO, UH......
...... WHATEVER. JUST LOOK AFTER IT.
YOU CAN LEAVE IT TO ME!
.... CAN I REALLY?
......UH, DUDE?
START WALKING, PUNKS.
AND DON'T EVEN THINK ABOUT TRYING TO RUN.

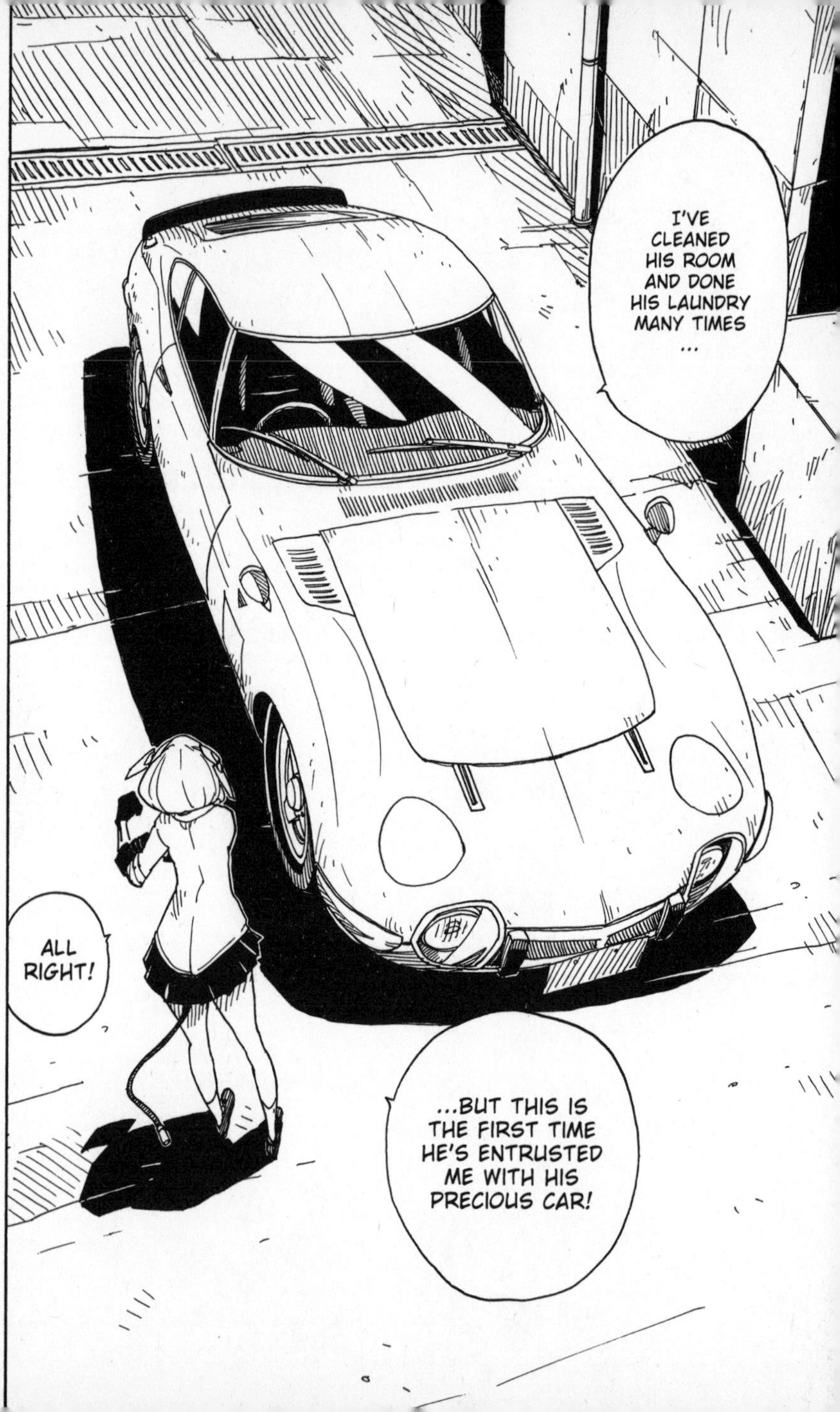
I'VE CLEANED HIS ROOM AND DONE HIS LAUNDRY MANY TIMES ...
...BUT THIS IS THE FIRST TIME HE'S ENTRUSTED ME WITH HIS PRECIOUS CAR!
ALL RIGHT!

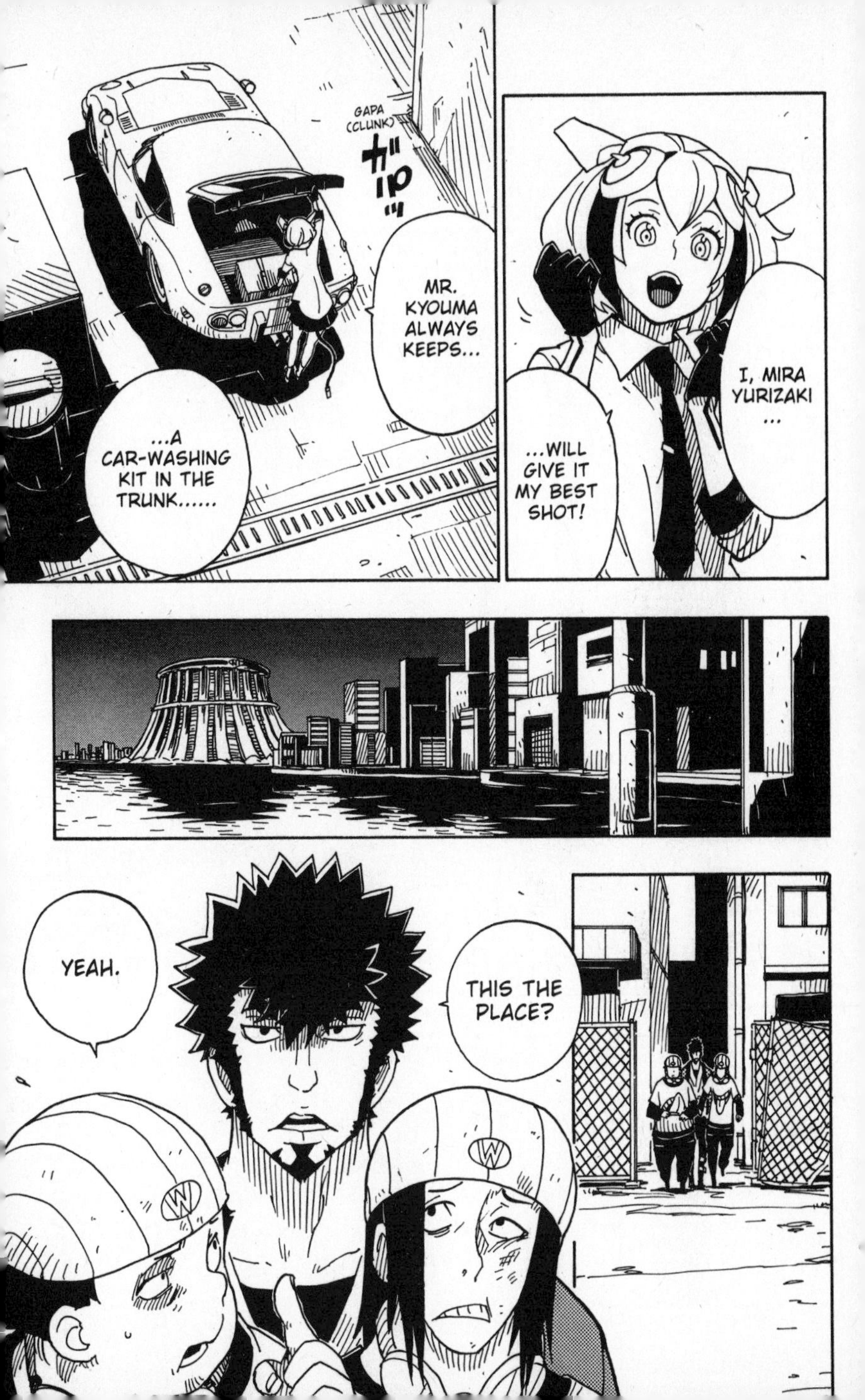

I, MIRA YURIZAKI ...
...WILL GIVE IT MY BEST SHOT!
GAPA (CLUNK)
MR. KYOUMA ALWAYS KEEPS...
...A CAR-WASHING KIT IN THE TRUNK......
THIS THE PLACE?
YEAH.

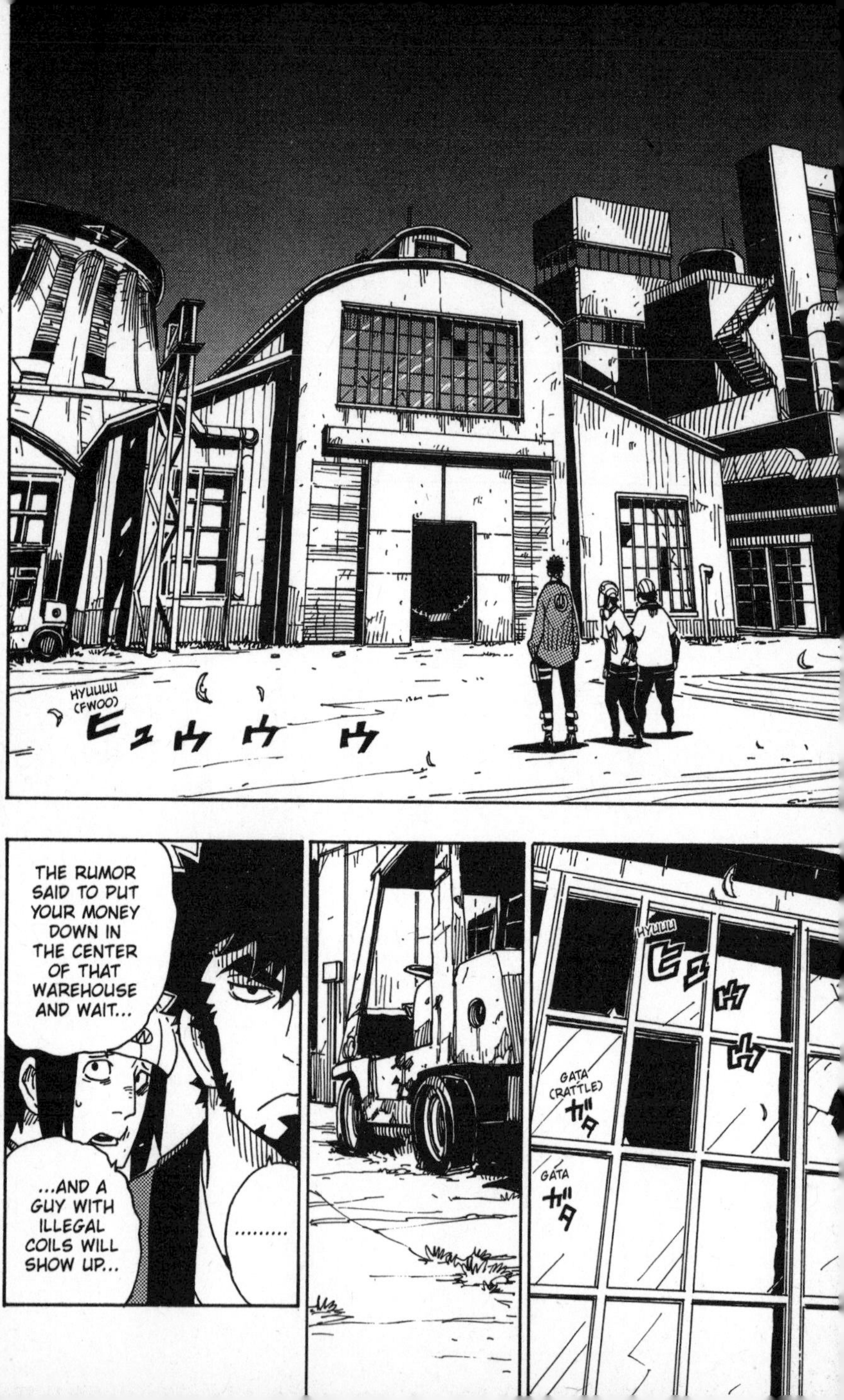
HYUUUU (FWOO)
ヒュウウウ
HYUUU
ヒュウウ
GATA (RATTLE)
ガタ
GATA
ガタ
THE RUMOR SAID TO PUT YOUR MONEY DOWN IN THE CENTER OF THAT WAREHOUSE AND WAIT...
...AND A GUY WITH ILLEGAL COILS WILL SHOW UP...
....

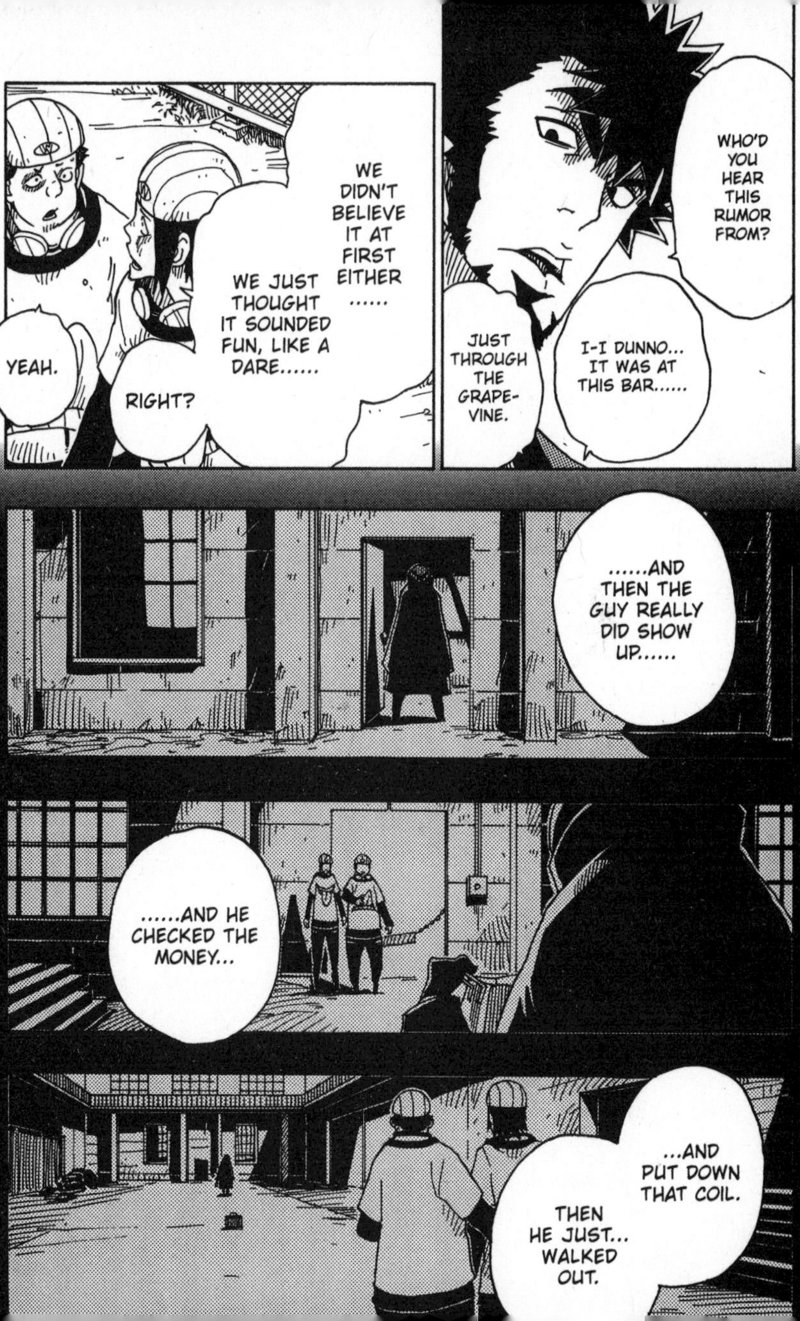
WHO'D YOU HEAR THIS RUMOR FROM?
I-I DUNNO... IT WAS AT THIS BAR......
JUST THROUGH THE GRAPE-VINE.
WE DIDN'T BELIEVE IT AT FIRST EITHER ......
WE JUST THOUGHT IT SOUNDED FUN, LIKE A DARE......
RIGHT?
YEAH.
......AND THEN THE GUY REALLY DID SHOW UP......
......AND HE CHECKED THE MONEY...
...AND PUT DOWN THAT COIL.
THEN HE JUST... WALKED OUT.

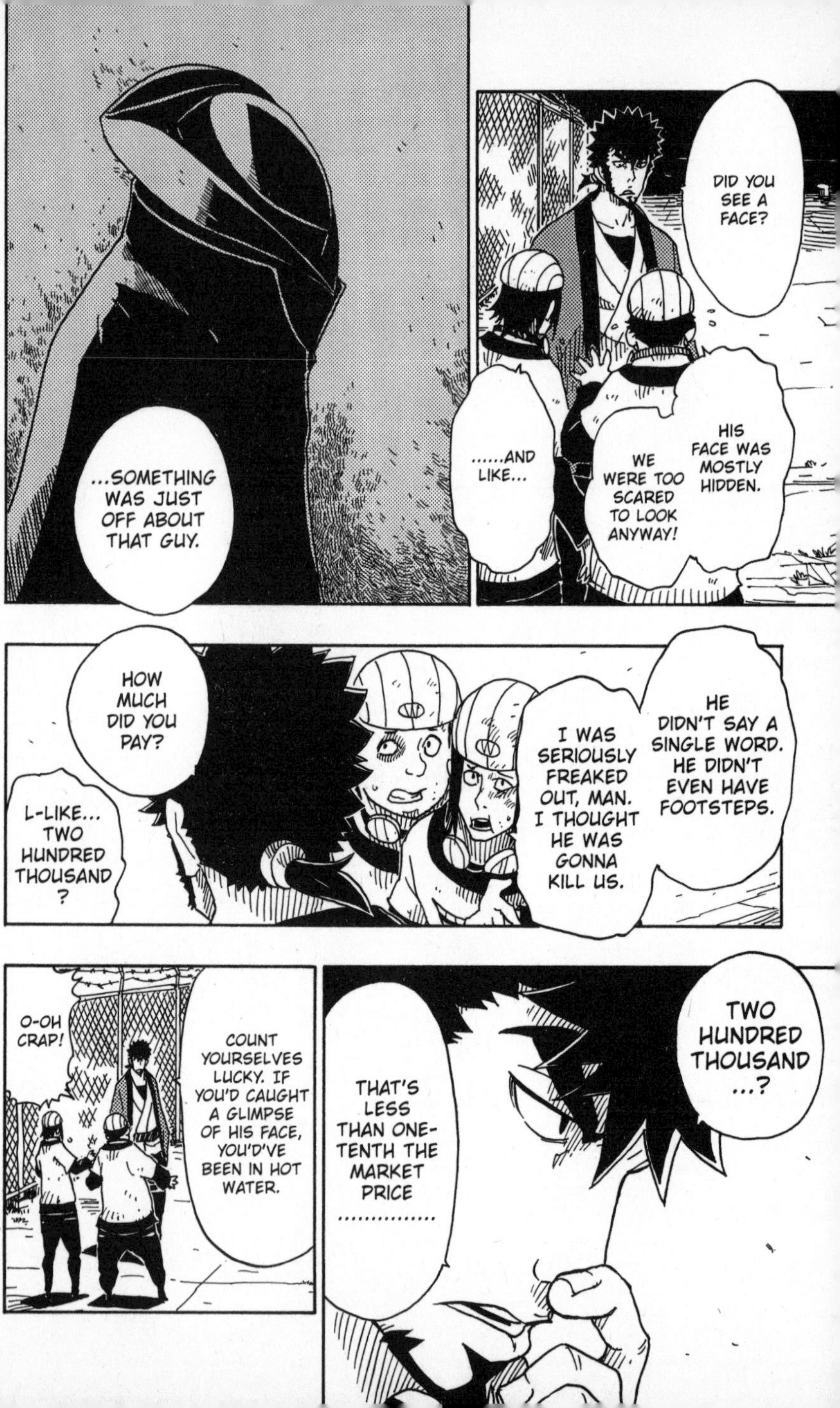
DID YOU SEE A FACE?
HIS FACE WAS MOSTLY HIDDEN.
WE WERE TOO SCARED TO LOOK ANYWAY!
......AND LIKE...
...SOMETHING WAS JUST OFF ABOUT THAT GUY.
HE DIDN'T SAY A SINGLE WORD. HE DIDN'T EVEN HAVE FOOTSTEPS.
I WAS SERIOUSLY FREAKED OUT, MAN. I THOUGHT HE WAS GONNA KILL US.
HOW MUCH DID YOU PAY?
L-LIKE... TWO HUNDRED THOUSAND?
TWO HUNDRED THOUSAND...?
THAT'S LESS THAN ONE-TENTH THE MARKET PRICE ....
COUNT YOURSELVES LUCKY. IF YOU'D CAUGHT A GLIMPSE OF HIS FACE, YOU'D'VE BEEN IN HOT WATER.
O-OH CRAP!

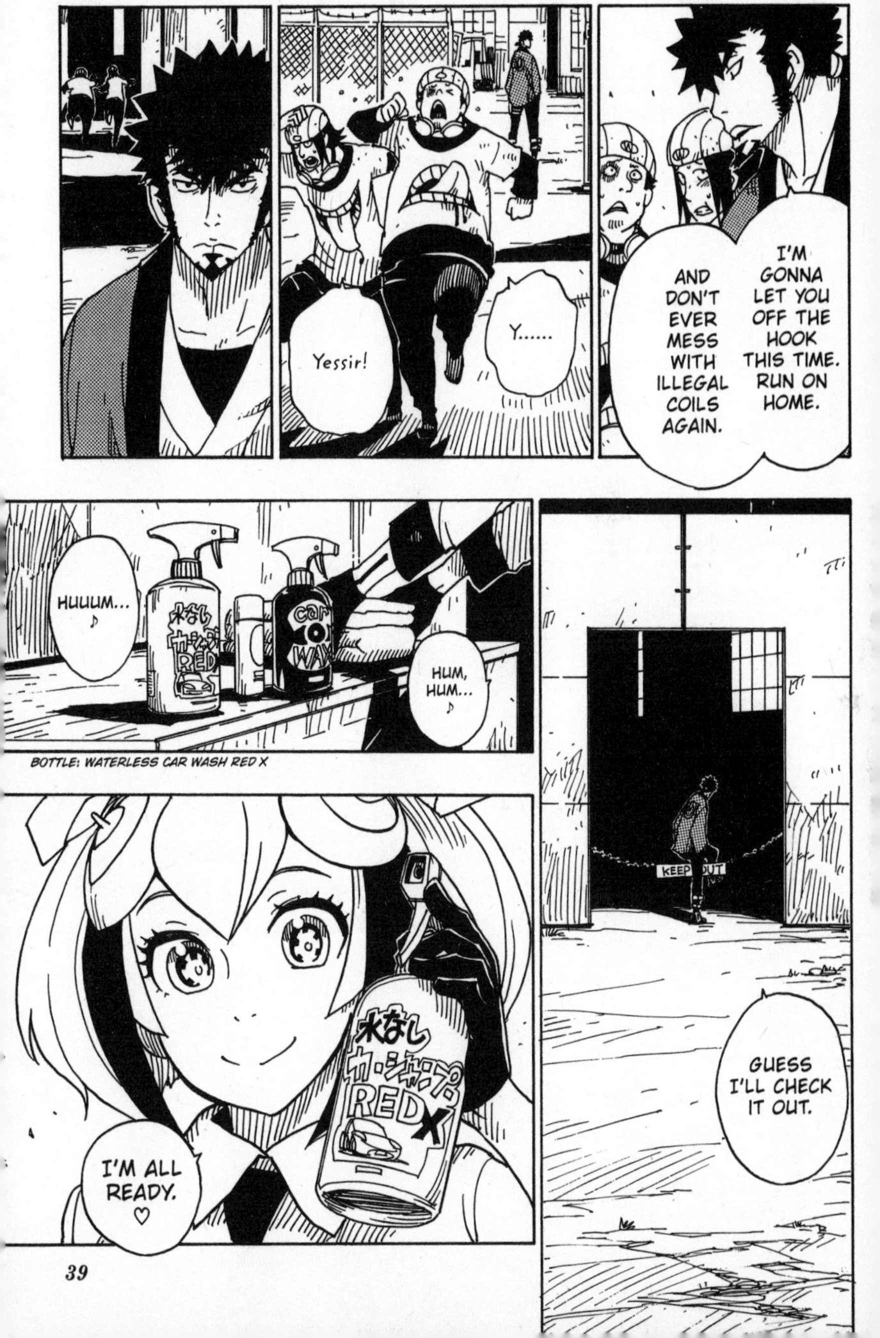
I'M GONNA LET YOU OFF THE HOOK THIS TIME. RUN ON HOME.
AND DON'T EVER MESS WITH ILLEGAL COILS AGAIN.
Y......
Yessir!
KEEP OUT
GUESS I'LL CHECK IT OUT.
HUUUM... ♪
HUM, HUM... ♪
I'M ALL READY. ♡

BOTTLE: WATERLESS CAR WASH RED X

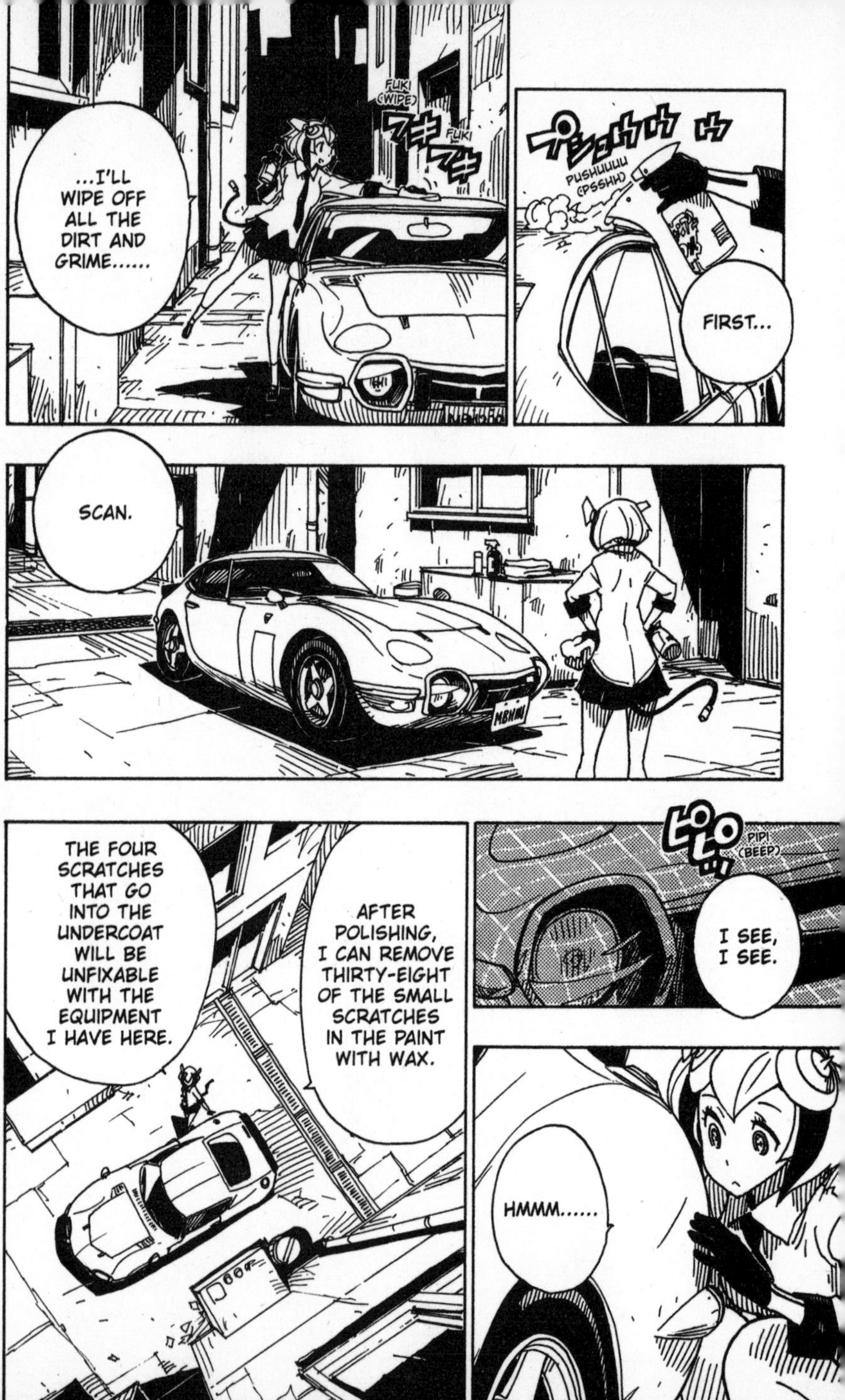
PUSHUUUU (PSSHH)
FIRST...
FUKI (WIPE)
FUKI
...I'LL WIPE OFF ALL THE DIRT AND GRIME......
SCAN.
PIPI (BEEP)
I SEE, I SEE.
HMMM......
AFTER POLISHING, I CAN REMOVE THIRTY-EIGHT OF THE SMALL SCRATCHES IN THE PAINT WITH WAX.
THE FOUR SCRATCHES THAT GO INTO THE UNDERCOAT WILL BE UNFIXABLE WITH THE EQUIPMENT I HAVE HERE.

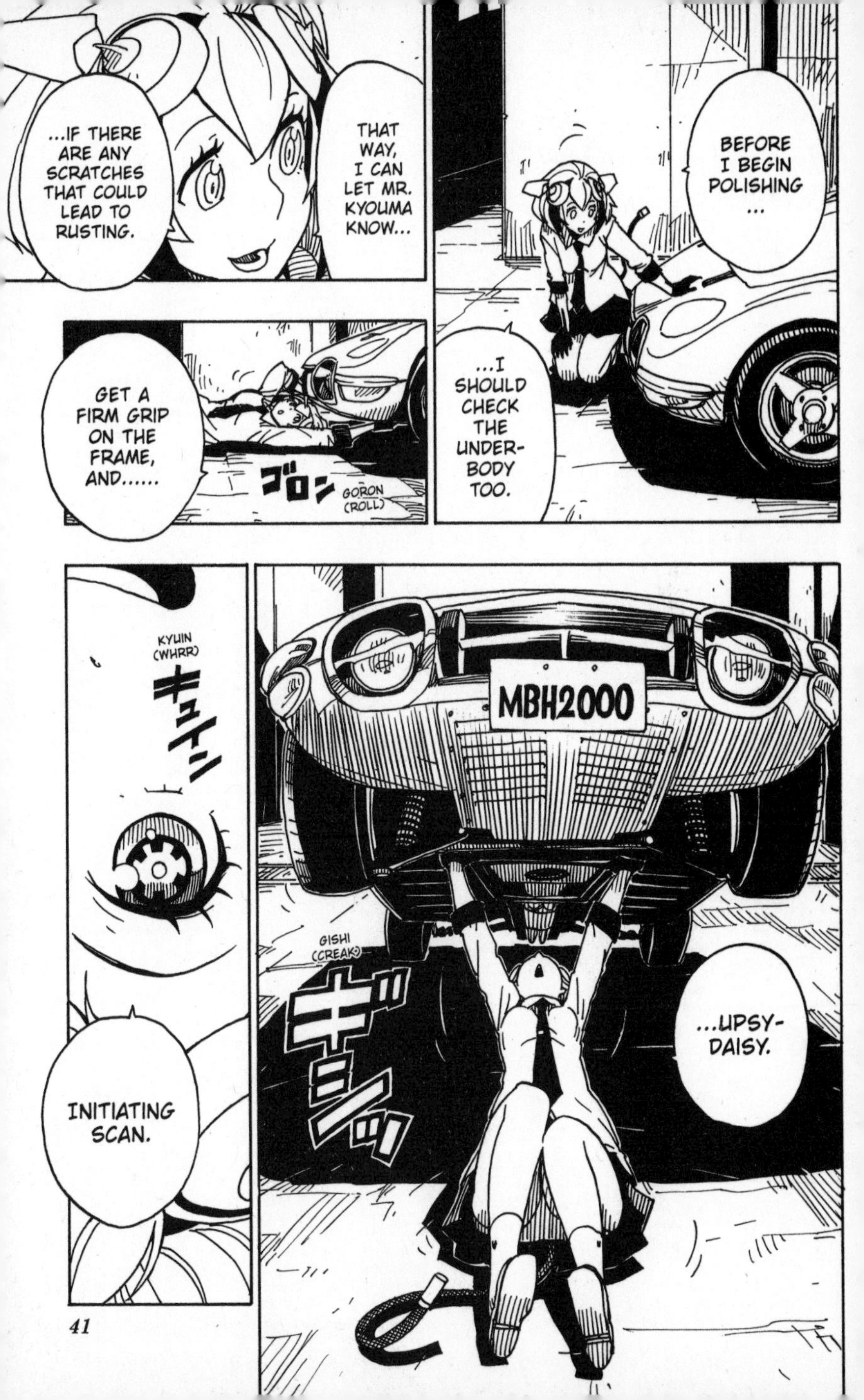
BEFORE I BEGIN POLISHING...
...I SHOULD CHECK THE UNDER-BODY TOO.
THAT WAY, I CAN LET MR. KYOUMA KNOW...
...IF THERE ARE ANY SCRATCHES THAT COULD LEAD TO RUSTING.
GET A FIRM GRIP ON THE FRAME, AND......
ゴロン GORON (ROLL)
MBH2000
ギシッ GISHI (CREAK)
...UPSY-DAISY.
キュイン KYUIN (WHRR)
INITIATING SCAN.

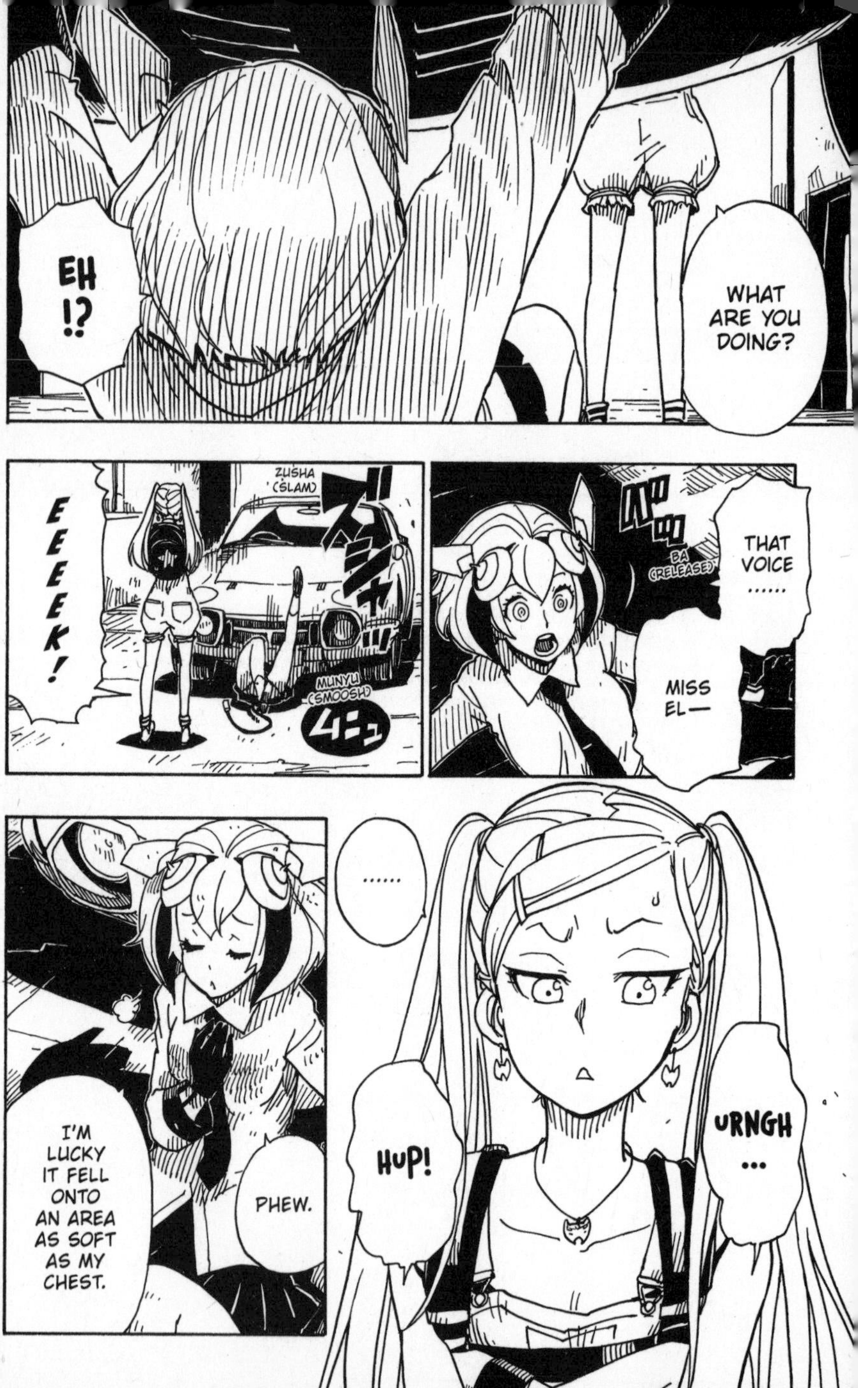
WHAT ARE YOU DOING?
EH!?
BA (RELEASE)
THAT VOICE ......
MISS EL—
ZUSHA (SLAM)
EEEEEK!
MUNYU (SMOOSH)
......
URNGH ...
HUP!
PHEW.
I'M LUCKY IT FELL ONTO AN AREA AS SOFT AS MY CHEST.

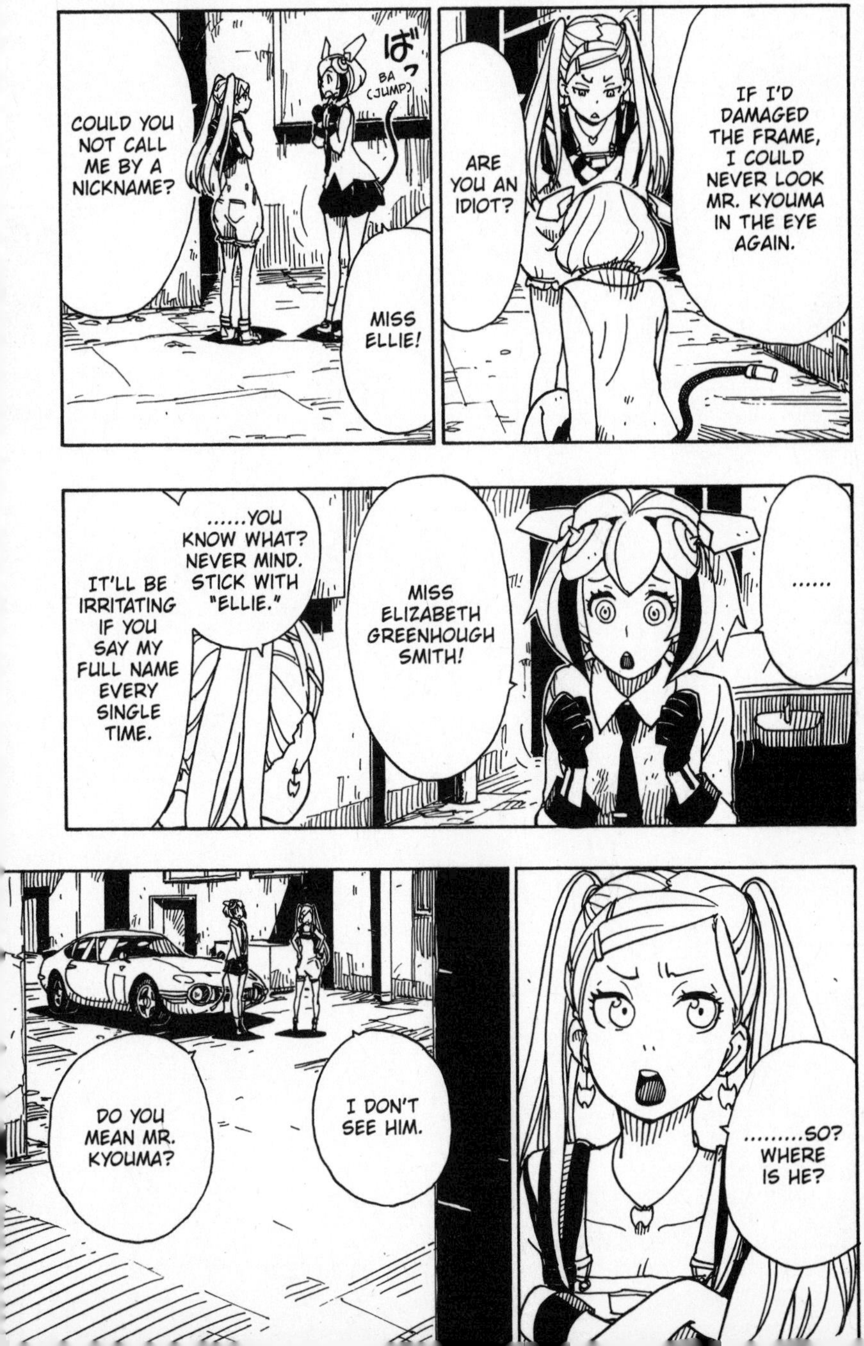
IF I'D DAMAGED THE FRAME, I COULD NEVER LOOK MR. KYOUMA IN THE EYE AGAIN.
ARE YOU AN IDIOT?
ばっ
BA (JUMP)
MISS ELLIE!
COULD YOU NOT CALL ME BY A NICKNAME?
......
MISS ELIZABETH GREENHOUGH SMITH!
......YOU KNOW WHAT? NEVER MIND. STICK WITH "ELLIE."
IT'LL BE IRRITATING IF YOU SAY MY FULL NAME EVERY SINGLE TIME.
.........SO? WHERE IS HE?
I DON'T SEE HIM.
DO YOU MEAN MR. KYOUMA?

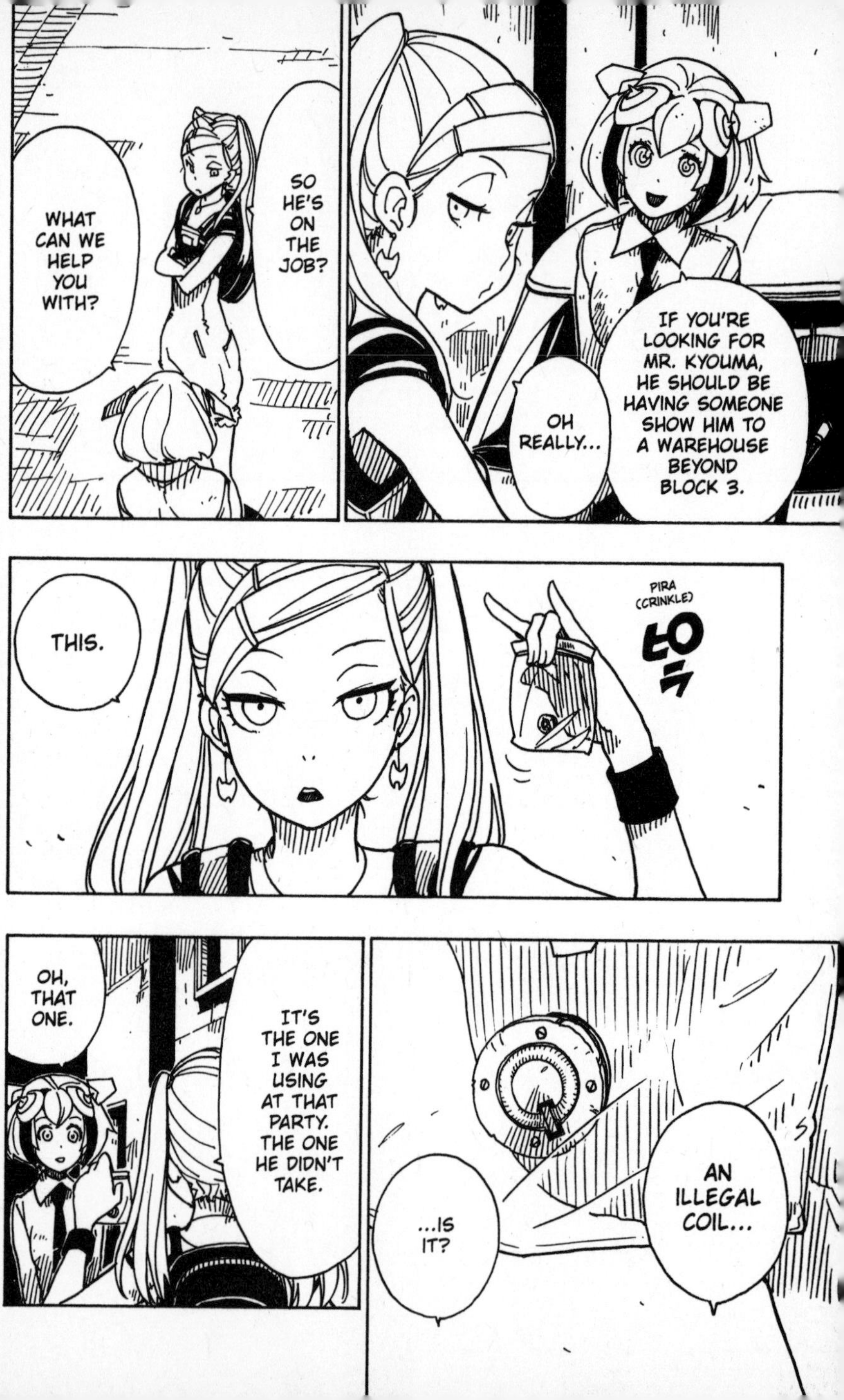
IF YOU'RE LOOKING FOR MR. KYOUMA, HE SHOULD BE HAVING SOMEONE SHOW HIM TO A WAREHOUSE BEYOND BLOCK 3.
OH REALLY...
SO HE'S ON THE JOB?
WHAT CAN WE HELP YOU WITH?
PIRA (CRINKLE)
ピラ
THIS.
AN ILLEGAL COIL...
...IS IT?
IT'S THE ONE I WAS USING AT THAT PARTY. THE ONE HE DIDN'T TAKE.
OH, THAT ONE.

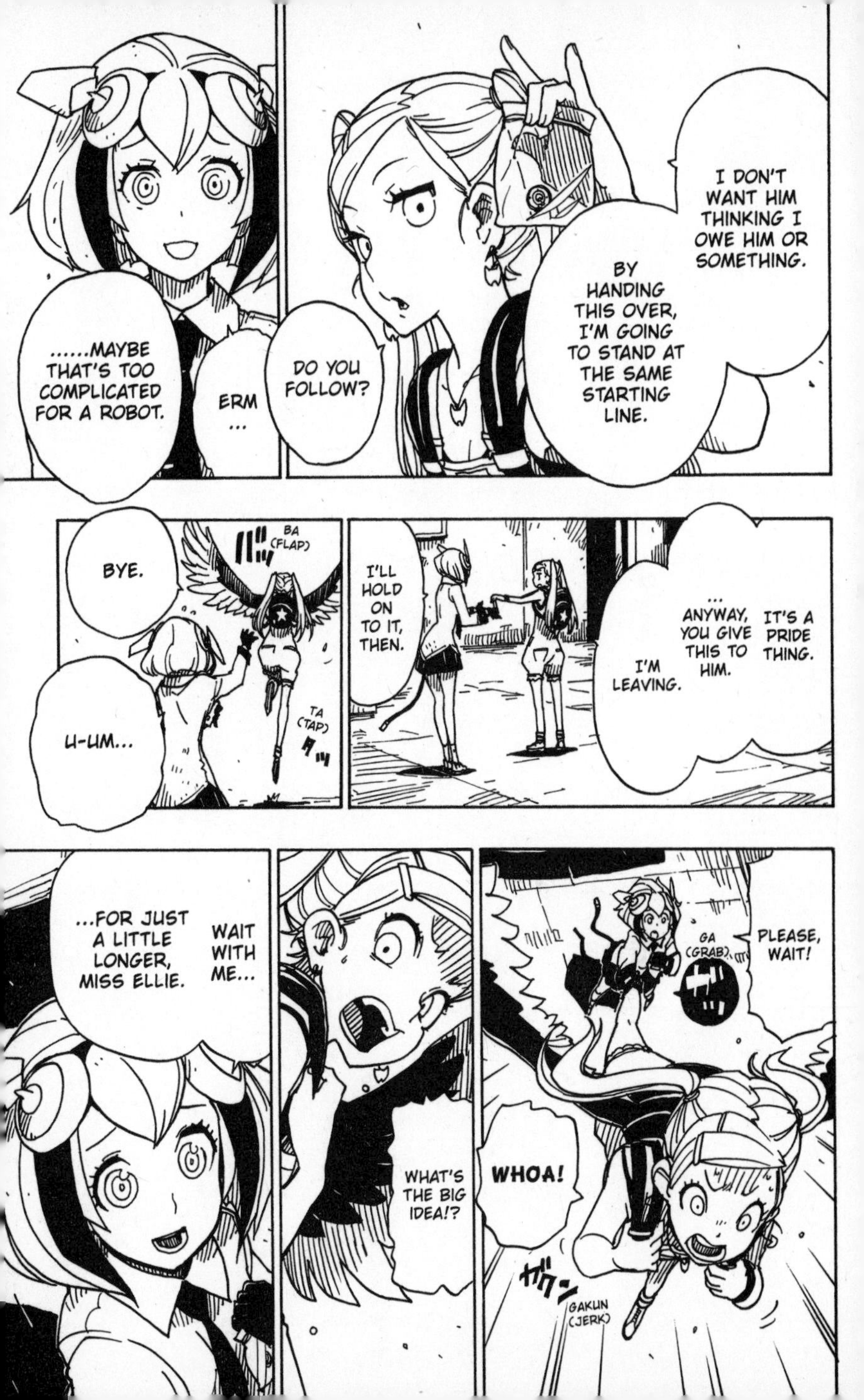
I DON'T WANT HIM THINKING I OWE HIM OR SOMETHING.
BY HANDING THIS OVER, I'M GOING TO STAND AT THE SAME STARTING LINE.
DO YOU FOLLOW?
ERM ...
......MAYBE THAT'S TOO COMPLICATED FOR A ROBOT.
IT'S A PRIDE THING.
... ANYWAY, YOU GIVE THIS TO HIM.
I'M LEAVING.
I'LL HOLD ON TO IT, THEN.
BYE.
BA (FLAP)
TA (TAP)
U-UM...
PLEASE, WAIT!
GA (GRAB)
WHOA!
GAKUN (JERK)
WHAT'S THE BIG IDEA!?
WAIT WITH ME...
...FOR JUST A LITTLE LONGER, MISS ELLIE.

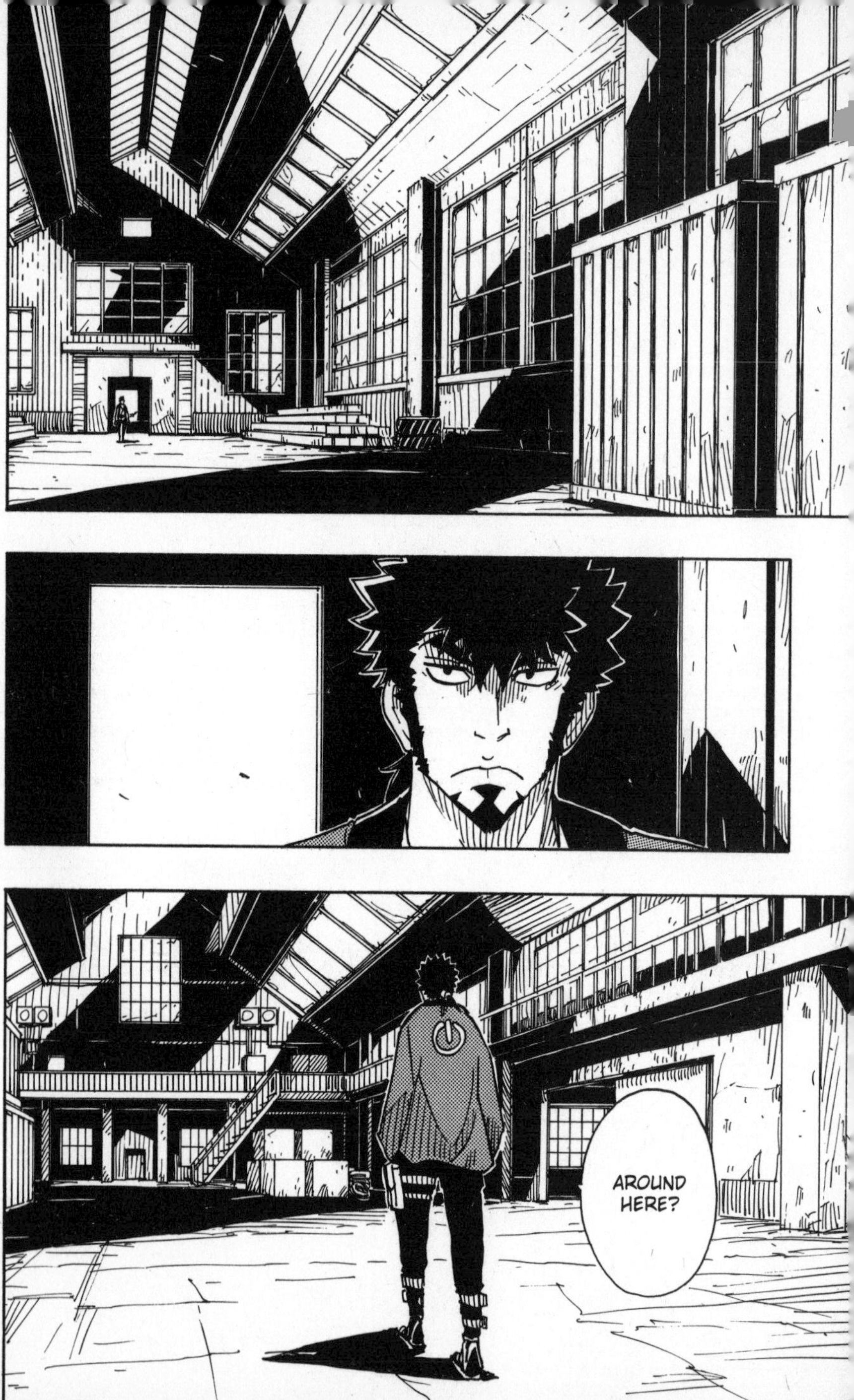
AROUND HERE?

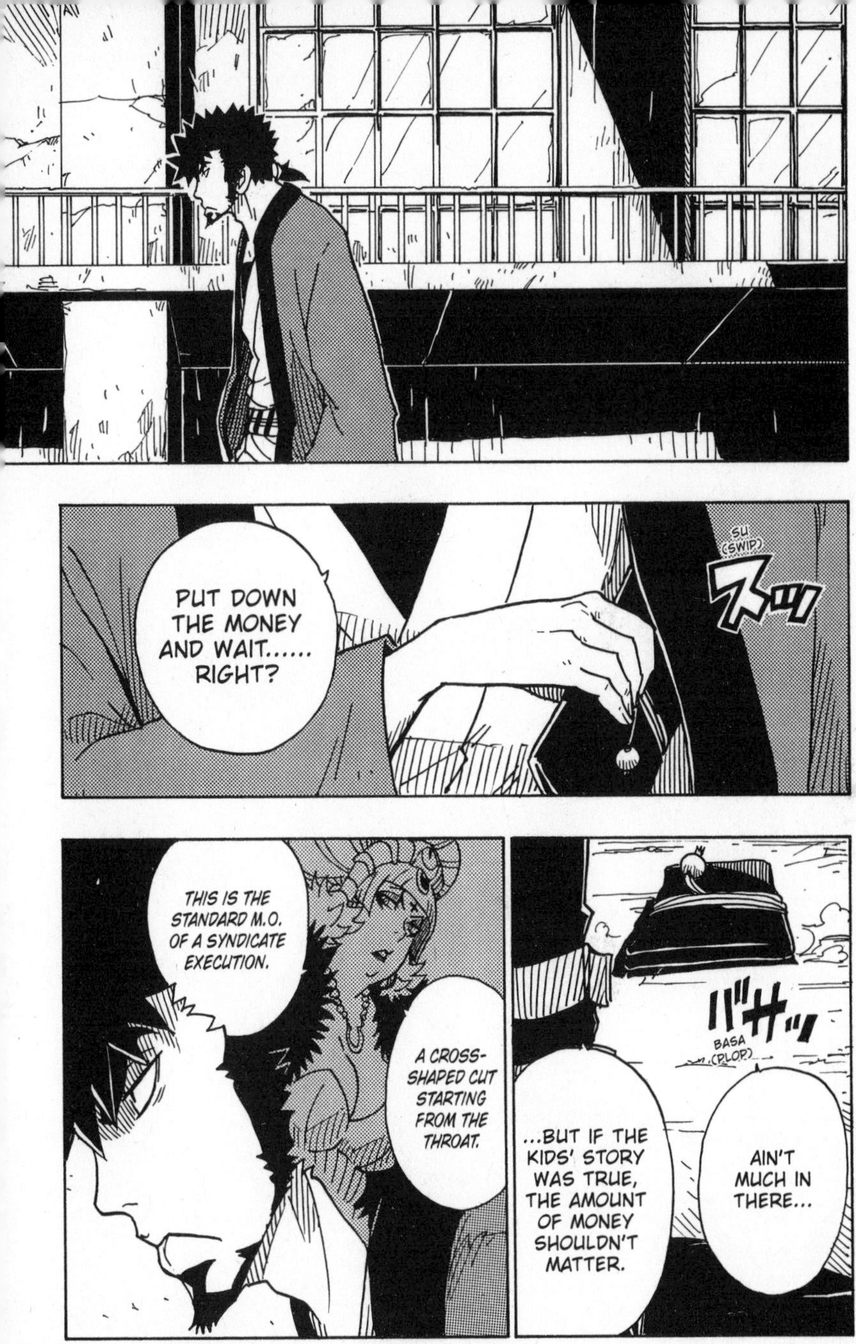
SU
(SWIP)
スッ
PUT DOWN THE MONEY AND WAIT...... RIGHT?
バサッ
BASA
(PLOP)
AIN'T MUCH IN THERE...
...BUT IF THE KIDS' STORY WAS TRUE, THE AMOUNT OF MONEY SHOULDN'T MATTER.
THIS IS THE STANDARD M.O. OF A SYNDICATE EXECUTION.
A CROSS-SHAPED CUT STARTING FROM THE THROAT.

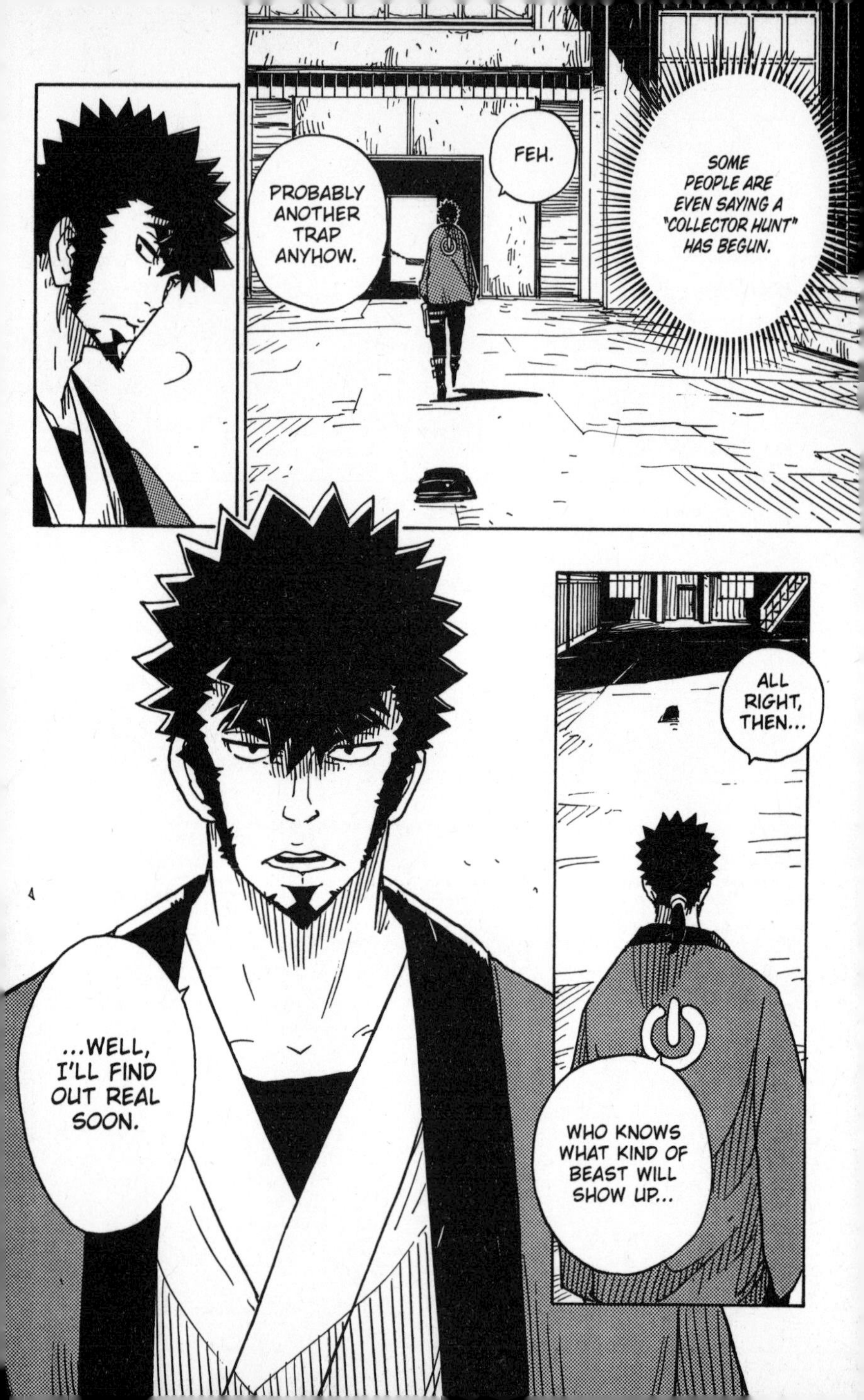
SOME PEOPLE ARE EVEN SAYING A "COLLECTOR HUNT" HAS BEGUN.
FEH.
PROBABLY ANOTHER TRAP ANYHOW.
ALL RIGHT, THEN...
WHO KNOWS WHAT KIND OF BEAST WILL SHOW UP...
...WELL, I'LL FIND OUT REAL SOON.

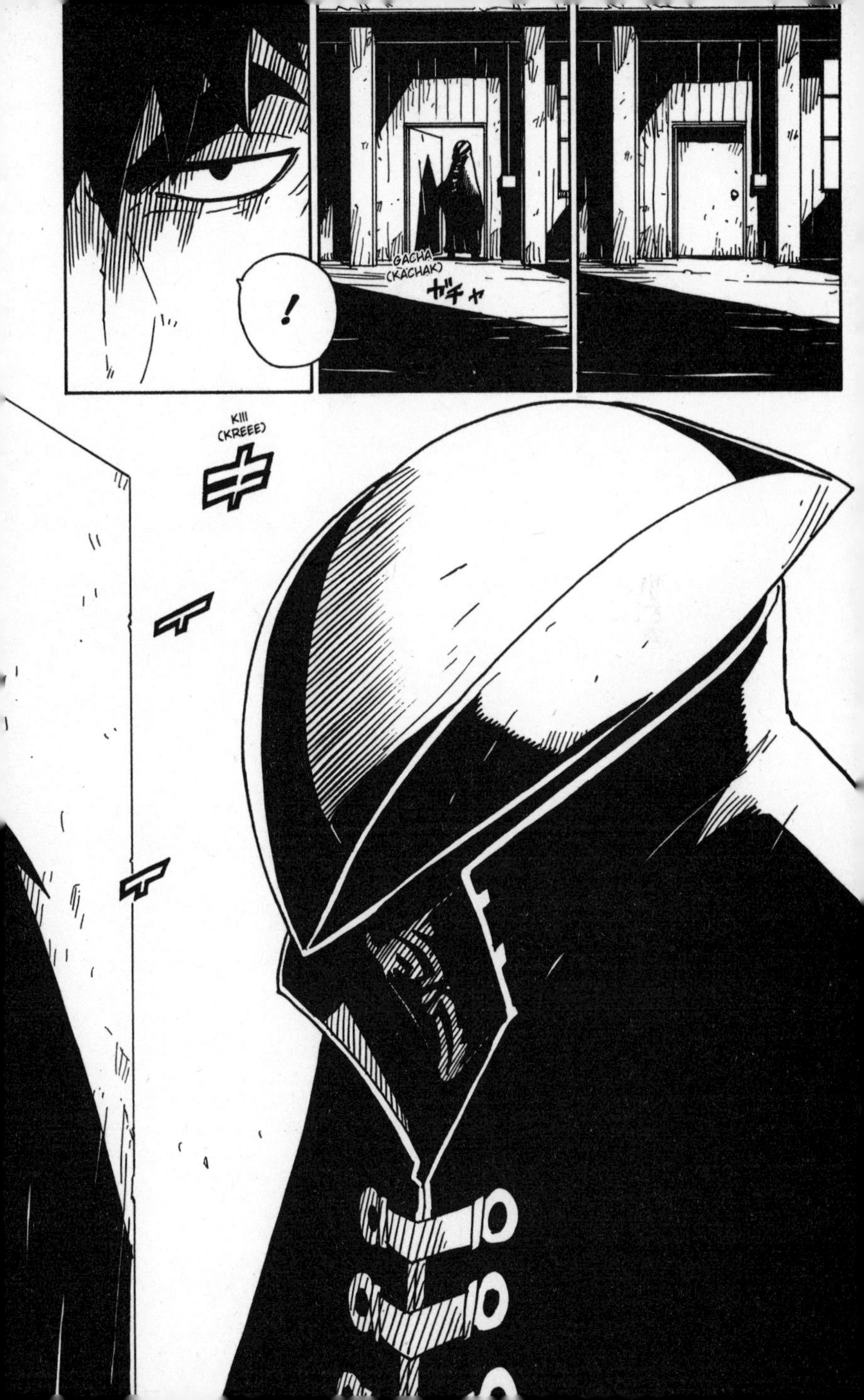
GACHA (KACHAK)
ガチャ
!
KIII (KREEE)
キィィ

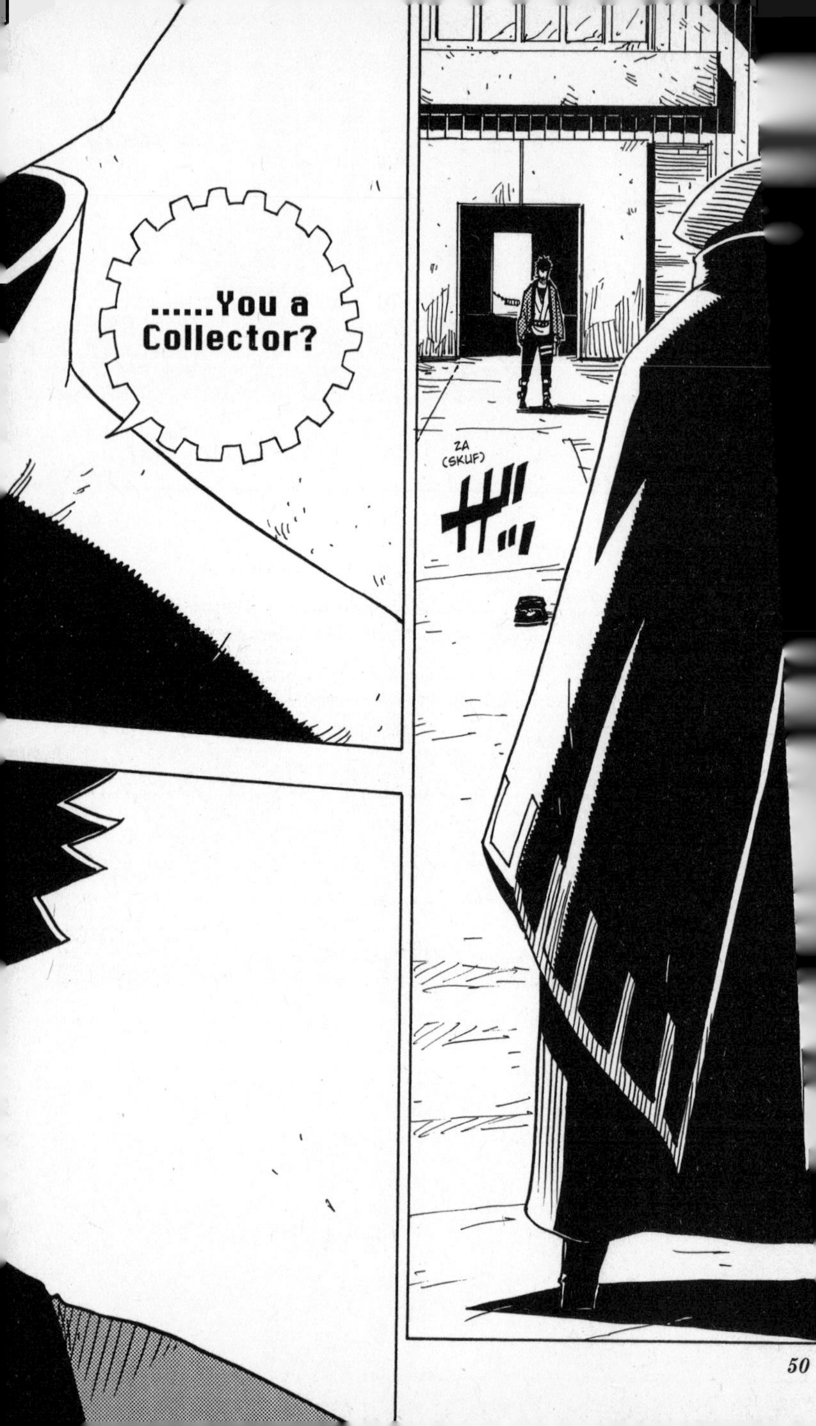
ZA
(SKUF)
ザッ
......You a Collector?

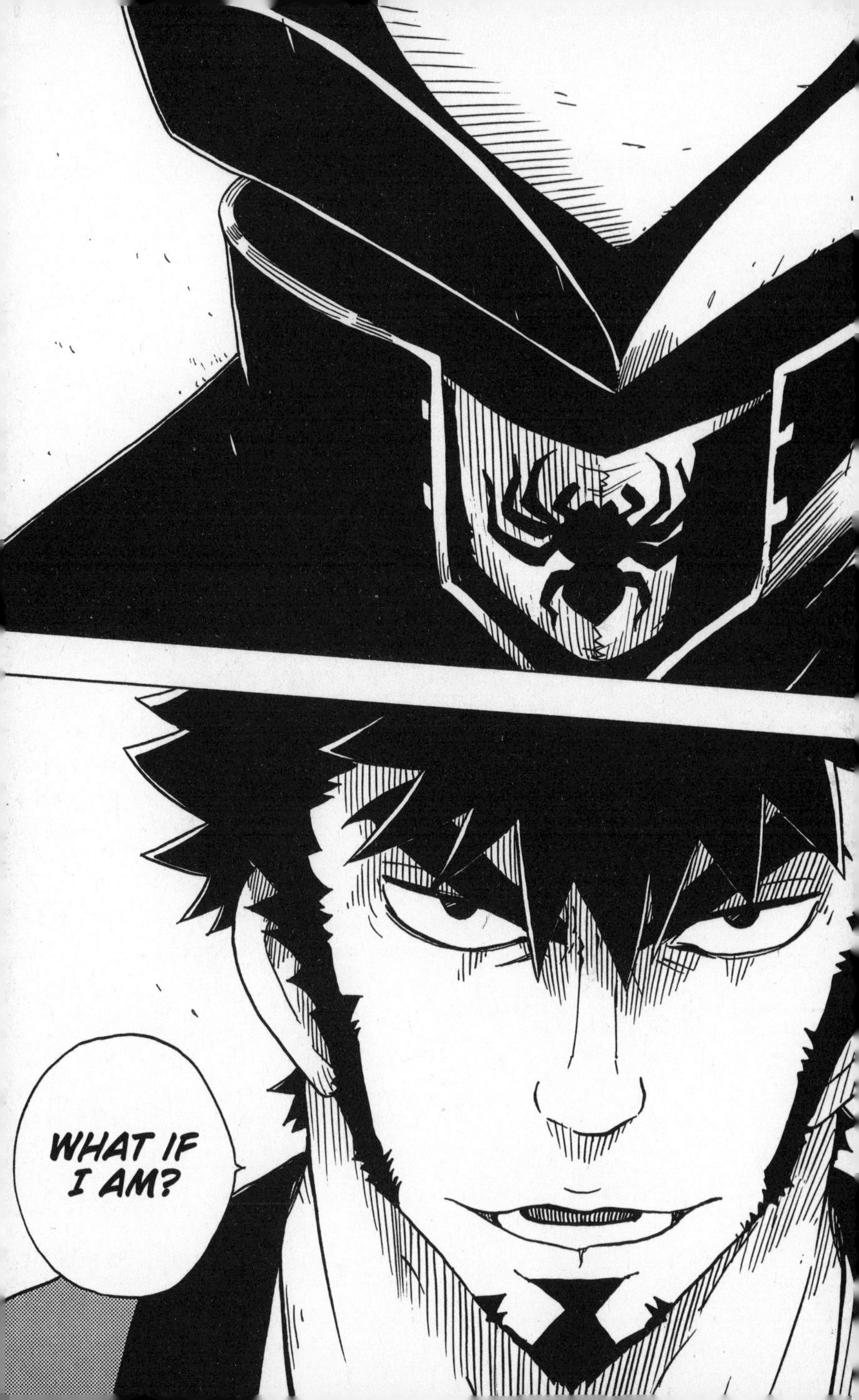
WHAT IF I AM?

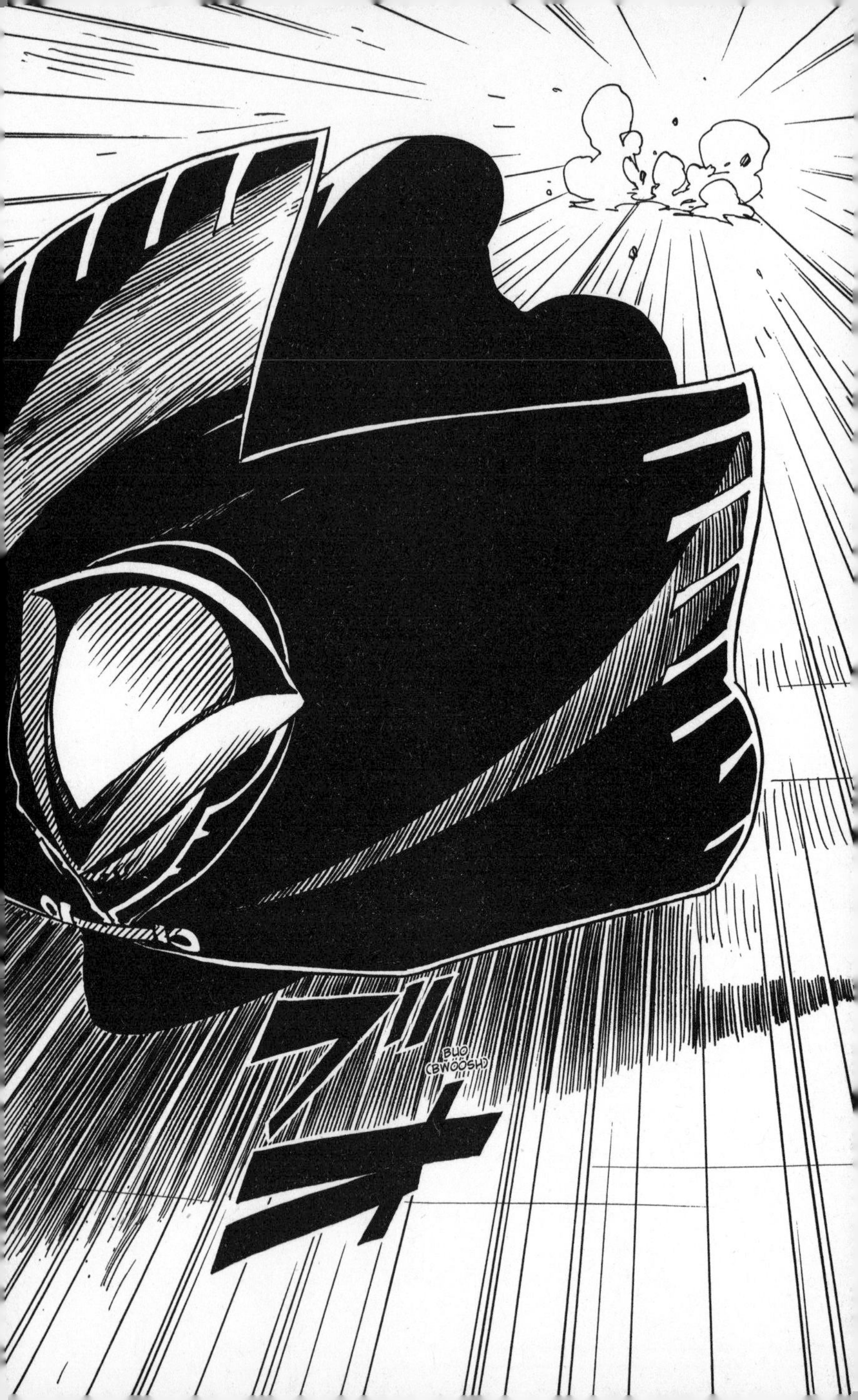
ブオ
BUO
(BWOOSH)

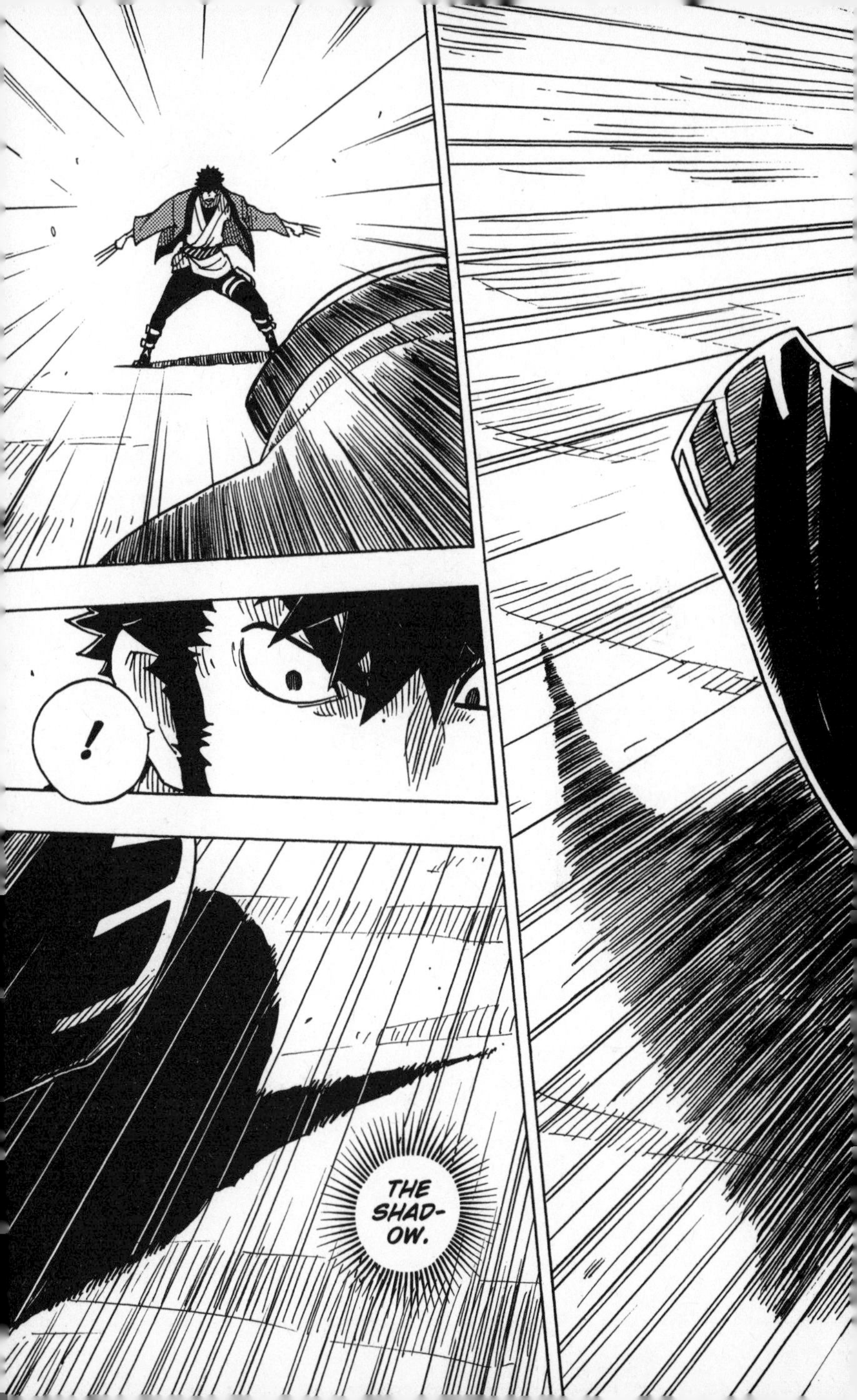
!
THE SHAD-OW.

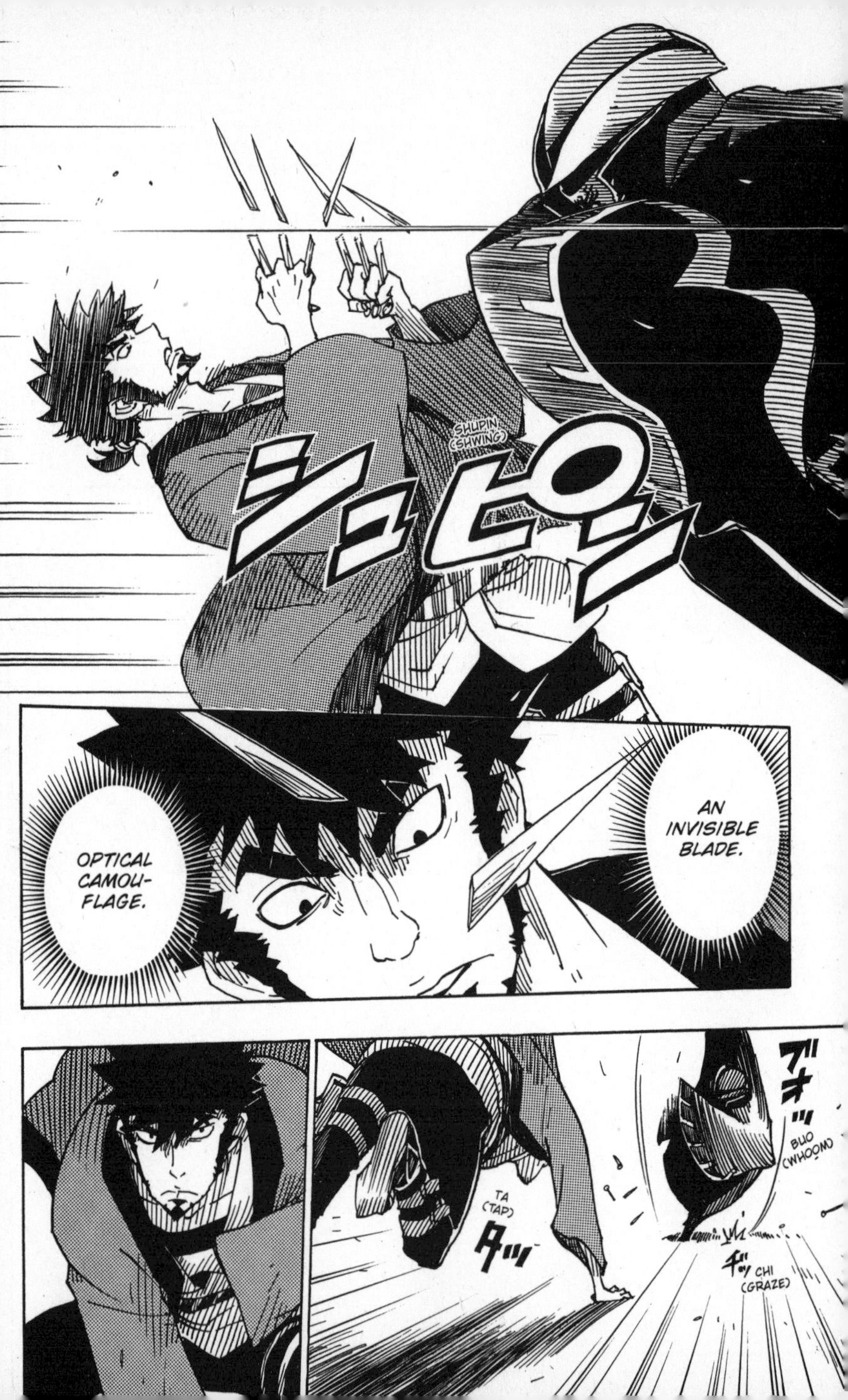
SHUPIN (SHWING)
シュピン
AN INVISIBLE BLADE.
OPTICAL CAMOUFLAGE.
ブオッ
BUO (WHOOM)
TA (TAP)
タッ
チッ
CHI (GRAZE)

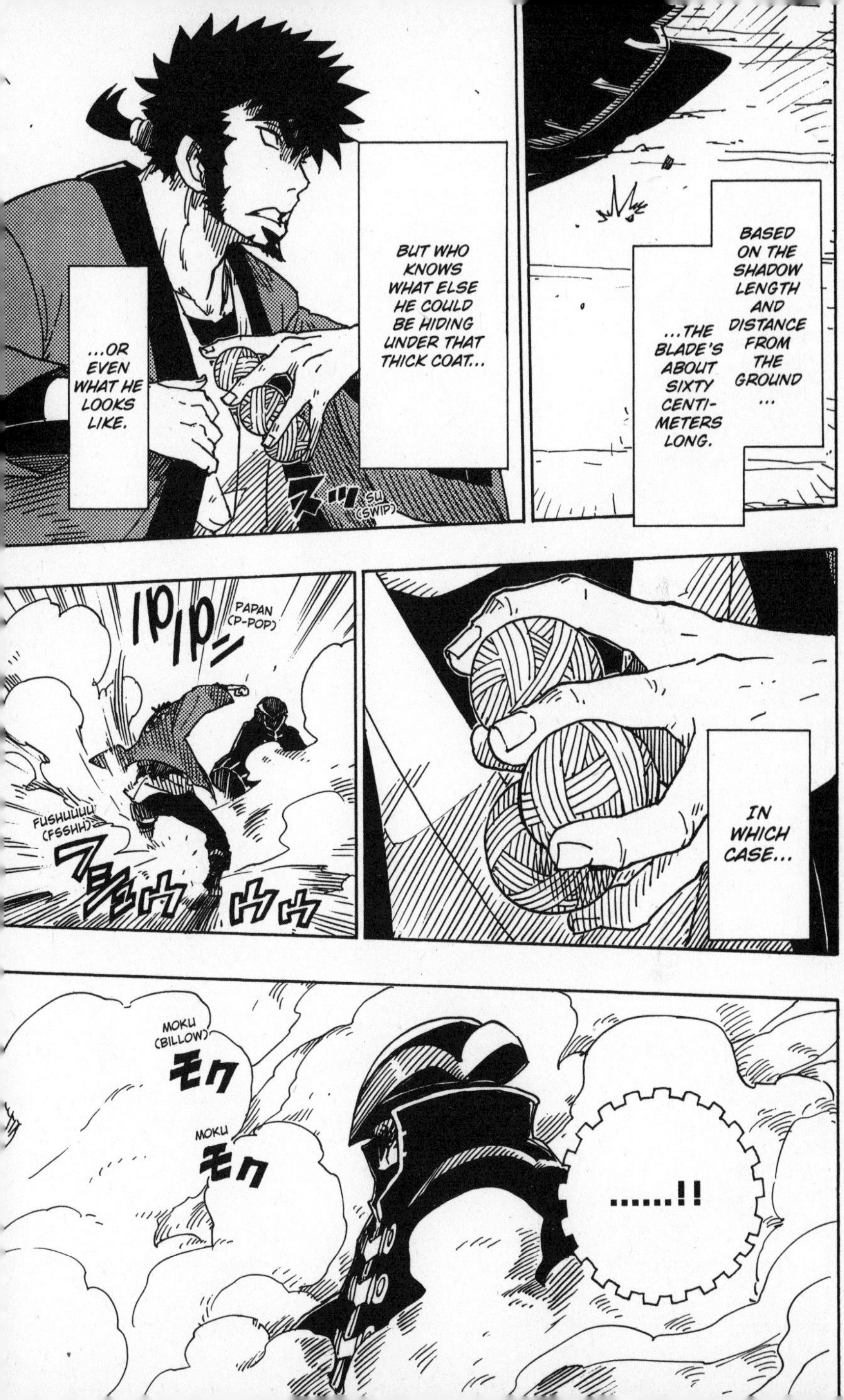
BASED ON THE SHADOW LENGTH AND DISTANCE FROM THE GROUND...
...THE BLADE'S ABOUT SIXTY CENTI-METERS LONG.
BUT WHO KNOWS WHAT ELSE HE COULD BE HIDING UNDER THAT THICK COAT...
...OR EVEN WHAT HE LOOKS LIKE.
SU (SWIP)
IN WHICH CASE...
PAPAN (P-POP)
FUSHUUUU (FSSHH)
......!!
MOKU (BILLOW)
MOKU

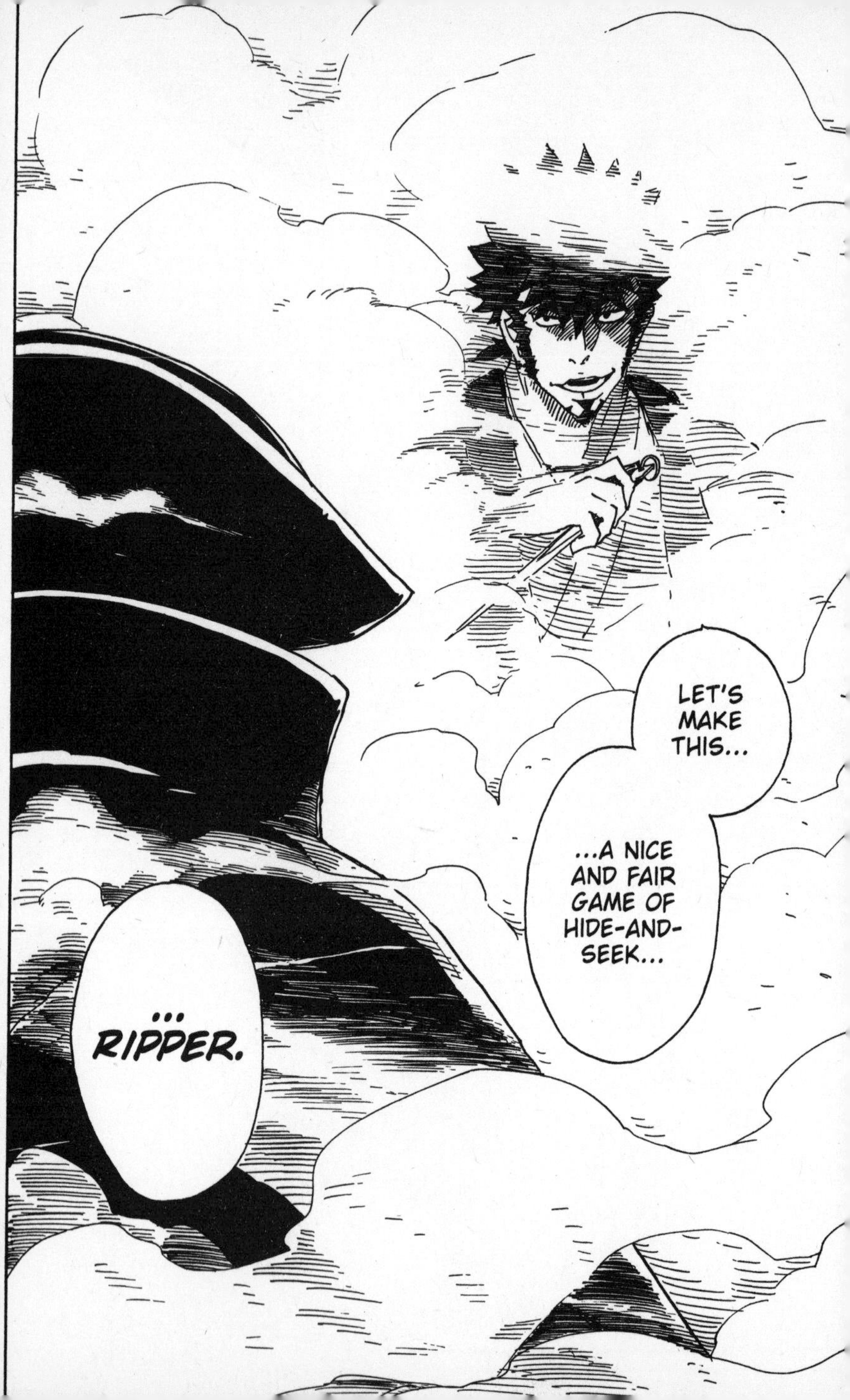
LET'S MAKE THIS...
...A NICE AND FAIR GAME OF HIDE-AND-SEEK...
...RIPPER.

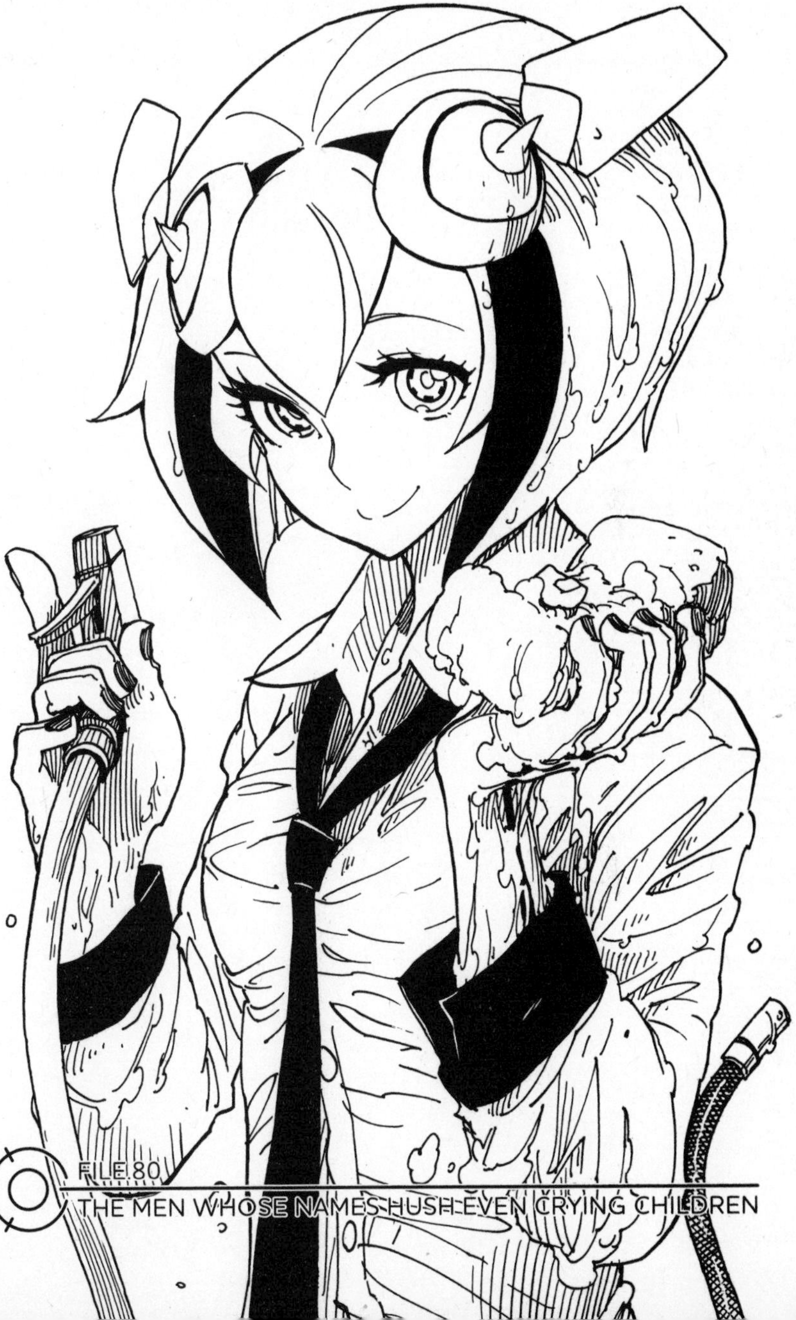

FILE.80
THE MEN WHOSE NAMES HUSH EVEN CRYING CHILDREN

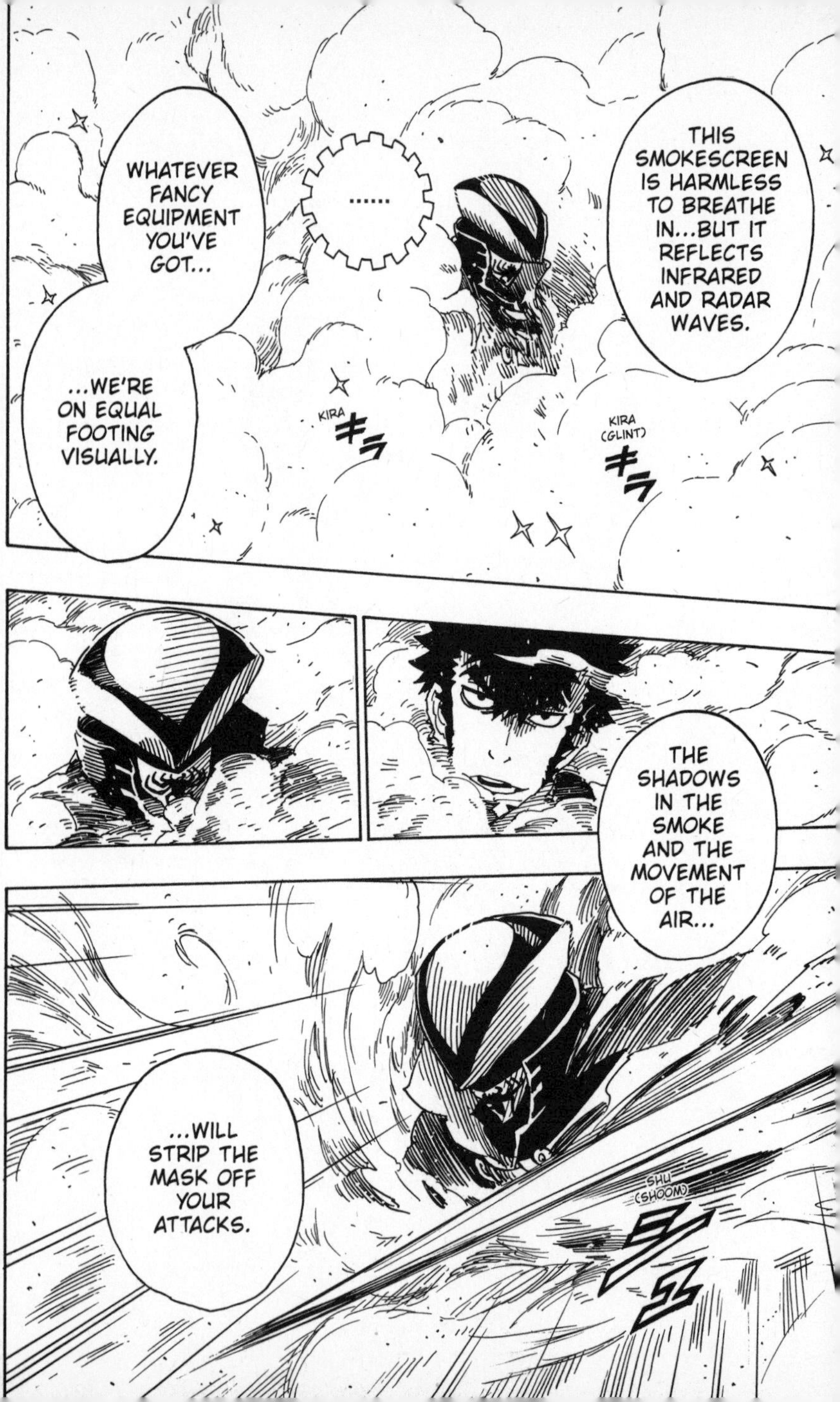
THIS SMOKESCREEN IS HARMLESS TO BREATHE IN...BUT IT REFLECTS INFRARED AND RADAR WAVES.
......
WHATEVER FANCY EQUIPMENT YOU'VE GOT...
...WE'RE ON EQUAL FOOTING VISUALLY.
KIRA (GLINT)
キラ
KIRA
キラ
THE SHADOWS IN THE SMOKE AND THE MOVEMENT OF THE AIR...
...WILL STRIP THE MASK OFF YOUR ATTACKS.
SHU (SHOOM)
シュ

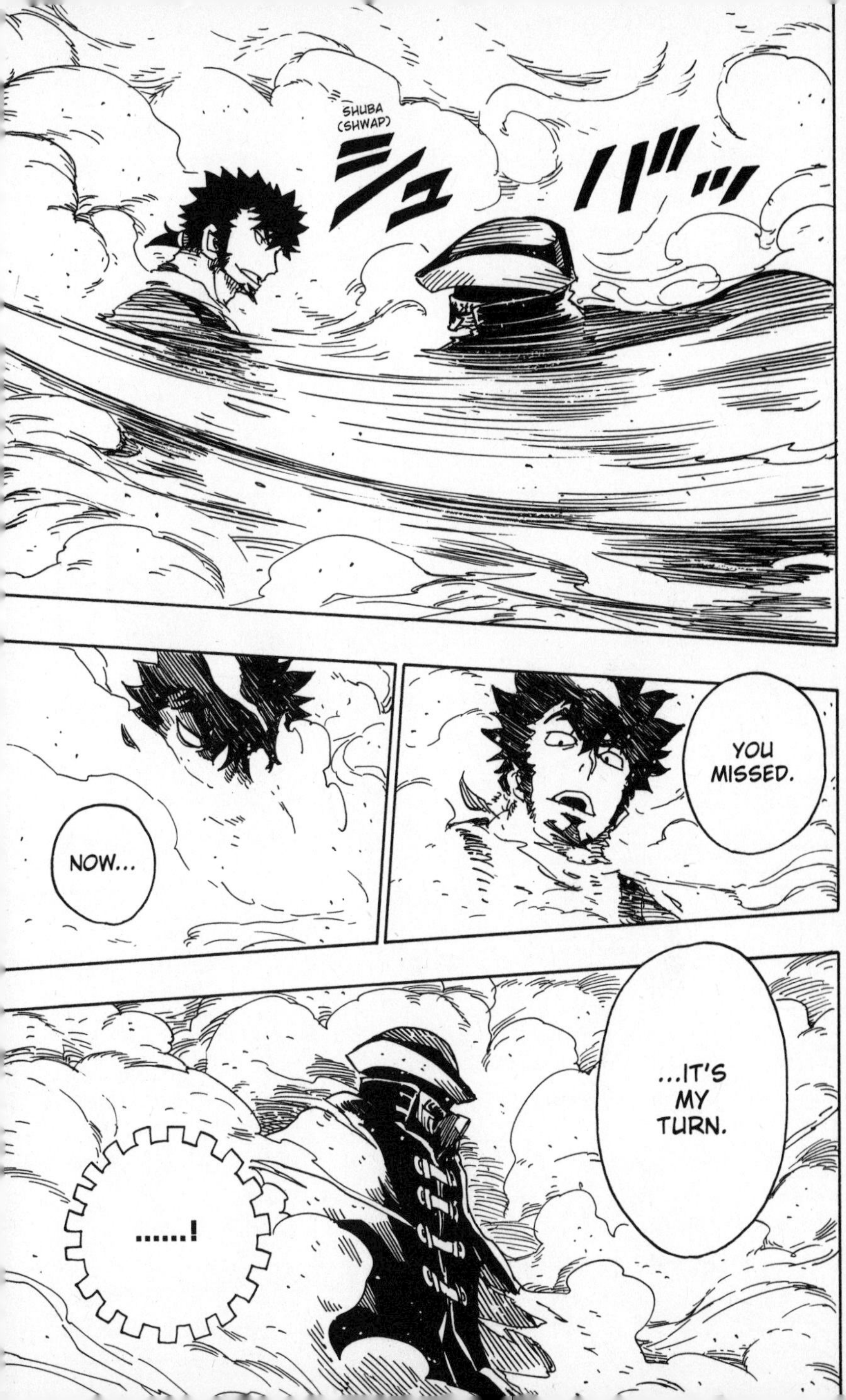
SHUBA (SHWAP)
シュバッ
YOU MISSED.
NOW...
...IT'S MY TURN.
......!

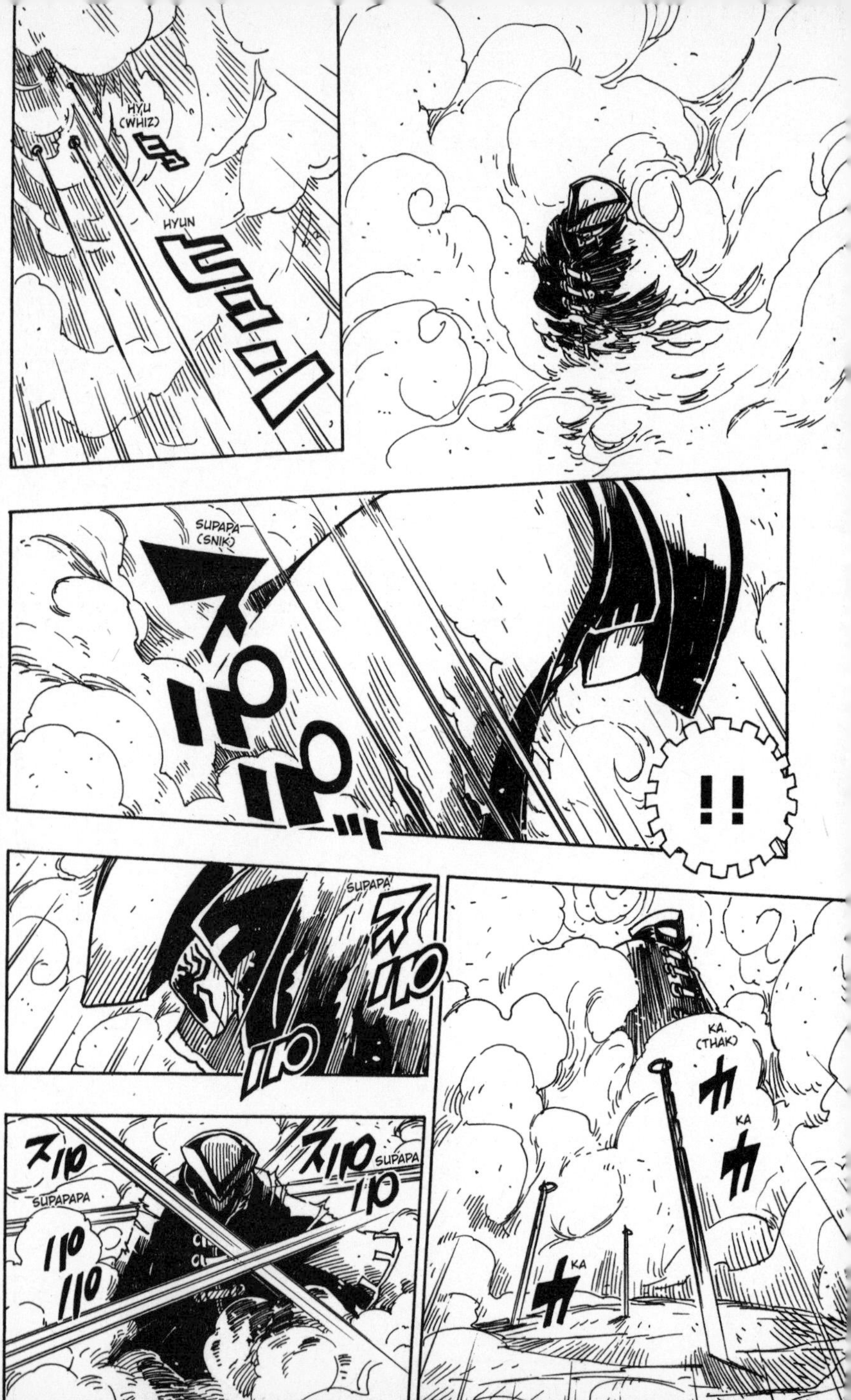
HYU (WHIZ)
HYUN
SUPAPA (SNIK)
!!
KA. (THAK)
KA
KA
SUPAPA
SUPAPA
SUPAPAPA

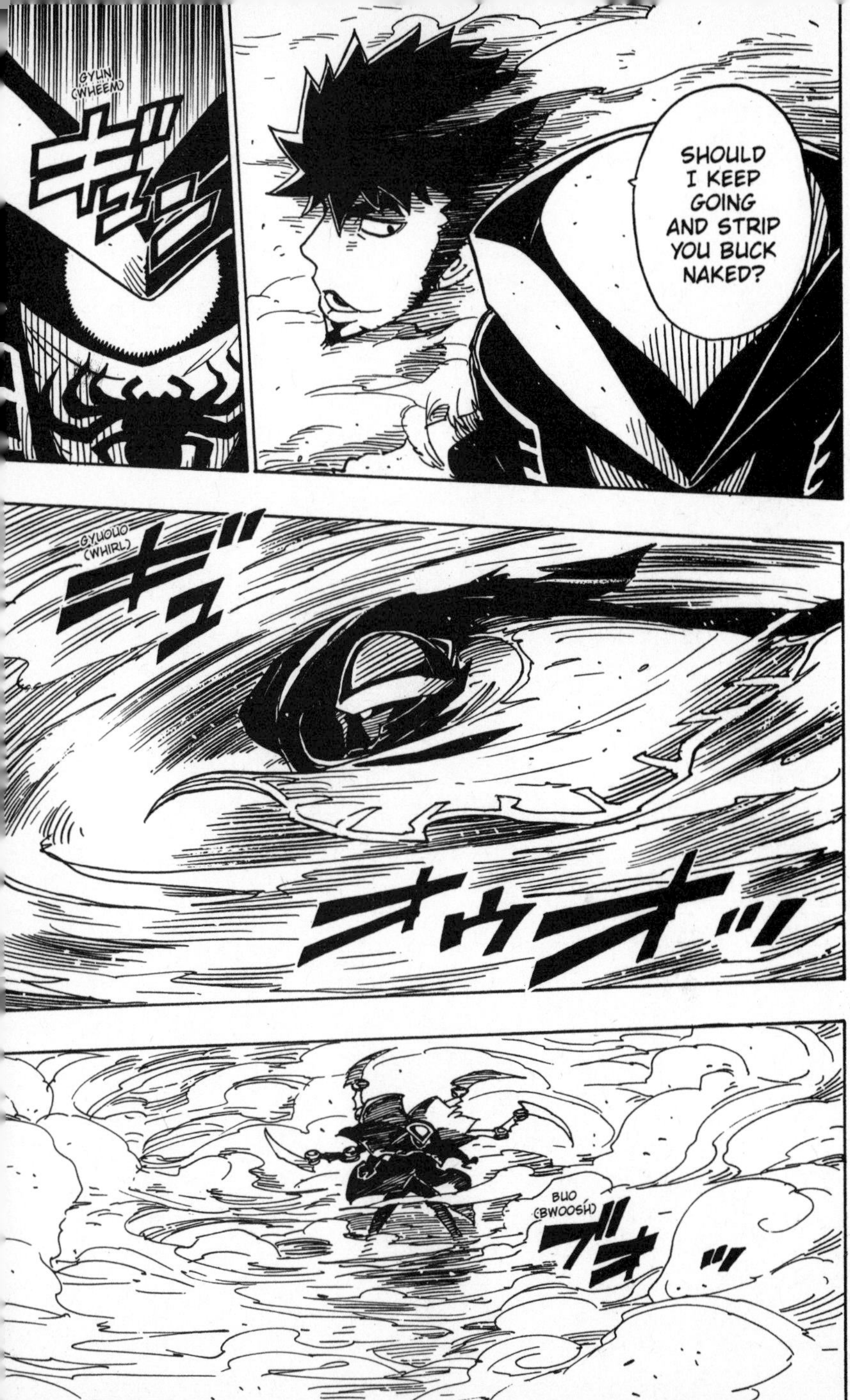
SHOULD I KEEP GOING AND STRIP YOU BUCK NAKED?
GYUN (WHEEM)
GYUOUO (WHIRL)
BUO (BWOOSH)

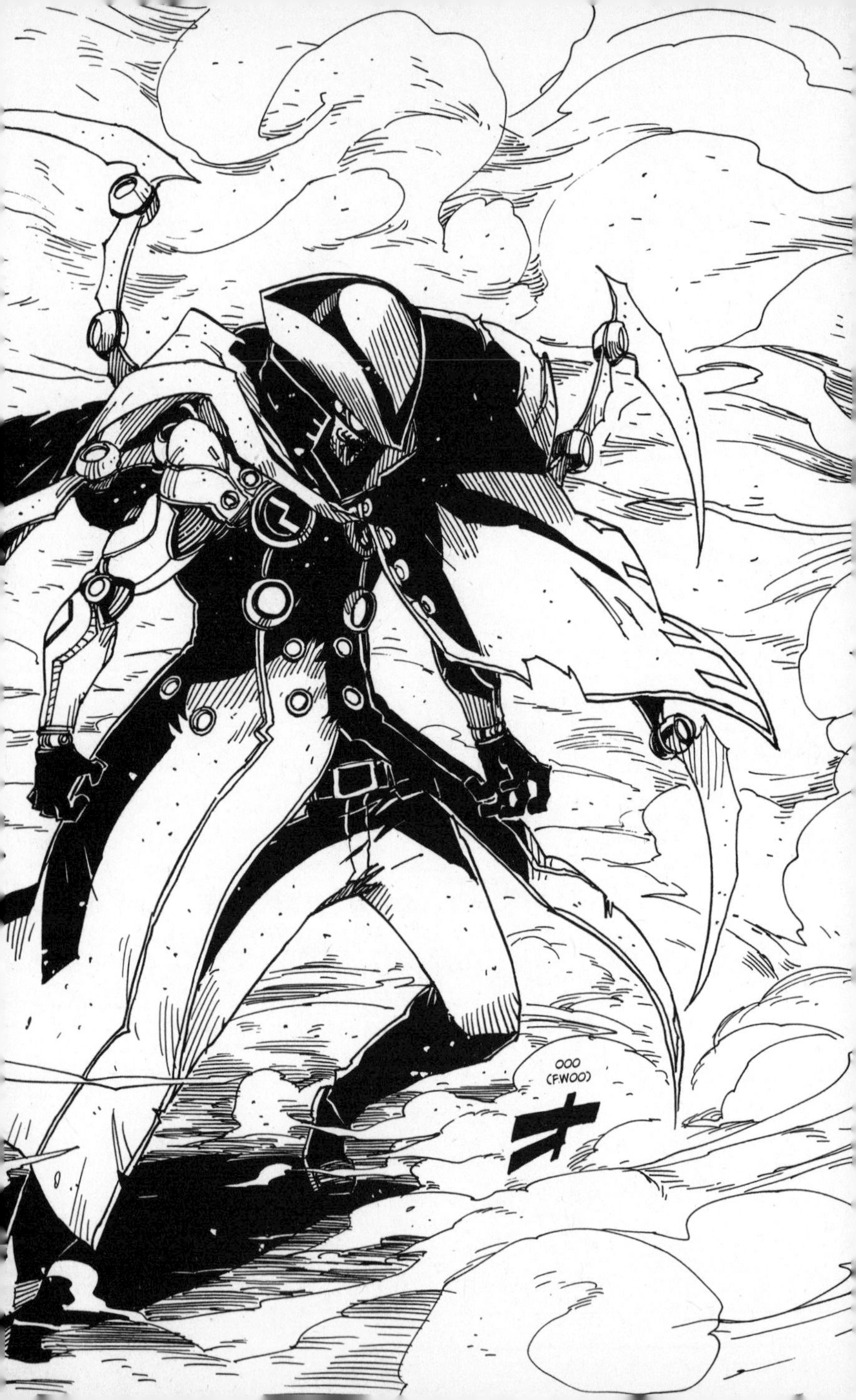
OOO
(F.WOO)

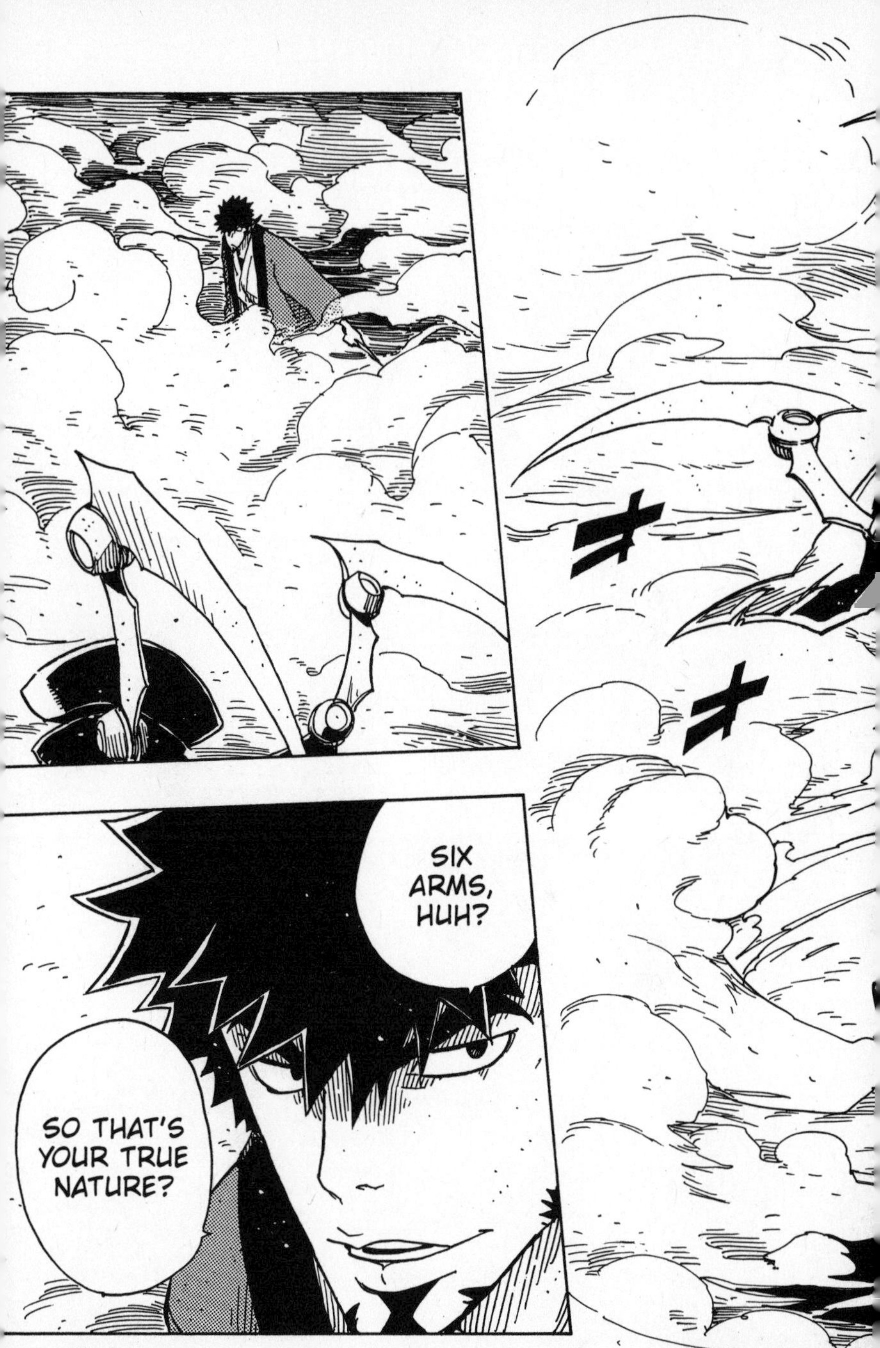
SIX ARMS, HUH?
SO THAT'S YOUR TRUE NATURE?

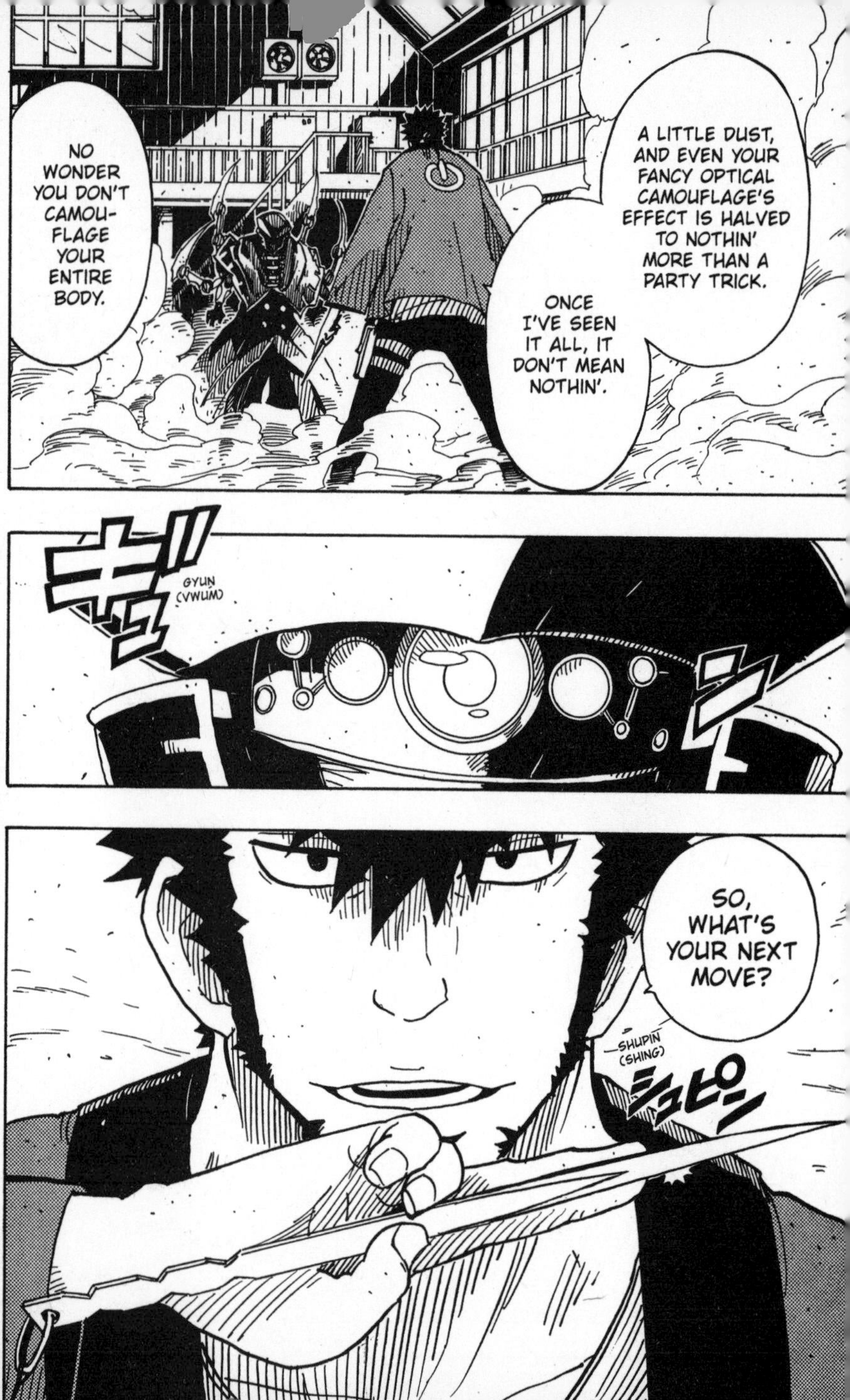

A LITTLE DUST, AND EVEN YOUR FANCY OPTICAL CAMOUFLAGE'S EFFECT IS HALVED TO NOTHIN' MORE THAN A PARTY TRICK.
ONCE I'VE SEEN IT ALL, IT DON'T MEAN NOTHIN'.
NO WONDER YOU DON'T CAMOU-FLAGE YOUR ENTIRE BODY.
GYUN (VWUM)
SO, WHAT'S YOUR NEXT MOVE?
SHUPIN (SHING)

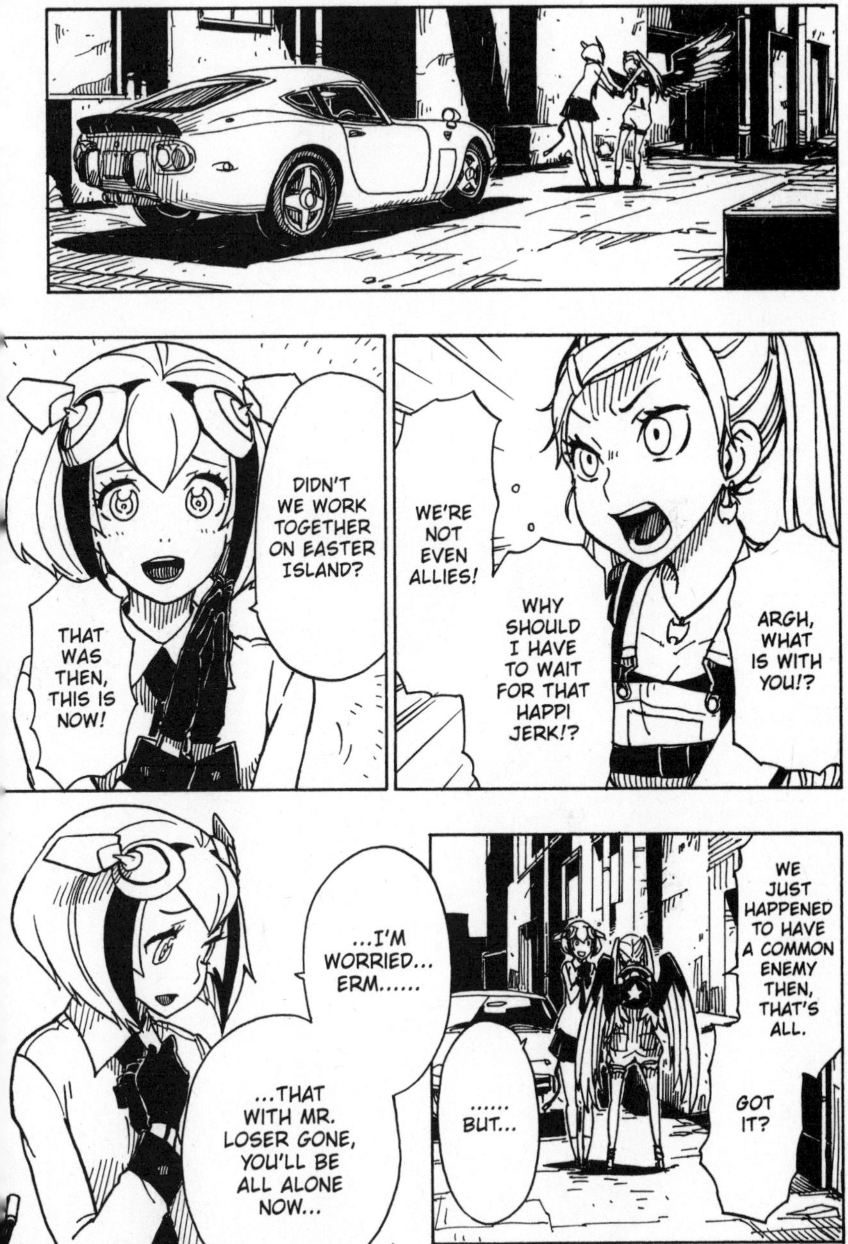
ARGH, WHAT IS WITH YOU!?
WHY SHOULD I HAVE TO WAIT FOR THAT HAPPI JERK!?
WE'RE NOT EVEN ALLIES!
DIDN'T WE WORK TOGETHER ON EASTER ISLAND?
THAT WAS THEN, THIS IS NOW!
WE JUST HAPPENED TO HAVE A COMMON ENEMY THEN, THAT'S ALL.
GOT IT?
...... BUT...
...I'M WORRIED... ERM......
...THAT WITH MR. LOSER GONE, YOU'LL BE ALL ALONE NOW...

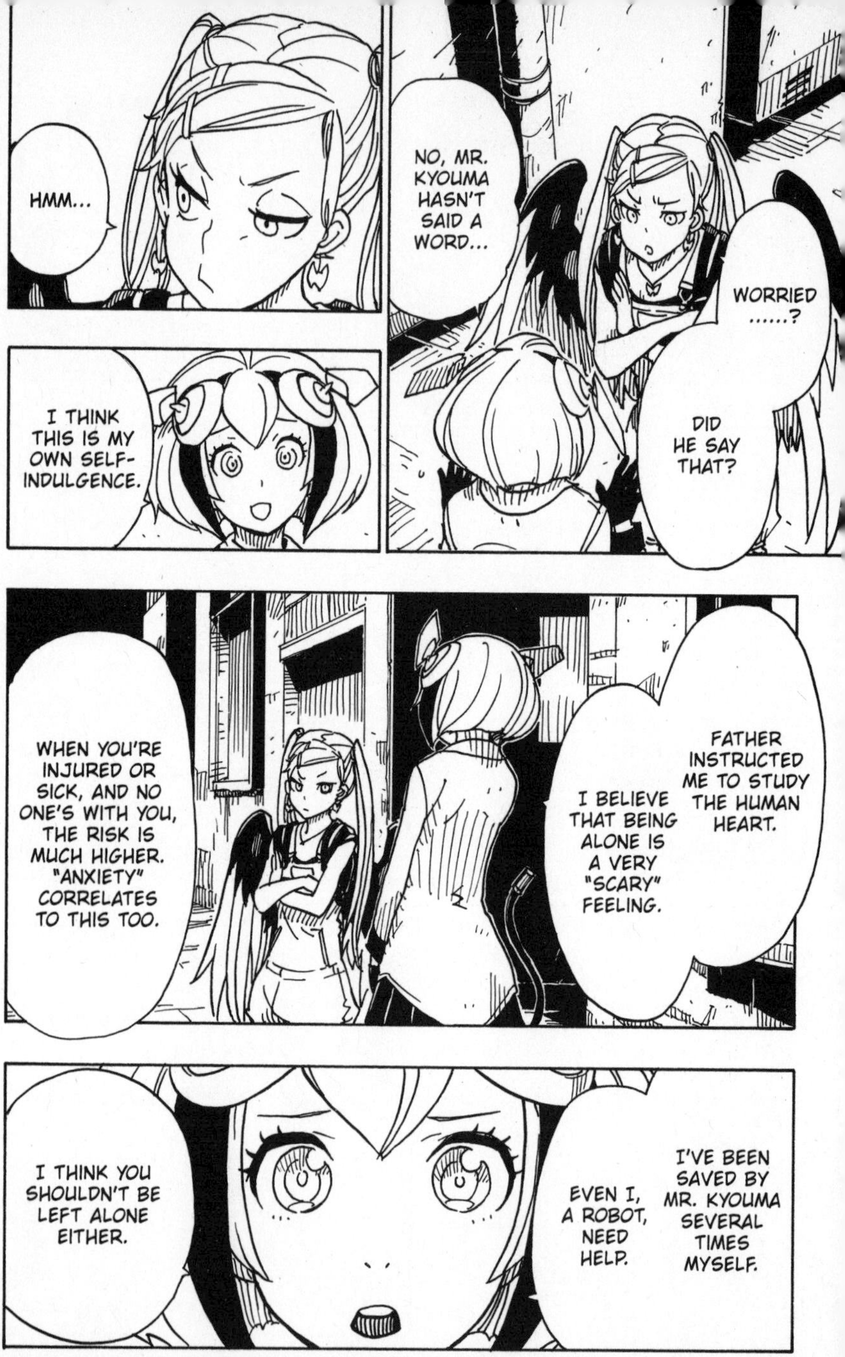
WORRIED ......?
DID HE SAY THAT?
NO, MR. KYOUMA HASN'T SAID A WORD...
HMM...
I THINK THIS IS MY OWN SELF-INDULGENCE.
FATHER INSTRUCTED ME TO STUDY THE HUMAN HEART.
I BELIEVE THAT BEING ALONE IS A VERY "SCARY" FEELING.
WHEN YOU'RE INJURED OR SICK, AND NO ONE'S WITH YOU, THE RISK IS MUCH HIGHER. "ANXIETY" CORRELATES TO THIS TOO.
I'VE BEEN SAVED BY MR. KYOUMA SEVERAL TIMES MYSELF.
EVEN I, A ROBOT, NEED HELP.
I THINK YOU SHOULDN'T BE LEFT ALONE EITHER.

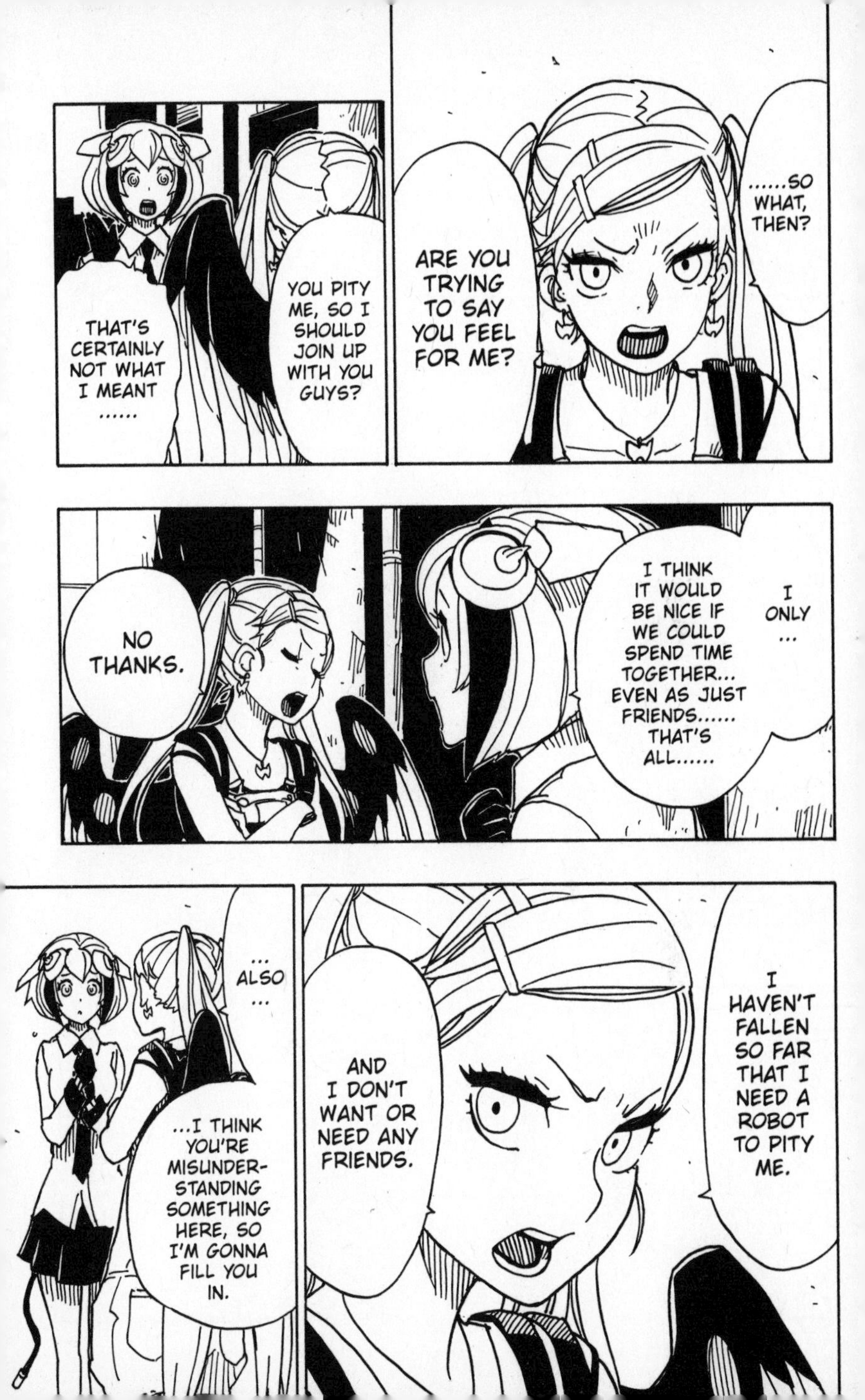
......SO WHAT, THEN?
ARE YOU TRYING TO SAY YOU FEEL FOR ME?
YOU PITY ME, SO I SHOULD JOIN UP WITH YOU GUYS?
THAT'S CERTAINLY NOT WHAT I MEANT ......
I ONLY ...
I THINK IT WOULD BE NICE IF WE COULD SPEND TIME TOGETHER... EVEN AS JUST FRIENDS...... THAT'S ALL......
NO THANKS.
I HAVEN'T FALLEN SO FAR THAT I NEED A ROBOT TO PITY ME.
AND I DON'T WANT OR NEED ANY FRIENDS.
... ALSO ...
...I THINK YOU'RE MISUNDER-STANDING SOMETHING HERE, SO I'M GONNA FILL YOU IN.

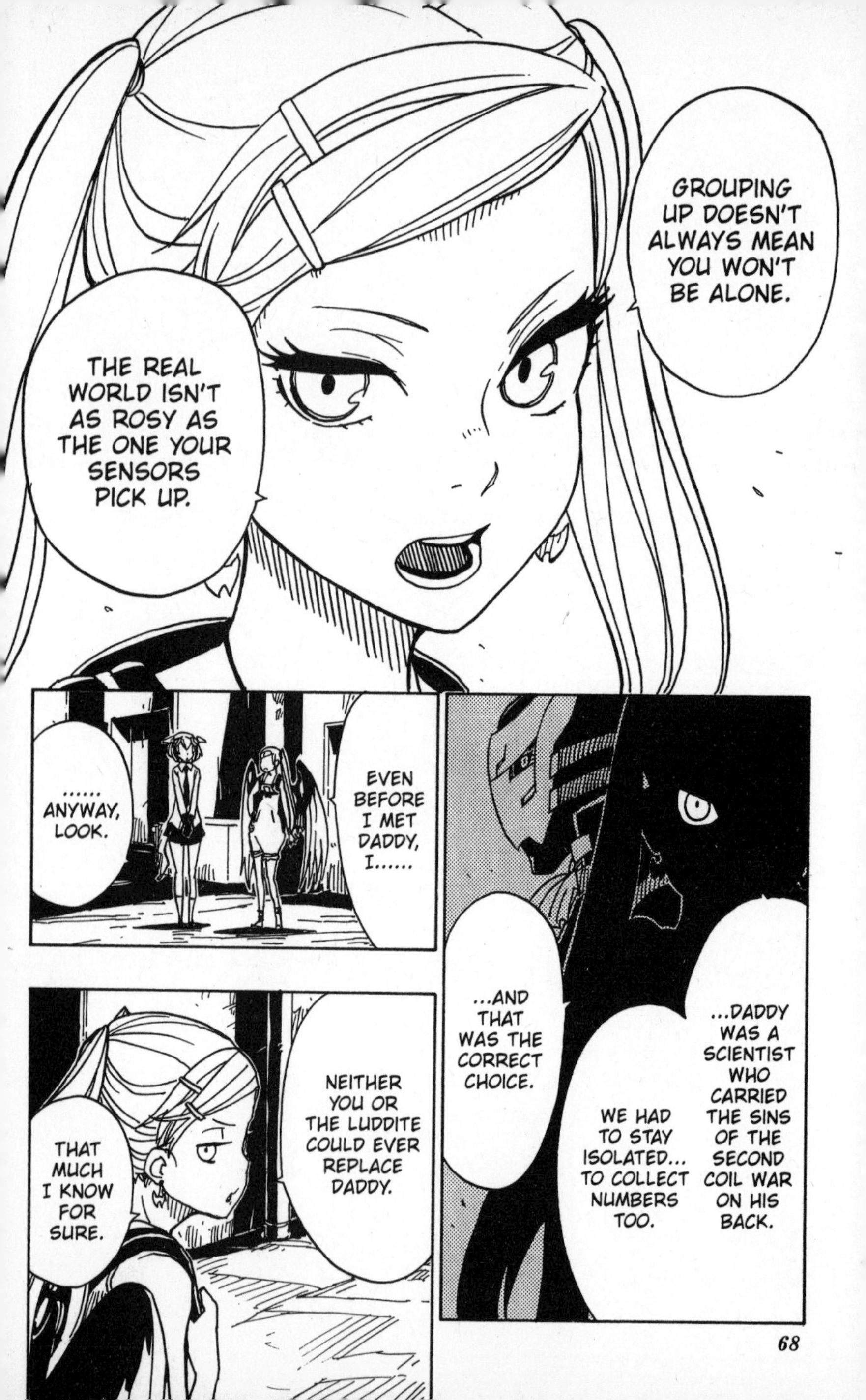
GROUPING UP DOESN'T ALWAYS MEAN YOU WON'T BE ALONE.
THE REAL WORLD ISN'T AS ROSY AS THE ONE YOUR SENSORS PICK UP.
...DADDY WAS A SCIENTIST WHO CARRIED THE SINS OF THE SECOND COIL WAR ON HIS BACK.
WE HAD TO STAY ISOLATED... TO COLLECT NUMBERS TOO.
...AND THAT WAS THE CORRECT CHOICE.
EVEN BEFORE I MET DADDY, I......
...... ANYWAY, LOOK.
NEITHER YOU OR THE LUDDITE COULD EVER REPLACE DADDY.
THAT MUCH I KNOW FOR SURE.

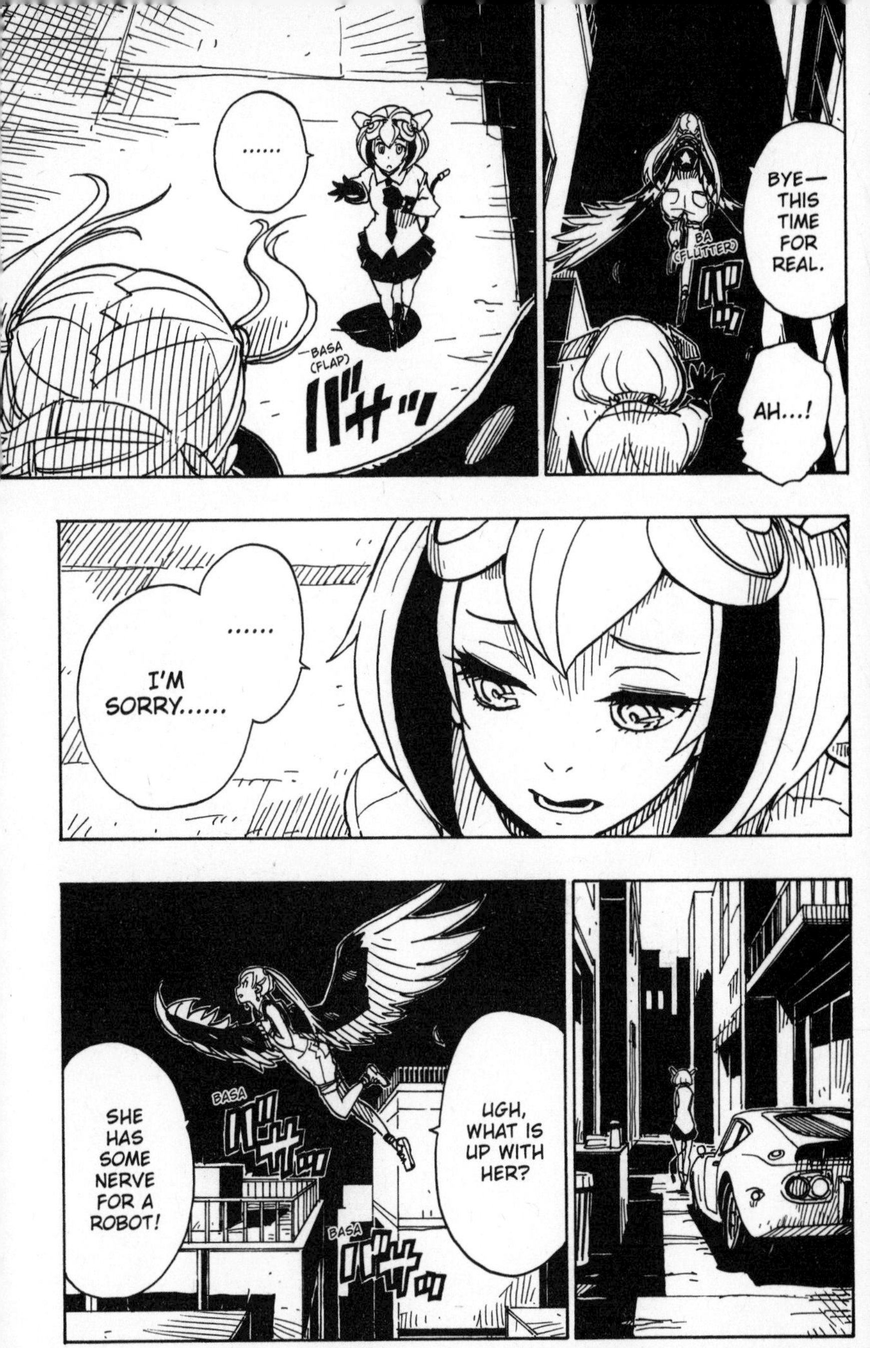
BYE— THIS TIME FOR REAL.
BA (FLUTTER)
AH...!
......
BASA (FLAP)
...... I'M SORRY......
UGH, WHAT IS UP WITH HER?
BASA
SHE HAS SOME NERVE FOR A ROBOT!
BASA

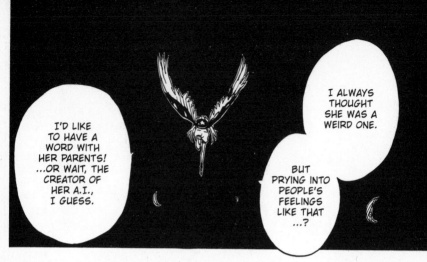

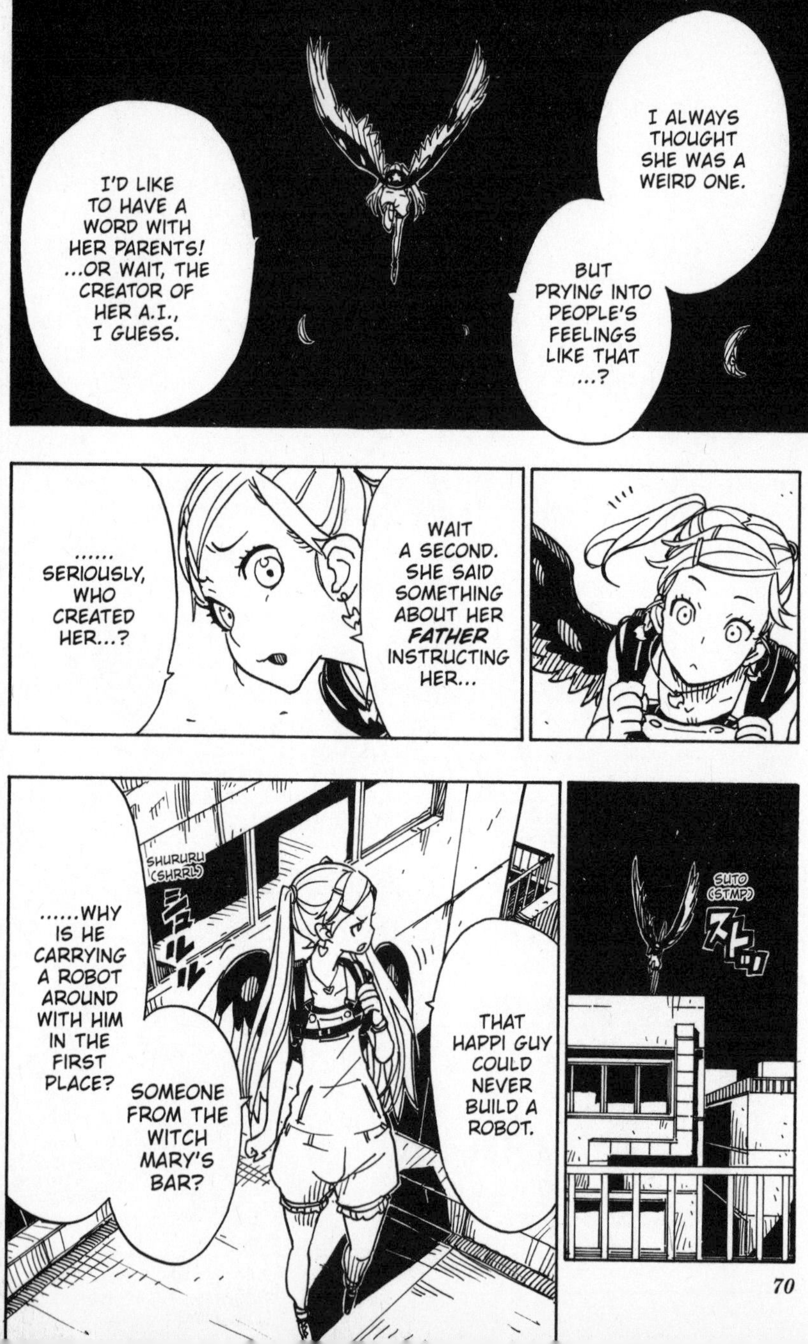
I ALWAYS THOUGHT SHE WAS A WEIRD ONE.
BUT PRYING INTO PEOPLE'S FEELINGS LIKE THAT ...?
I'D LIKE TO HAVE A WORD WITH HER PARENTS! ...OR WAIT, THE CREATOR OF HER A.I., I GUESS.
WAIT A SECOND. SHE SAID SOMETHING ABOUT HER ***FATHER*** INSTRUCTING HER...
...... SERIOUSLY, WHO CREATED HER...?
SUTO (STMP)
SHURURU (SHRRL)
THAT HAPPI GUY COULD NEVER BUILD A ROBOT.
......WHY IS HE CARRYING A ROBOT AROUND WITH HIM IN THE FIRST PLACE?
SOMEONE FROM THE WITCH MARY'S BAR?

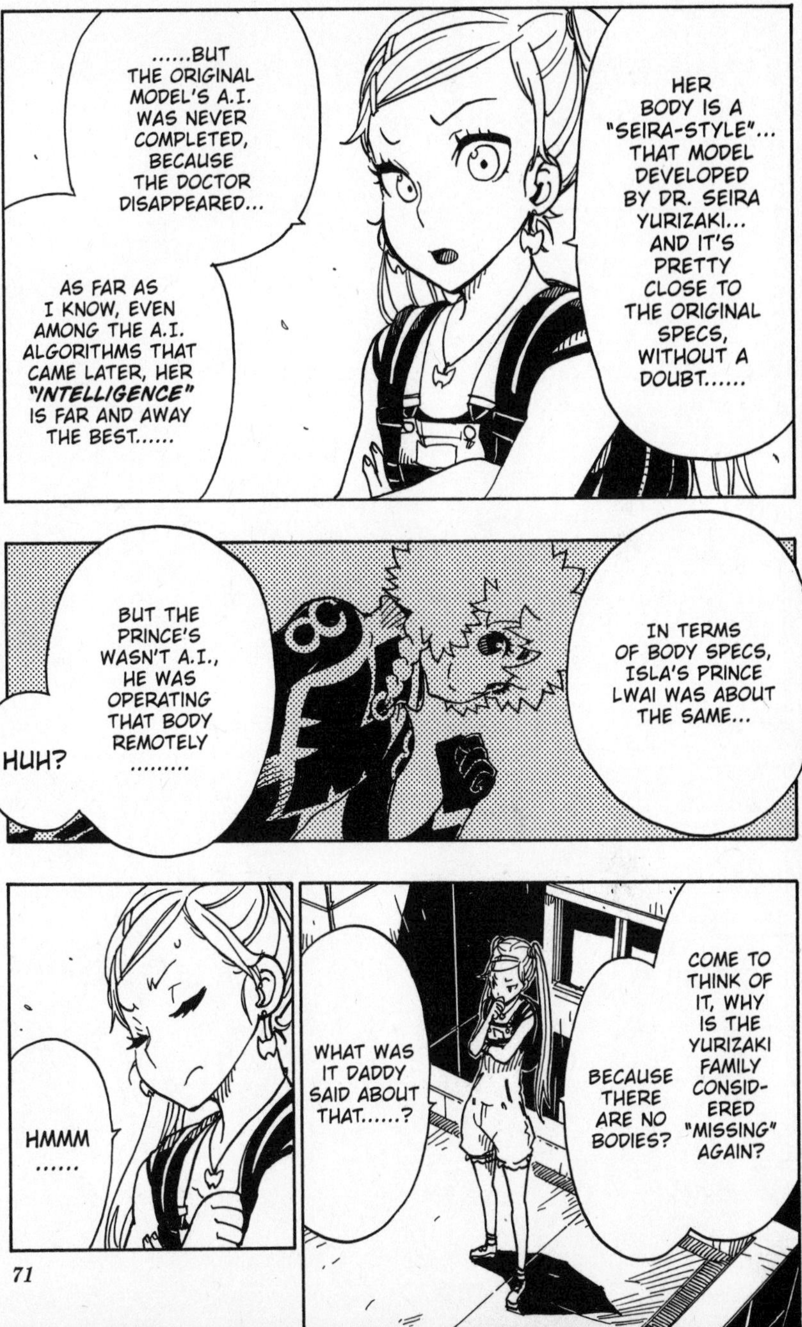
HER BODY IS A "SEIRA-STYLE"... THAT MODEL DEVELOPED BY DR. SEIRA YURIZAKI... AND IT'S PRETTY CLOSE TO THE ORIGINAL SPECS, WITHOUT A DOUBT......
......BUT THE ORIGINAL MODEL'S A.I. WAS NEVER COMPLETED, BECAUSE THE DOCTOR DISAPPEARED...
AS FAR AS I KNOW, EVEN AMONG THE A.I. ALGORITHMS THAT CAME LATER, HER *"INTELLIGENCE"* IS FAR AND AWAY THE BEST......
IN TERMS OF BODY SPECS, ISLA'S PRINCE LWAI WAS ABOUT THE SAME...
BUT THE PRINCE'S WASN'T A.I., HE WAS OPERATING THAT BODY REMOTELY ....
HUH?
COME TO THINK OF IT, WHY IS THE YURIZAKI FAMILY CONSIDERED "MISSING" AGAIN?
BECAUSE THERE ARE NO BODIES?
WHAT WAS IT DADDY SAID ABOUT THAT......?
HMMM ......

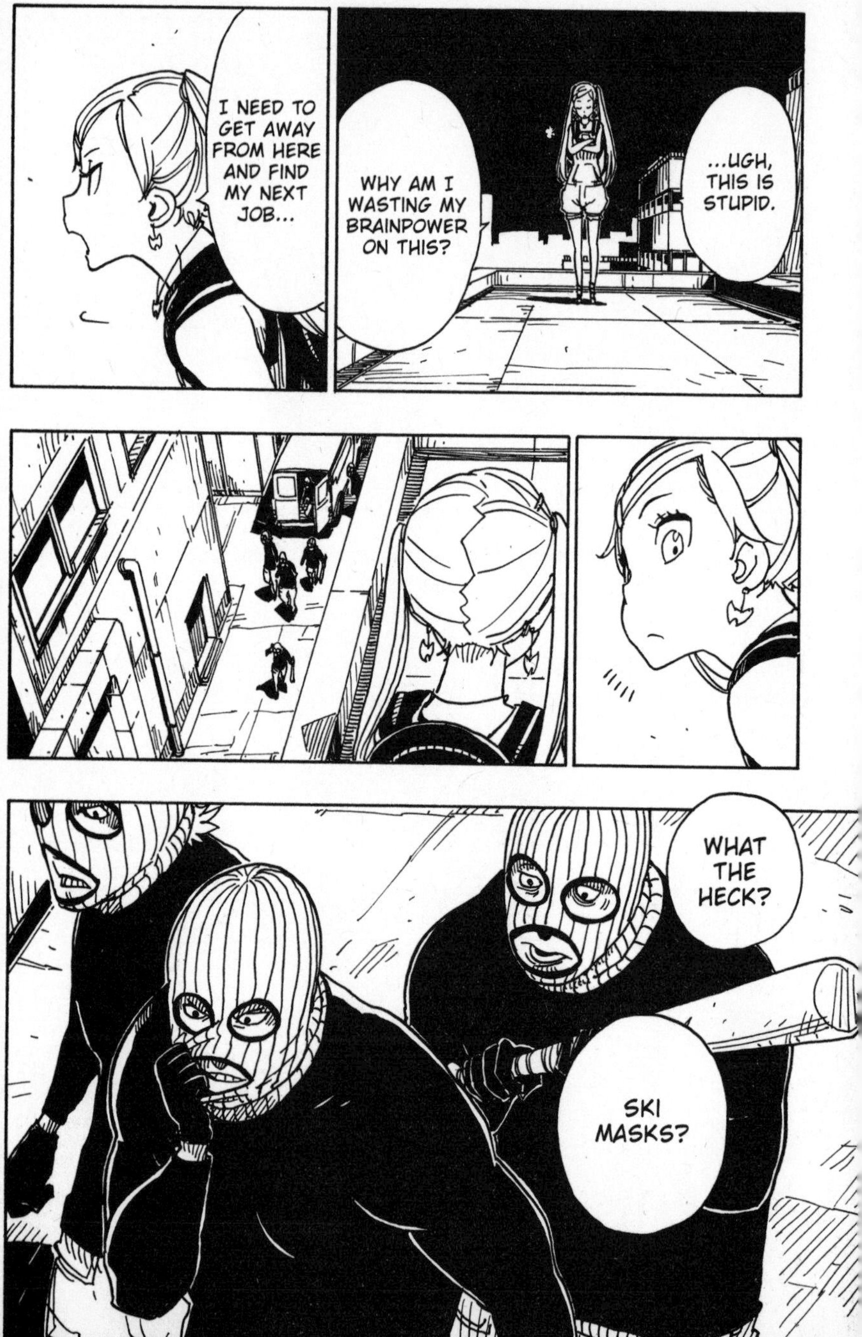
...UGH, THIS IS STUPID.
WHY AM I WASTING MY BRAINPOWER ON THIS?
I NEED TO GET AWAY FROM HERE AND FIND MY NEXT JOB...
WHAT THE HECK?
SKI MASKS?

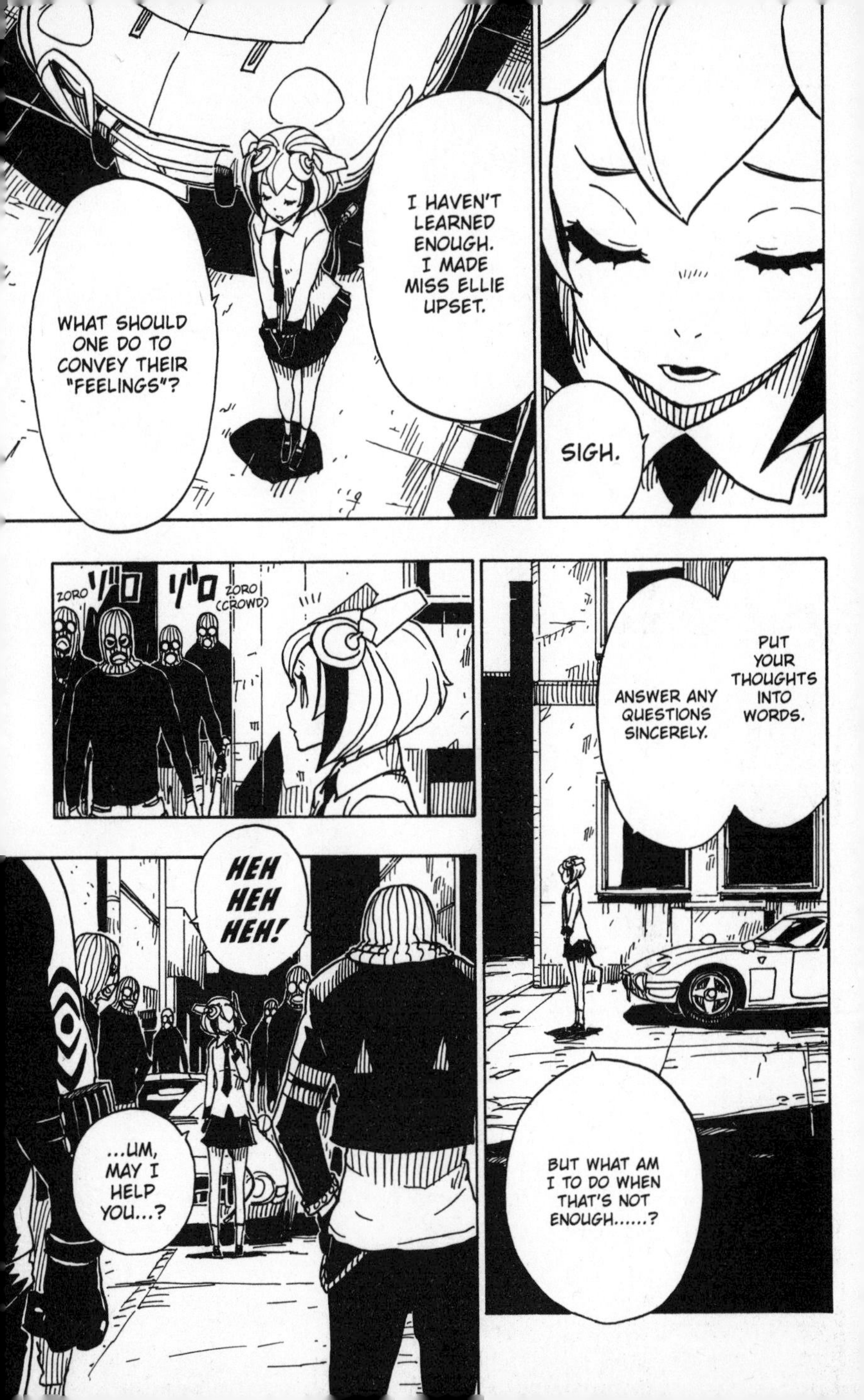
SIGH.
I HAVEN'T LEARNED ENOUGH. I MADE MISS ELLIE UPSET.
WHAT SHOULD ONE DO TO CONVEY THEIR "FEELINGS"?
PUT YOUR THOUGHTS INTO WORDS.
ANSWER ANY QUESTIONS SINCERELY.
BUT WHAT AM I TO DO WHEN THAT'S NOT ENOUGH......?
ゾロ ZORO (CROWD)
ゾロ ZORO
HEH HEH HEH!
...UM, MAY I HELP YOU...?

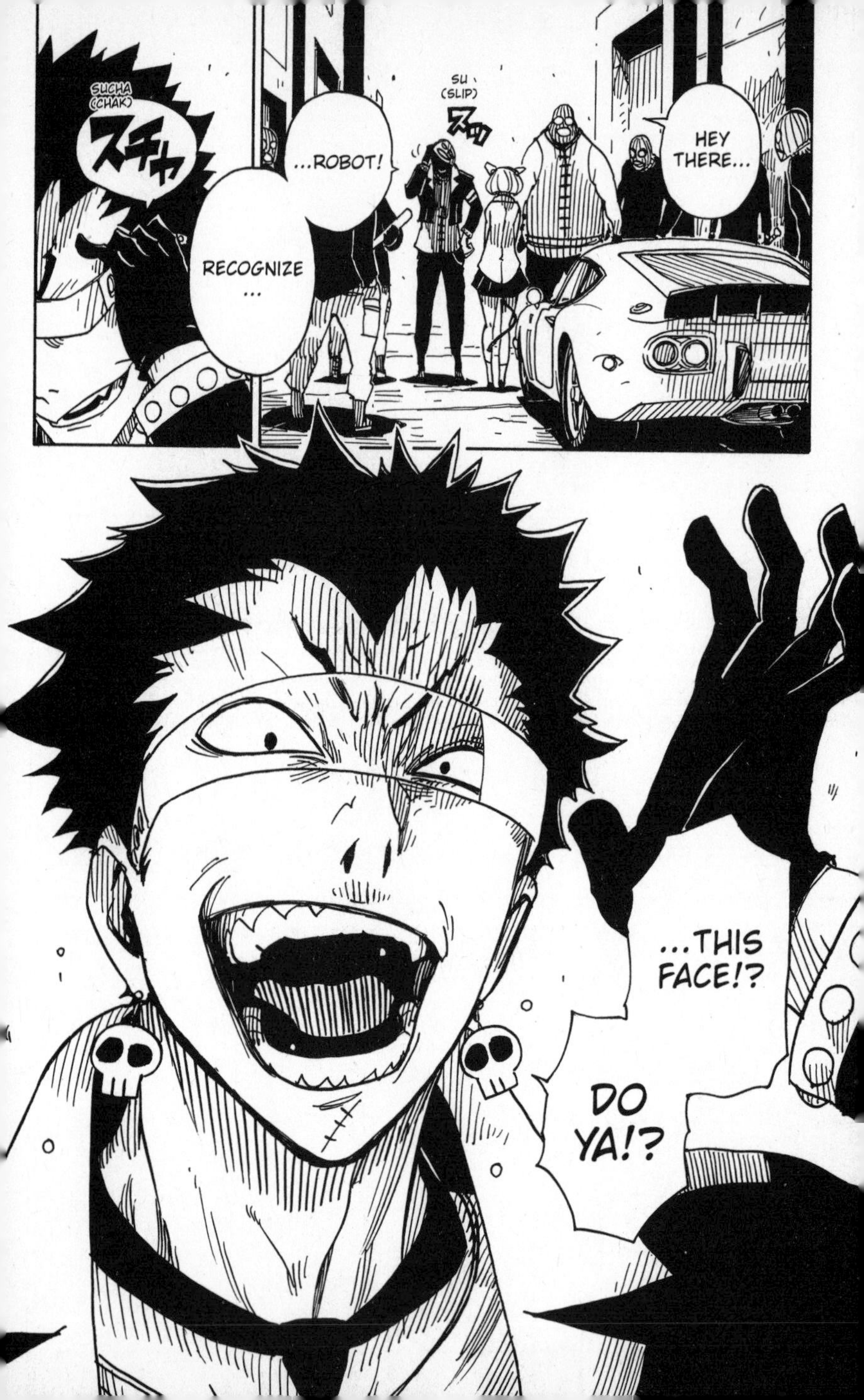
HEY THERE...
SU (SLIP)
スッ
...ROBOT!
RECOGNIZE ...
SUCHA (CHAK)
スチャ
...THIS FACE!?
DO YA!?

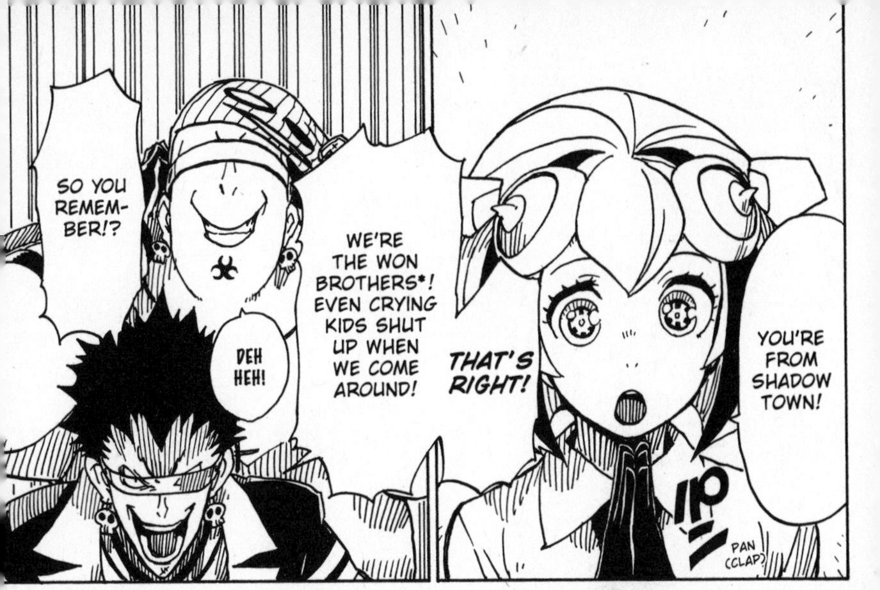
YOU'RE FROM SHADOW TOWN!
PAN (CLAP)
THAT'S RIGHT!
WE'RE THE WON BROTHERS*! EVEN CRYING KIDS SHUT UP WHEN WE COME AROUND!
DEH HEH!
SO YOU REMEMBER!?

*SEE FILE 1.

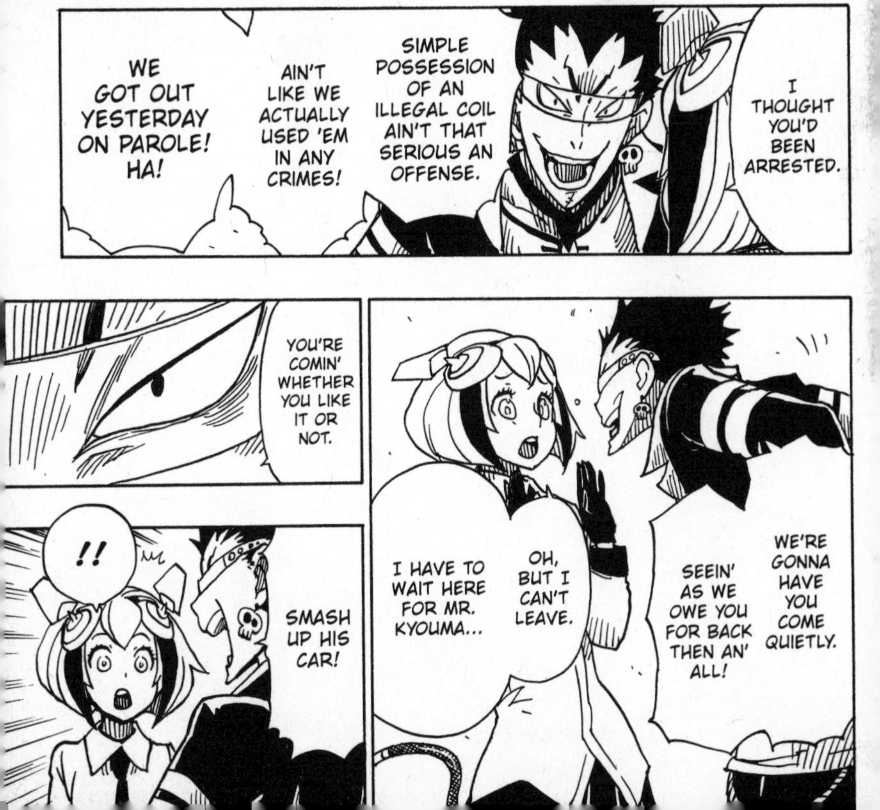
I THOUGHT YOU'D BEEN ARRESTED.
SIMPLE POSSESSION OF AN ILLEGAL COIL AIN'T THAT SERIOUS AN OFFENSE.
AIN'T LIKE WE ACTUALLY USED 'EM IN ANY CRIMES!
WE GOT OUT YESTERDAY ON PAROLE! HA!
WE'RE GONNA HAVE YOU COME QUIETLY.
SEEIN' AS WE OWE YOU FOR BACK THEN AN' ALL!
OH, BUT I CAN'T LEAVE.
I HAVE TO WAIT HERE FOR MR. KYOUMA...
YOU'RE COMIN' WHETHER YOU LIKE IT OR NOT.
!!
SMASH UP HIS CAR!

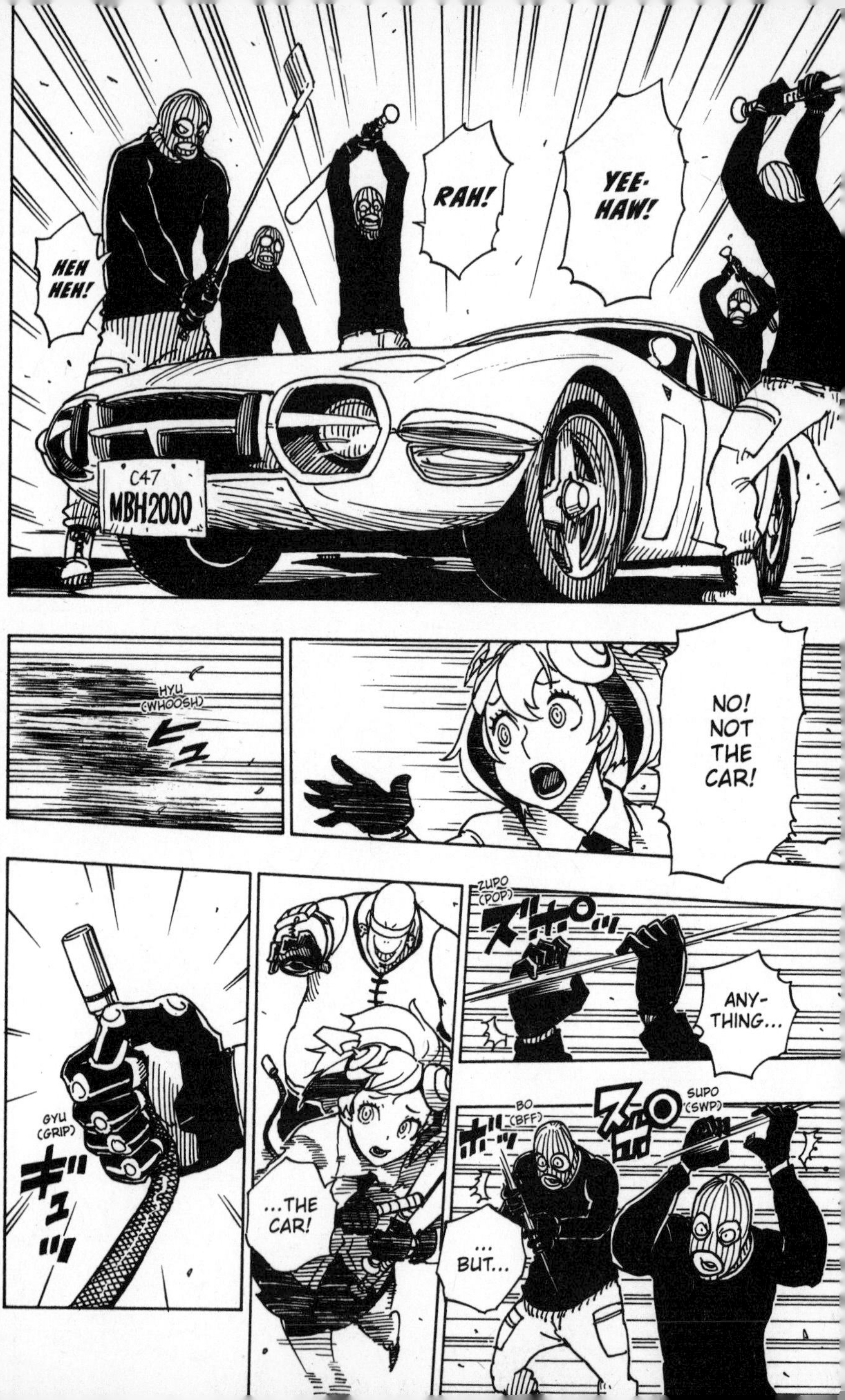

YEE-HAW!
RAH!
HEH HEH!
NO! NOT THE CAR!
HYU (WHOOSH)
ZUPO (POP)
ANY-THING...
SUPO (SWP)
BO (BFF)
... BUT...
...THE CAR!
GYU (GRIP)

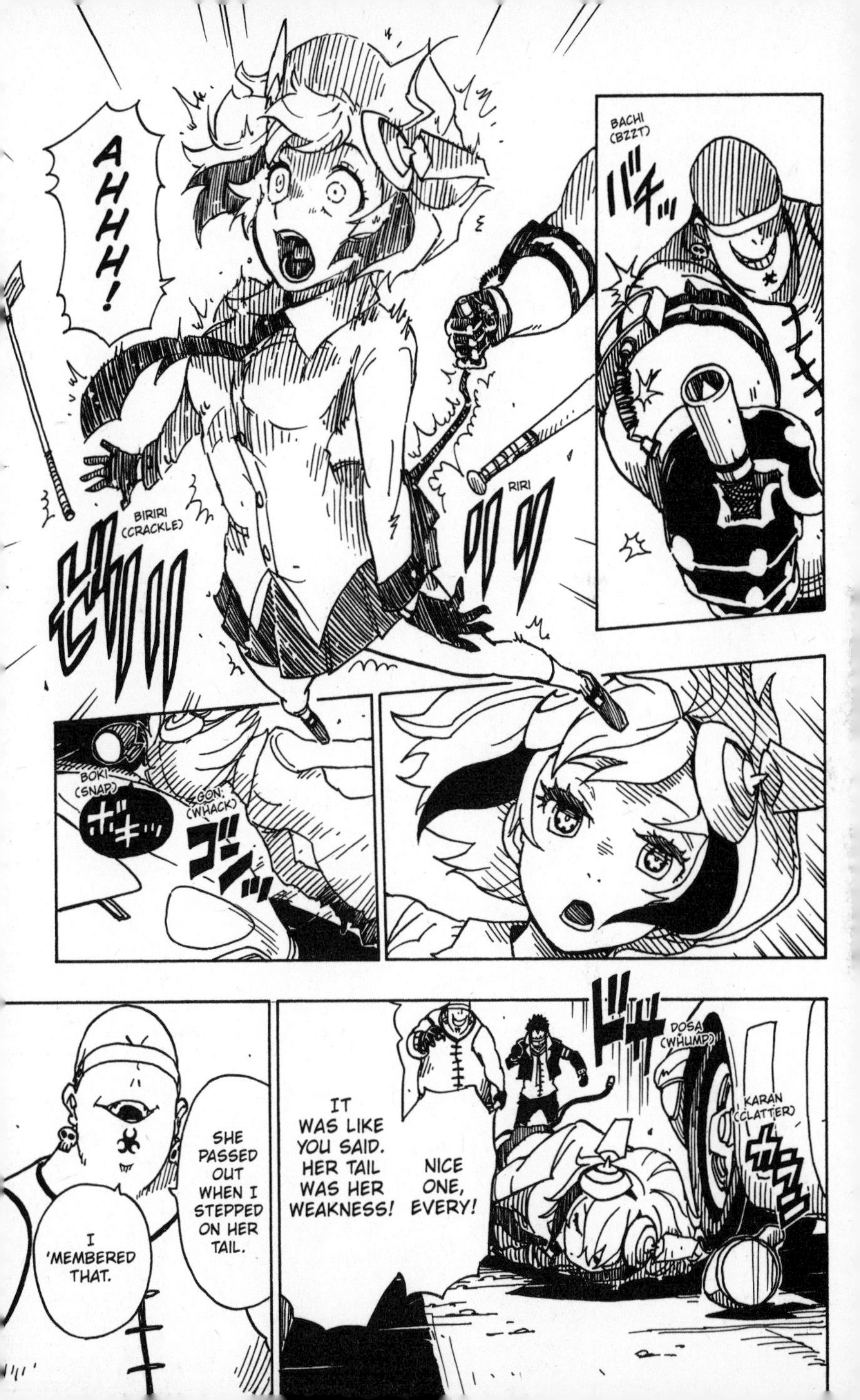
BACHI (BZZT)
バチッ
AHHHH!
RIRI
リリ
BIRIRI (CRACKLE)
ビリリ
GON (WHACK)
ゴンッ
BOKI (SNAP)
ボキッ
DOSA (WHUMP)
ドサ
KARAN (CLATTER)
カラン
NICE ONE, EVERY!
IT WAS LIKE YOU SAID. HER TAIL WAS HER WEAKNESS!
SHE PASSED OUT WHEN I STEPPED ON HER TAIL.
I 'MEMBERED THAT.

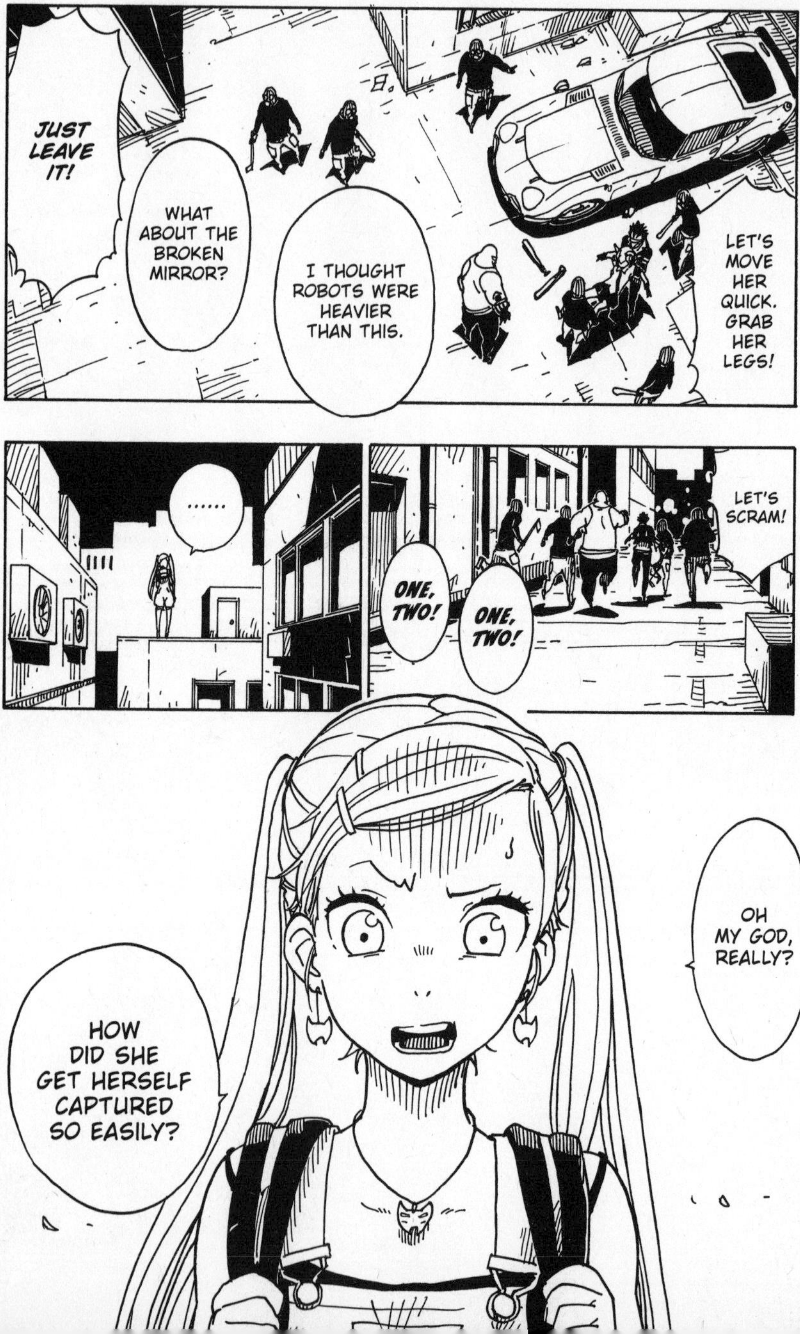
LET'S MOVE HER QUICK. GRAB HER LEGS!
I THOUGHT ROBOTS WERE HEAVIER THAN THIS.
WHAT ABOUT THE BROKEN MIRROR?
JUST LEAVE IT!
LET'S SCRAM!
ONE, TWO!
ONE, TWO!
......
OH MY GOD, REALLY?
HOW DID SHE GET HERSELF CAPTURED SO EASILY?

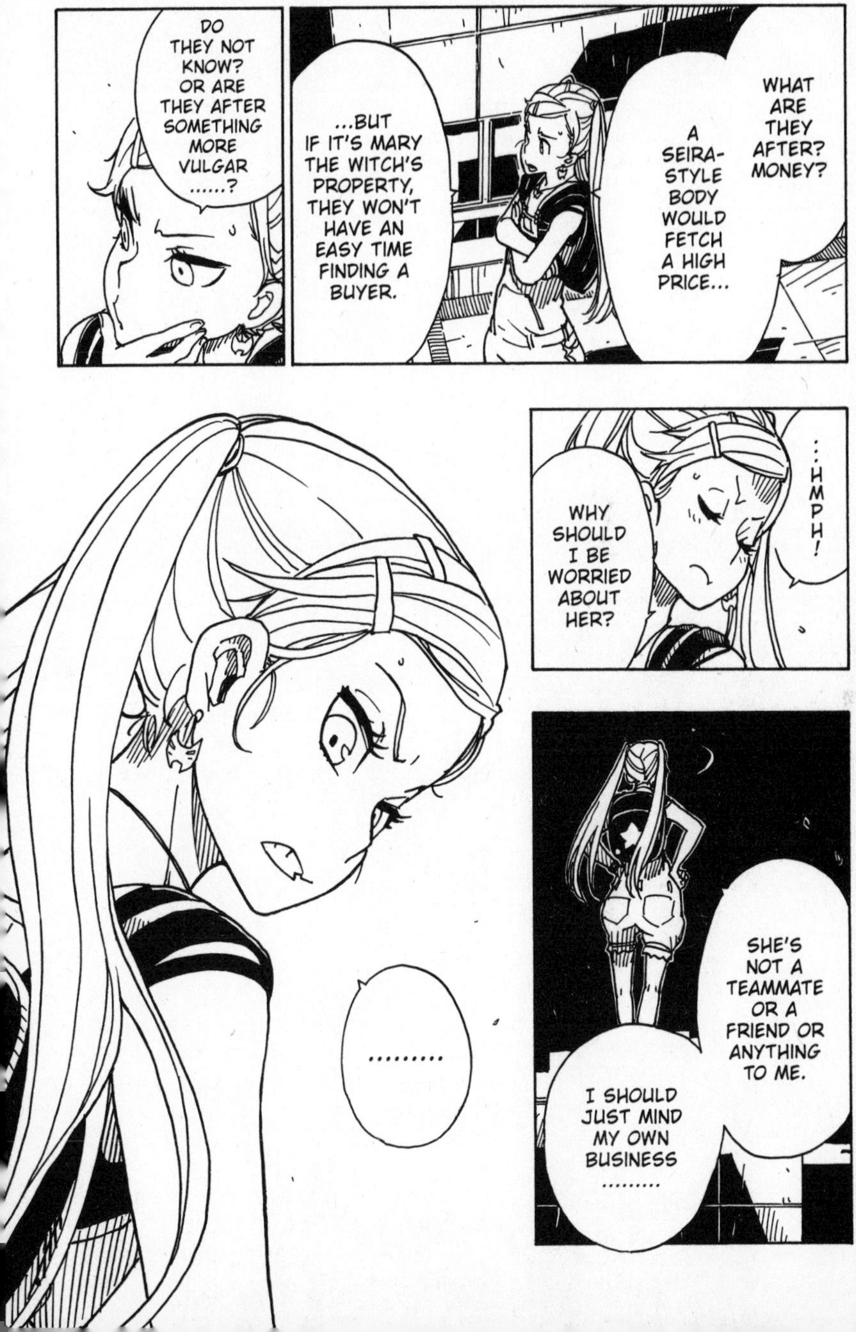

WHAT ARE THEY AFTER? MONEY?
A SEIRA-STYLE BODY WOULD FETCH A HIGH PRICE...
...BUT IF IT'S MARY THE WITCH'S PROPERTY, THEY WON'T HAVE AN EASY TIME FINDING A BUYER.
DO THEY NOT KNOW? OR ARE THEY AFTER SOMETHING MORE VULGAR ......?
...HMPH!
WHY SHOULD I BE WORRIED ABOUT HER?
SHE'S NOT A TEAMMATE OR A FRIEND OR ANYTHING TO ME.
I SHOULD JUST MIND MY OWN BUSINESS ....
....

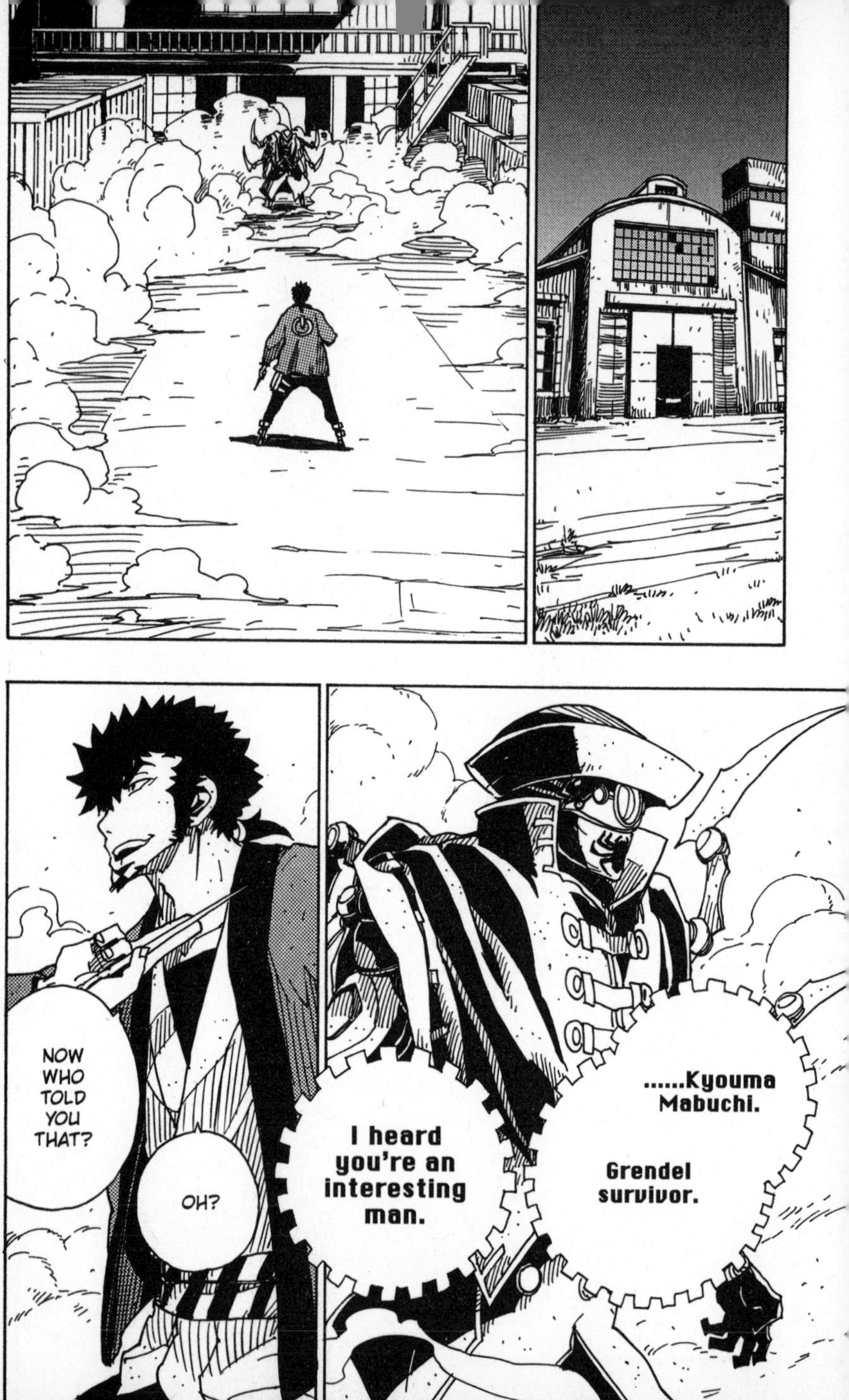
......Kyouma Mabuchi.
Grendel survivor.
I heard you're an interesting man.
OH?
NOW WHO TOLD YOU THAT?

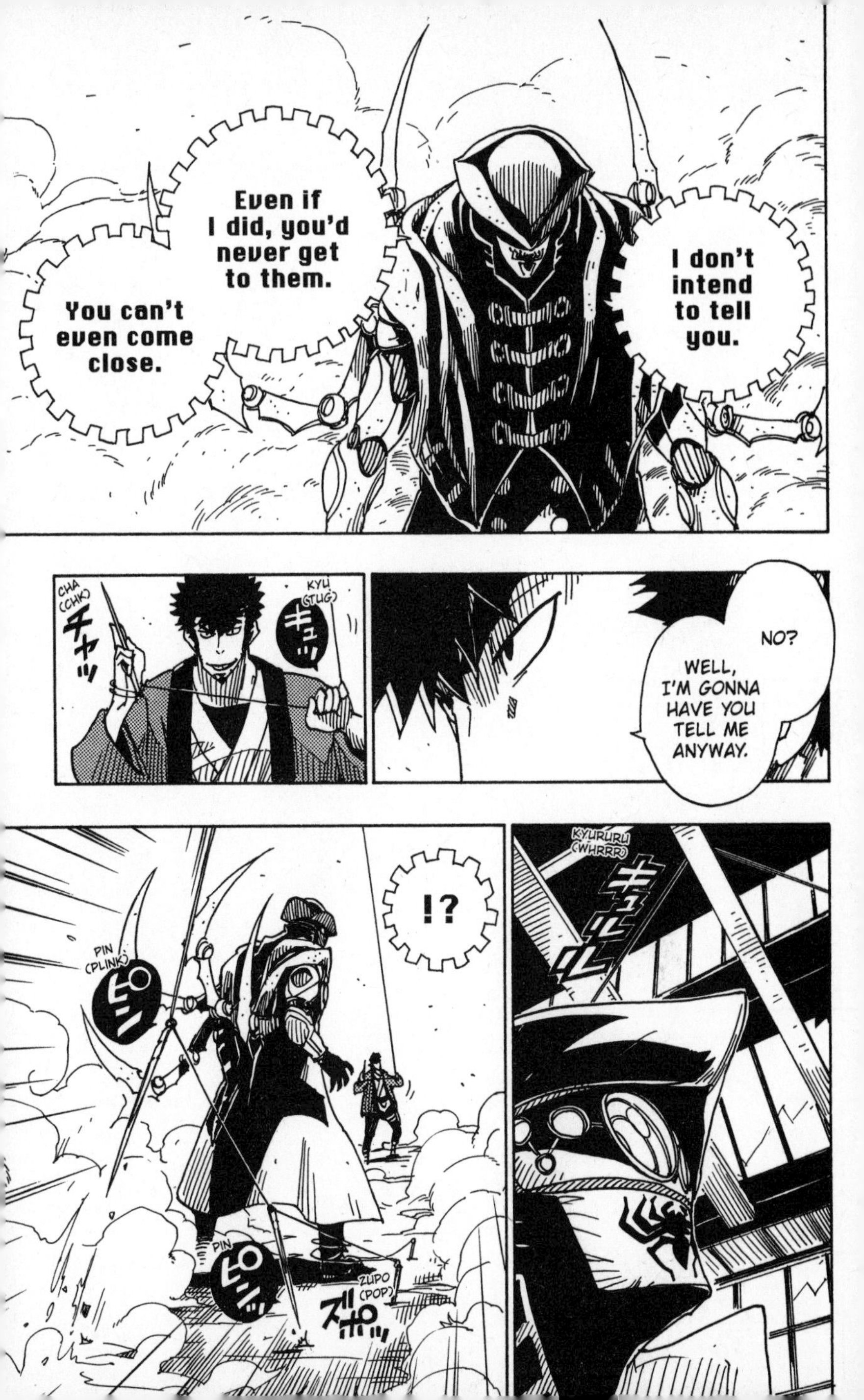
I don't intend to tell you.
Even if I did, you'd never get to them.
You can't even come close.
NO?
WELL, I'M GONNA HAVE YOU TELL ME ANYWAY.
KYU (TUG) キュッ
CHA (CHK) チャッ
KYURURU (WHRRR) キュルル
!?
PIN (PLINK) ピン
PIN ピン
ZUPO (POP) ズポッ

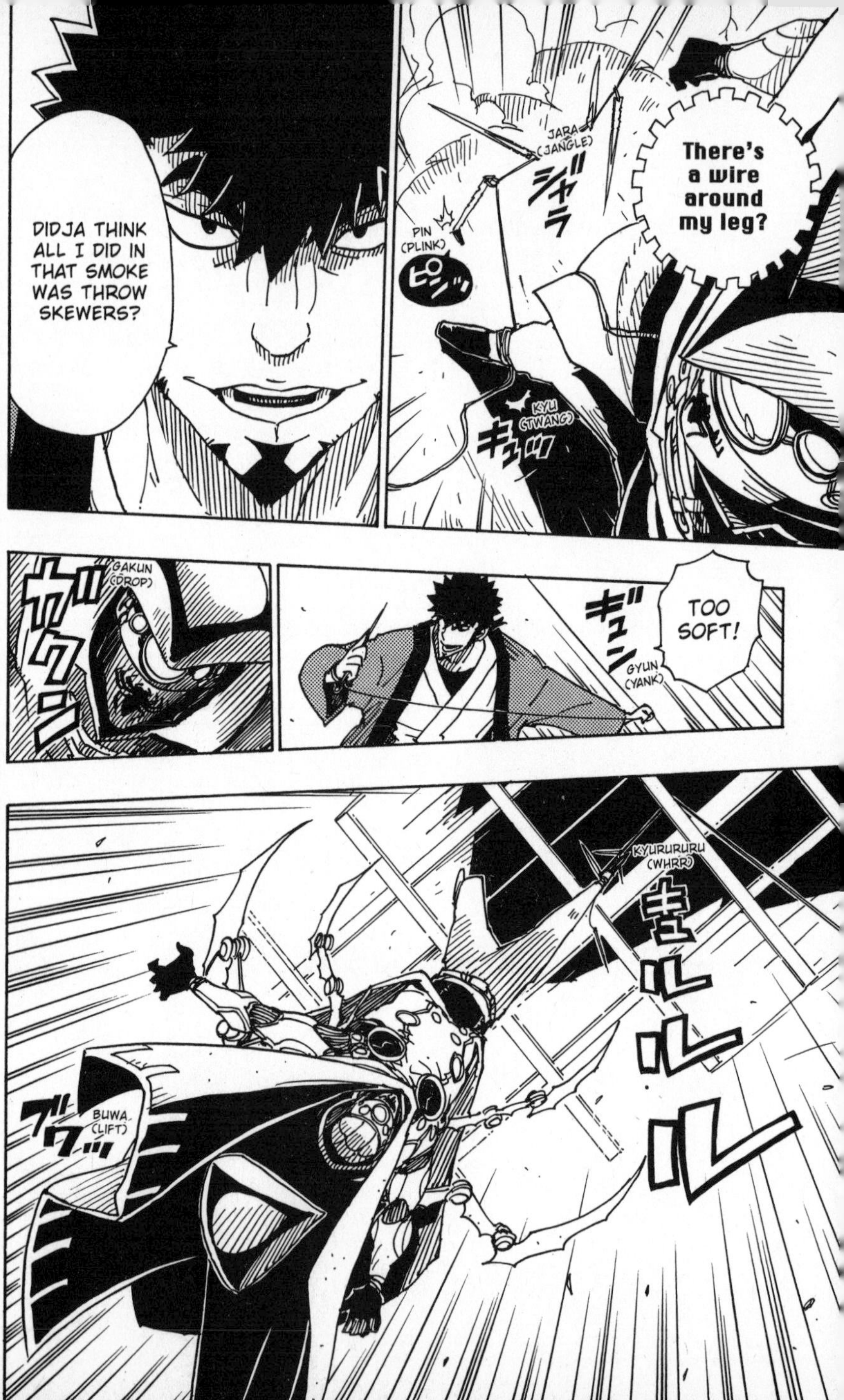
There's a wire around my leg?
JARA (JANGLE)
ジャラ
PIN (PLINK)
ピンッ
KYU (TWANG)
ギュッ
DIDJA THINK ALL I DID IN THAT SMOKE WAS THROW SKEWERS?
TOO SOFT!
GYUN (YANK)
ギュン
GAKUN (DROP)
ガクン
KYURURURU (WHRR)
BUWA (LIFT)
ブワッ

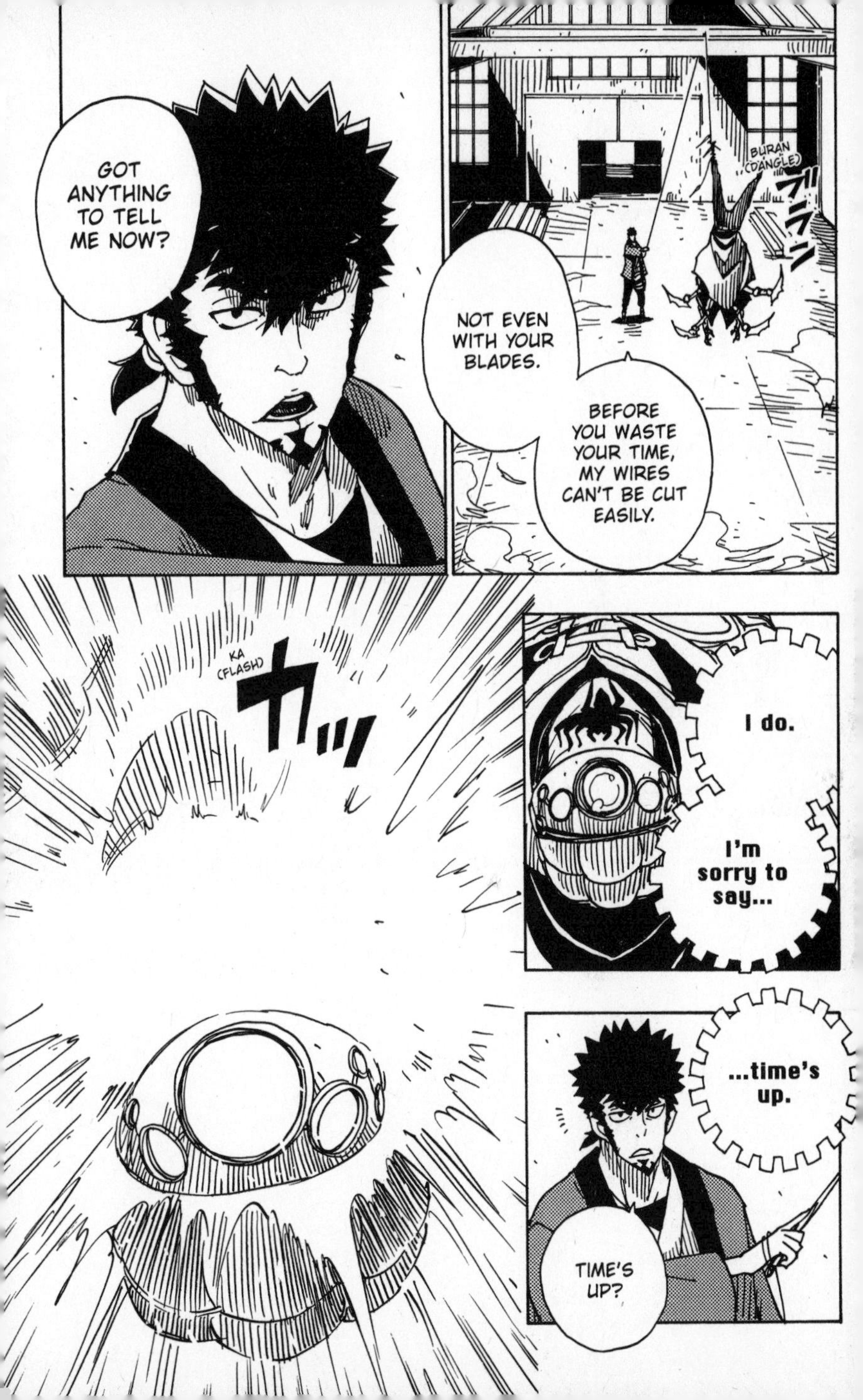
BURAN (DANGLE)
ブラン
BEFORE YOU WASTE YOUR TIME, MY WIRES CAN'T BE CUT EASILY.
NOT EVEN WITH YOUR BLADES.
GOT ANYTHING TO TELL ME NOW?
I do.
I'm sorry to say...
...time's up.
TIME'S UP?
KA (FLASH)
カッ

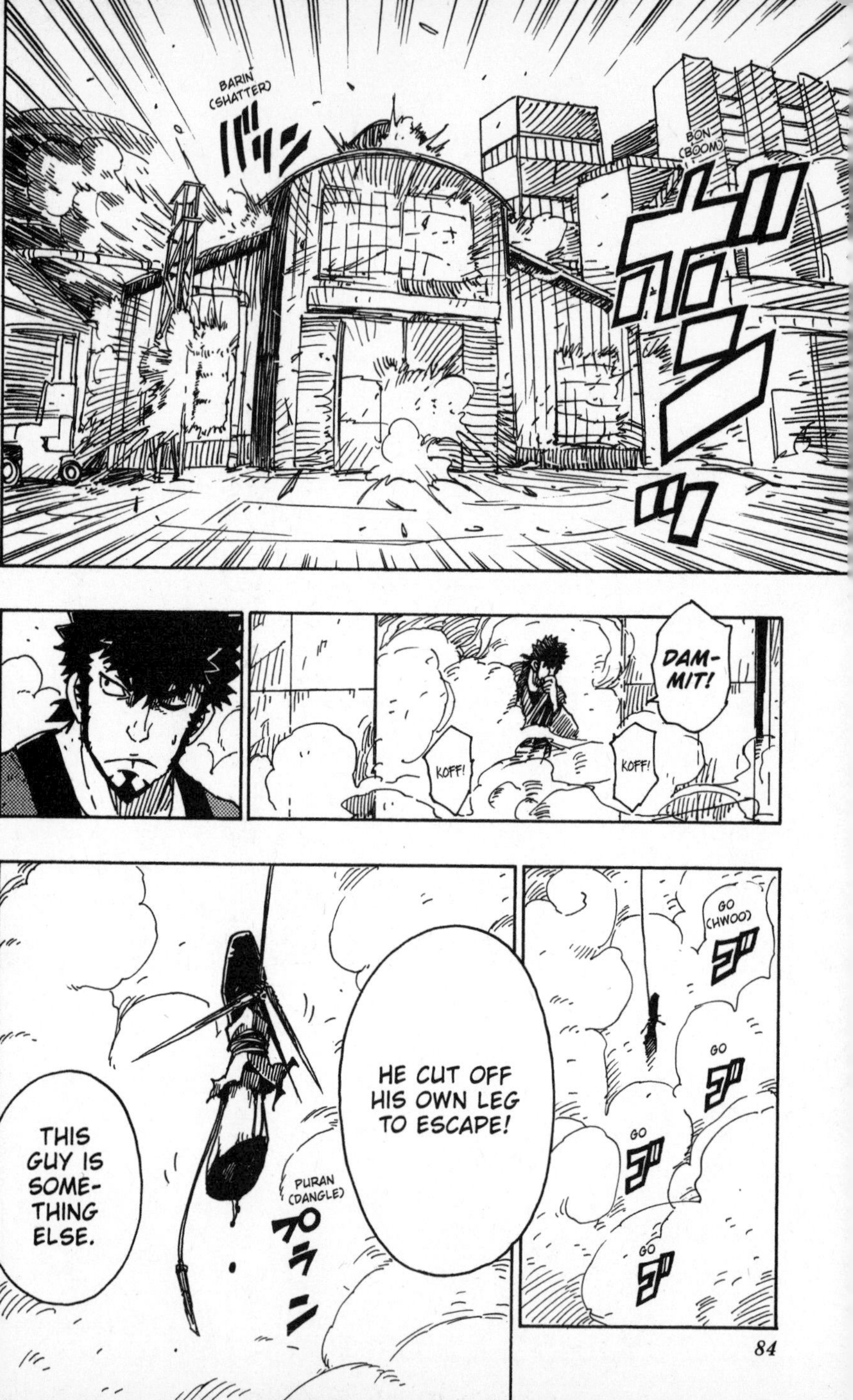
BON (BOOM)
BARIN (SHATTER)
DAM-MIT!
KOFF!
KOFF!
GO (CHWOO)
GO
GO
GO
HE CUT OFF HIS OWN LEG TO ESCAPE!
PURAN (DANGLE)
THIS GUY IS SOME-THING ELSE.

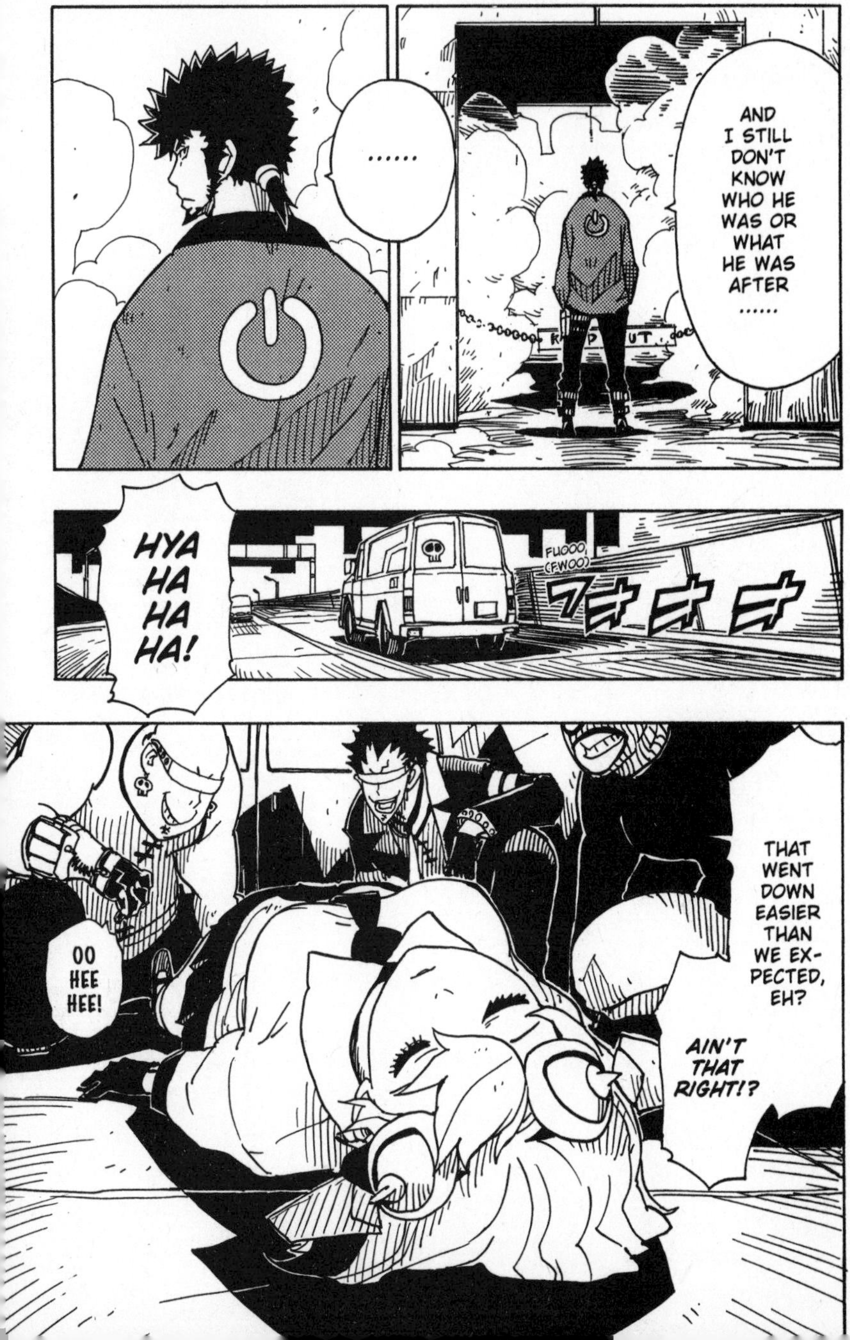
AND I STILL DON'T KNOW WHO HE WAS OR WHAT HE WAS AFTER ......
......
FUOOO (FWOO)
HYA HA HA HA!
THAT WENT DOWN EASIER THAN WE EX-PECTED, EH?
AIN'T THAT RIGHT!?
OO HEE HEE!

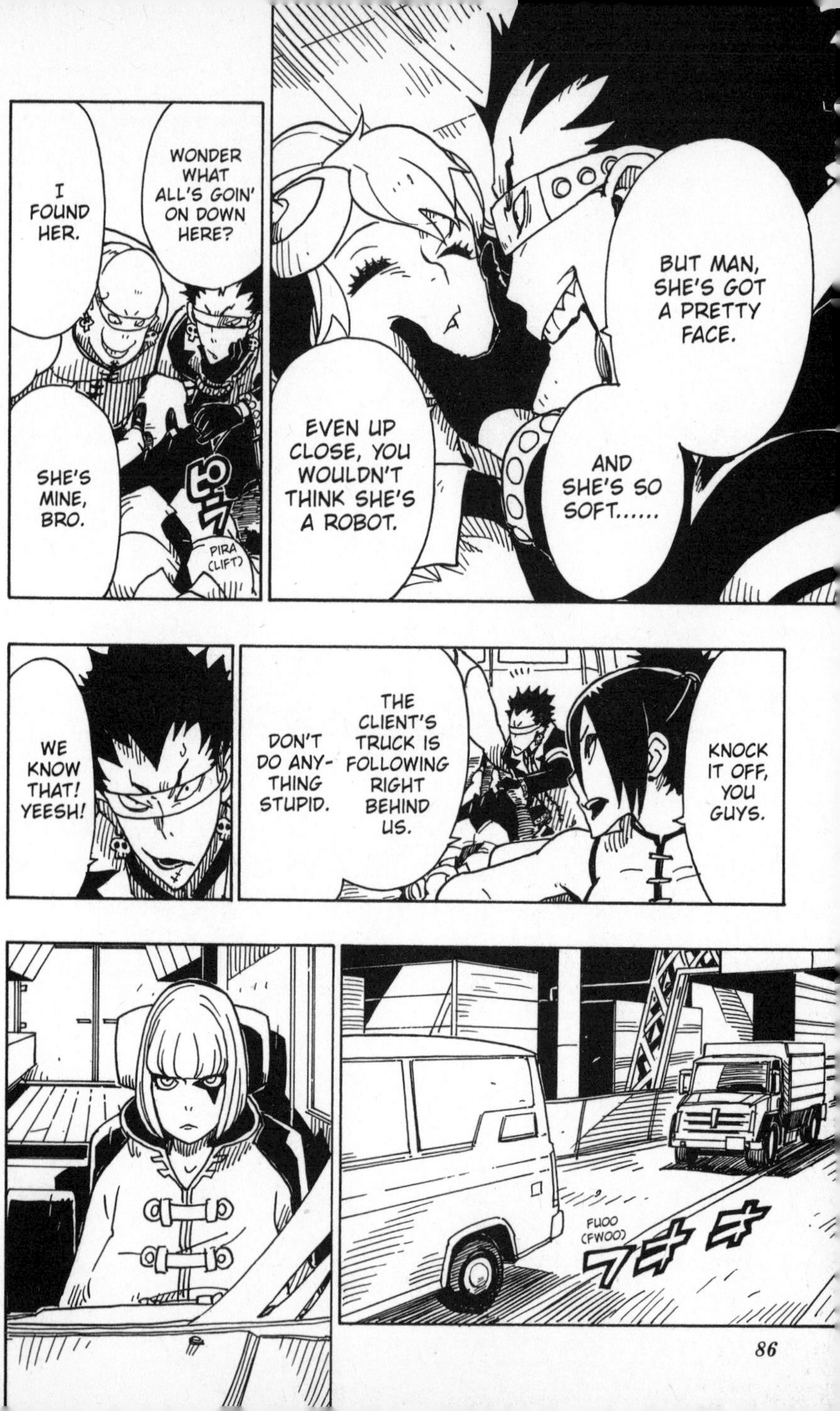
BUT MAN, SHE'S GOT A PRETTY FACE.
AND SHE'S SO SOFT......
EVEN UP CLOSE, YOU WOULDN'T THINK SHE'S A ROBOT.
WONDER WHAT ALL'S GOIN' ON DOWN HERE?
I FOUND HER.
SHE'S MINE, BRO.
PIRA (LIFT)
KNOCK IT OFF, YOU GUYS.
THE CLIENT'S TRUCK IS FOLLOWING RIGHT BEHIND US.
DON'T DO ANY-THING STUPID.
WE KNOW THAT! YEESH!
FUOO (FWOO)

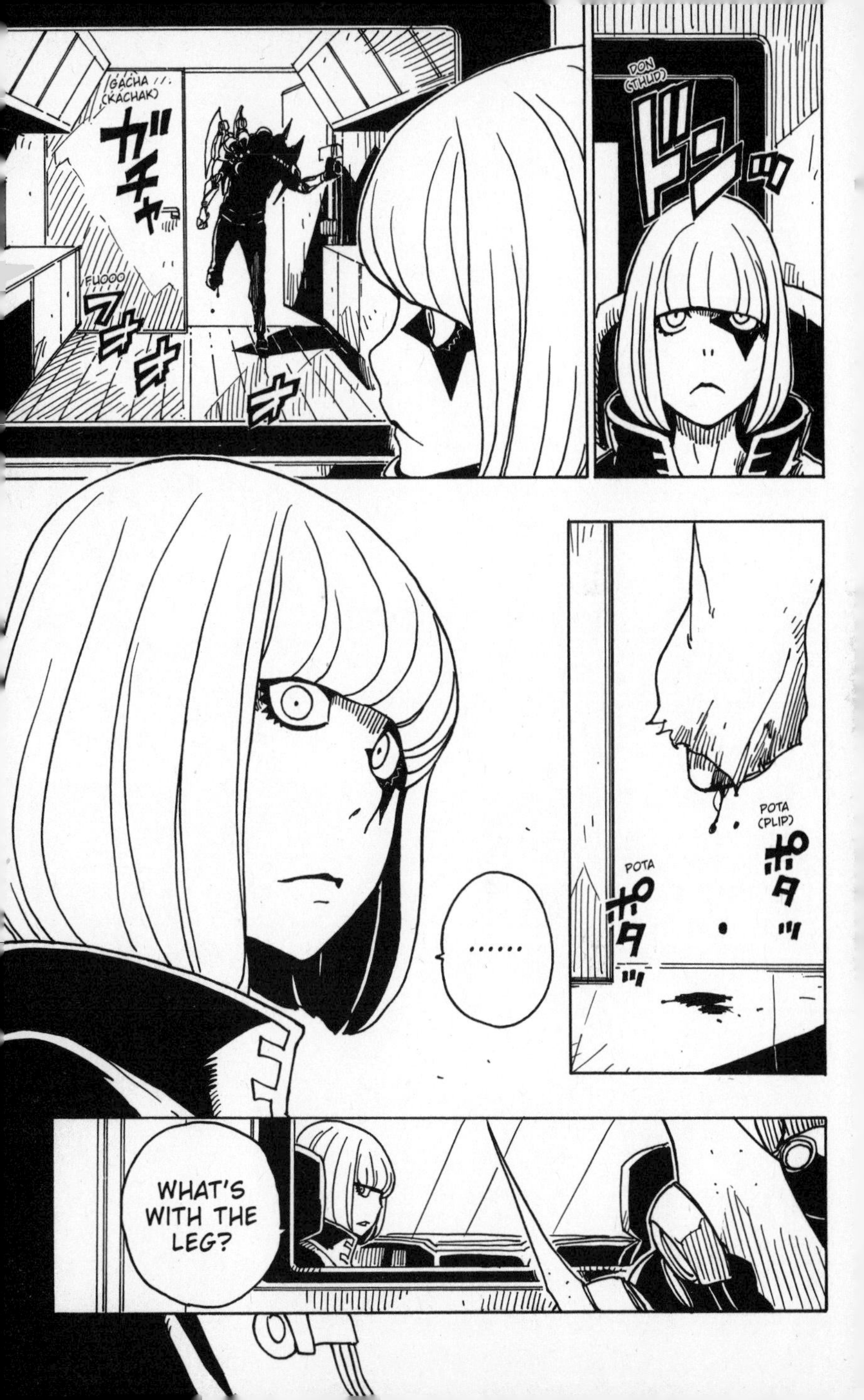
DON (THUD)
ドンッ
GACHA (KACHAK)
ガチャ
FUOOO
POTA (PLIP)
ポタッ
POTA
ポタッ
......
WHAT'S WITH THE LEG?

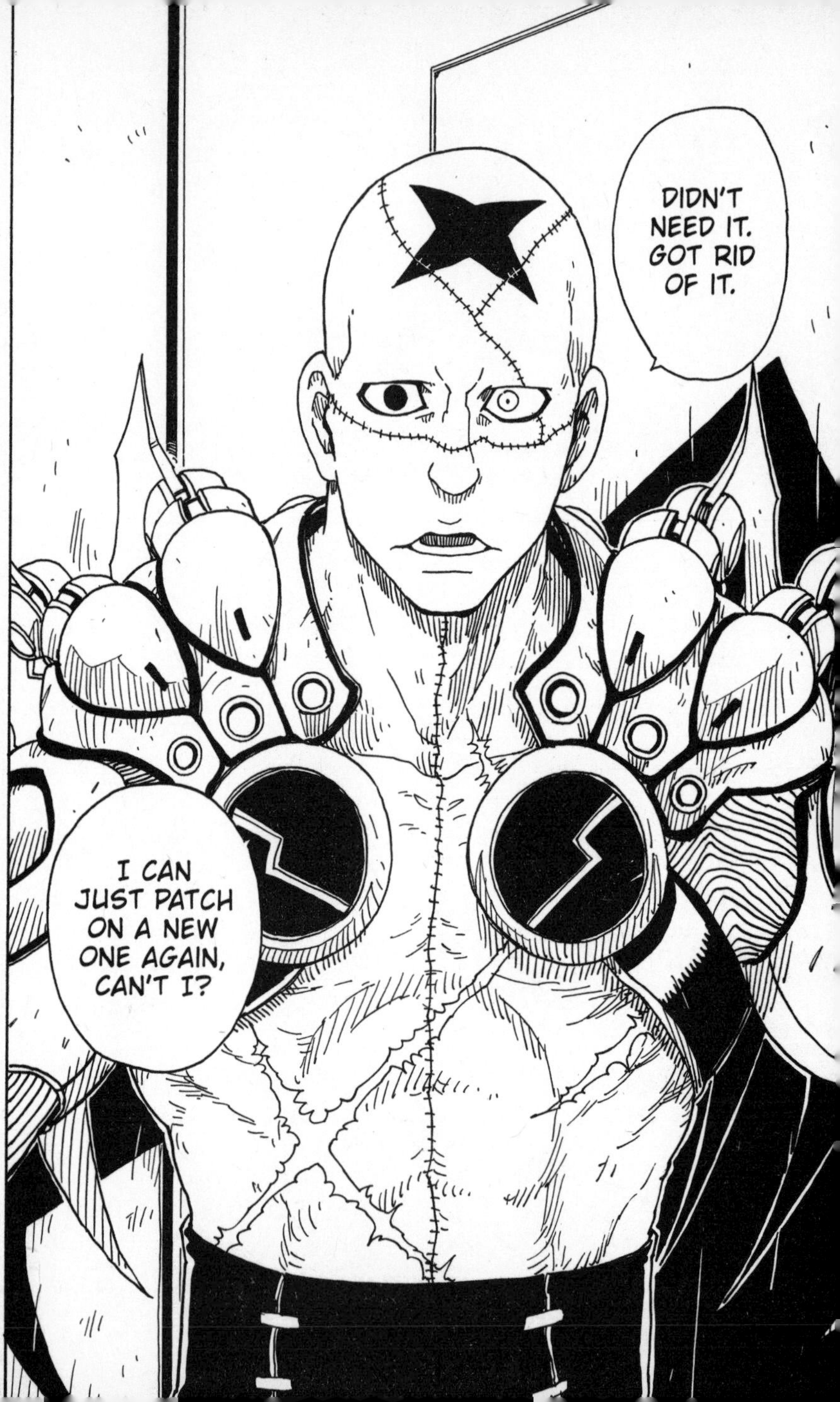
DIDN'T NEED IT. GOT RID OF IT.
I CAN JUST PATCH ON A NEW ONE AGAIN, CAN'T I?

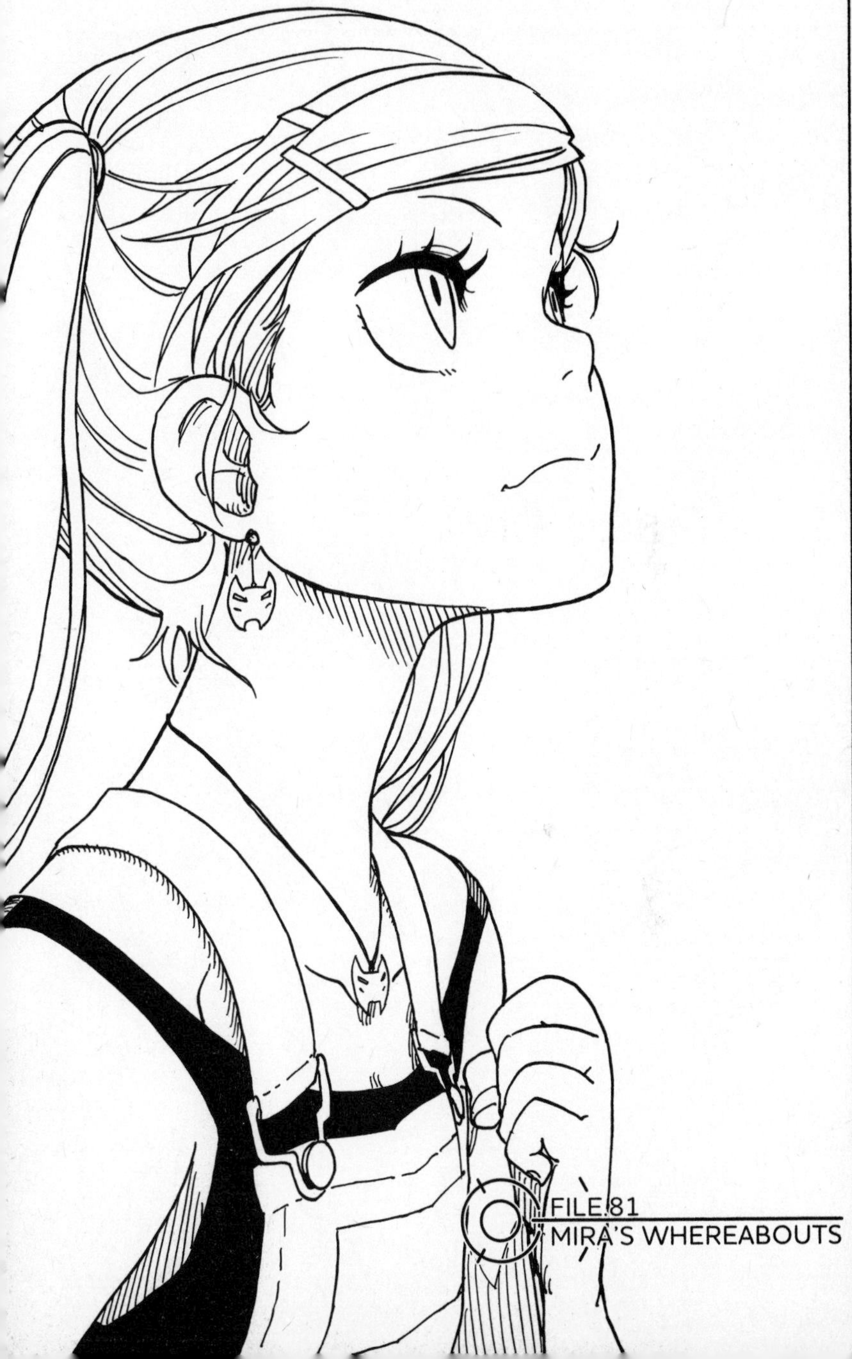
FILE.81
MIRA'S WHEREABOUTS

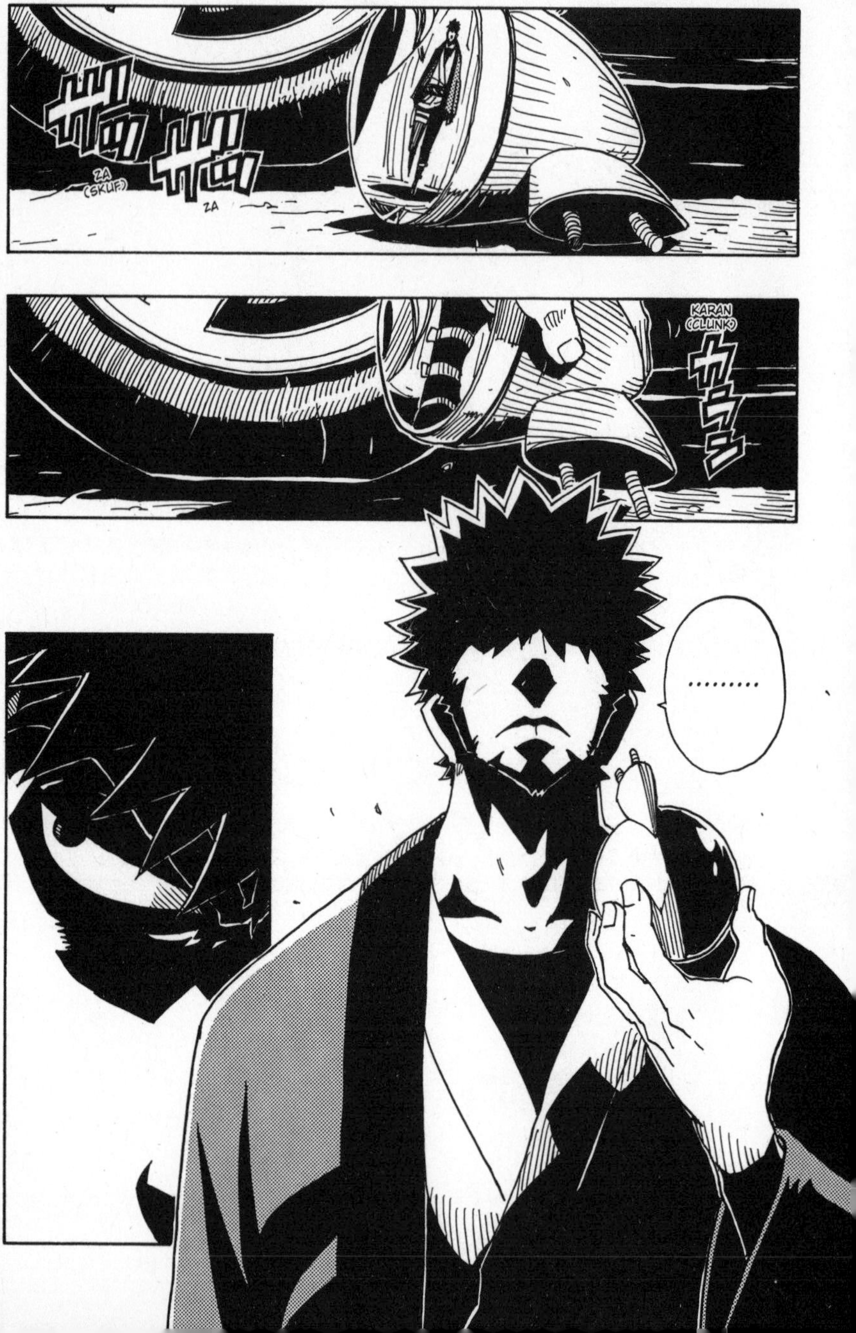

ザッ
ザッ
ZA
(SKUF)
ZA
KARAN
(CLUNK)
カラン
....

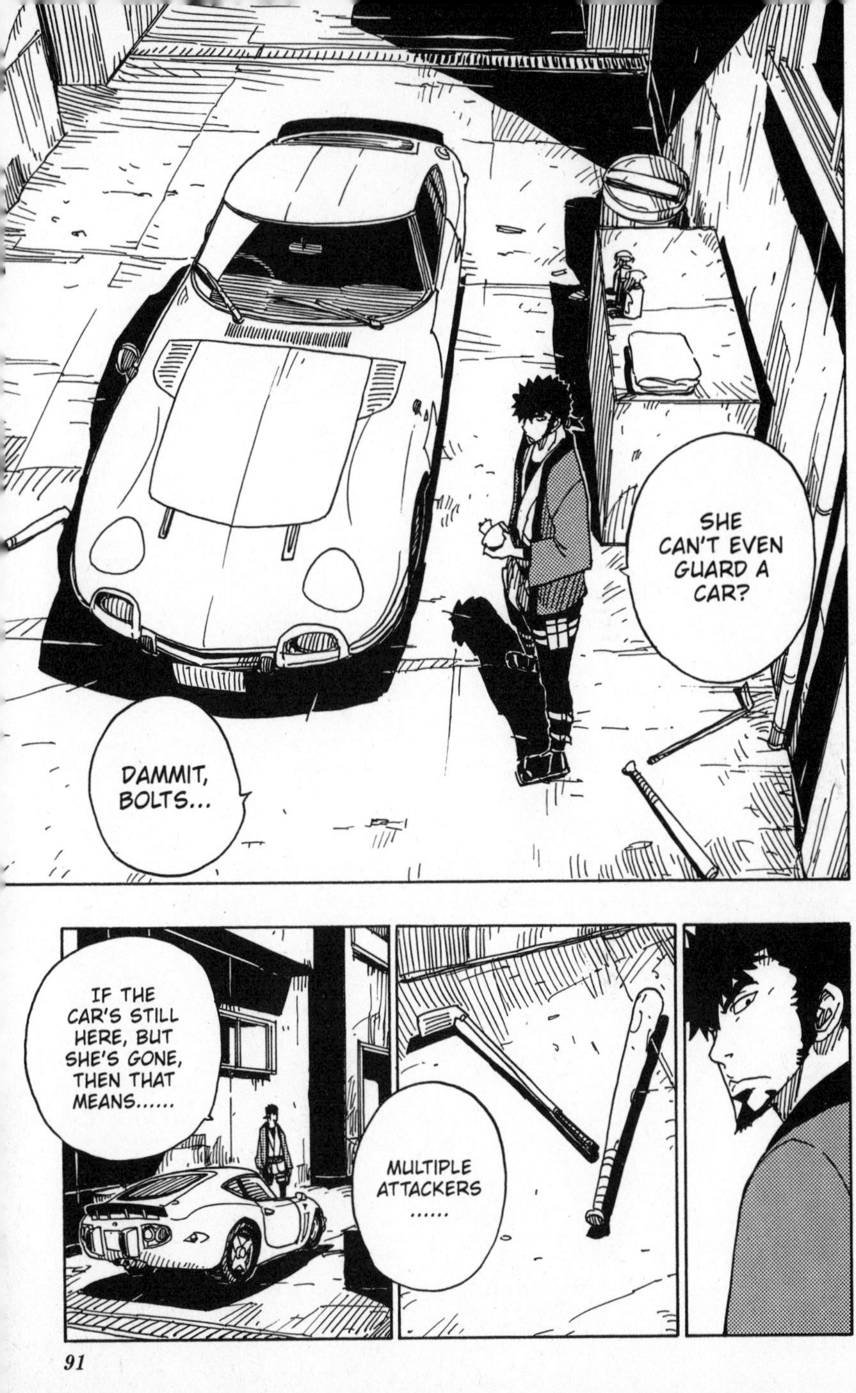
DAMMIT, BOLTS...
SHE CAN'T EVEN GUARD A CAR?
IF THE CAR'S STILL HERE, BUT SHE'S GONE, THEN THAT MEANS......
MULTIPLE ATTACKERS ......

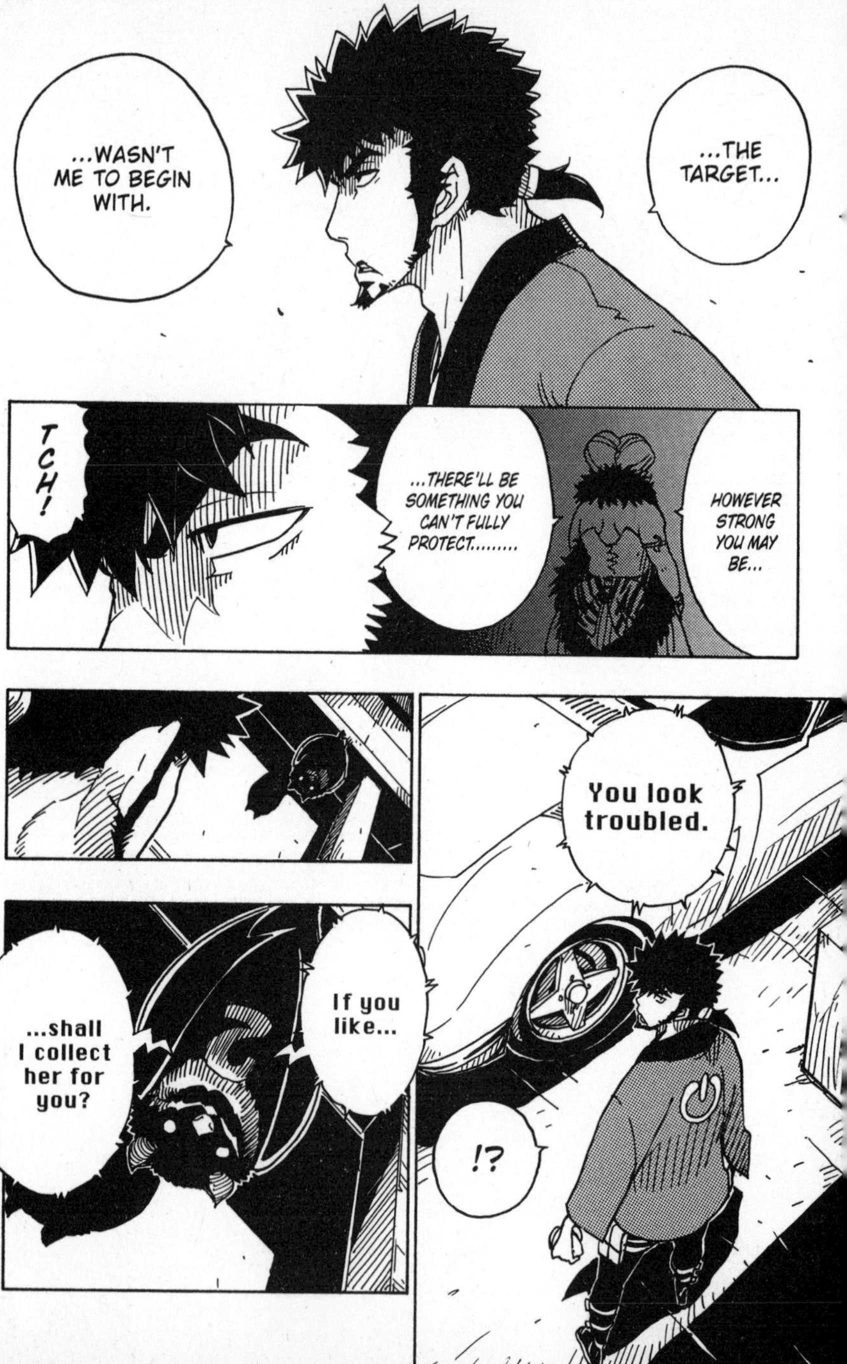
...THE TARGET...
...WASN'T ME TO BEGIN WITH.
HOWEVER STRONG YOU MAY BE...
...THERE'LL BE SOMETHING YOU CAN'T FULLY PROTECT........
TCH!
You look troubled.
!?
If you like...
...shall I collect her for you?

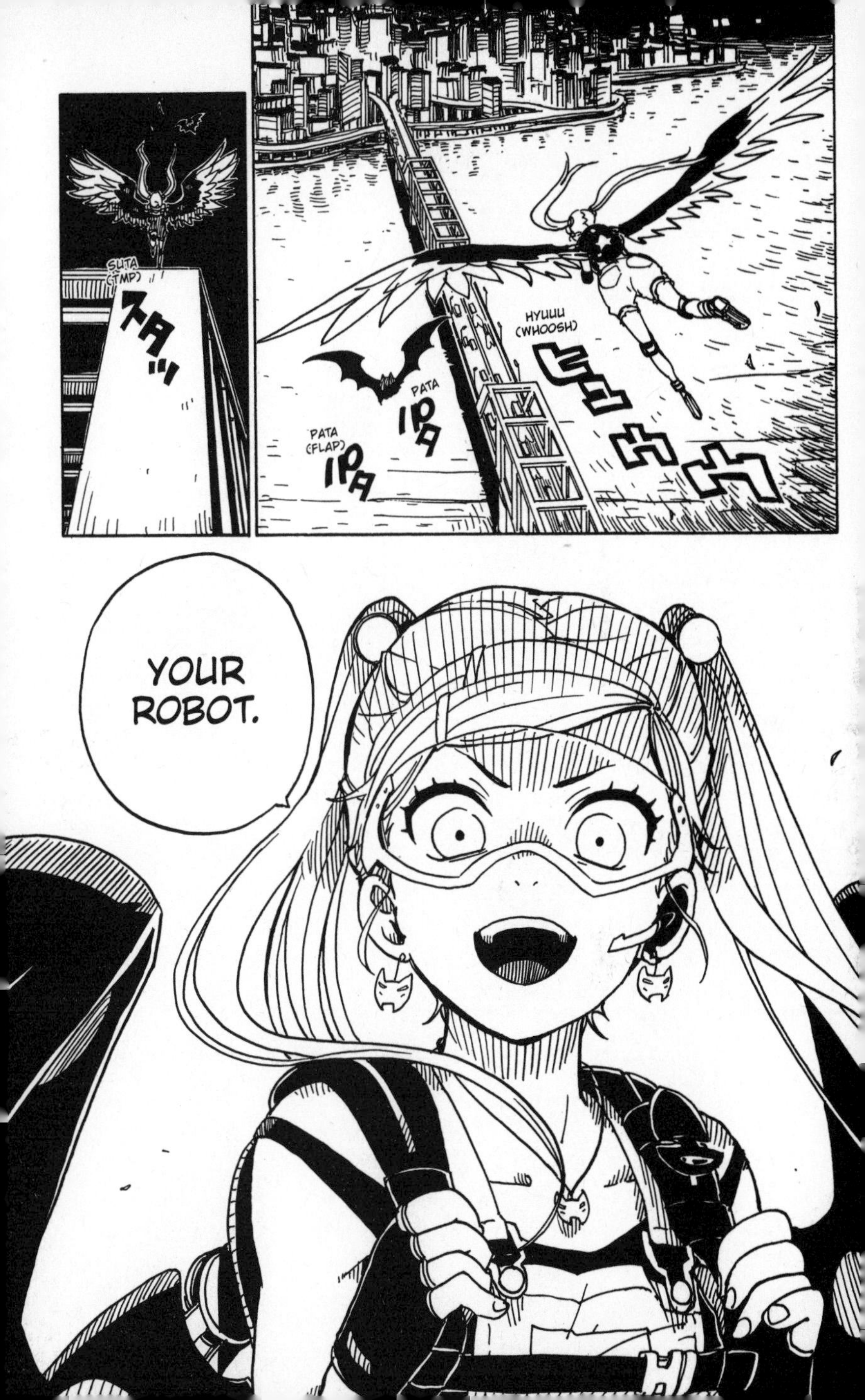
HYUUU (WHOOSH)
PATA
PATA (FLAP)
SUTA (TMP)
YOUR ROBOT.

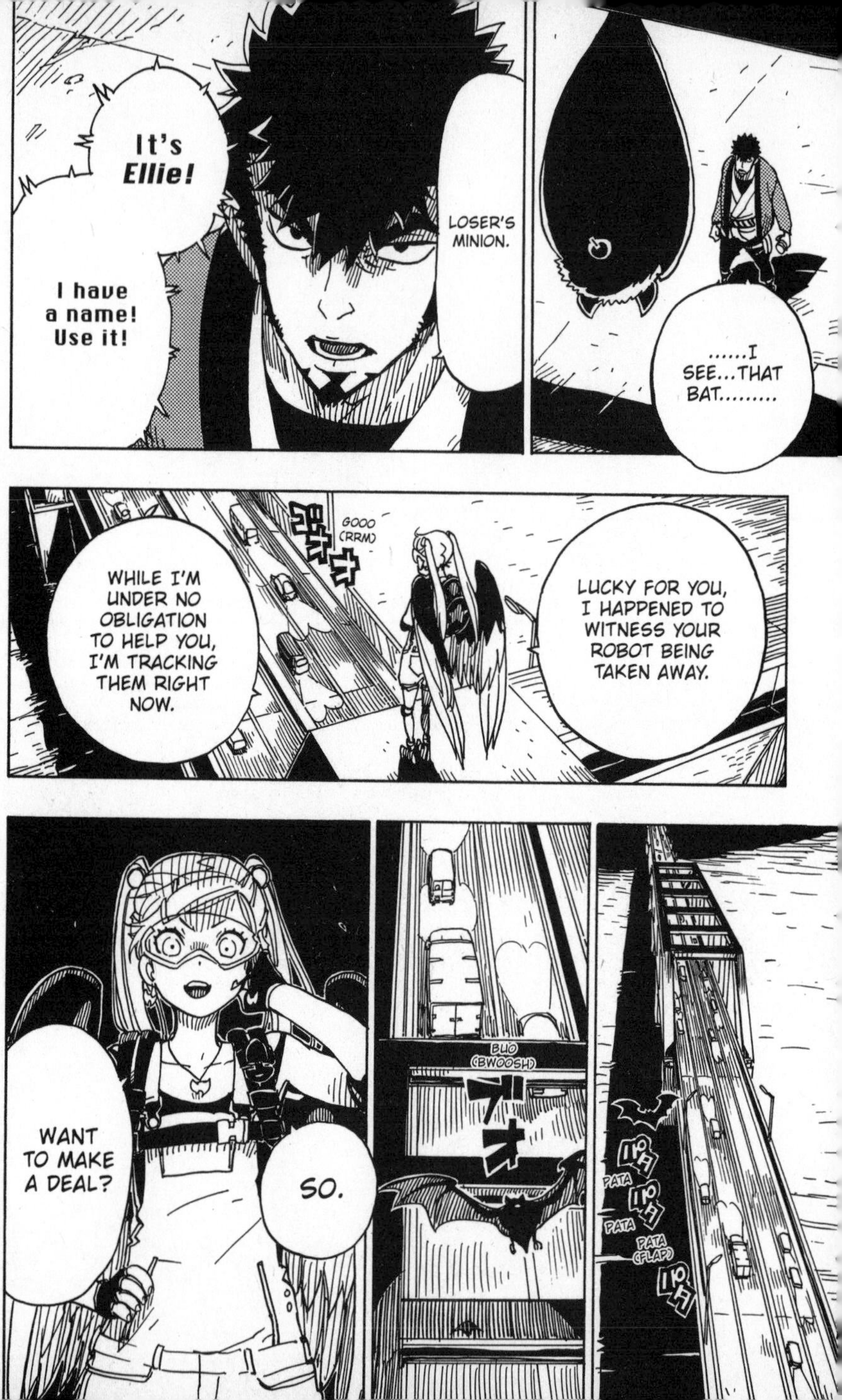

......I SEE...THAT BAT.........
LOSER'S MINION.
It's *Ellie!*
I have a name! Use it!
LUCKY FOR YOU, I HAPPENED TO WITNESS YOUR ROBOT BEING TAKEN AWAY.
GOOO (RRM)
WHILE I'M UNDER NO OBLIGATION TO HELP YOU, I'M TRACKING THEM RIGHT NOW.
PATA
PATA
PATA (FLAP)
BUO (BWOOSH)
SO.
WANT TO MAKE A DEAL?

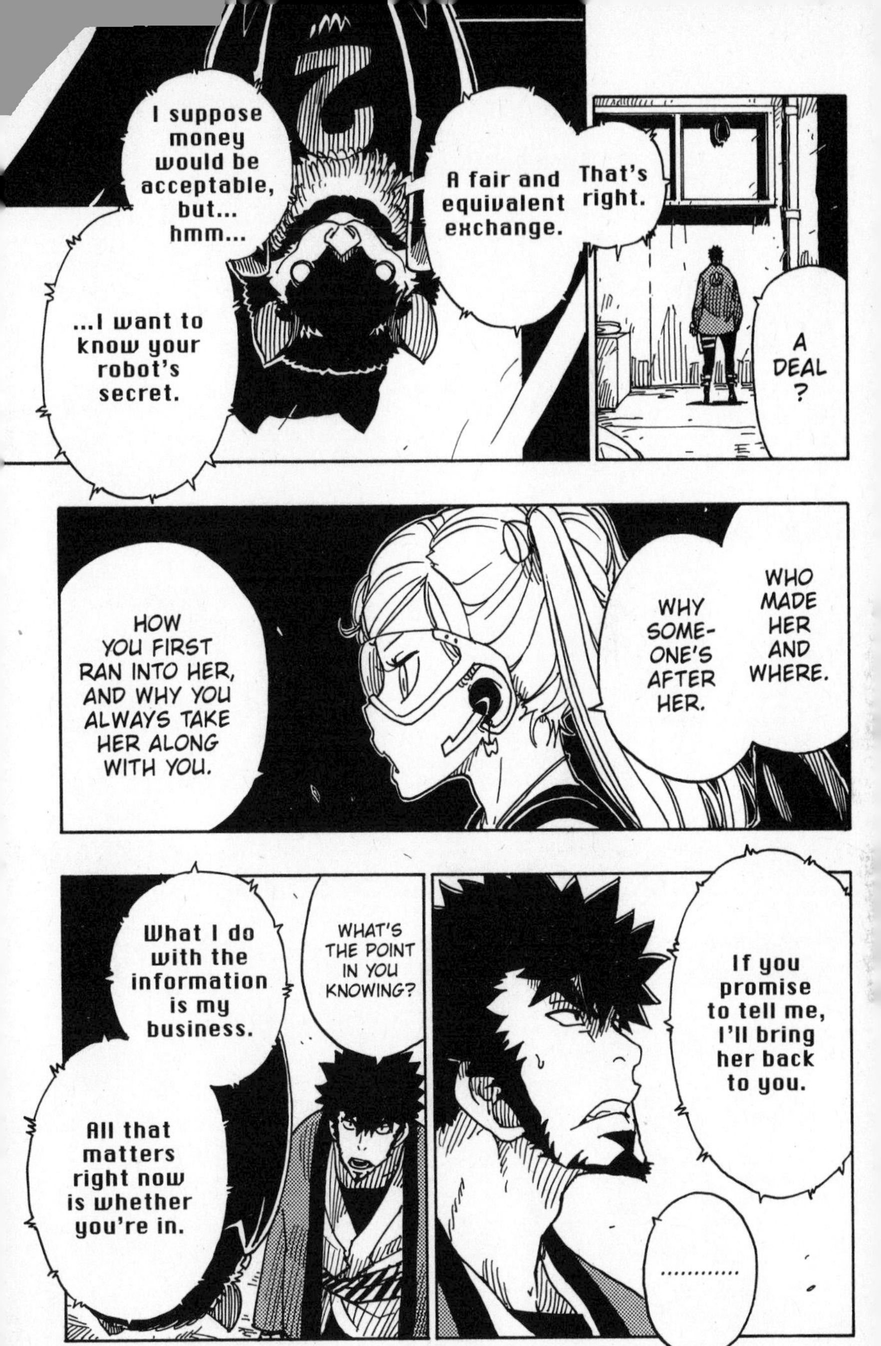
A DEAL?
That's right.
A fair and equivalent exchange.
I suppose money would be acceptable, but... hmm...
...I want to know your robot's secret.
WHO MADE HER AND WHERE.
WHY SOME-ONE'S AFTER HER.
HOW YOU FIRST RAN INTO HER, AND WHY YOU ALWAYS TAKE HER ALONG WITH YOU.
If you promise to tell me, I'll bring her back to you.
....
WHAT'S THE POINT IN YOU KNOWING?
What I do with the information is my business.
All that matters right now is whether you're in.

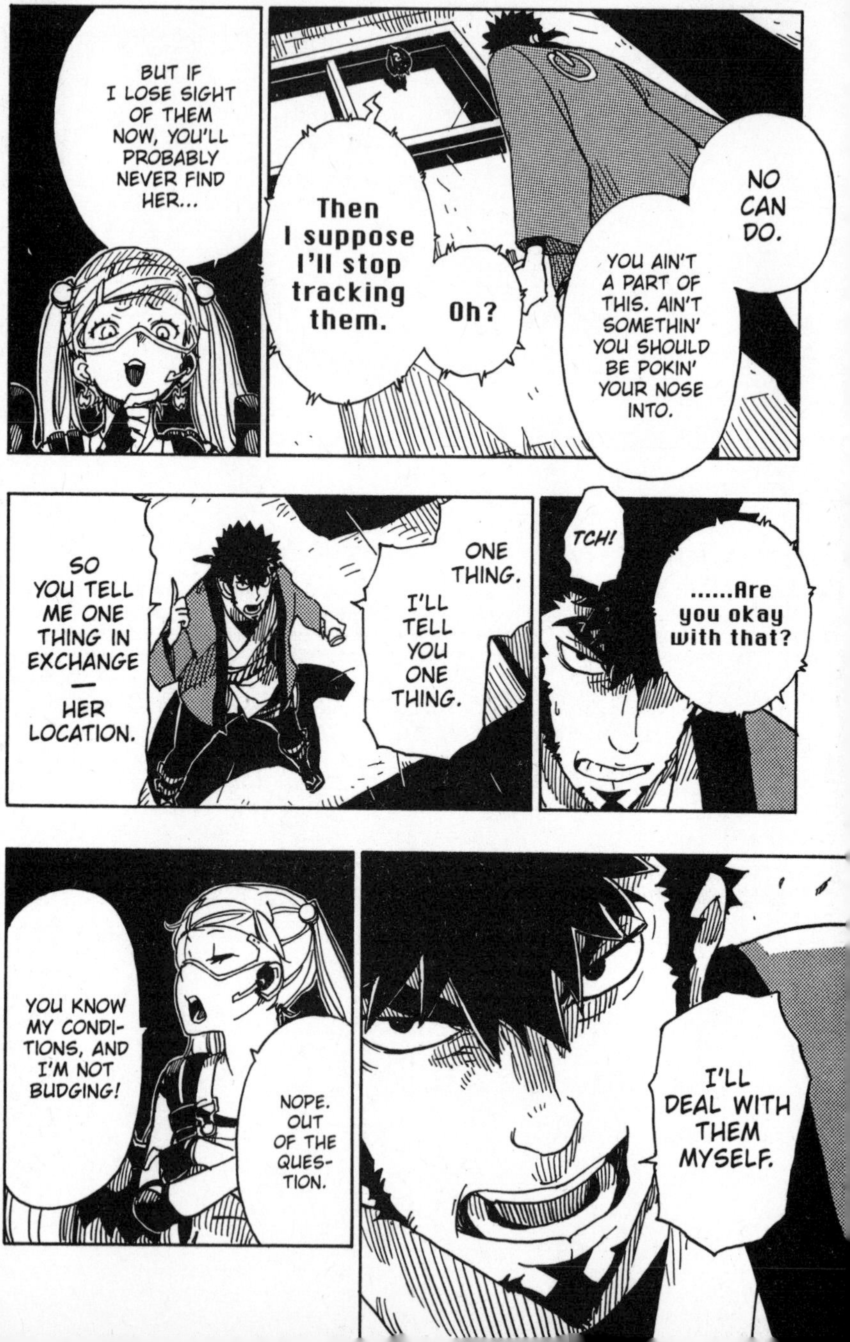
NO CAN DO.
YOU AIN'T A PART OF THIS. AIN'T SOMETHIN' YOU SHOULD BE POKIN' YOUR NOSE INTO.
Oh?
Then I suppose I'll stop tracking them.
BUT IF I LOSE SIGHT OF THEM NOW, YOU'LL PROBABLY NEVER FIND HER...
TCH!
......Are you okay with that?
ONE THING.
I'LL TELL YOU ONE THING.
SO YOU TELL ME ONE THING IN EXCHANGE — HER LOCATION.
I'LL DEAL WITH THEM MYSELF.
NOPE. OUT OF THE QUESTION.
YOU KNOW MY CONDITIONS, AND I'M NOT BUDGING!

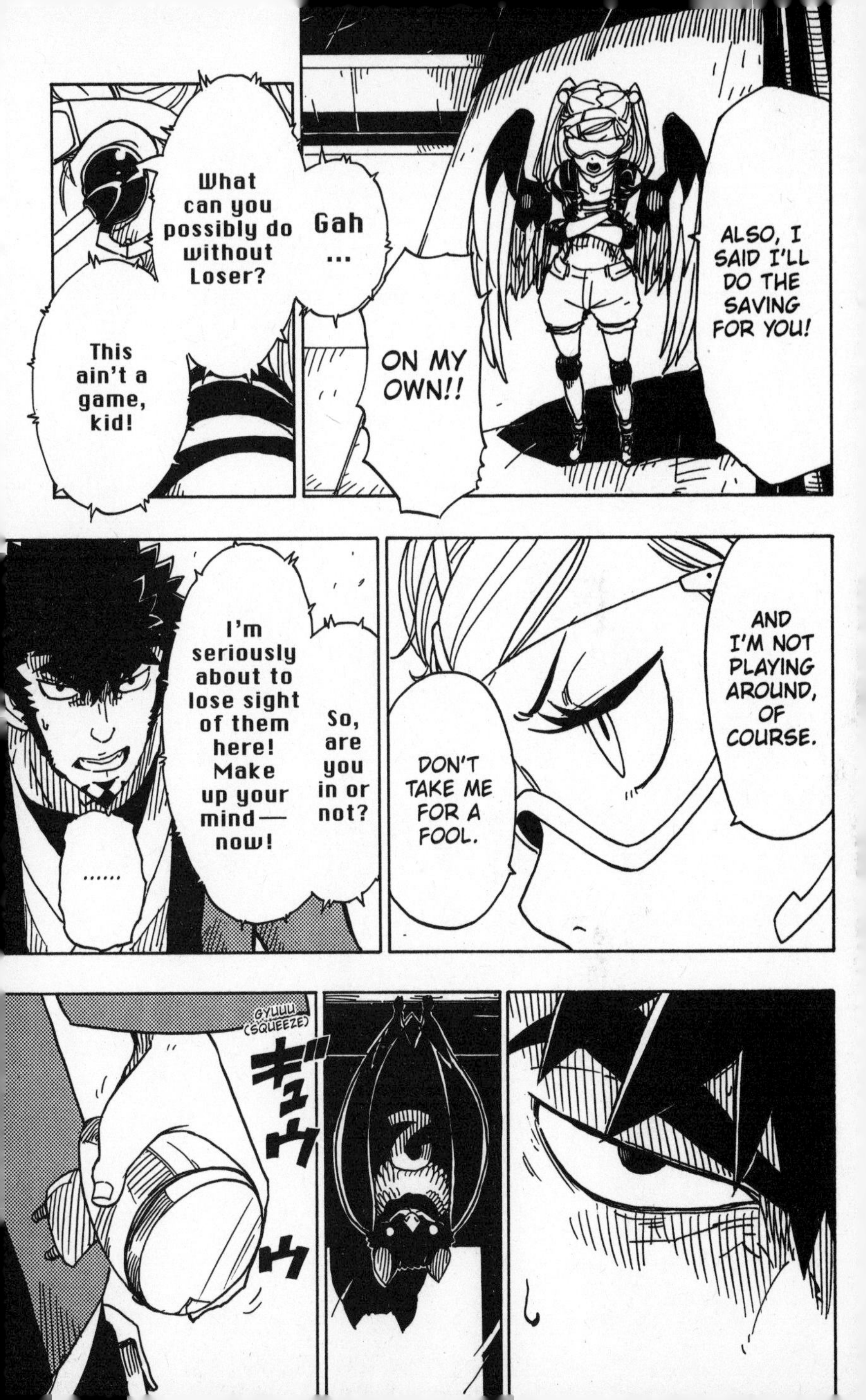
ALSO, I SAID I'LL DO THE SAVING FOR YOU!
ON MY OWN!!
Gah ...
What can you possibly do without Loser?
This ain't a game, kid!
AND I'M NOT PLAYING AROUND, OF COURSE.
DON'T TAKE ME FOR A FOOL.
I'm seriously about to lose sight of them here! Make up your mind—now!
So, are you in or not?
......
GYUUU (SQUEEZE)
ギュウウ

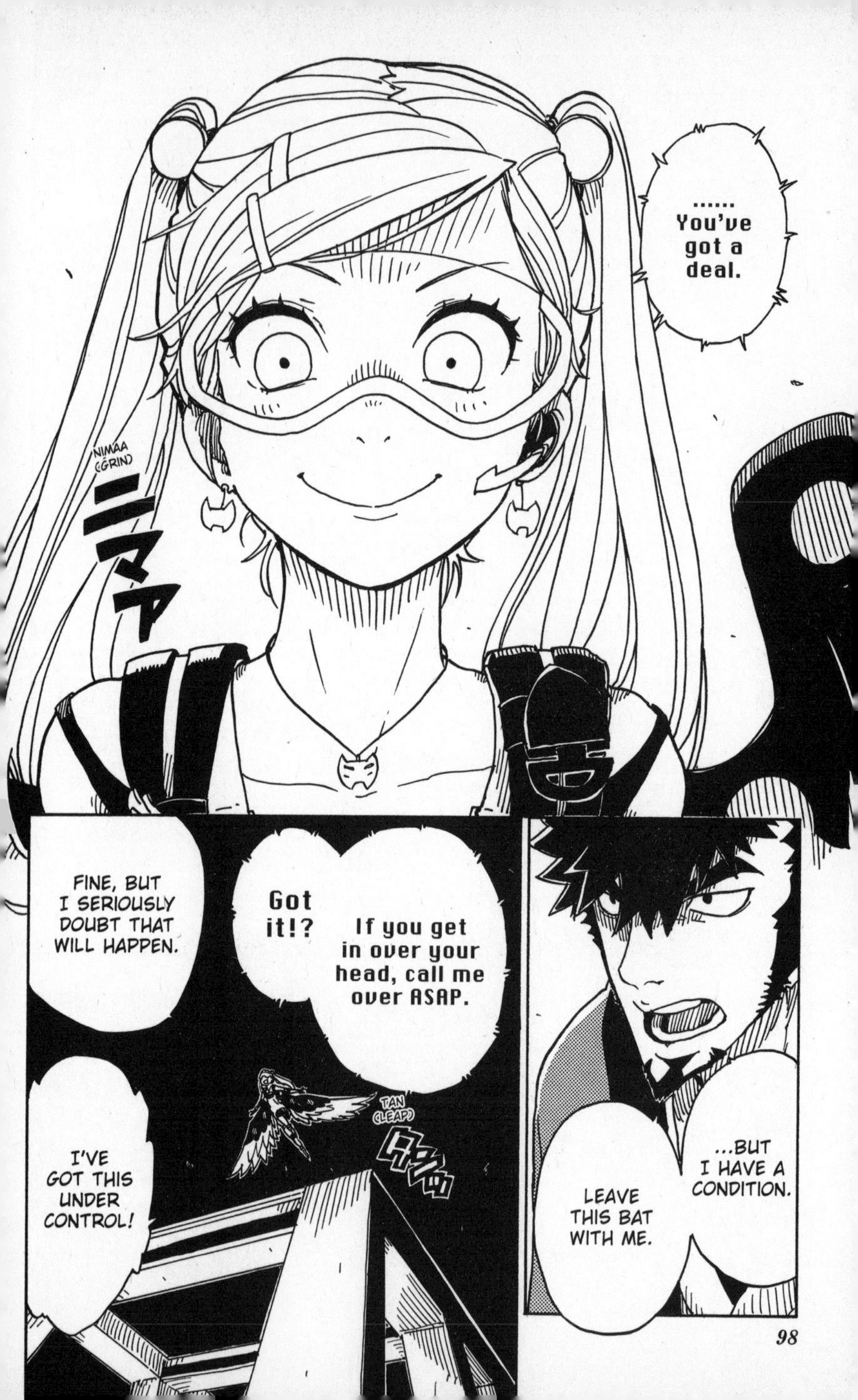

...... You've got a deal.
NIMAA (GRIN)
...BUT I HAVE A CONDITION.
LEAVE THIS BAT WITH ME.
If you get in over your head, call me over ASAP.
Got it!?
FINE, BUT I SERIOUSLY DOUBT THAT WILL HAPPEN.
TAN (LEAP)
I'VE GOT THIS UNDER CONTROL!

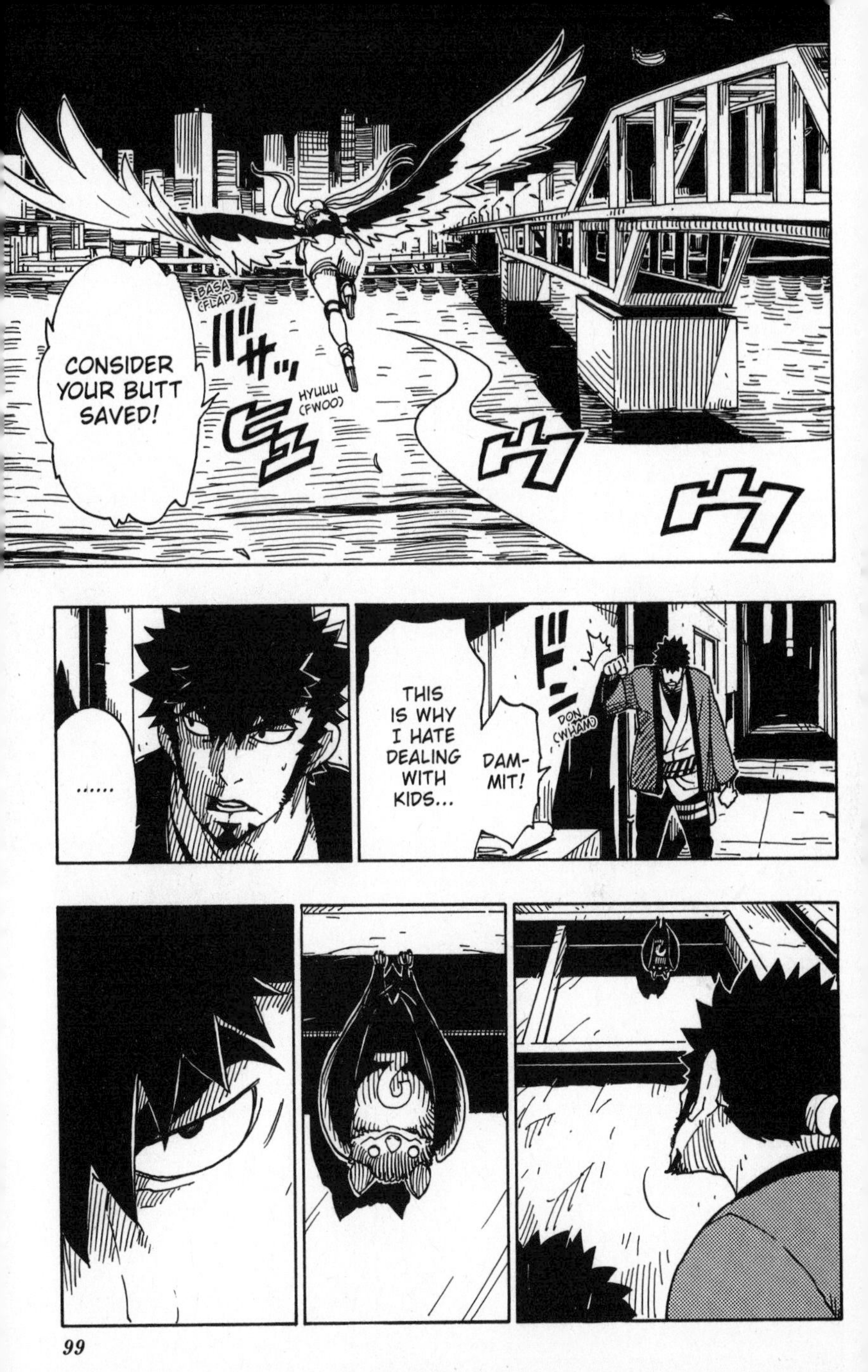

HYUUU (FWOO)
BASA (FLAP)
CONSIDER YOUR BUTT SAVED!
DON (WHAM)
DAM-MIT!
THIS IS WHY I HATE DEALING WITH KIDS...
......

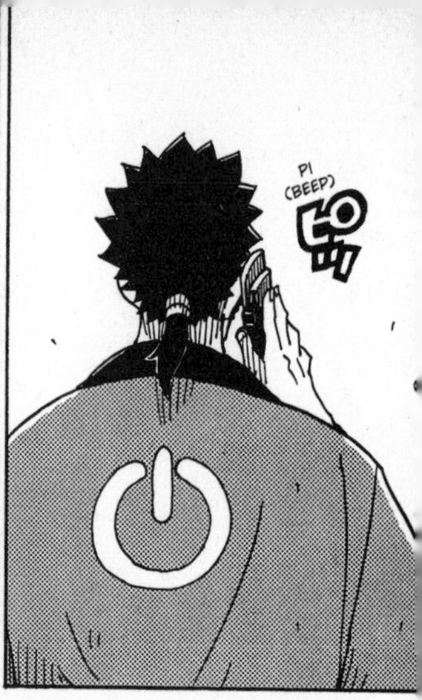
PI
(BEEP)
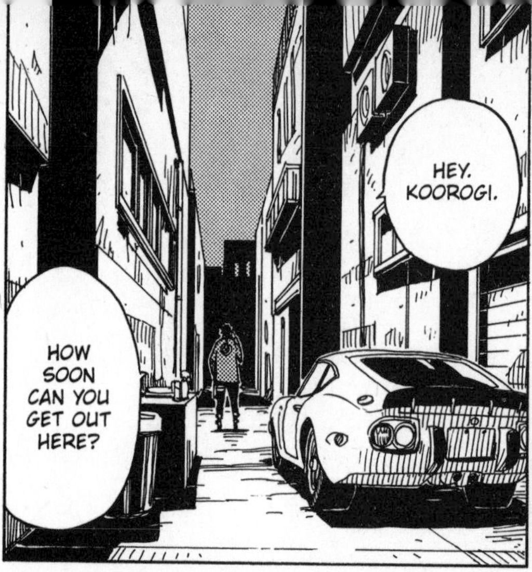
HEY. KOOROGI.
HOW SOON CAN YOU GET OUT HERE?
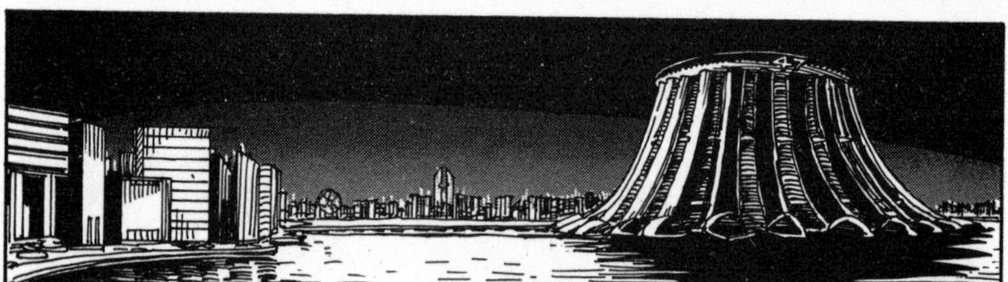
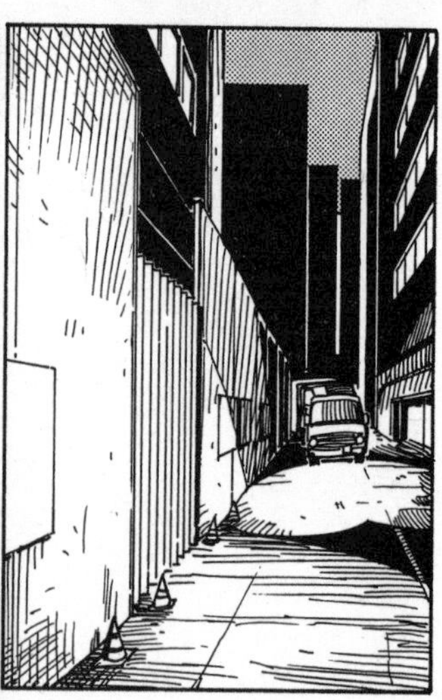
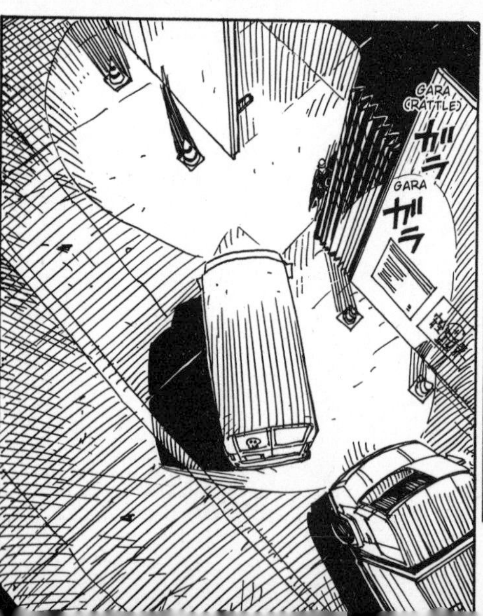
GARA
(RATTLE)
GARA

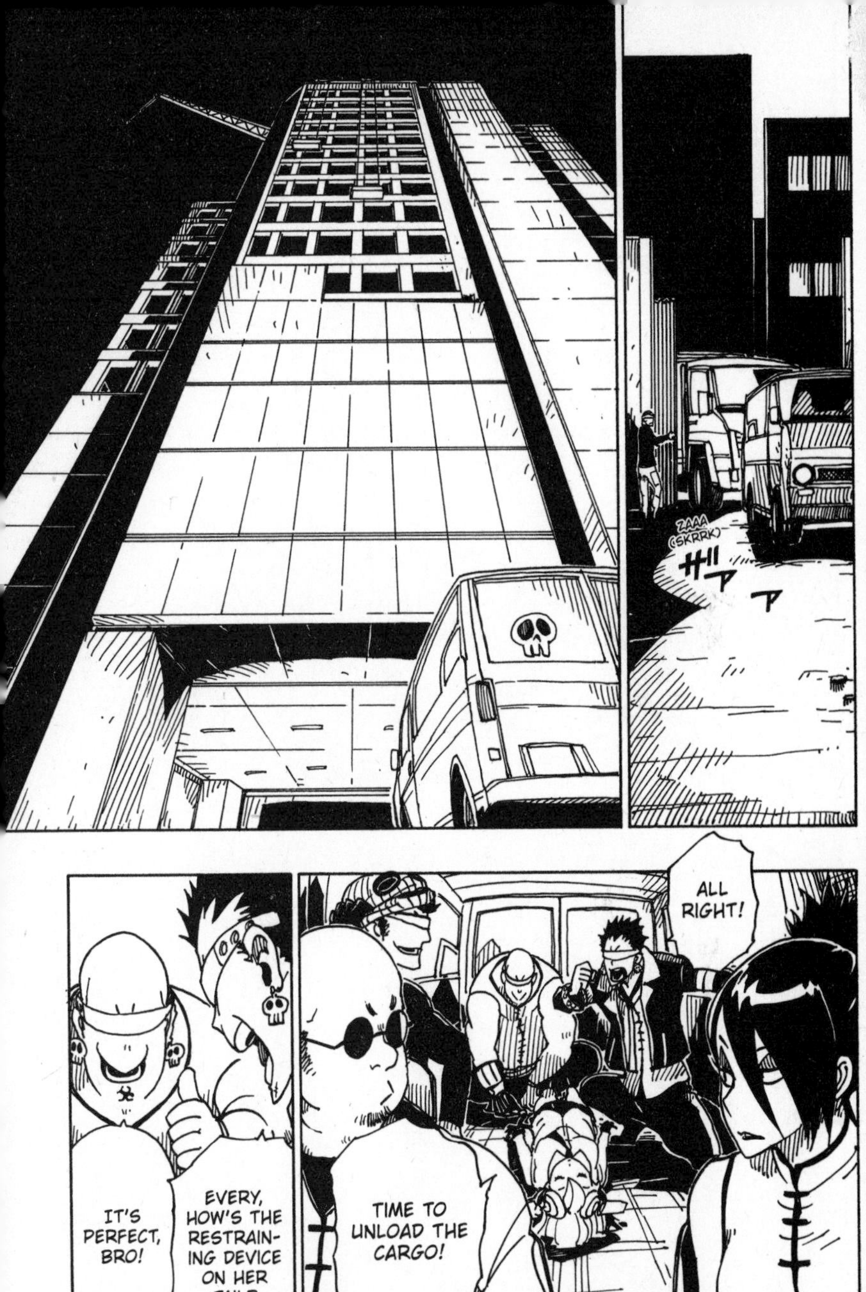
ZAAA (SKRRK)
ザァァ
ALL RIGHT!
TIME TO UNLOAD THE CARGO!
EVERY, HOW'S THE RESTRAINING DEVICE ON HER TAIL?
IT'S PERFECT, BRO!

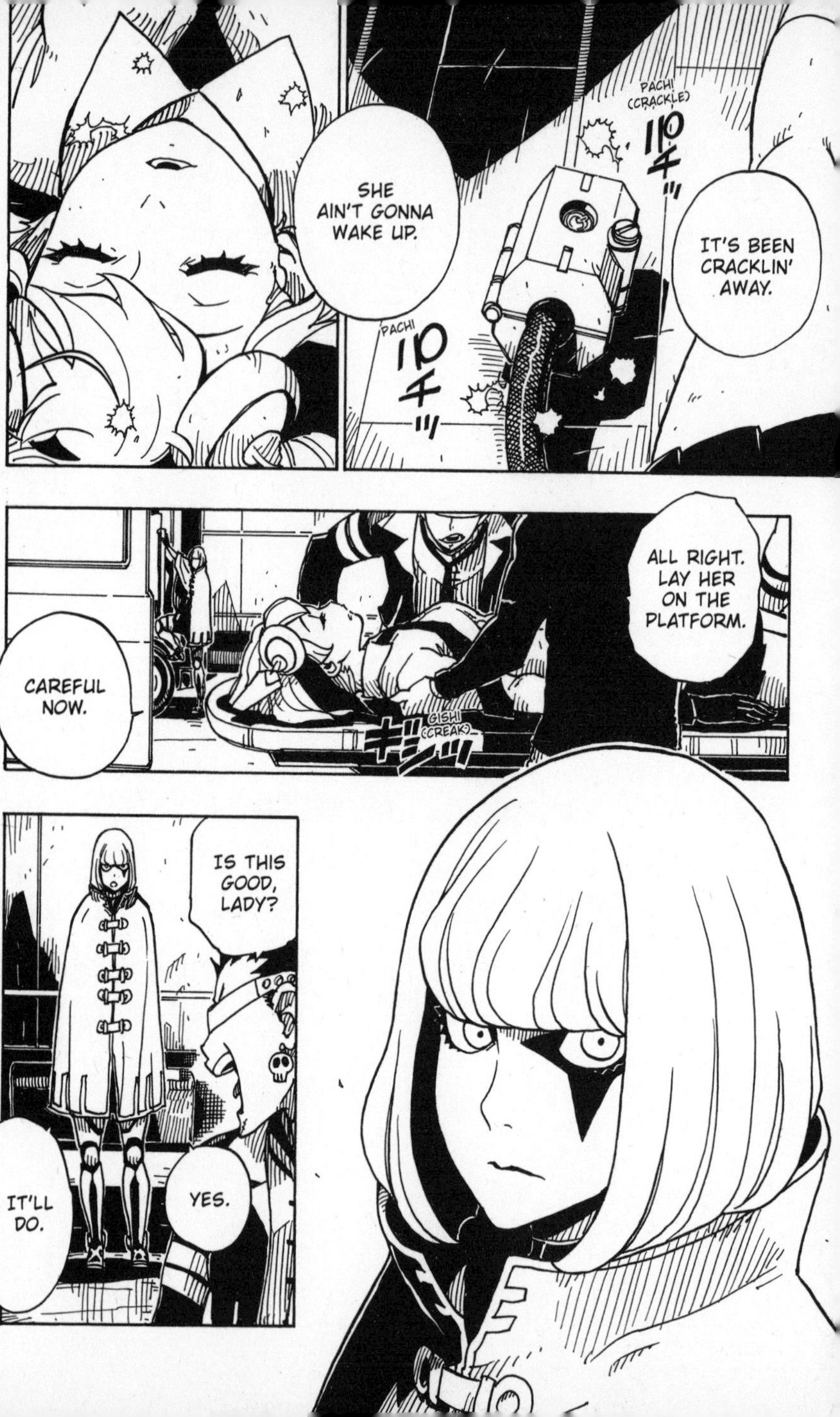
PACHI (CRACKLE)
IT'S BEEN CRACKLIN' AWAY.
SHE AIN'T GONNA WAKE UP.
PACHI
ALL RIGHT. LAY HER ON THE PLATFORM.
GISHI (CREAK)
CAREFUL NOW.
IS THIS GOOD, LADY?
YES.
IT'LL DO.

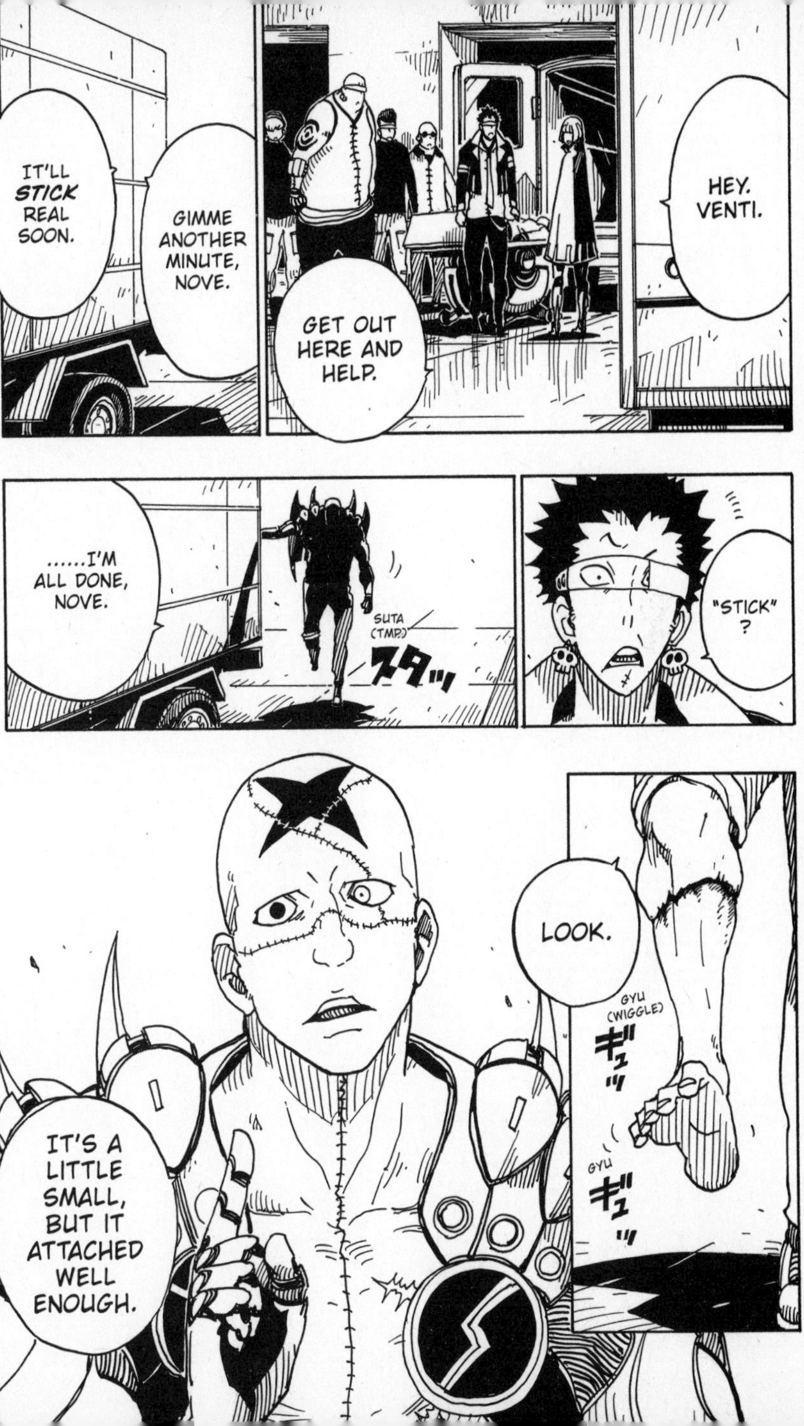
HEY. VENTI.
GET OUT HERE AND HELP.
GIMME ANOTHER MINUTE, NOVE.
IT'LL *STICK* REAL SOON.
"STICK" ?
......I'M ALL DONE, NOVE.
SUTA (TMP.)
スタッ
LOOK.
GYU (WIGGLE)
ギュッ
GYU
ギュッ
IT'S A LITTLE SMALL, BUT IT ATTACHED WELL ENOUGH.

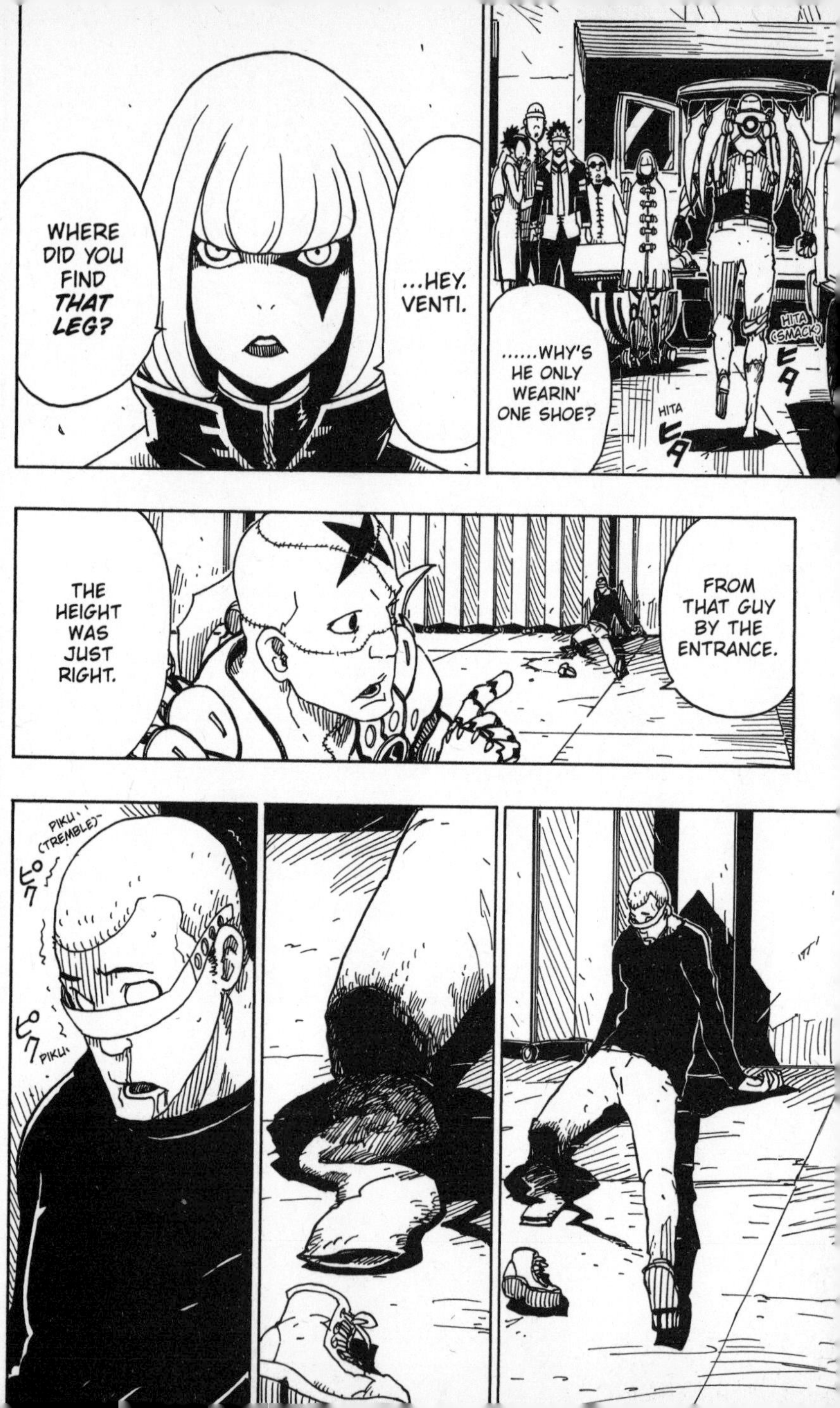

......WHY'S HE ONLY WEARIN' ONE SHOE?
HITA (SMACK)
HITA
...HEY. VENTI.
WHERE DID YOU FIND *THAT LEG?*
FROM THAT GUY BY THE ENTRANCE.
THE HEIGHT WAS JUST RIGHT.
PIKU (TREMBLE)
PIKU

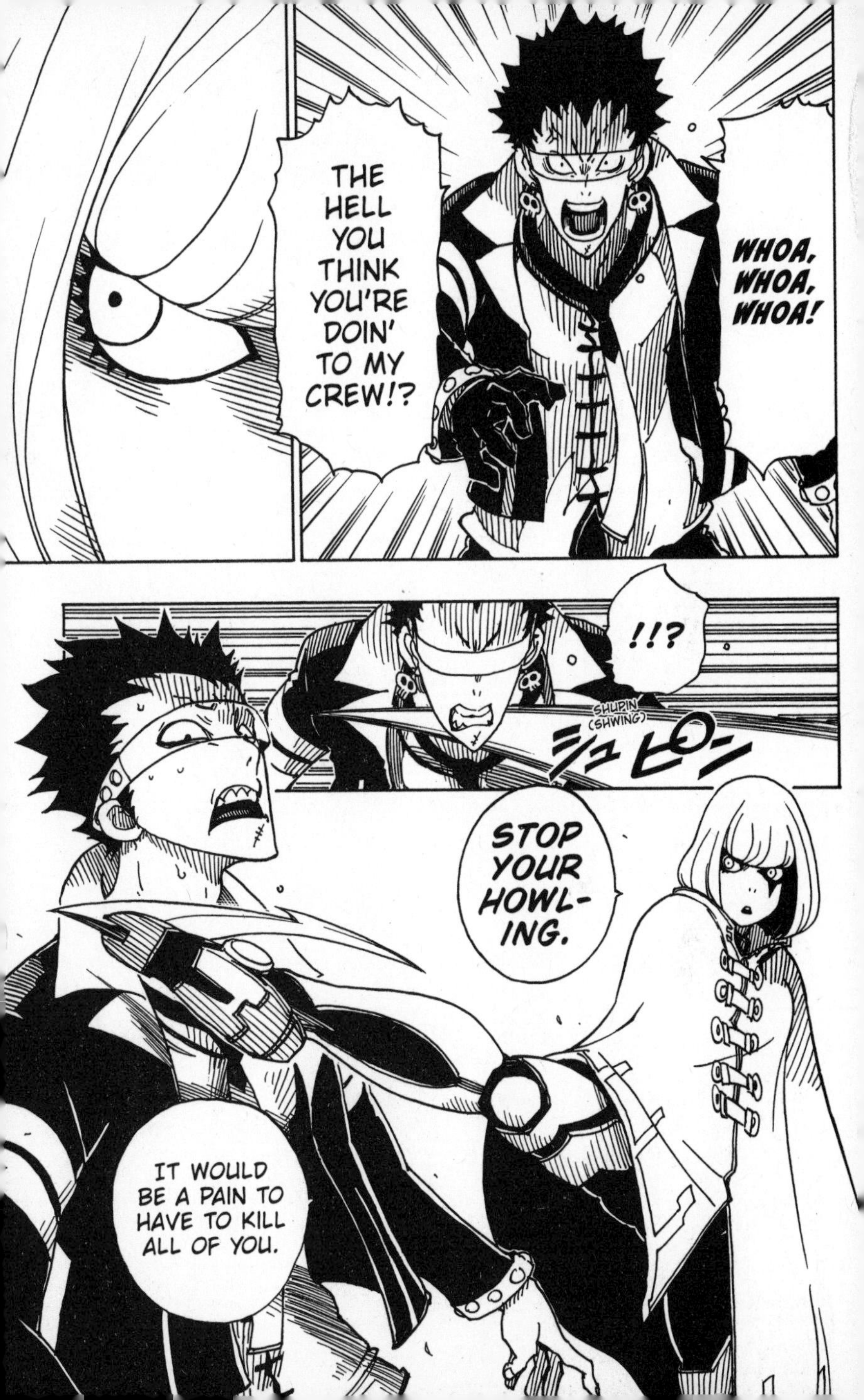
WHOA, WHOA, WHOA!
THE HELL YOU THINK YOU'RE DOIN' TO MY CREW!?
!!?
SHUPIN (SHWING)
シュピーン
STOP YOUR HOWL-ING.
IT WOULD BE A PAIN TO HAVE TO KILL ALL OF YOU.

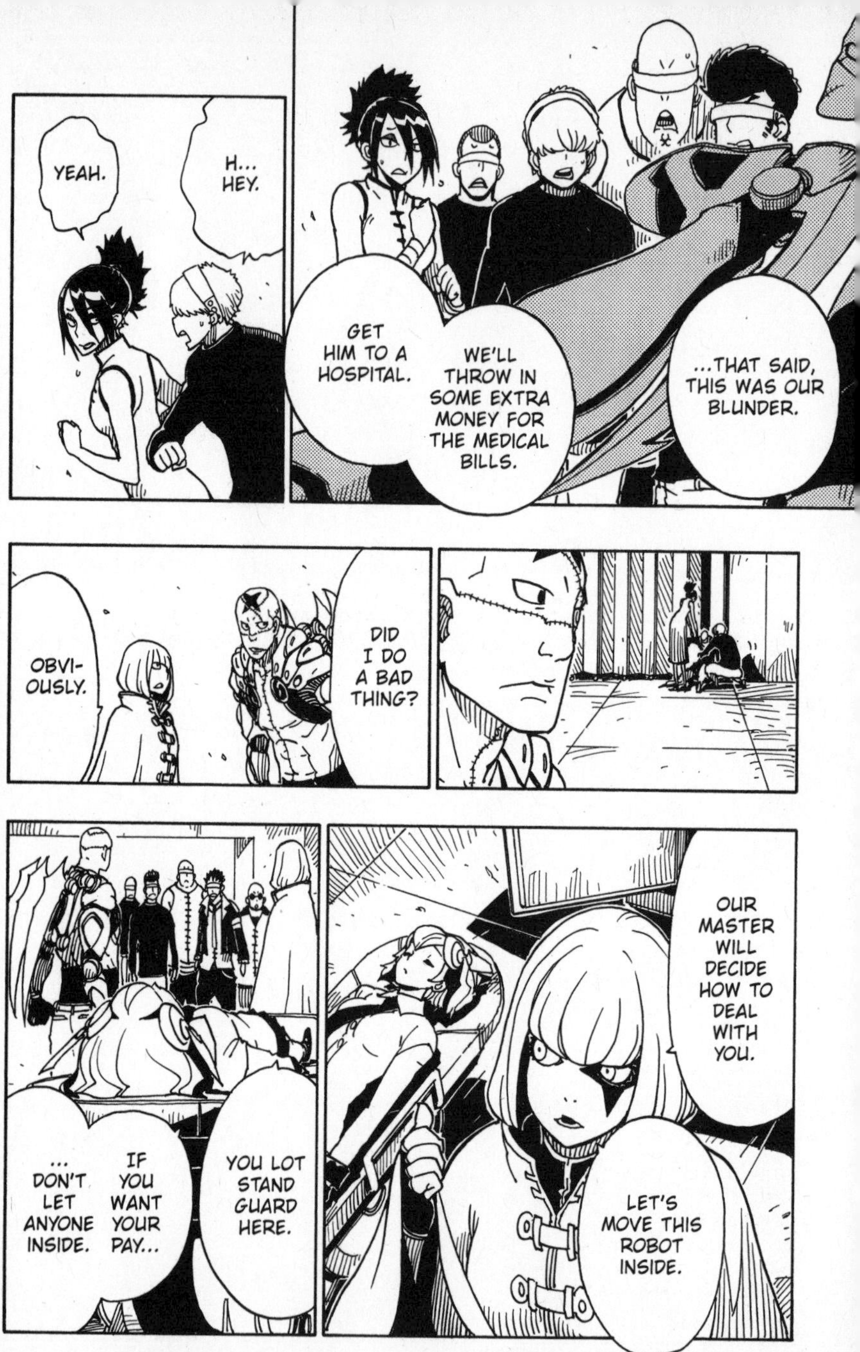
...THAT SAID, THIS WAS OUR BLUNDER.
WE'LL THROW IN SOME EXTRA MONEY FOR THE MEDICAL BILLS.
GET HIM TO A HOSPITAL.
H... HEY.
YEAH.
DID I DO A BAD THING?
OBVIOUSLY.
OUR MASTER WILL DECIDE HOW TO DEAL WITH YOU.
LET'S MOVE THIS ROBOT INSIDE.
YOU LOT STAND GUARD HERE.
IF YOU WANT YOUR PAY...
...DON'T LET ANYONE INSIDE.

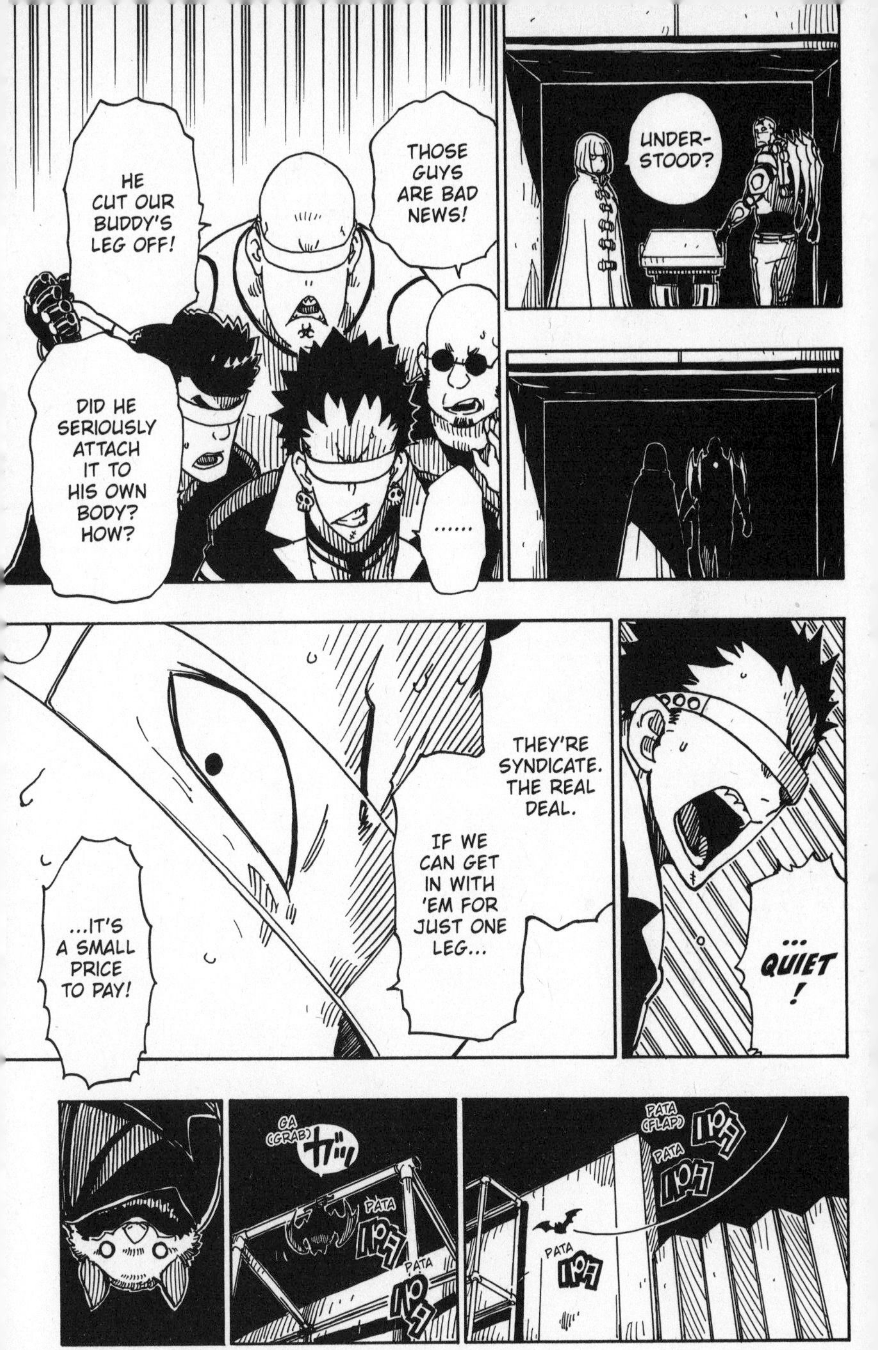
UNDER-STOOD?
THOSE GUYS ARE BAD NEWS!
HE CUT OUR BUDDY'S LEG OFF!
DID HE SERIOUSLY ATTACH IT TO HIS OWN BODY? HOW?
......
...QUIET!
THEY'RE SYNDICATE. THE REAL DEAL.
IF WE CAN GET IN WITH 'EM FOR JUST ONE LEG...
...IT'S A SMALL PRICE TO PAY!
PATA (FLAP)
PATA
PATA
GA (GRAB)
PATA
PATA

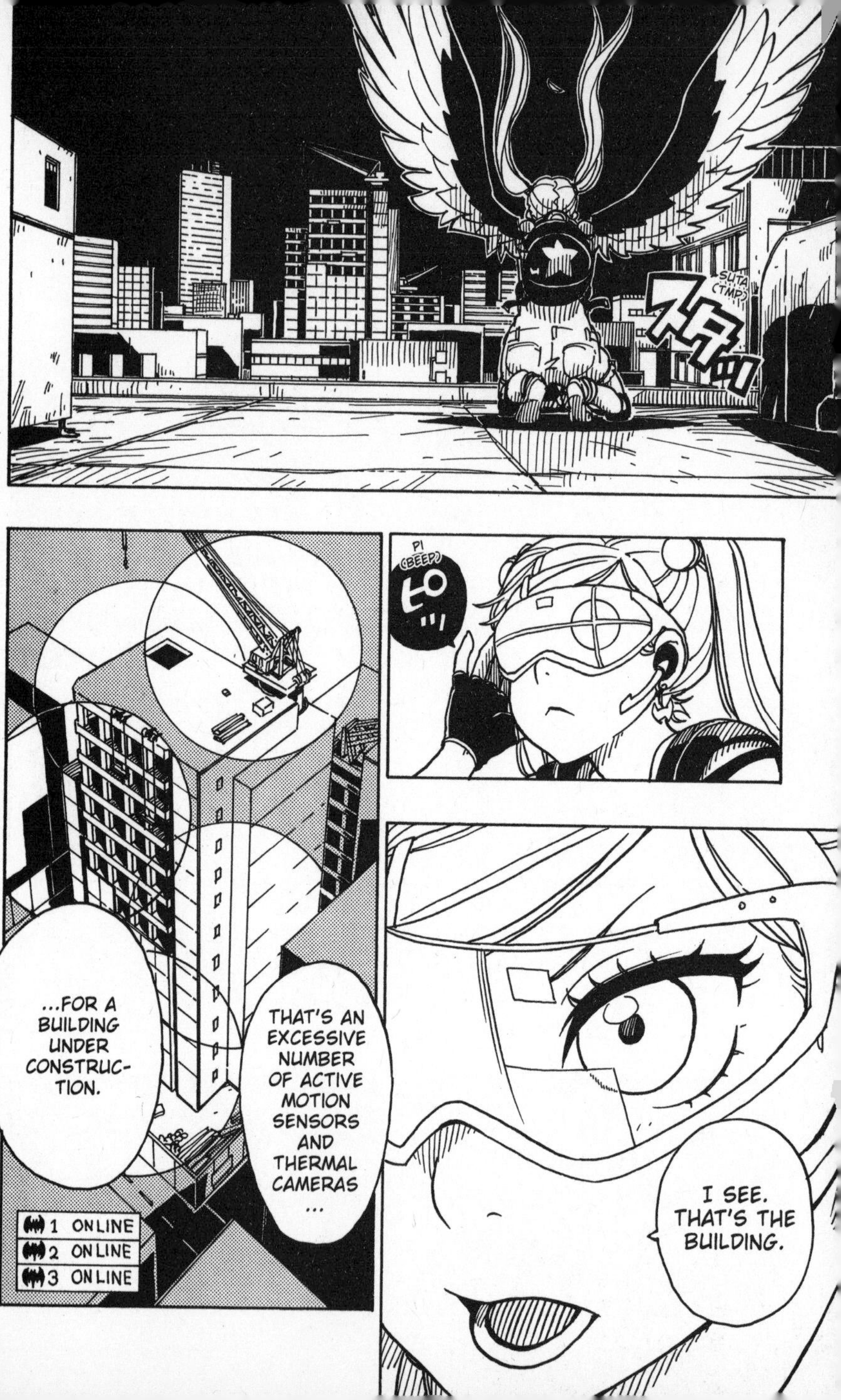
SUTA (TMP)
スタッ
PI (BEEP)
ピッ
I SEE. THAT'S THE BUILDING.
THAT'S AN EXCESSIVE NUMBER OF ACTIVE MOTION SENSORS AND THERMAL CAMERAS...
...FOR A BUILDING UNDER CONSTRUC-TION.
1 ONLINE
2 ONLINE
3 ONLINE

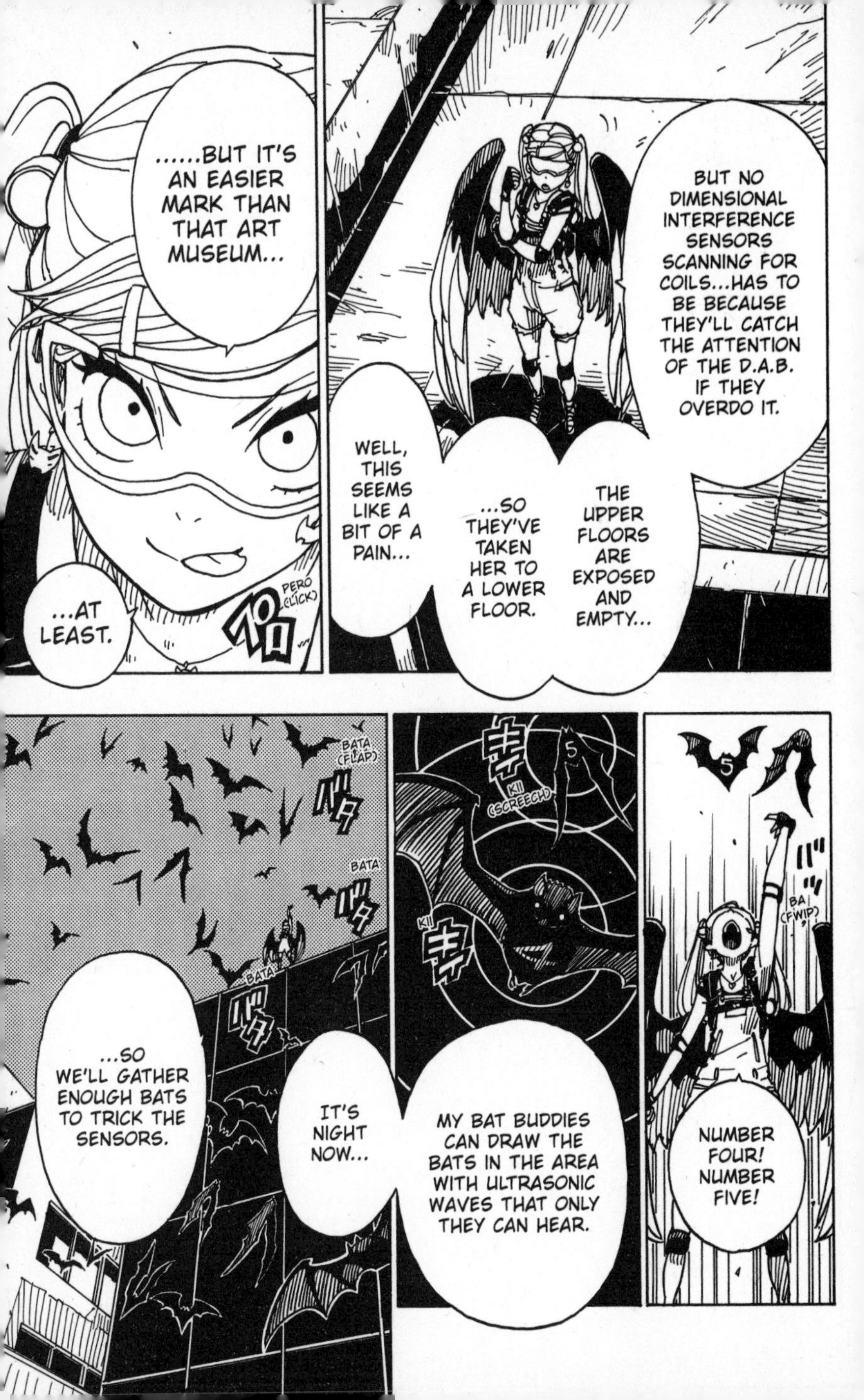
BUT NO DIMENSIONAL INTERFERENCE SENSORS SCANNING FOR COILS...HAS TO BE BECAUSE THEY'LL CATCH THE ATTENTION OF THE D.A.B. IF THEY OVERDO IT.
THE UPPER FLOORS ARE EXPOSED AND EMPTY...
...SO THEY'VE TAKEN HER TO A LOWER FLOOR.
WELL, THIS SEEMS LIKE A BIT OF A PAIN...
......BUT IT'S AN EASIER MARK THAN THAT ART MUSEUM...
PERO (LICK)
...AT LEAST.
BA (FWIP)
NUMBER FOUR! NUMBER FIVE!
KII (SCREECH)
KII
MY BAT BUDDIES CAN DRAW THE BATS IN THE AREA WITH ULTRASONIC WAVES THAT ONLY THEY CAN HEAR.
IT'S NIGHT NOW...
BATA (FLAP)
BATA
BATA
...SO WE'LL GATHER ENOUGH BATS TO TRICK THE SENSORS.

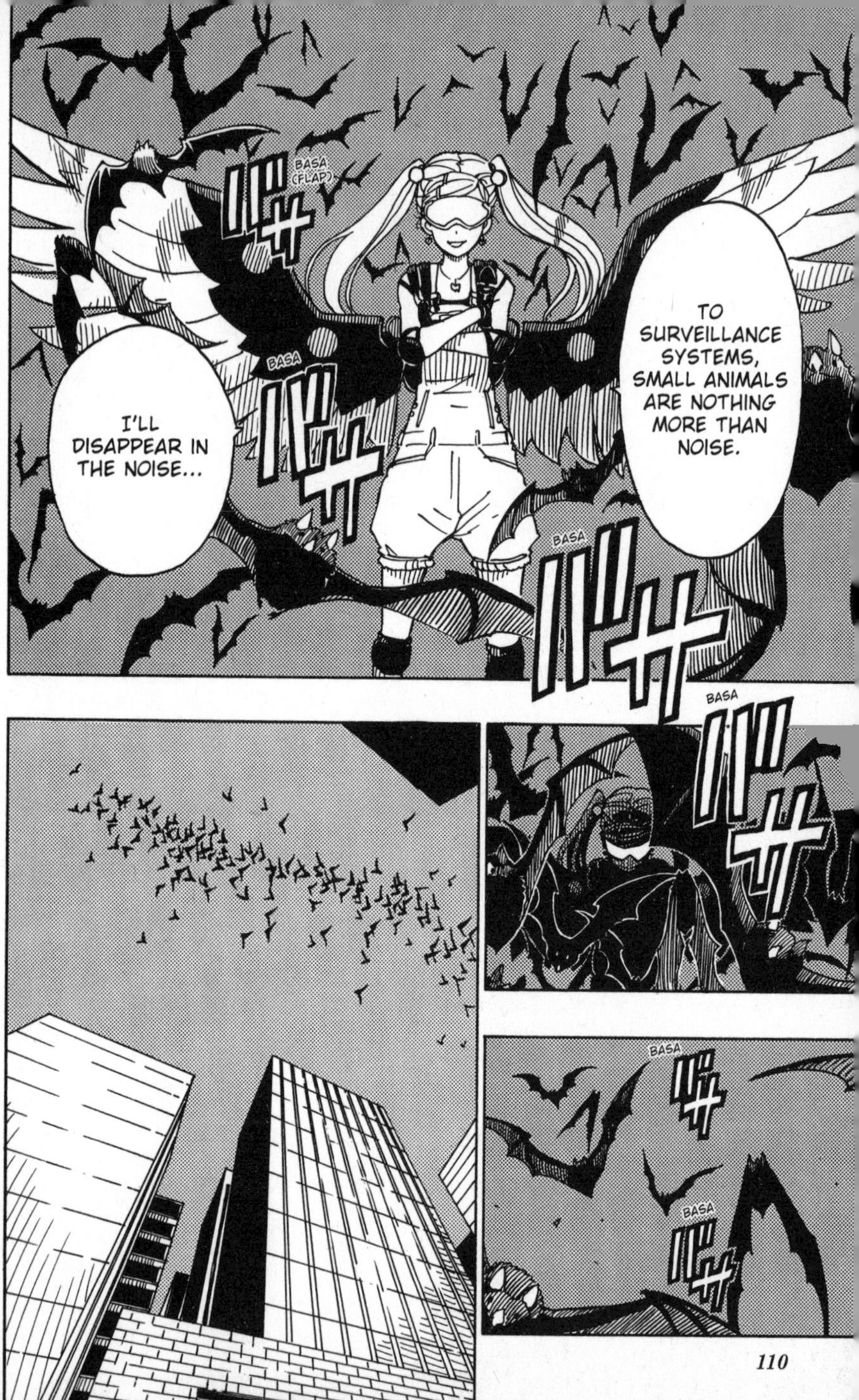
TO SURVEILLANCE SYSTEMS, SMALL ANIMALS ARE NOTHING MORE THAN NOISE.
BASA (FLAP)
BASA
I'LL DISAPPEAR IN THE NOISE...
BASA
BASA
BASA
BASA

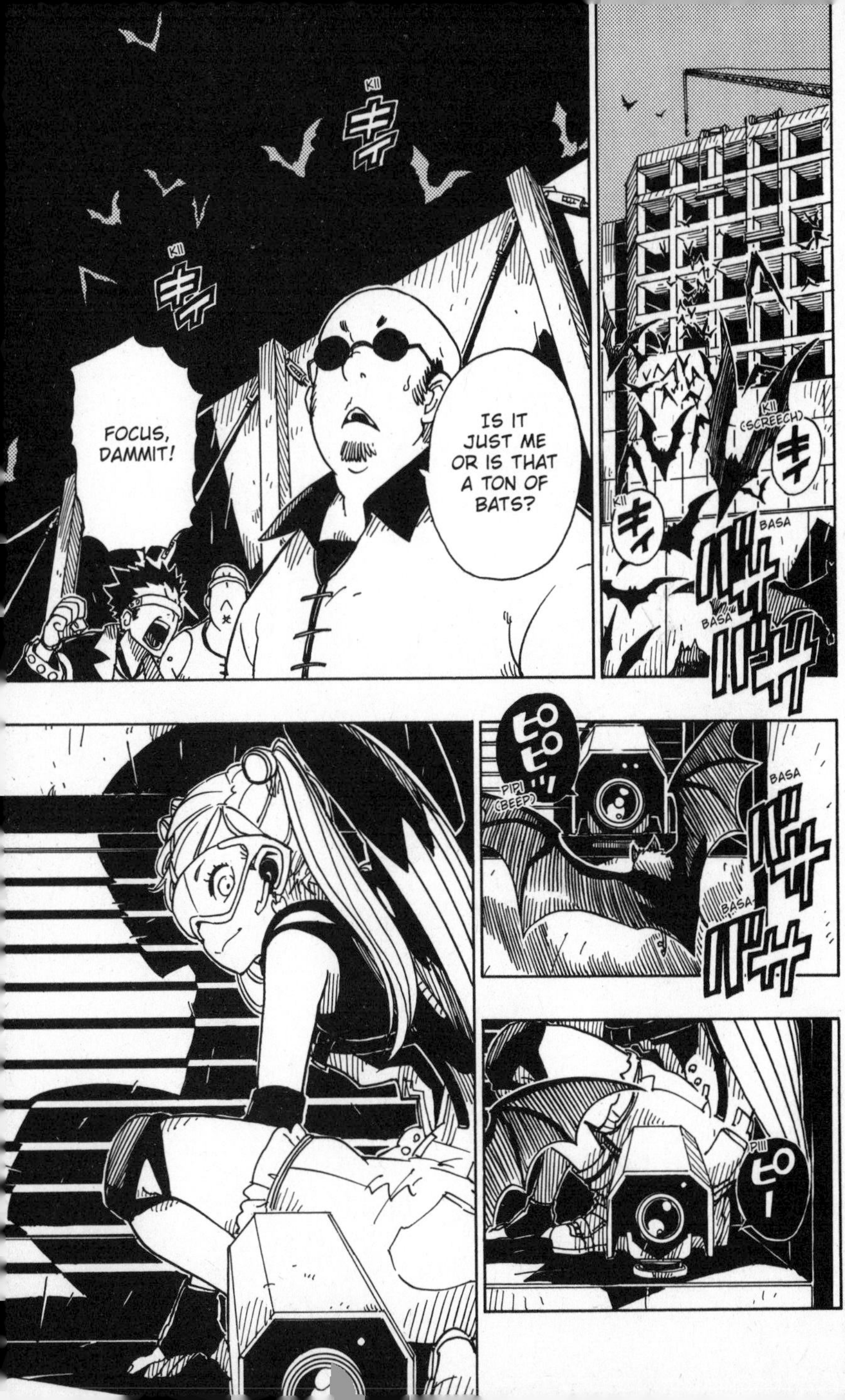

KII (SCREECH)
KII
BASA
BASA
IS IT JUST ME OR IS THAT A TON OF BATS?
FOCUS, DAMMIT!
KII
KII
PIPI (BEEP)
BASA
BASA
PIII

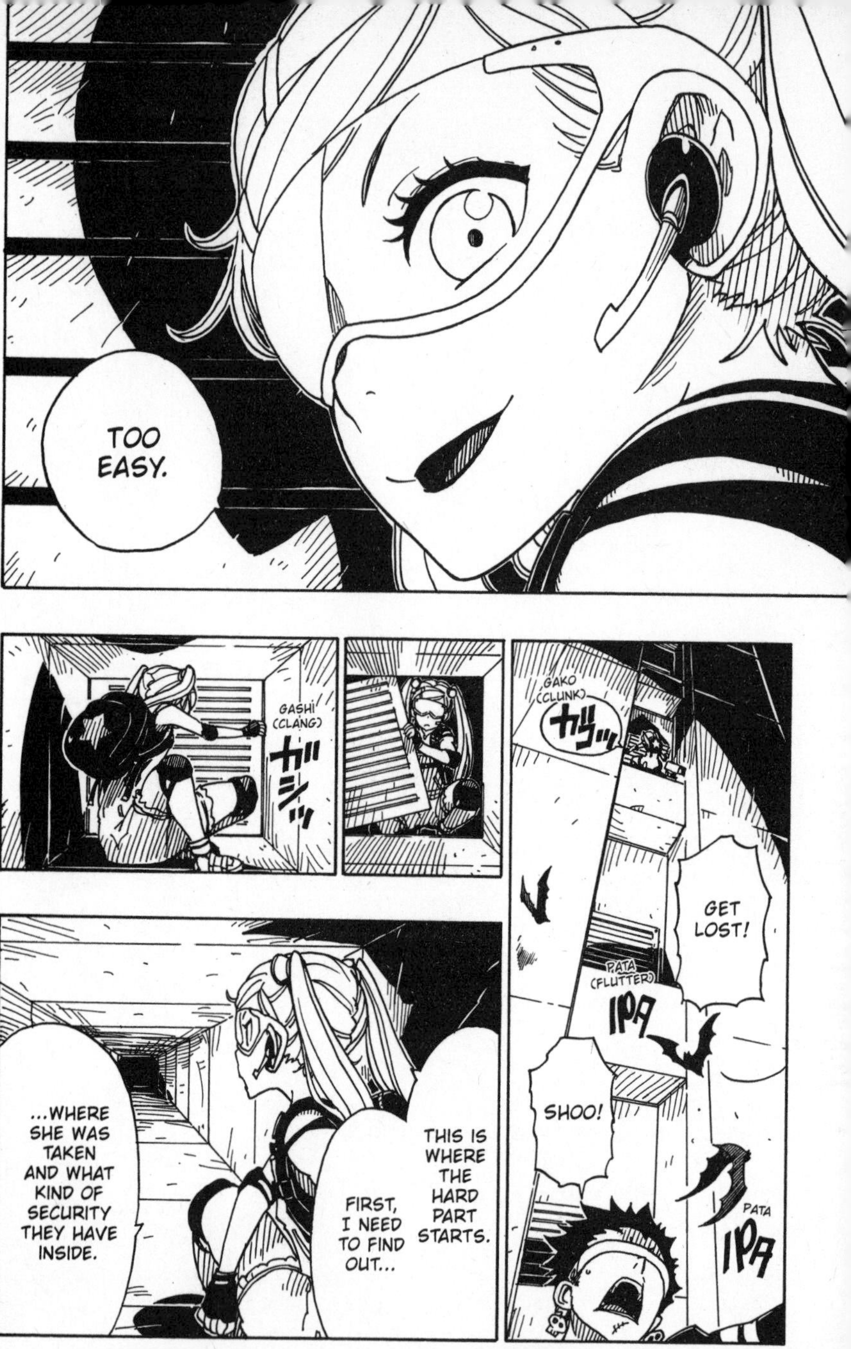
TOO EASY.
GAKO (CLUNK)
GET LOST!
PATA (FLUTTER)
SHOO!
PATA
GASHI (CLANG)
THIS IS WHERE THE HARD PART STARTS.
FIRST, I NEED TO FIND OUT...
...WHERE SHE WAS TAKEN AND WHAT KIND OF SECURITY THEY HAVE INSIDE.

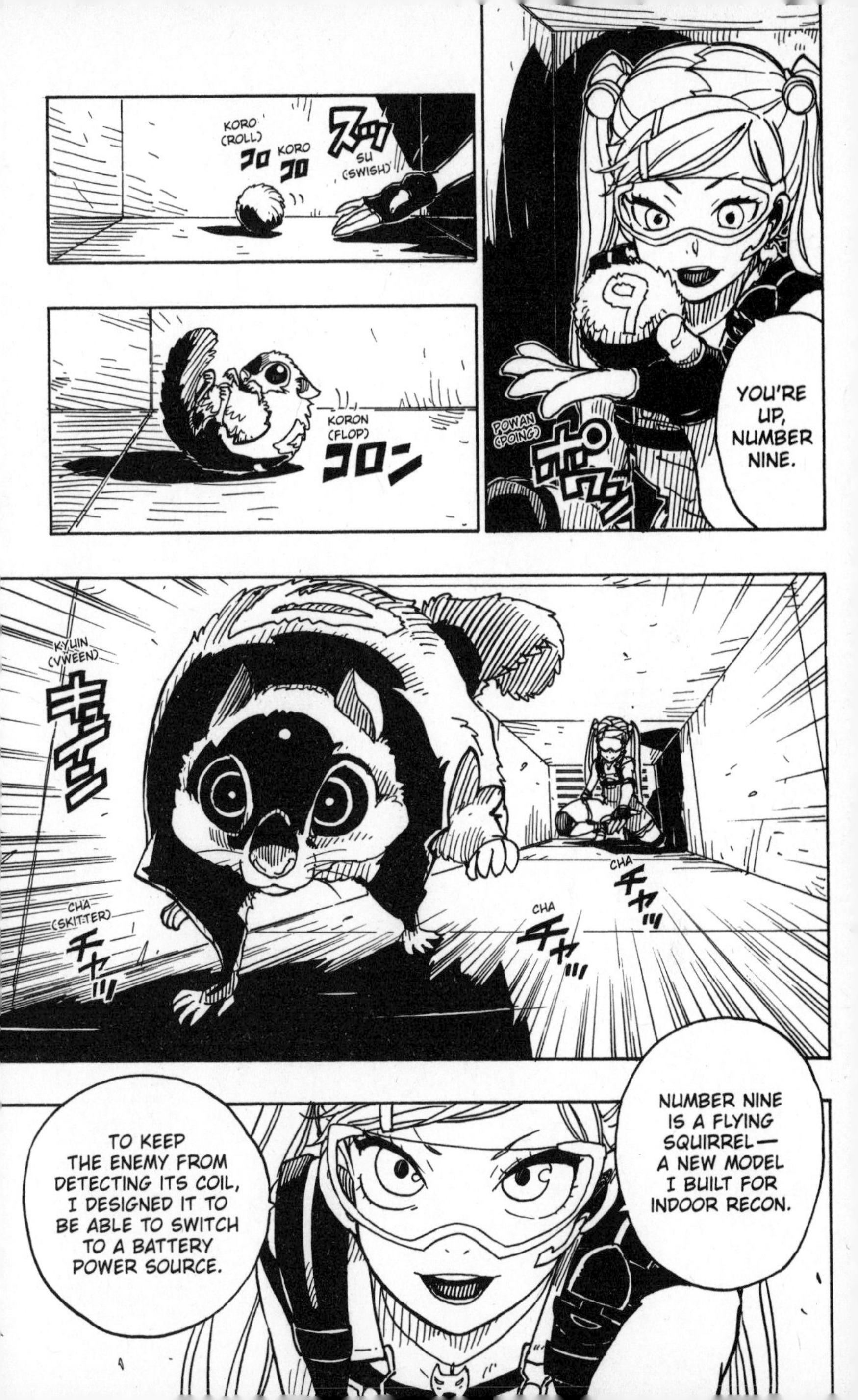
YOU'RE UP, NUMBER NINE.
POWAN (POING)
SU (SWISH)
KORO (ROLL) KORO
KORON (FLOP)
KYUIN (VWEEN)
CHA
CHA
CHA (SKIT-TER)
NUMBER NINE IS A FLYING SQUIRREL— A NEW MODEL I BUILT FOR INDOOR RECON.
TO KEEP THE ENEMY FROM DETECTING ITS COIL, I DESIGNED IT TO BE ABLE TO SWITCH TO A BATTERY POWER SOURCE.

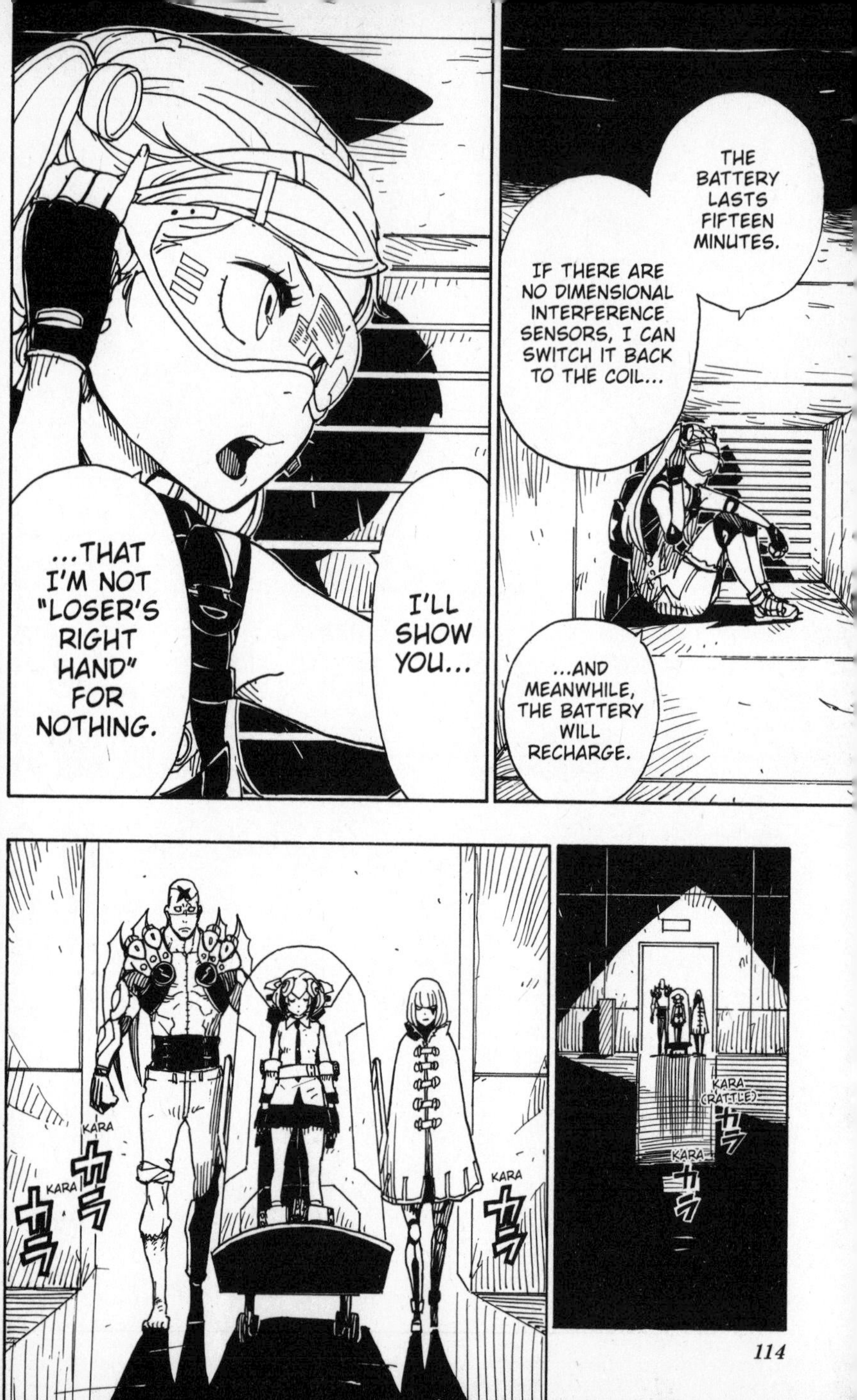
THE BATTERY LASTS FIFTEEN MINUTES.
IF THERE ARE NO DIMENSIONAL INTERFERENCE SENSORS, I CAN SWITCH IT BACK TO THE COIL...
...AND MEANWHILE, THE BATTERY WILL RECHARGE.
I'LL SHOW YOU...
...THAT I'M NOT "LOSER'S RIGHT HAND" FOR NOTHING.
KARA (RATTLE)
カラ
KARA
カラ
KARA
カラ
KARA
カラ
KARA
カラ

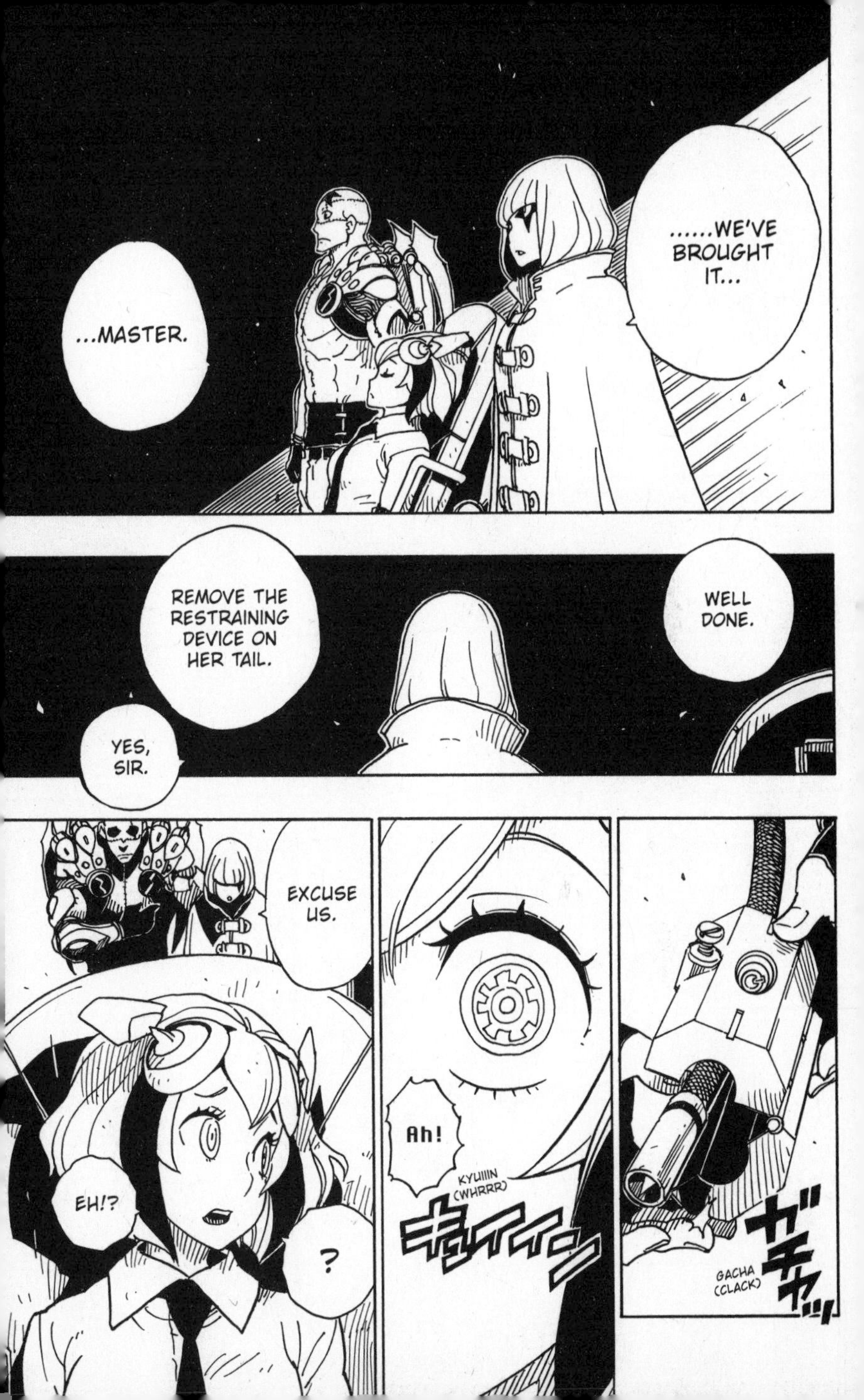
......WE'VE BROUGHT IT...
...MASTER.
WELL DONE.
REMOVE THE RESTRAINING DEVICE ON HER TAIL.
YES, SIR.
GACHA (CLACK)
Ah!
KYUIIIN (WHRRR)
EXCUSE US.
EH!?
?

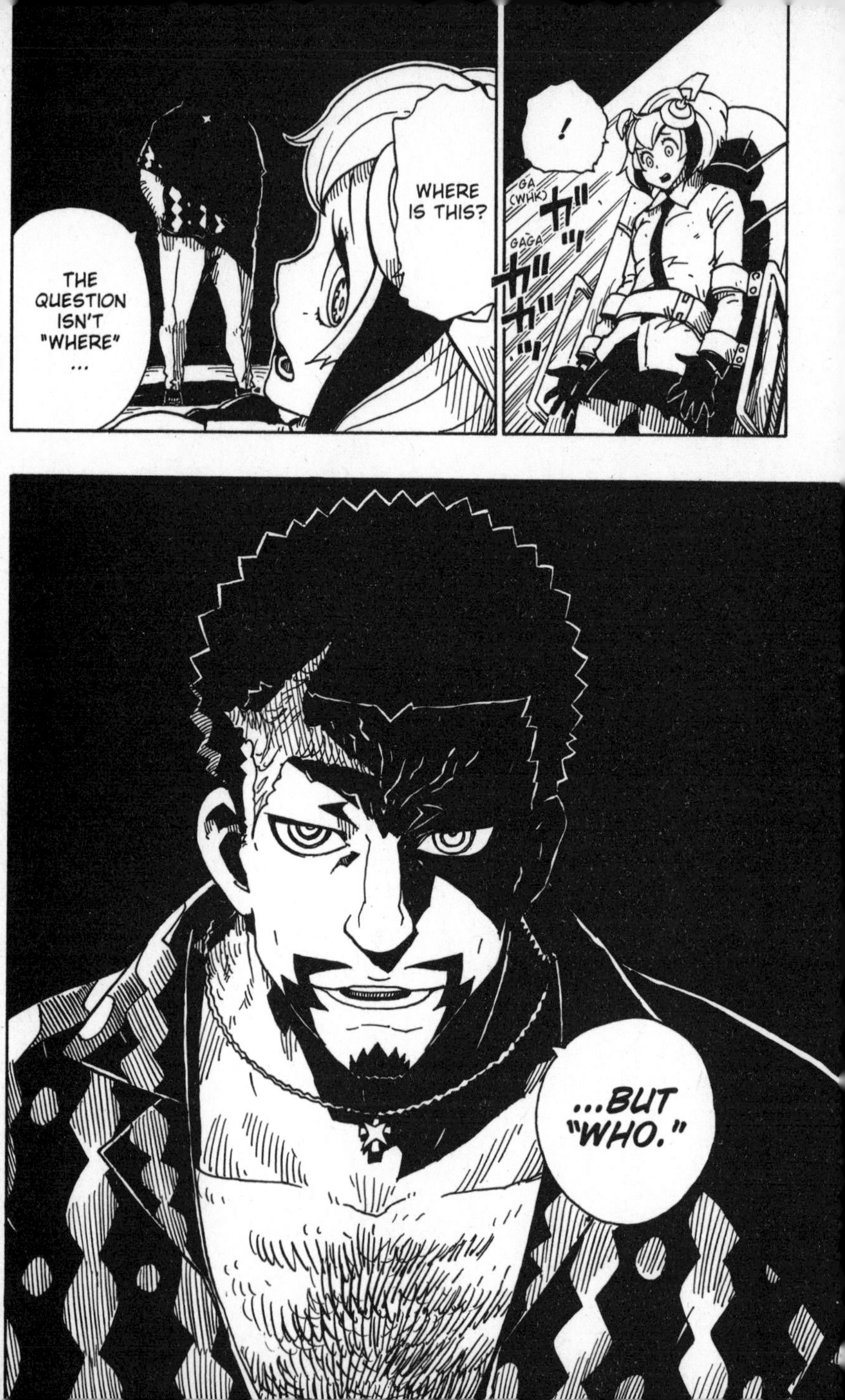
!
GA (WHK)
ガッ
GAGA
ガガッ
WHERE IS THIS?
THE QUESTION ISN'T "WHERE"...
...BUT "WHO."

Dimension W

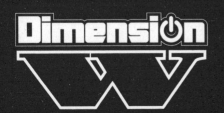

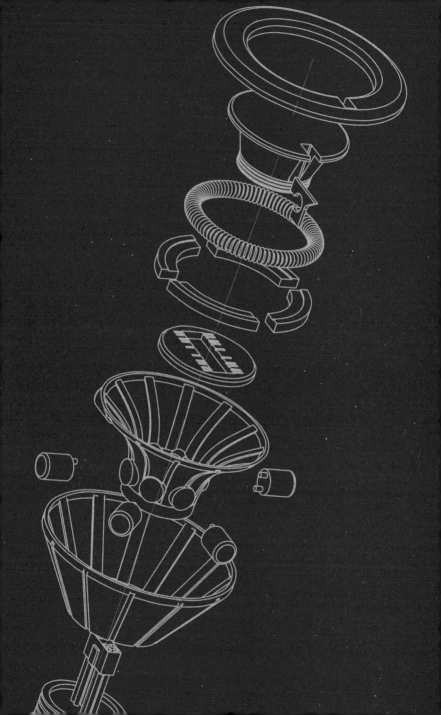

FILE.82
SWORD OF EUDOS

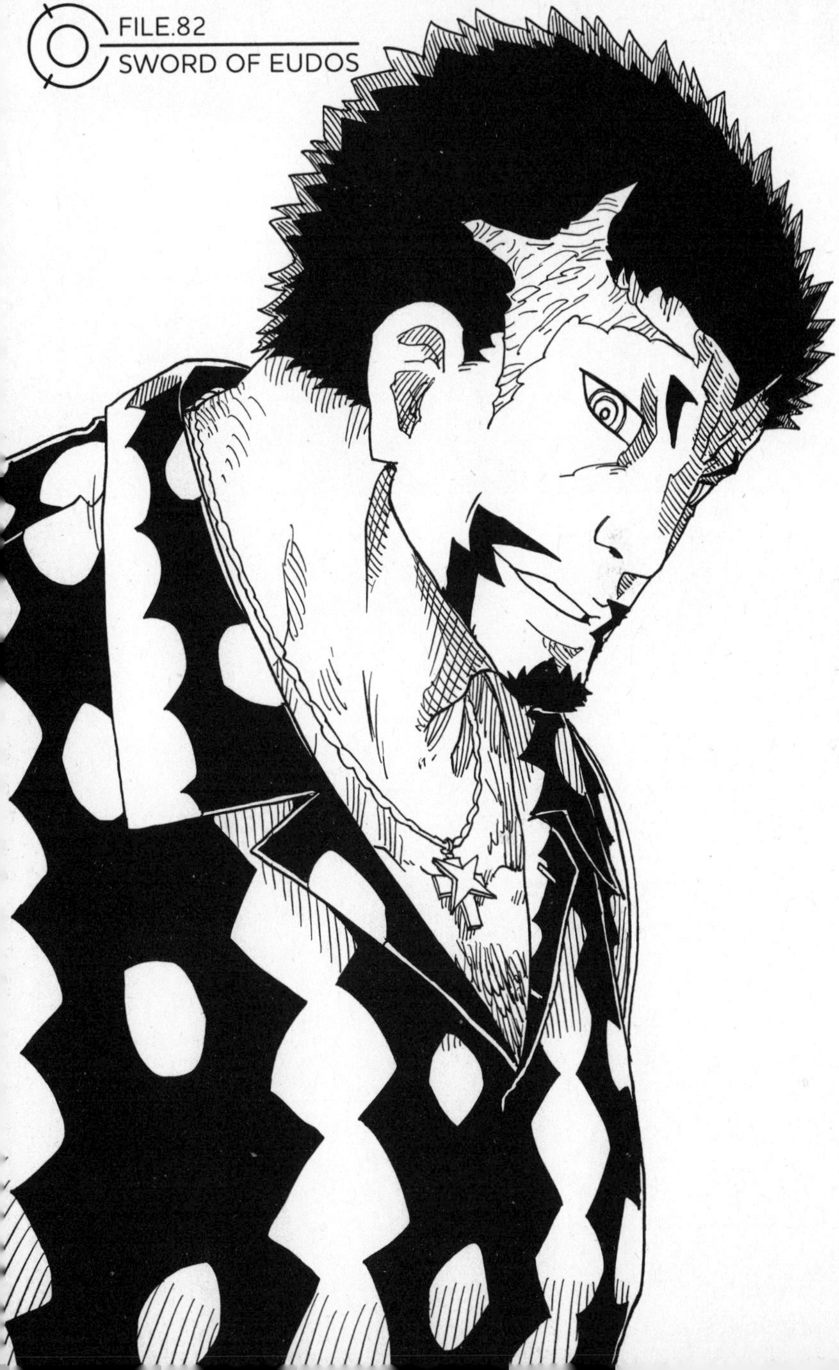

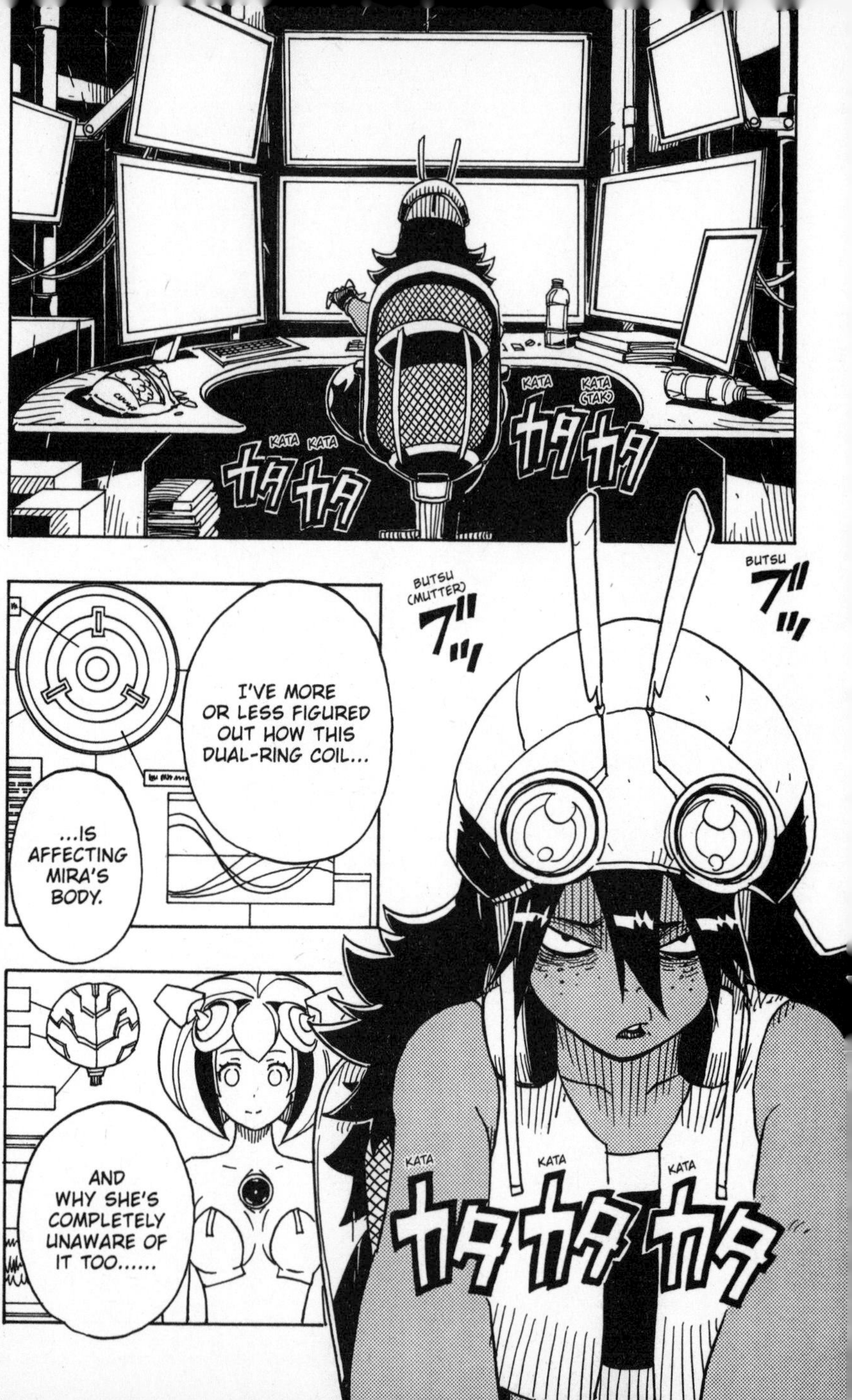
KATA KATA (TAK)
カタカタ
KATA KATA
カタカタ
BUTSU
ブツ
BUTSU (MUTTER)
ブツ
KATA KATA KATA
カタカタカタ
I'VE MORE OR LESS FIGURED OUT HOW THIS DUAL-RING COIL...
...IS AFFECTING MIRA'S BODY.
AND WHY SHE'S COMPLETELY UNAWARE OF IT TOO......

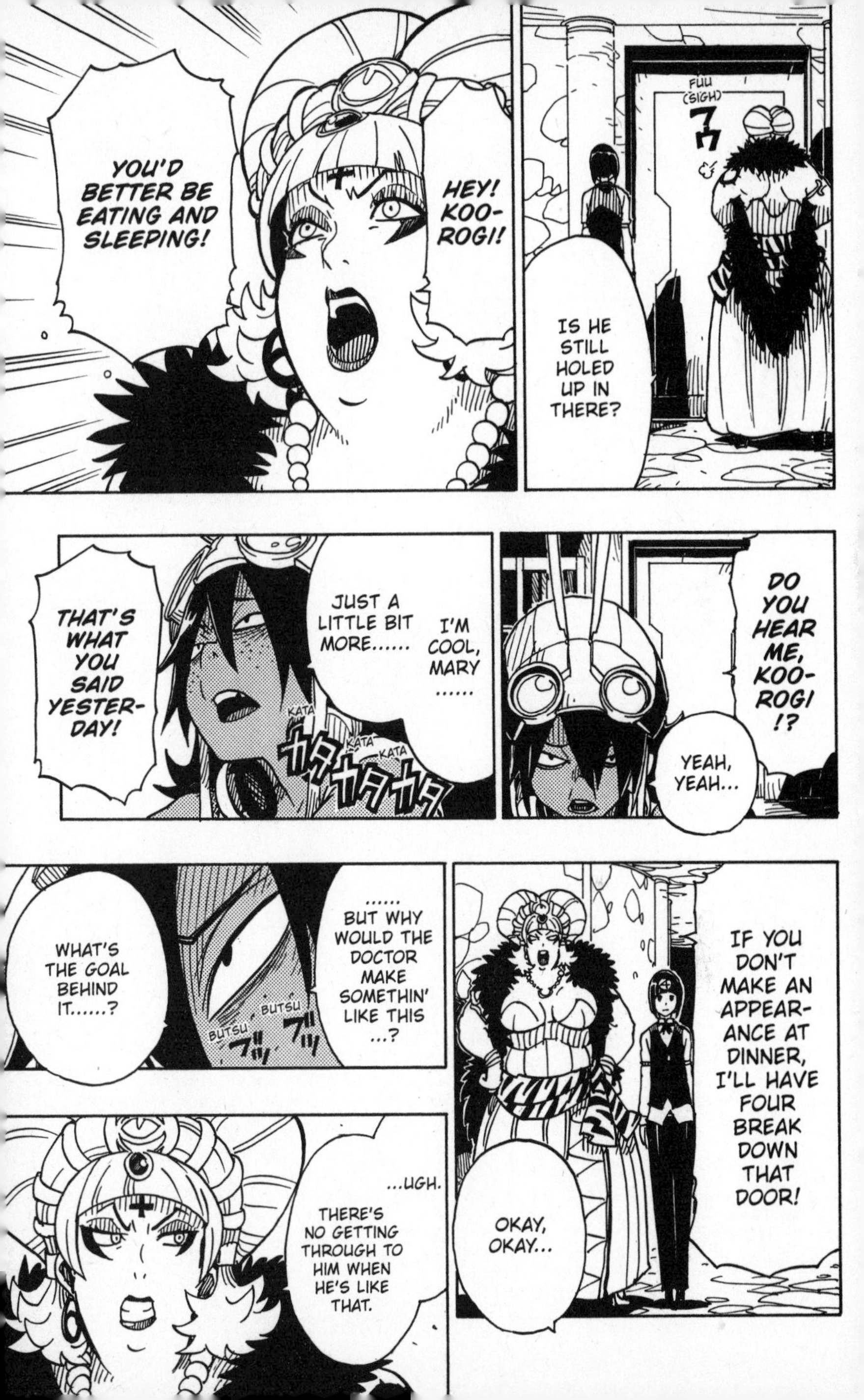

FUU (SIGH)
IS HE STILL HOLED UP IN THERE?
HEY! KOO-ROGI!
YOU'D BETTER BE EATING AND SLEEPING!
DO YOU HEAR ME, KOO-ROGI!?
YEAH, YEAH...
I'M COOL, MARY ......
JUST A LITTLE BIT MORE......
THAT'S WHAT YOU SAID YESTER-DAY!
KATA KATA KATA KATA
IF YOU DON'T MAKE AN APPEAR-ANCE AT DINNER, I'LL HAVE FOUR BREAK DOWN THAT DOOR!
OKAY, OKAY...
...... BUT WHY WOULD THE DOCTOR MAKE SOMETHIN' LIKE THIS ...?
BUTSU BUTSU
WHAT'S THE GOAL BEHIND IT......?
...UGH.
THERE'S NO GETTING THROUGH TO HIM WHEN HE'S LIKE THAT.

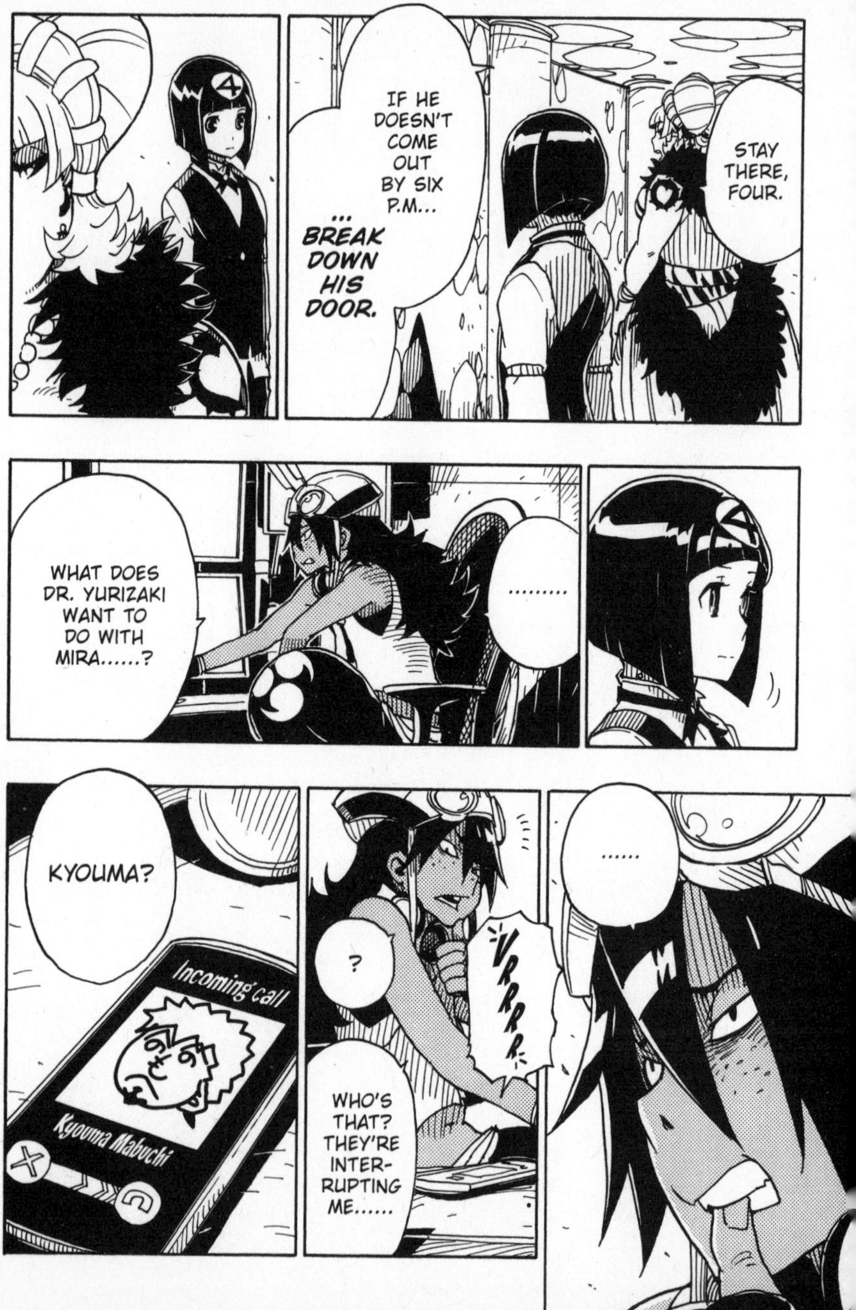
STAY THERE, FOUR.
IF HE DOESN'T COME OUT BY SIX P.M...
...BREAK DOWN HIS DOOR.
....
WHAT DOES DR. YURIZAKI WANT TO DO WITH MIRA......?
......
?
VRRRR
WHO'S THAT? THEY'RE INTER-RUPTING ME......
KYOUMA?
Incoming call
Kyouma Mabuchi

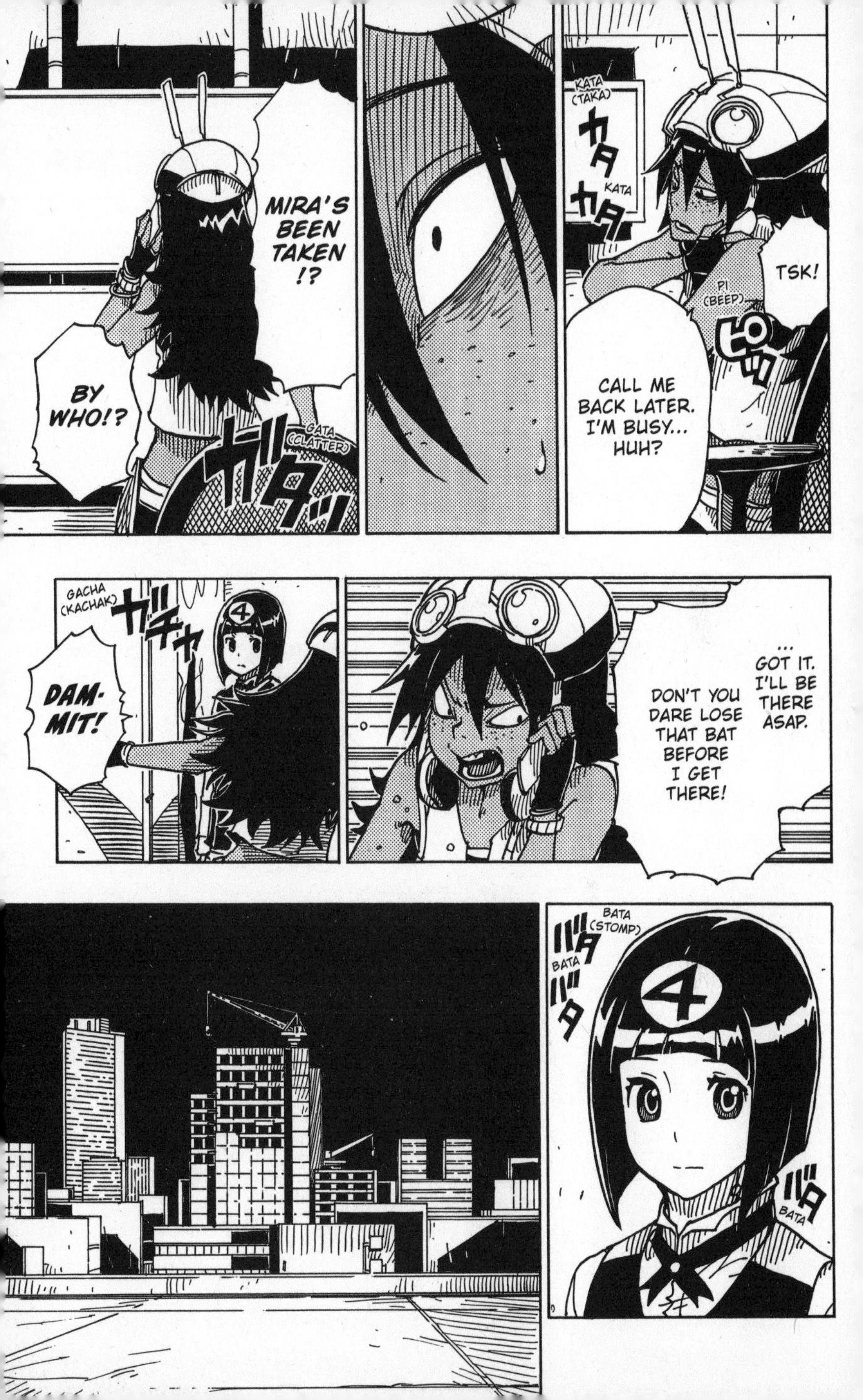
KATA (TAKA)
KATA
TSK!
PI (BEEP)
CALL ME BACK LATER. I'M BUSY... HUH?
MIRA'S BEEN TAKEN !?
BY WHO!?
GATA (CLATTER)
... GOT IT. I'LL BE THERE ASAP.
DON'T YOU DARE LOSE THAT BAT BEFORE I GET THERE!
GACHA (KACHAK)
DAM-MIT!
BATA (STOMP)
BATA
BATA

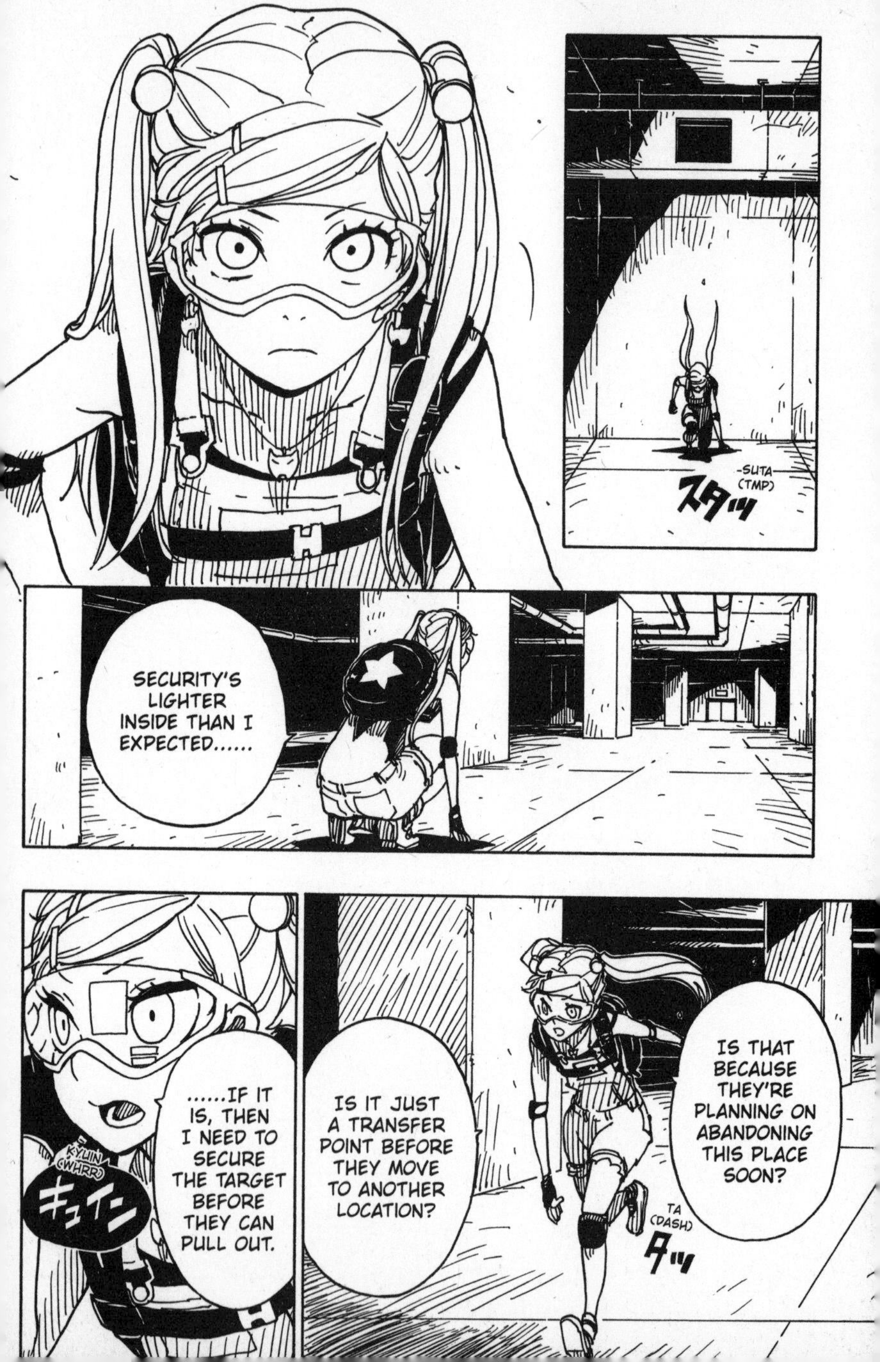
-SUTA (TMP)
スタッ
SECURITY'S LIGHTER INSIDE THAN I EXPECTED......
IS THAT BECAUSE THEY'RE PLANNING ON ABANDONING THIS PLACE SOON?
IS IT JUST A TRANSFER POINT BEFORE THEY MOVE TO ANOTHER LOCATION?
TA (DASH)
タッ
......IF IT IS, THEN I NEED TO SECURE THE TARGET BEFORE THEY CAN PULL OUT.
KYUIN (WHRR)
キュイン

KYUIN
CHA (SKITTER)
CHA
CHA
CHA
CHA
PITA (HALT)
KOSO (SNEAK)
KOSO

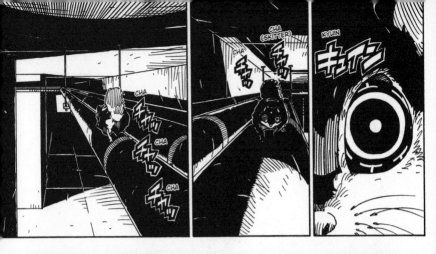

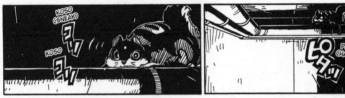

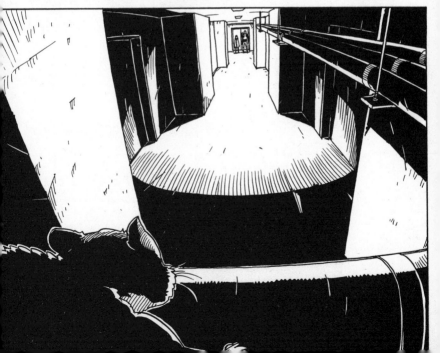

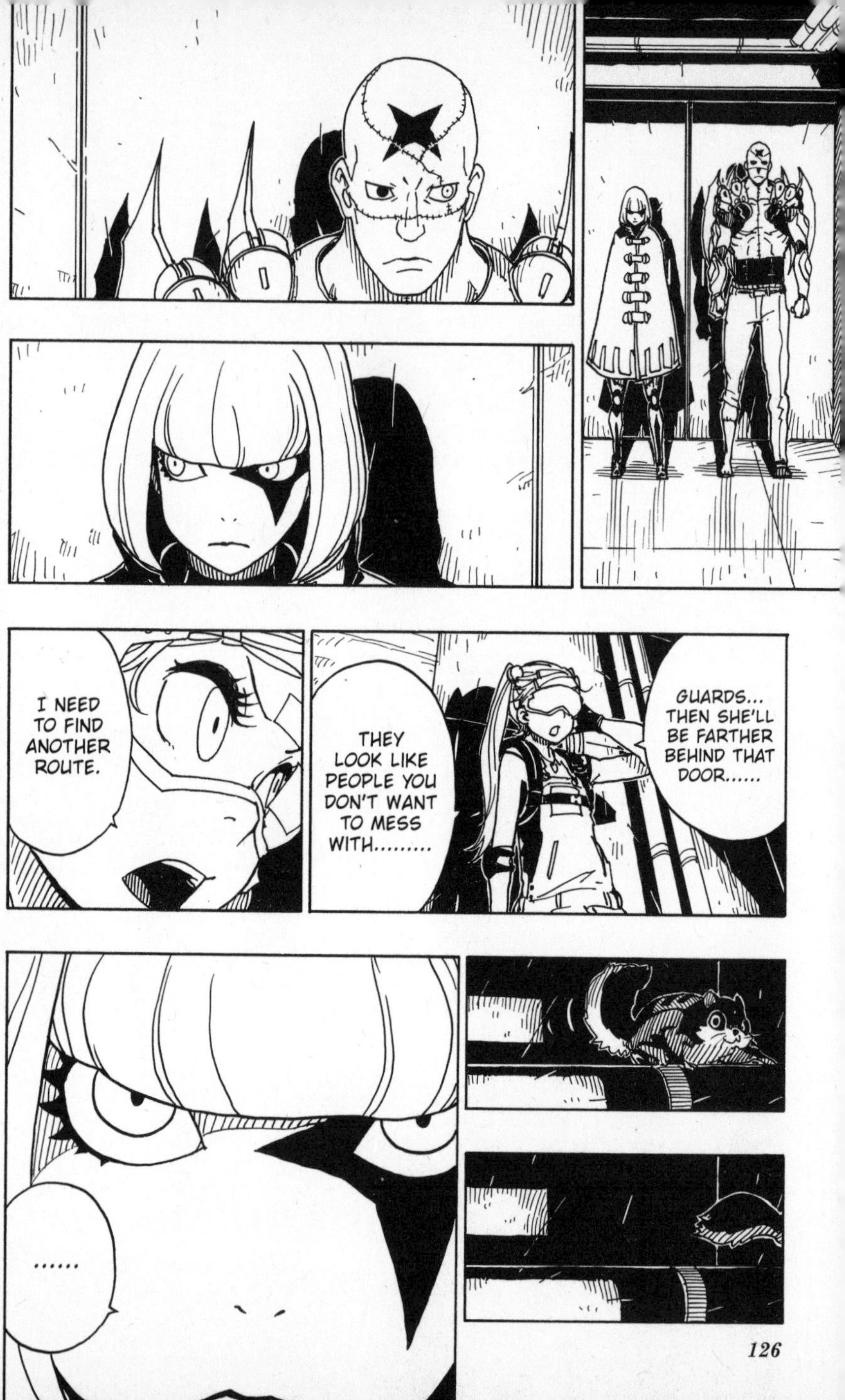
GUARDS... THEN SHE'LL BE FARTHER BEHIND THAT DOOR......
THEY LOOK LIKE PEOPLE YOU DON'T WANT TO MESS WITH.........
I NEED TO FIND ANOTHER ROUTE.
......

NAH......

WHAT IS IT, NOVE?

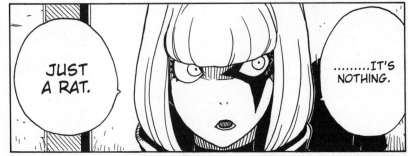

JUST A RAT.

.........IT'S NOTHING.

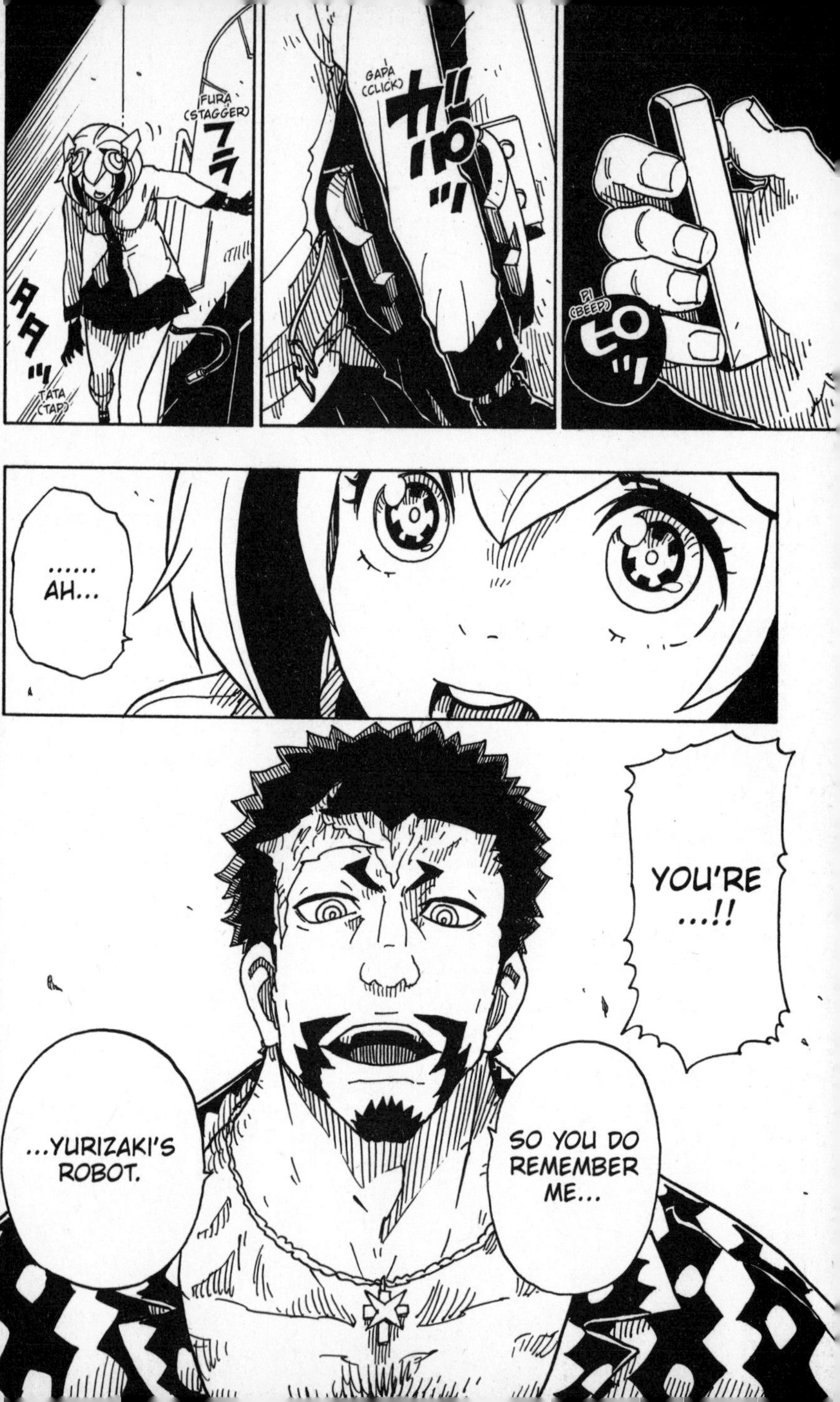
PI (BEEP)
GAPA (CLICK)
FURA (STAGGER)
TATA (TAP)
......AH...
YOU'RE ...!!
SO YOU DO REMEMBER ME...
...YURIZAKI'S ROBOT.

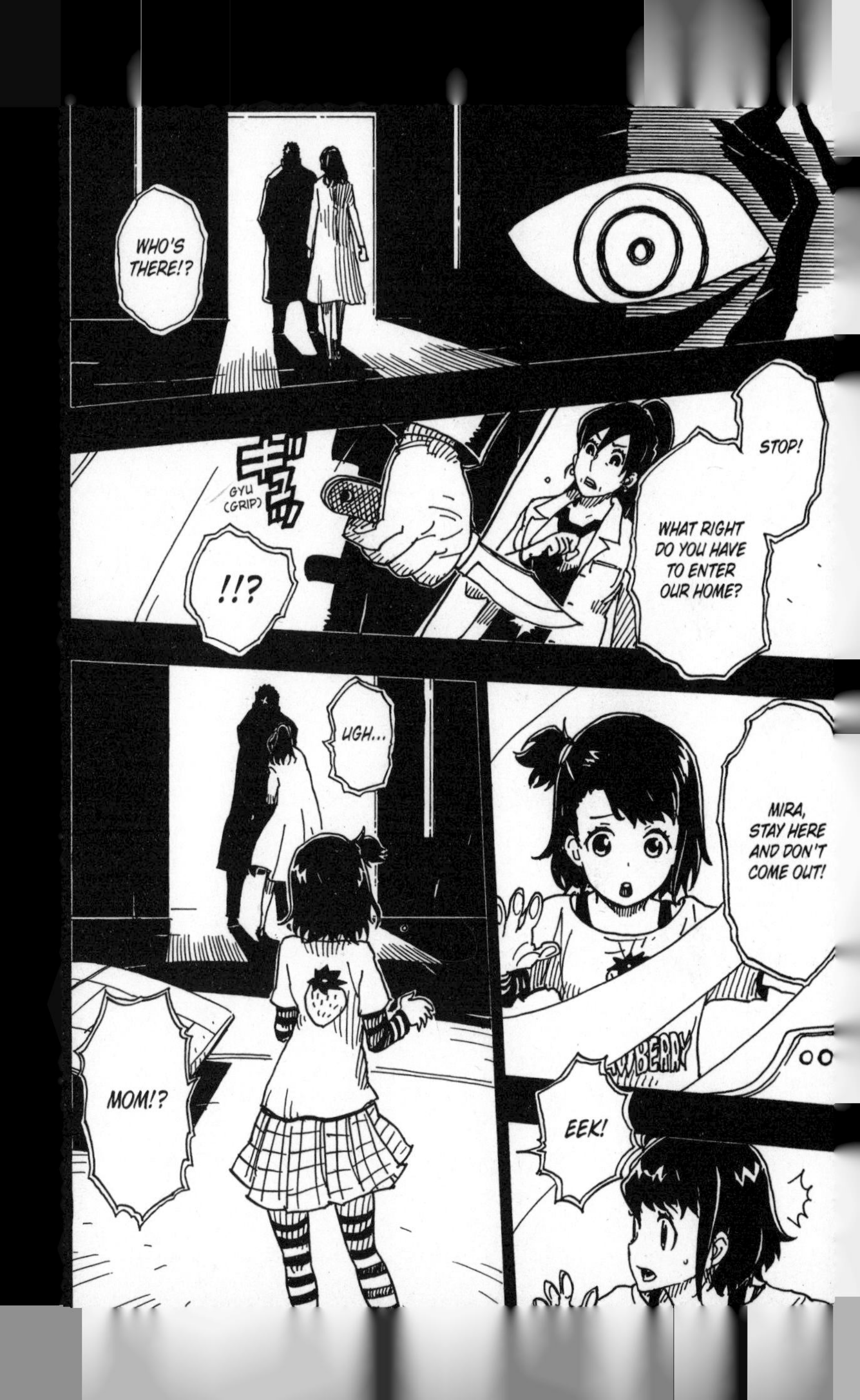
WHO'S THERE!?
STOP!
WHAT RIGHT DO YOU HAVE TO ENTER OUR HOME?
GYU (GRIP)
!!?
MIRA, STAY HERE AND DON'T COME OUT!
EEK!
UGH...
MOM!?

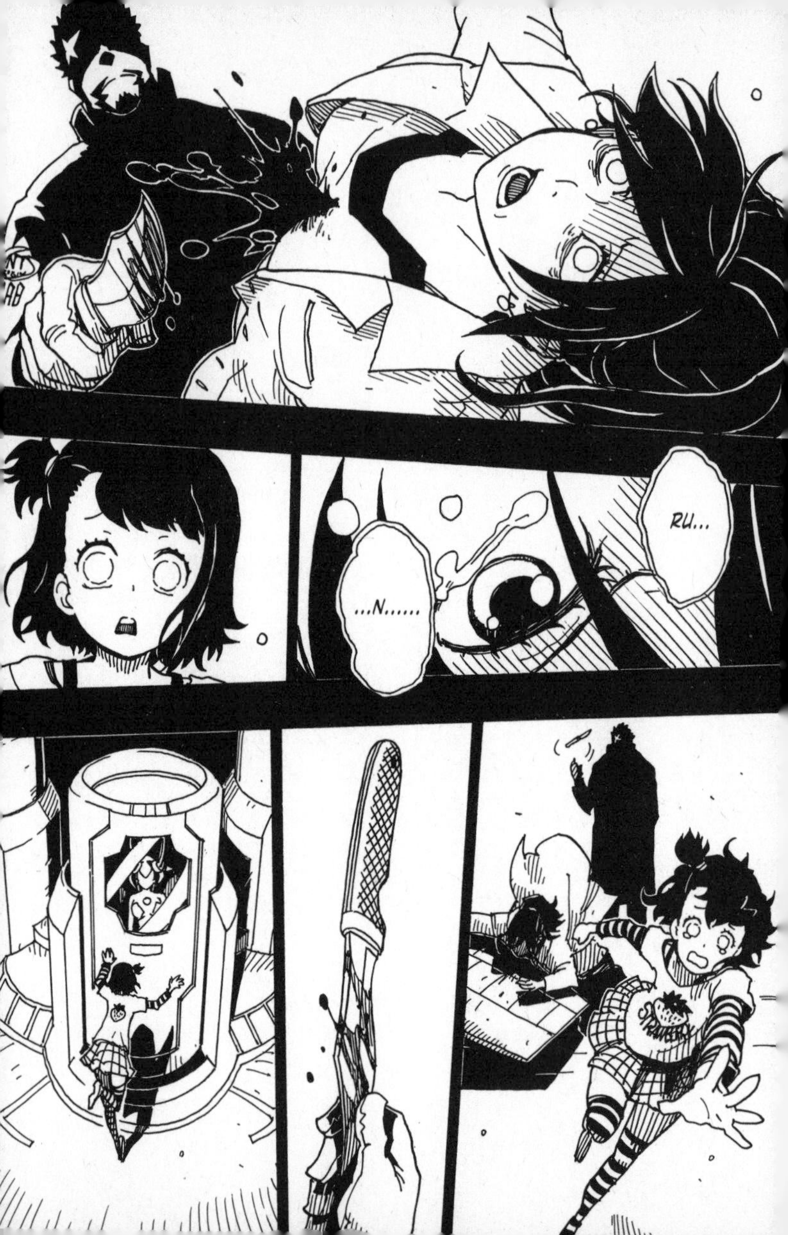
RU...
...N......

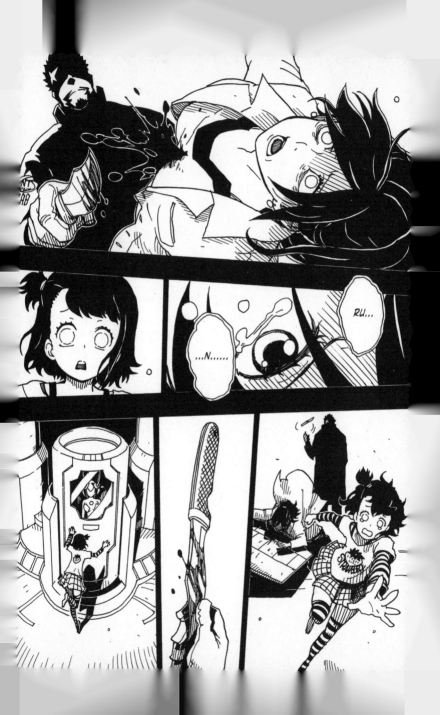

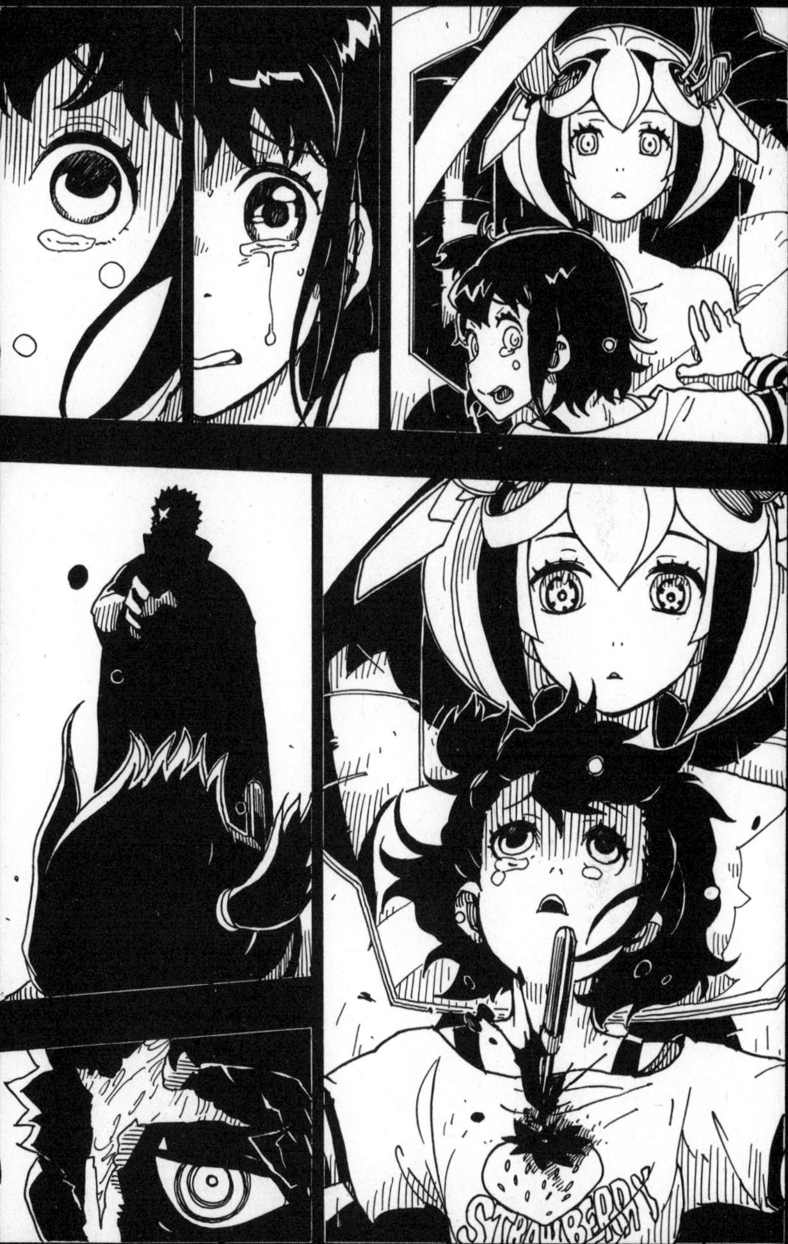
STRAWBERRY

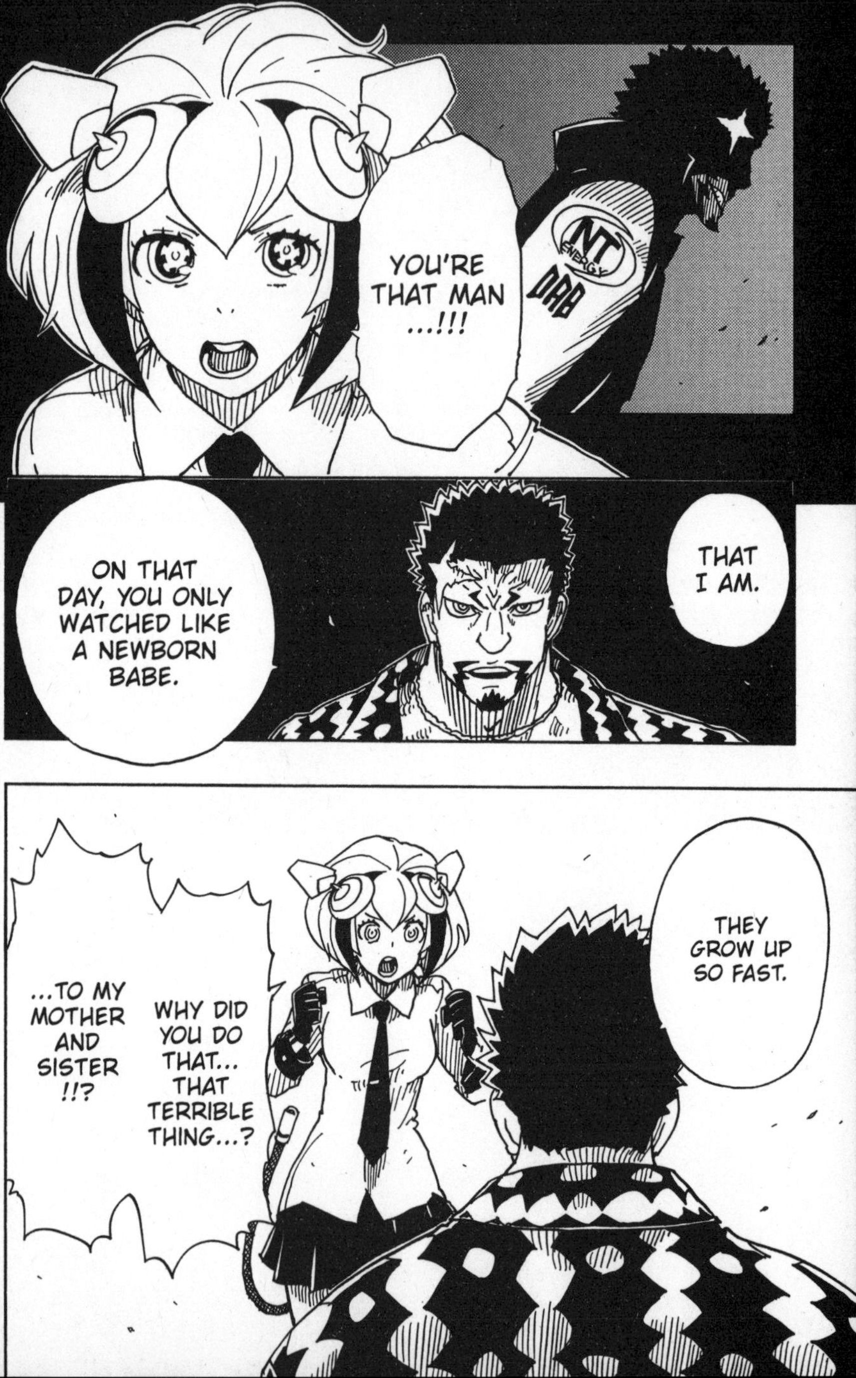
YOU'RE THAT MAN ...!!!
NT ENERGY
THAT I AM.
ON THAT DAY, YOU ONLY WATCHED LIKE A NEWBORN BABE.
THEY GROW UP SO FAST.
WHY DID YOU DO THAT... THAT TERRIBLE THING...?
...TO MY MOTHER AND SISTER !!?

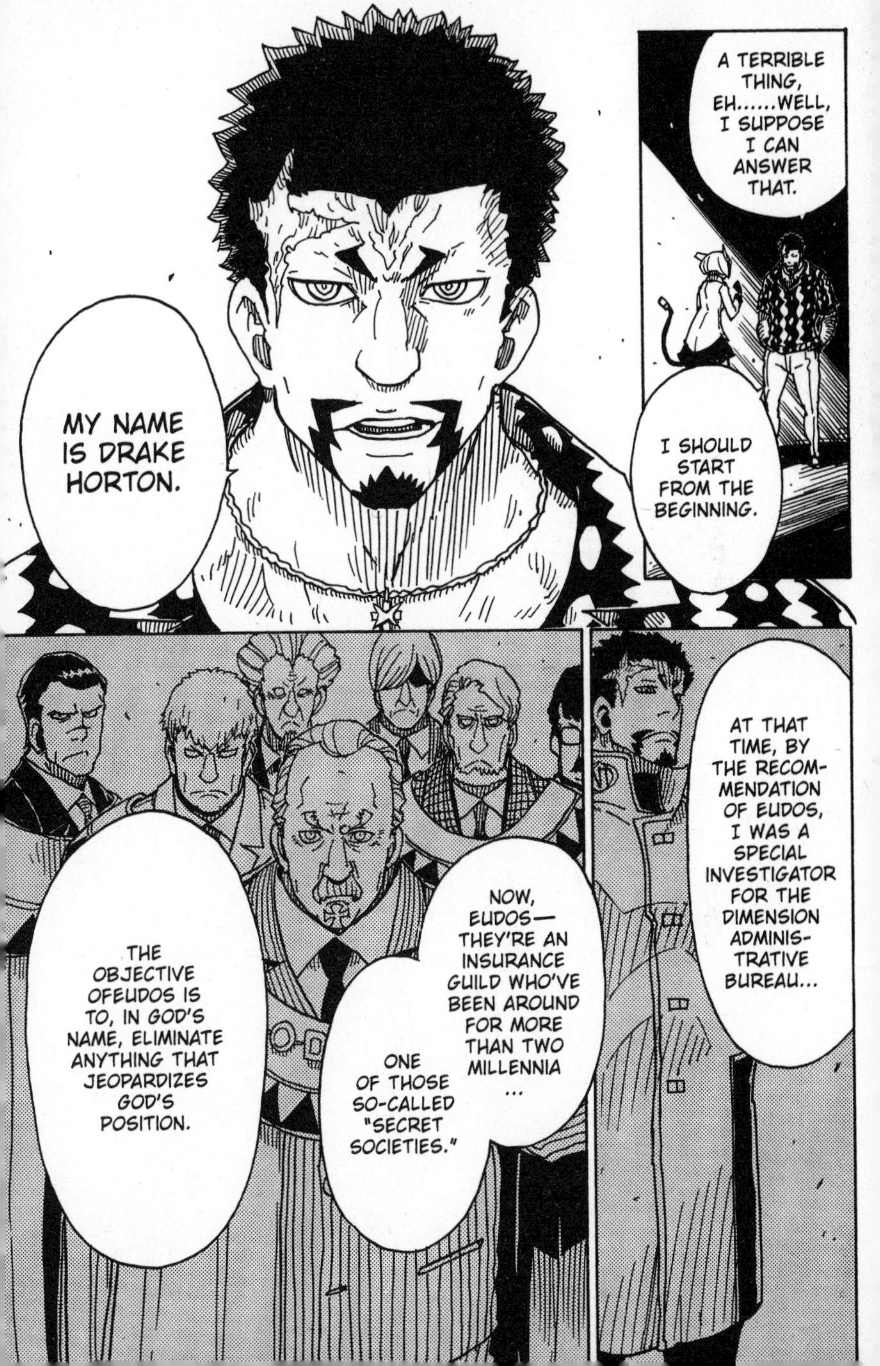
A TERRIBLE THING, EH......WELL, I SUPPOSE I CAN ANSWER THAT.
I SHOULD START FROM THE BEGINNING.
MY NAME IS DRAKE HORTON.
AT THAT TIME, BY THE RECOMMENDATION OF EUDOS, I WAS A SPECIAL INVESTIGATOR FOR THE DIMENSION ADMINISTRATIVE BUREAU...
NOW, EUDOS—THEY'RE AN INSURANCE GUILD WHO'VE BEEN AROUND FOR MORE THAN TWO MILLENNIA...
ONE OF THOSE SO-CALLED "SECRET SOCIETIES."
THE OBJECTIVE OFEUDOS IS TO, IN GOD'S NAME, ELIMINATE ANYTHING THAT JEOPARDIZES GOD'S POSITION.

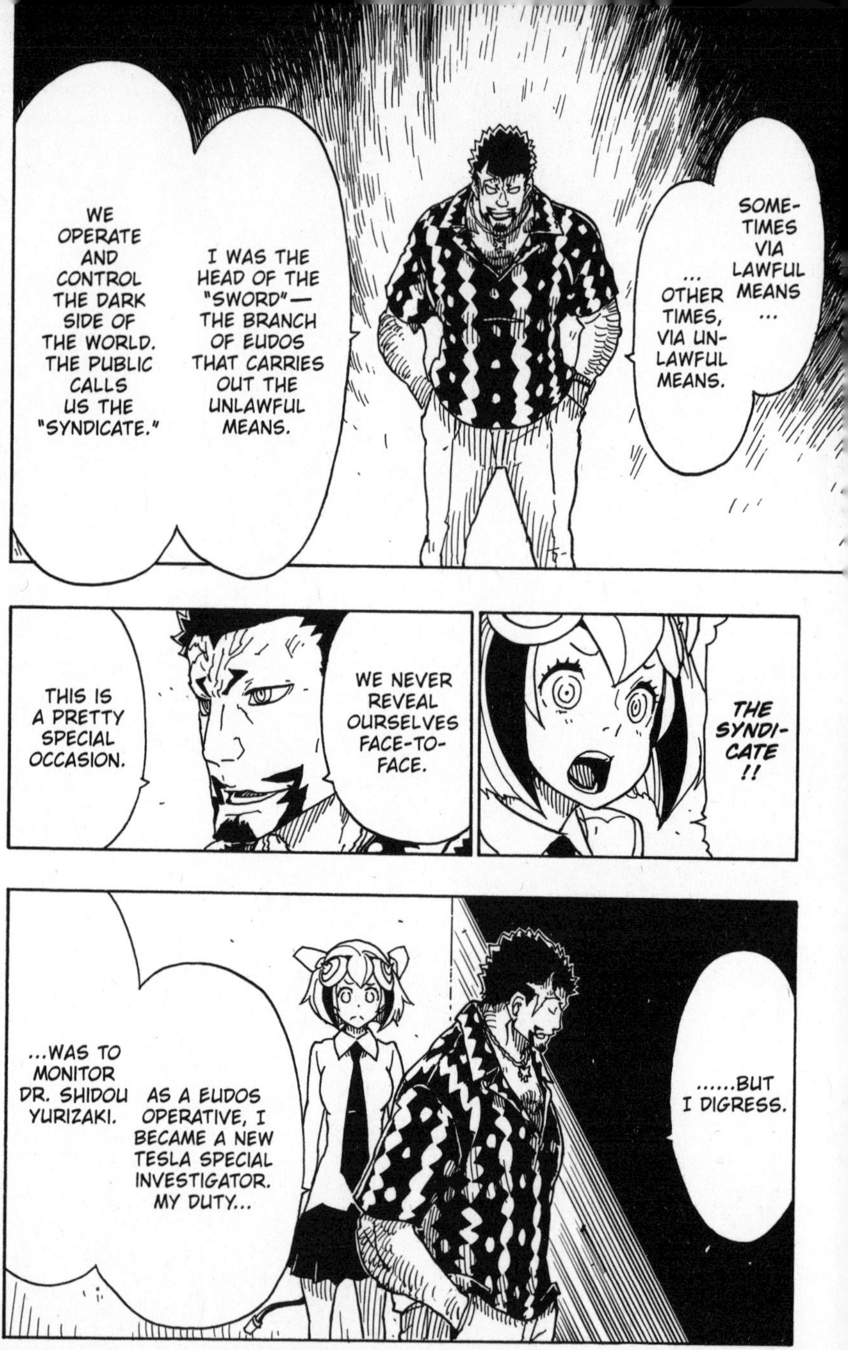
SOMETIMES VIA LAWFUL MEANS...
...OTHER TIMES, VIA UNLAWFUL MEANS.
I WAS THE HEAD OF THE "SWORD"—THE BRANCH OF EUDOS THAT CARRIES OUT THE UNLAWFUL MEANS.
WE OPERATE AND CONTROL THE DARK SIDE OF THE WORLD. THE PUBLIC CALLS US THE "SYNDICATE."
THE SYNDICATE!!
WE NEVER REVEAL OURSELVES FACE-TO-FACE.
THIS IS A PRETTY SPECIAL OCCASION.
......BUT I DIGRESS.
AS A EUDOS OPERATIVE, I BECAME A NEW TESLA SPECIAL INVESTIGATOR. MY DUTY...
...WAS TO MONITOR DR. SHIDOU YURIZAKI.

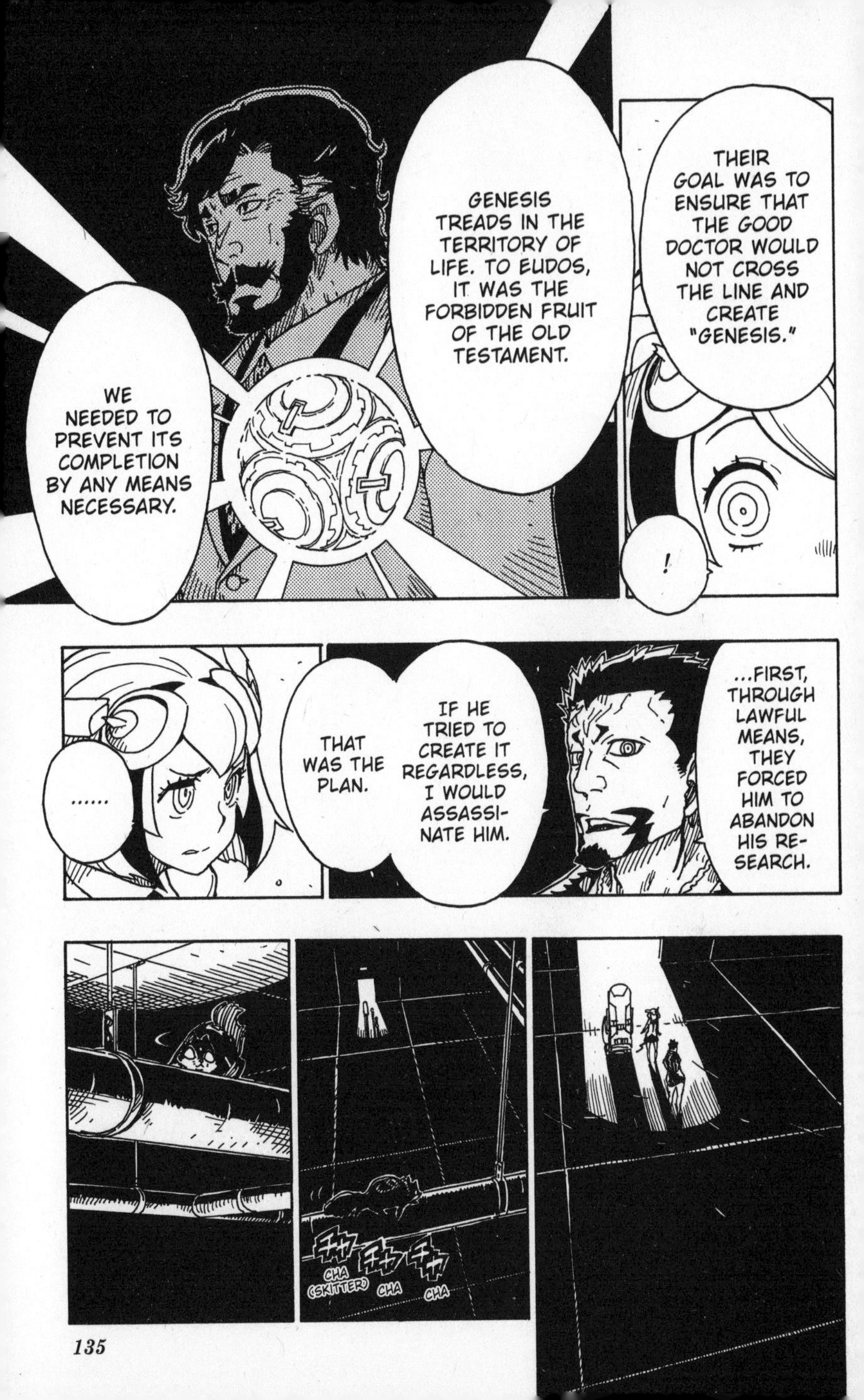
THEIR GOAL WAS TO ENSURE THAT THE GOOD DOCTOR WOULD NOT CROSS THE LINE AND CREATE "GENESIS."
!
GENESIS TREADS IN THE TERRITORY OF LIFE. TO EUDOS, IT WAS THE FORBIDDEN FRUIT OF THE OLD TESTAMENT.
WE NEEDED TO PREVENT ITS COMPLETION BY ANY MEANS NECESSARY.
...FIRST, THROUGH LAWFUL MEANS, THEY FORCED HIM TO ABANDON HIS RE-SEARCH.
IF HE TRIED TO CREATE IT REGARDLESS, I WOULD ASSASSI-NATE HIM.
THAT WAS THE PLAN.
......
チャ
CHA (SKITTER)
チャ
CHA
チャ
CHA

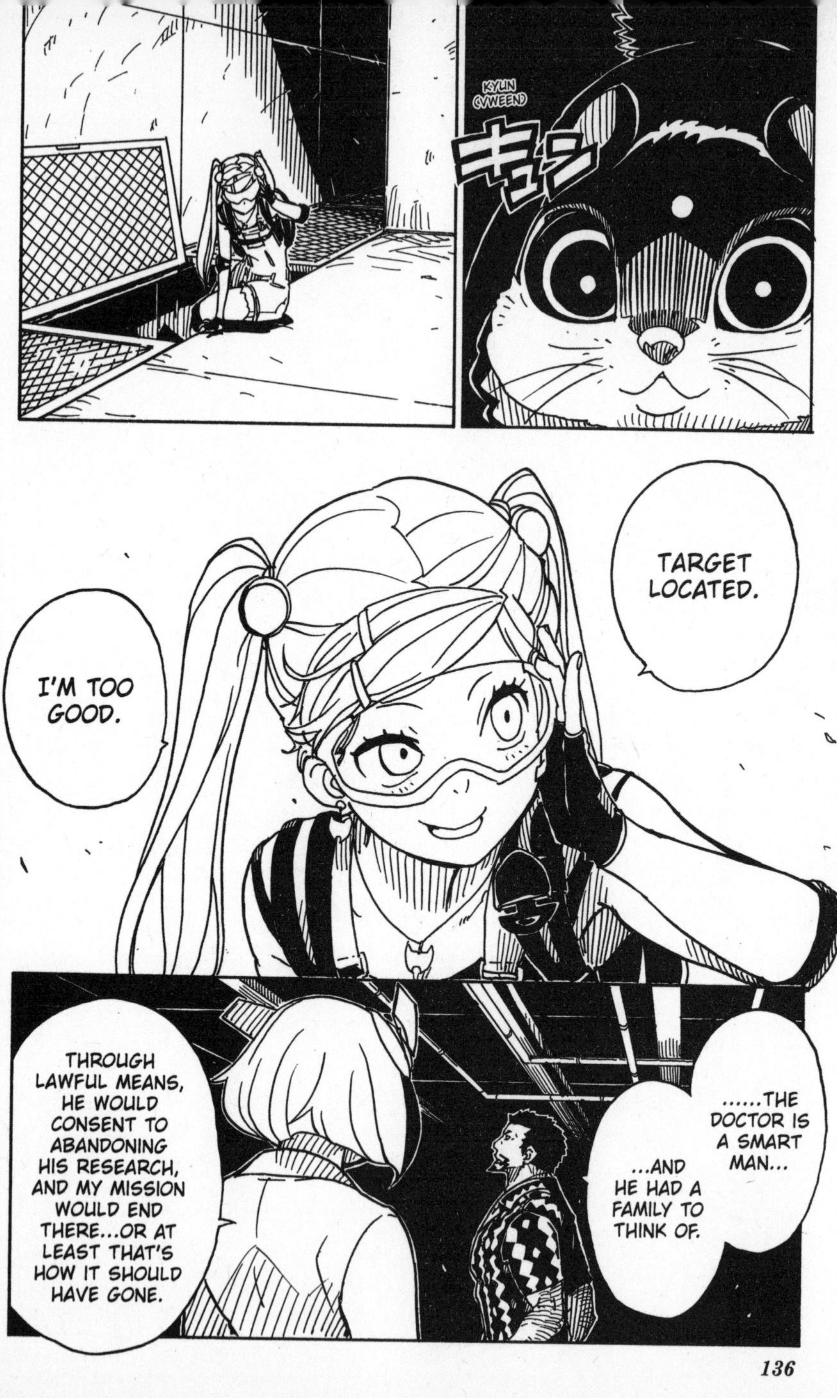
KYUN (VWEEN)
TARGET LOCATED.
I'M TOO GOOD.
......THE DOCTOR IS A SMART MAN...
...AND HE HAD A FAMILY TO THINK OF.
THROUGH LAWFUL MEANS, HE WOULD CONSENT TO ABANDONING HIS RESEARCH, AND MY MISSION WOULD END THERE...OR AT LEAST THAT'S HOW IT SHOULD HAVE GONE.

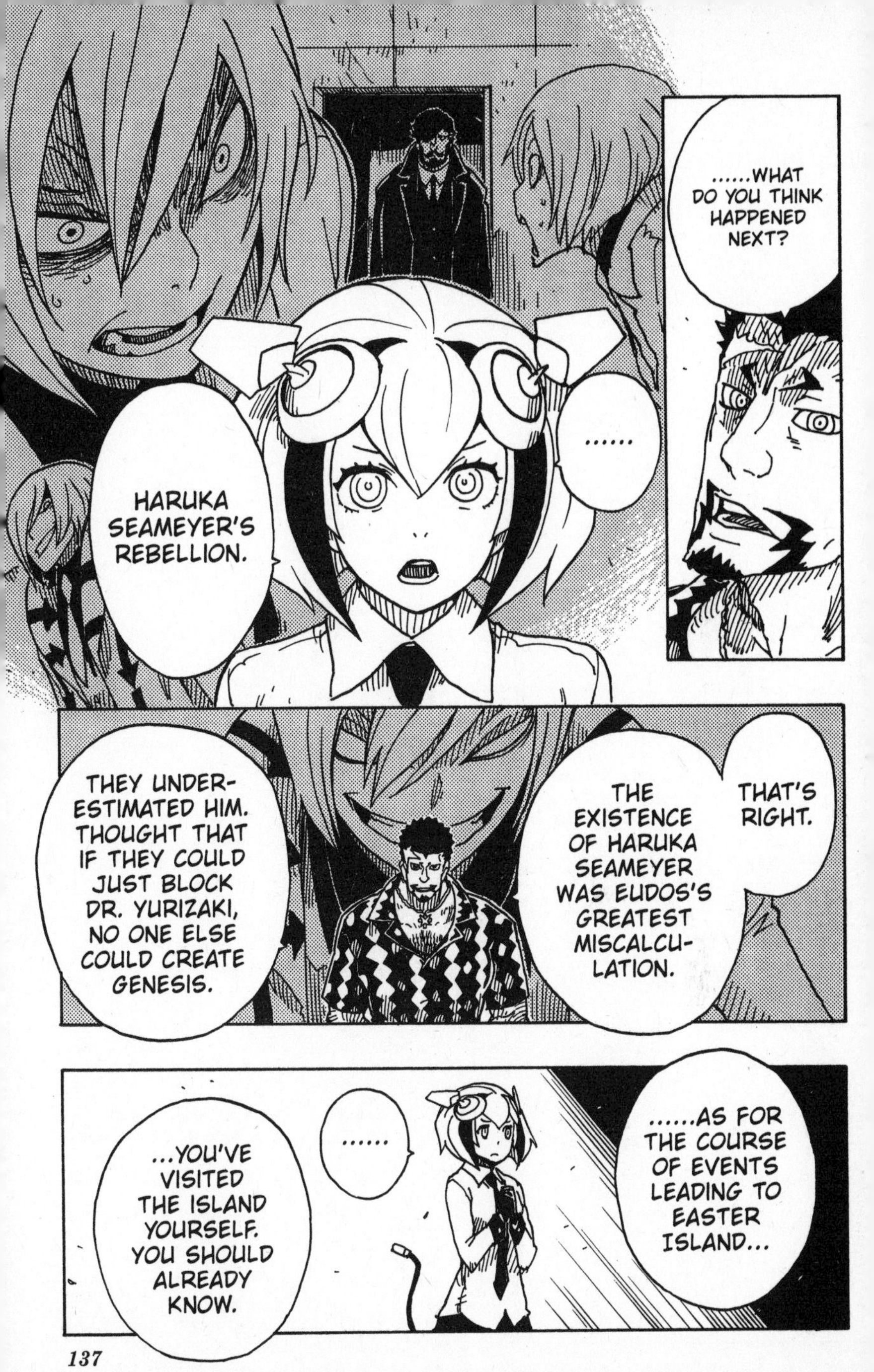
......WHAT DO YOU THINK HAPPENED NEXT?
......
HARUKA SEAMEYER'S REBELLION.
THAT'S RIGHT.
THE EXISTENCE OF HARUKA SEAMEYER WAS EUDOS'S GREATEST MISCALCU-LATION.
THEY UNDER-ESTIMATED HIM. THOUGHT THAT IF THEY COULD JUST BLOCK DR. YURIZAKI, NO ONE ELSE COULD CREATE GENESIS.
......AS FOR THE COURSE OF EVENTS LEADING TO EASTER ISLAND...
......
...YOU'VE VISITED THE ISLAND YOURSELF. YOU SHOULD ALREADY KNOW.

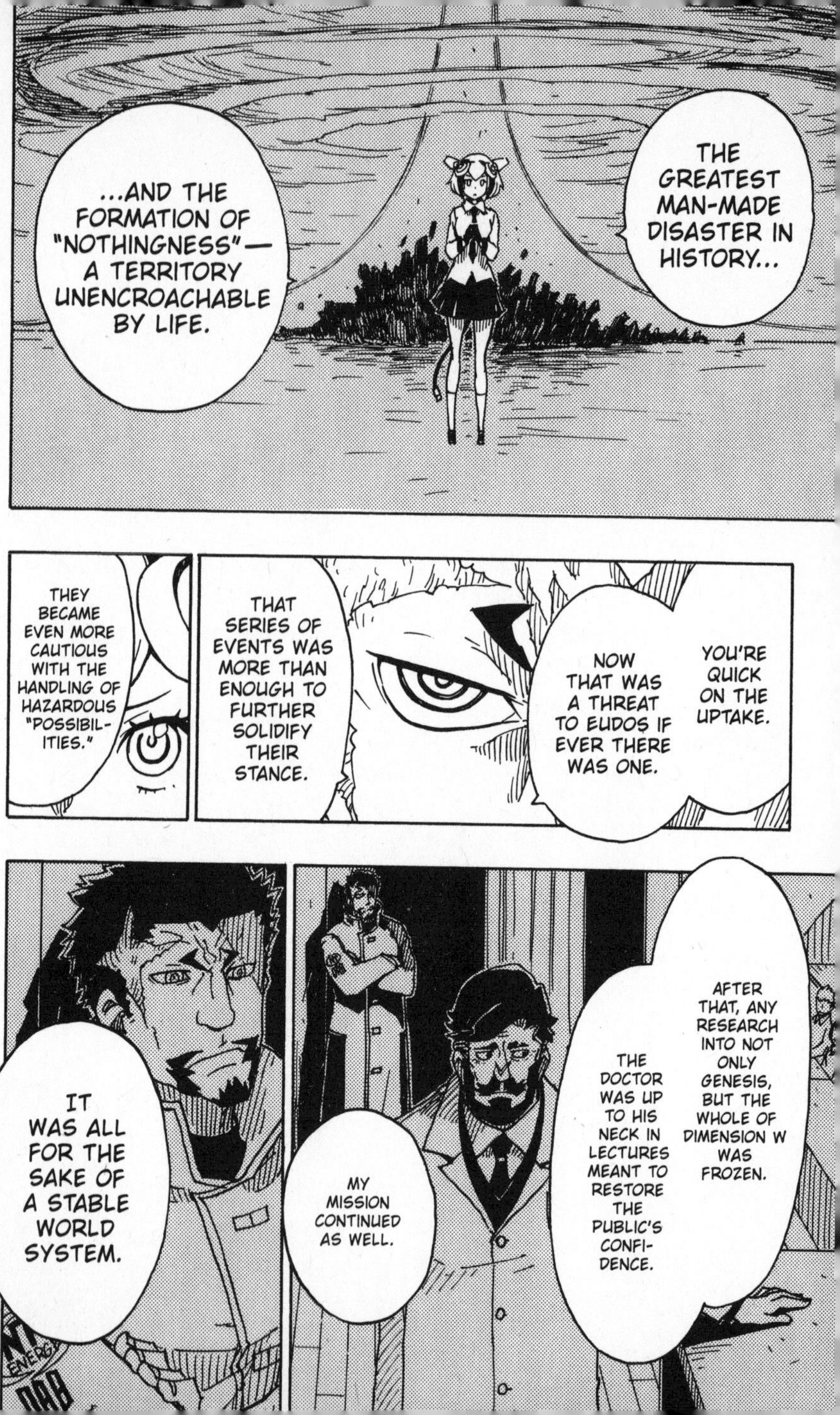
THE GREATEST MAN-MADE DISASTER IN HISTORY...
...AND THE FORMATION OF "NOTHINGNESS"—A TERRITORY UNENCROACHABLE BY LIFE.
YOU'RE QUICK ON THE UPTAKE.
NOW THAT WAS A THREAT TO EUDOS IF EVER THERE WAS ONE.
THAT SERIES OF EVENTS WAS MORE THAN ENOUGH TO FURTHER SOLIDIFY THEIR STANCE.
THEY BECAME EVEN MORE CAUTIOUS WITH THE HANDLING OF HAZARDOUS "POSSIBIL-ITIES."
AFTER THAT, ANY RESEARCH INTO NOT ONLY GENESIS, BUT THE WHOLE OF DIMENSION W WAS FROZEN.
THE DOCTOR WAS UP TO HIS NECK IN LECTURES MEANT TO RESTORE THE PUBLIC'S CONFI-DENCE.
MY MISSION CONTINUED AS WELL.
IT WAS ALL FOR THE SAKE OF A STABLE WORLD SYSTEM.

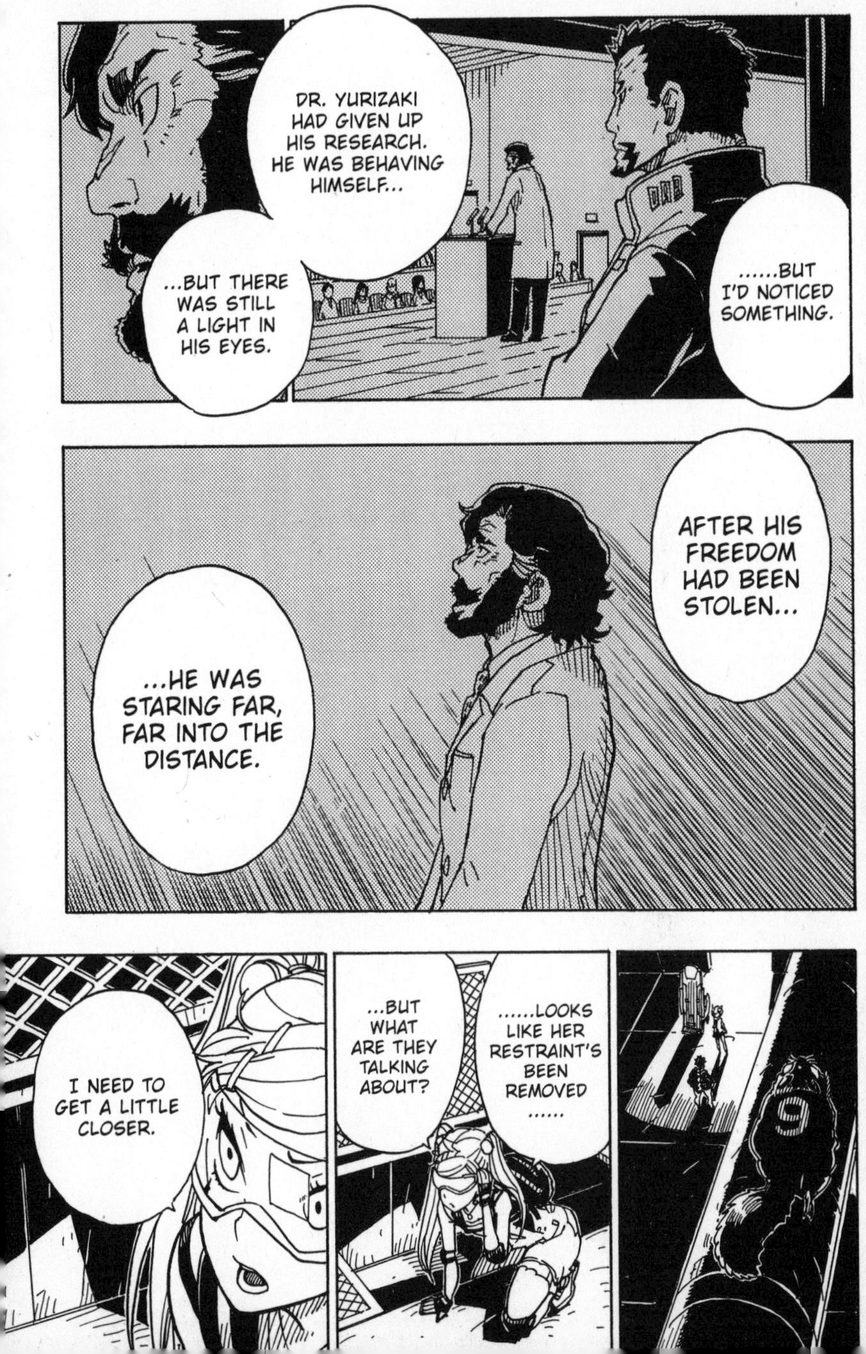
DR. YURIZAKI HAD GIVEN UP HIS RESEARCH. HE WAS BEHAVING HIMSELF...
......BUT I'D NOTICED SOMETHING.
...BUT THERE WAS STILL A LIGHT IN HIS EYES.
AFTER HIS FREEDOM HAD BEEN STOLEN...
...HE WAS STARING FAR, FAR INTO THE DISTANCE.
......LOOKS LIKE HER RESTRAINT'S BEEN REMOVED......
...BUT WHAT ARE THEY TALKING ABOUT?
I NEED TO GET A LITTLE CLOSER.

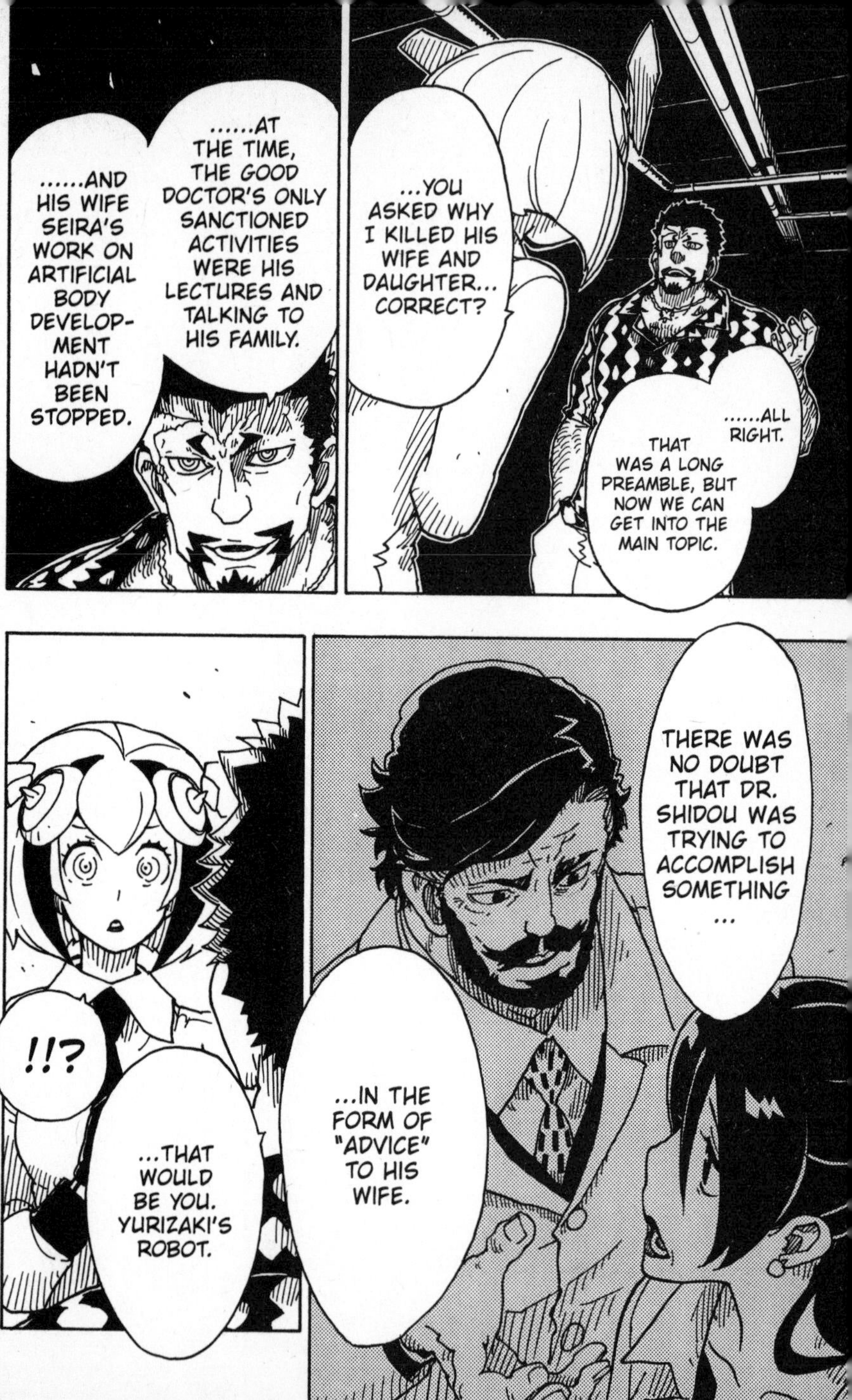
...YOU ASKED WHY I KILLED HIS WIFE AND DAUGHTER... CORRECT?
......ALL RIGHT.
THAT WAS A LONG PREAMBLE, BUT NOW WE CAN GET INTO THE MAIN TOPIC.
......AT THE TIME, THE GOOD DOCTOR'S ONLY SANCTIONED ACTIVITIES WERE HIS LECTURES AND TALKING TO HIS FAMILY.
......AND HIS WIFE SEIRA'S WORK ON ARTIFICIAL BODY DEVELOPMENT HADN'T BEEN STOPPED.
THERE WAS NO DOUBT THAT DR. SHIDOU WAS TRYING TO ACCOMPLISH SOMETHING ...
...IN THE FORM OF "ADVICE" TO HIS WIFE.
...THAT WOULD BE YOU. YURIZAKI'S ROBOT.
!!?

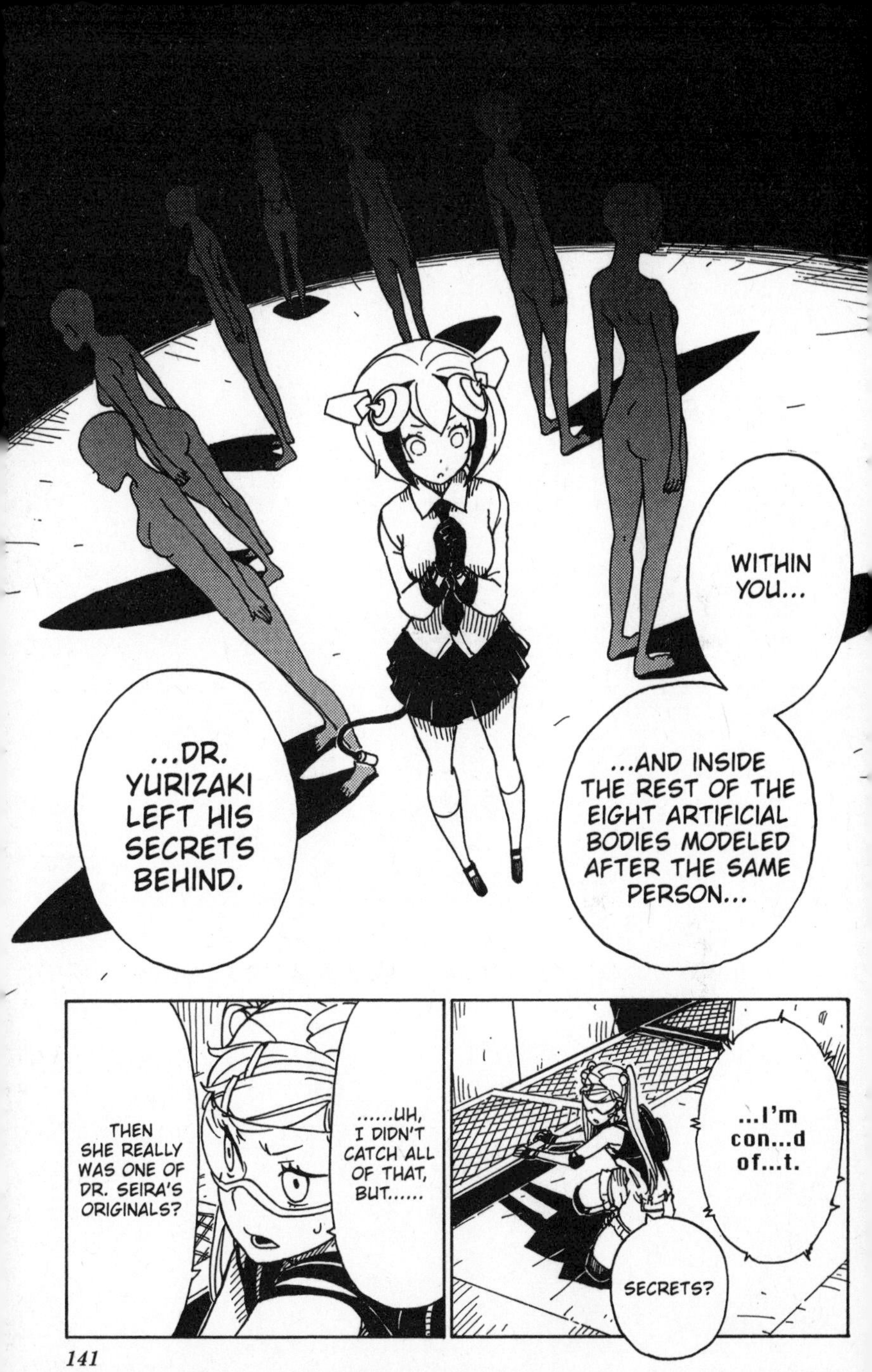
WITHIN YOU...
...AND INSIDE THE REST OF THE EIGHT ARTIFICIAL BODIES MODELED AFTER THE SAME PERSON...
...DR. YURIZAKI LEFT HIS SECRETS BEHIND.
...I'm con...d of...t.
SECRETS?
......UH, I DIDN'T CATCH ALL OF THAT, BUT......
THEN SHE REALLY WAS ONE OF DR. SEIRA'S ORIGINALS?

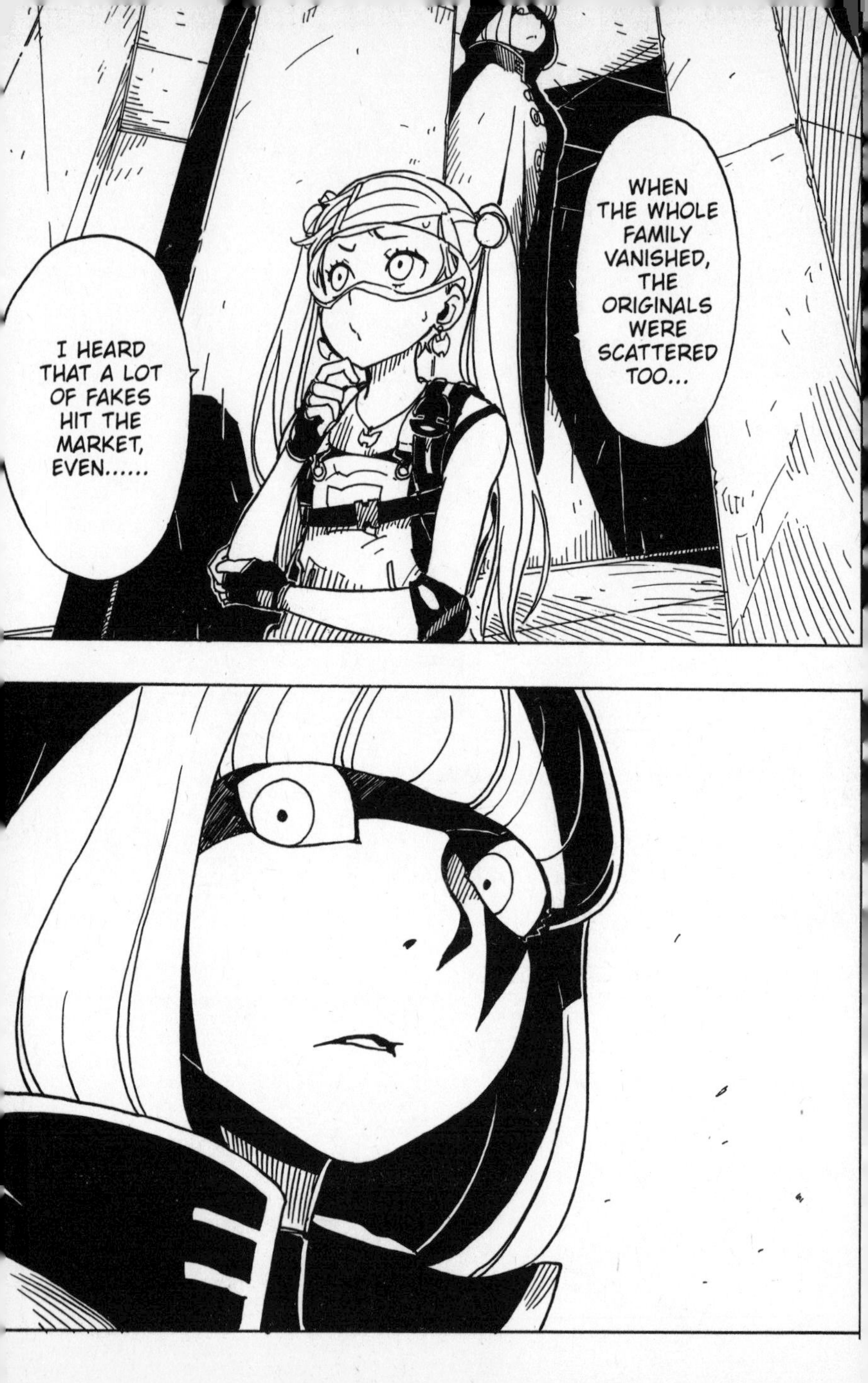
WHEN THE WHOLE FAMILY VANISHED, THE ORIGINALS WERE SCATTERED TOO...
I HEARD THAT A LOT OF FAKES HIT THE MARKET, EVEN......

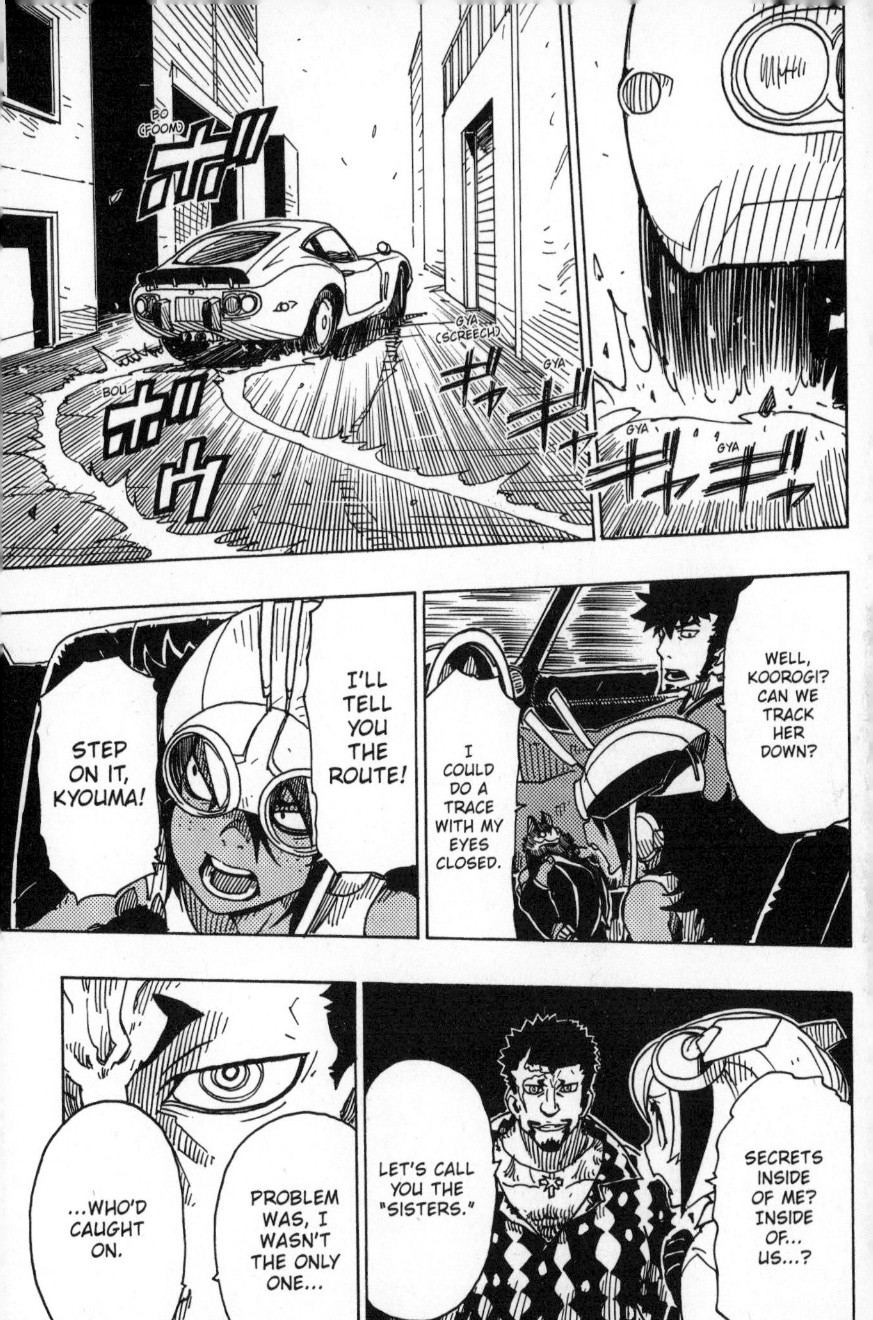
GYA
GYA
BO
(FOOM)
GYA
(SCREECH)
GYA
BOU
WELL, KOOROGI? CAN WE TRACK HER DOWN?
I COULD DO A TRACE WITH MY EYES CLOSED.
I'LL TELL YOU THE ROUTE!
STEP ON IT, KYOUMA!
SECRETS INSIDE OF ME? INSIDE OF... US...?
LET'S CALL YOU THE "SISTERS."
PROBLEM WAS, I WASN'T THE ONLY ONE...
...WHO'D CAUGHT ON.

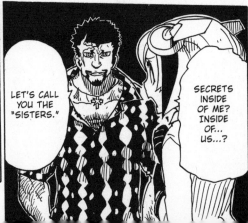

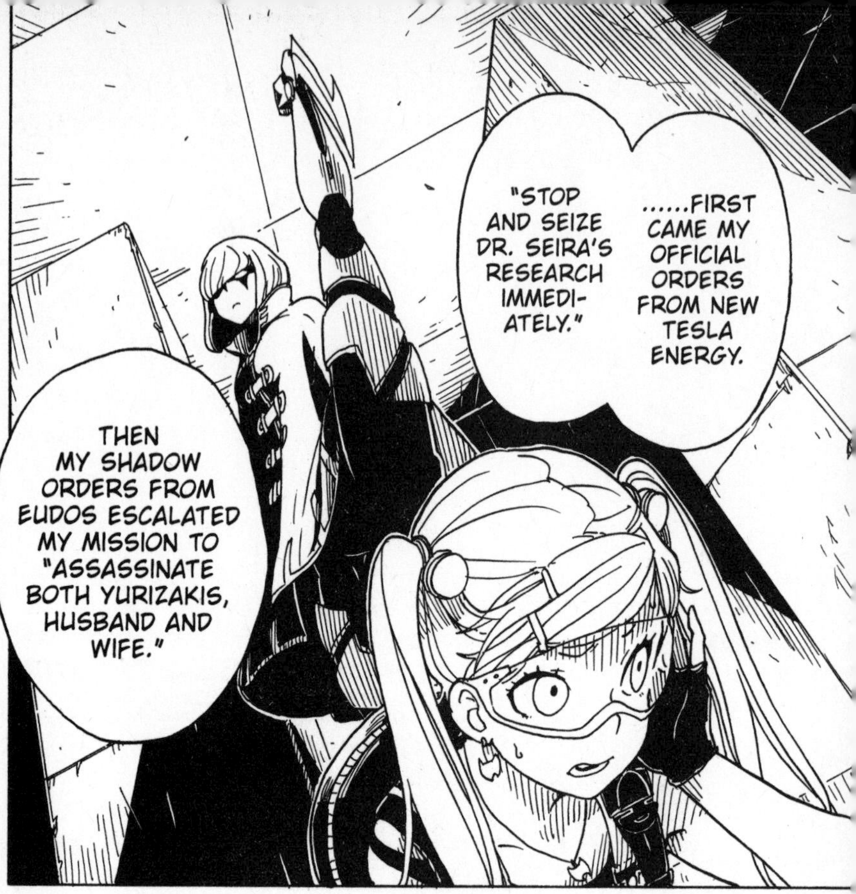
......FIRST CAME MY OFFICIAL ORDERS FROM NEW TESLA ENERGY.
"STOP AND SEIZE DR. SEIRA'S RESEARCH IMMEDI-ATELY."
THEN MY SHADOW ORDERS FROM EUDOS ESCALATED MY MISSION TO "ASSASSINATE BOTH YURIZAKIS, HUSBAND AND WIFE."

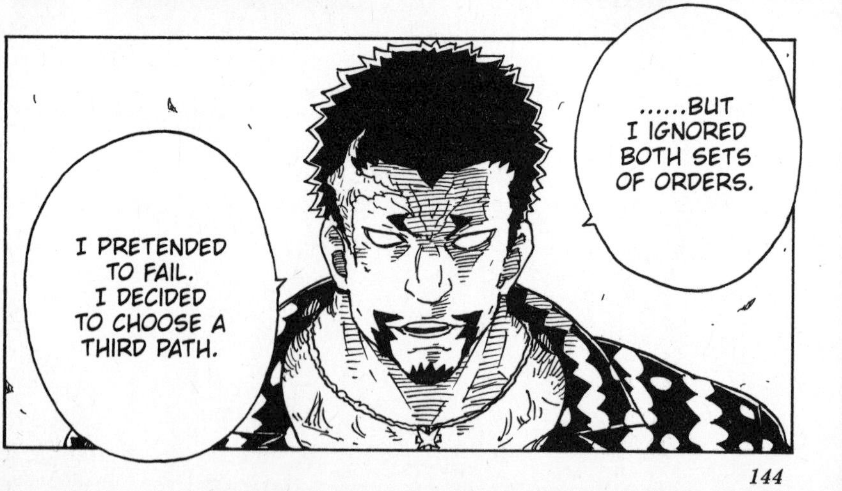
......BUT I IGNORED BOTH SETS OF ORDERS.
I PRETENDED TO FAIL. I DECIDED TO CHOOSE A THIRD PATH.

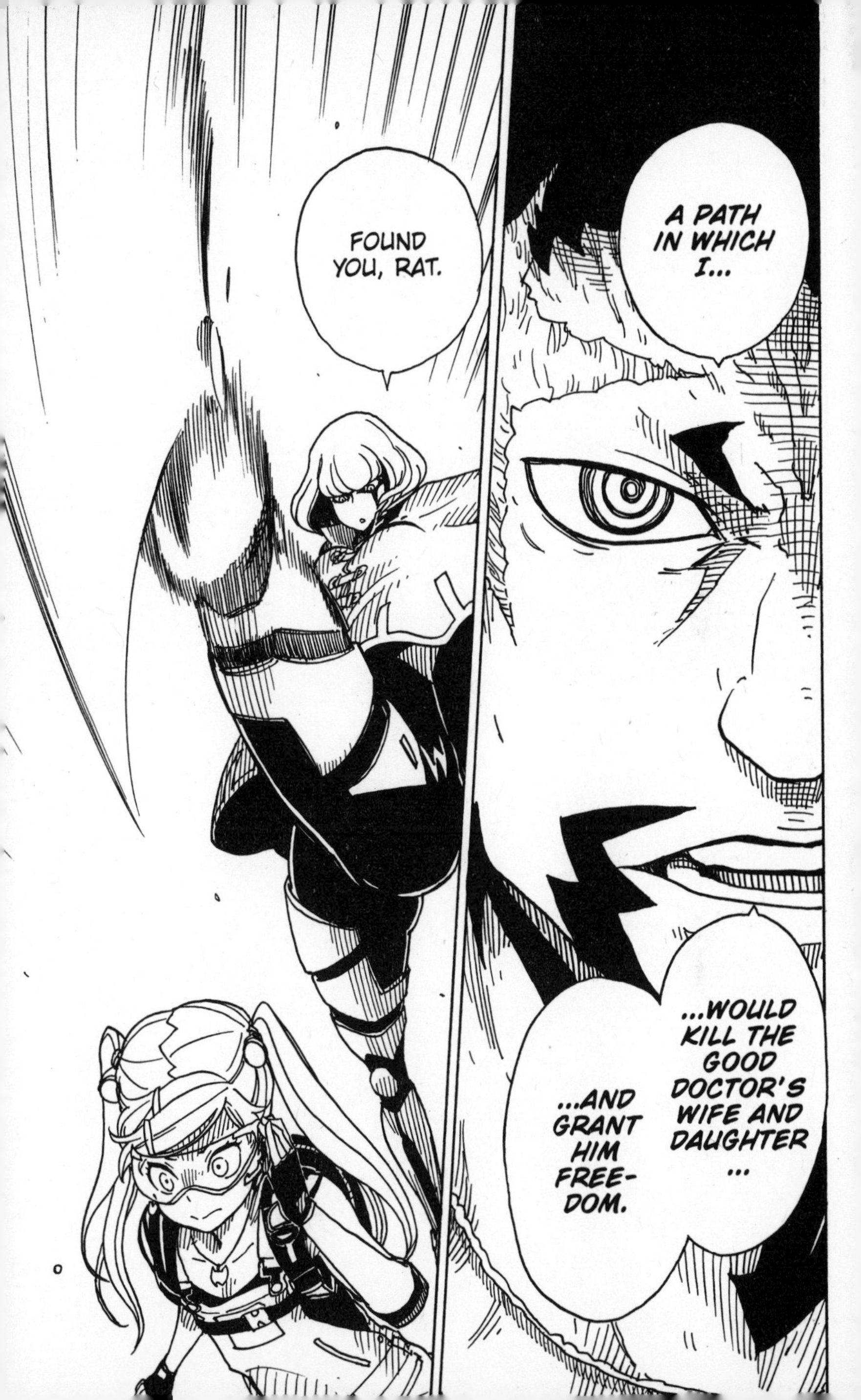
A PATH IN WHICH I...
...WOULD KILL THE GOOD DOCTOR'S WIFE AND DAUGHTER...
...AND GRANT HIM FREE-DOM.
FOUND YOU, RAT.

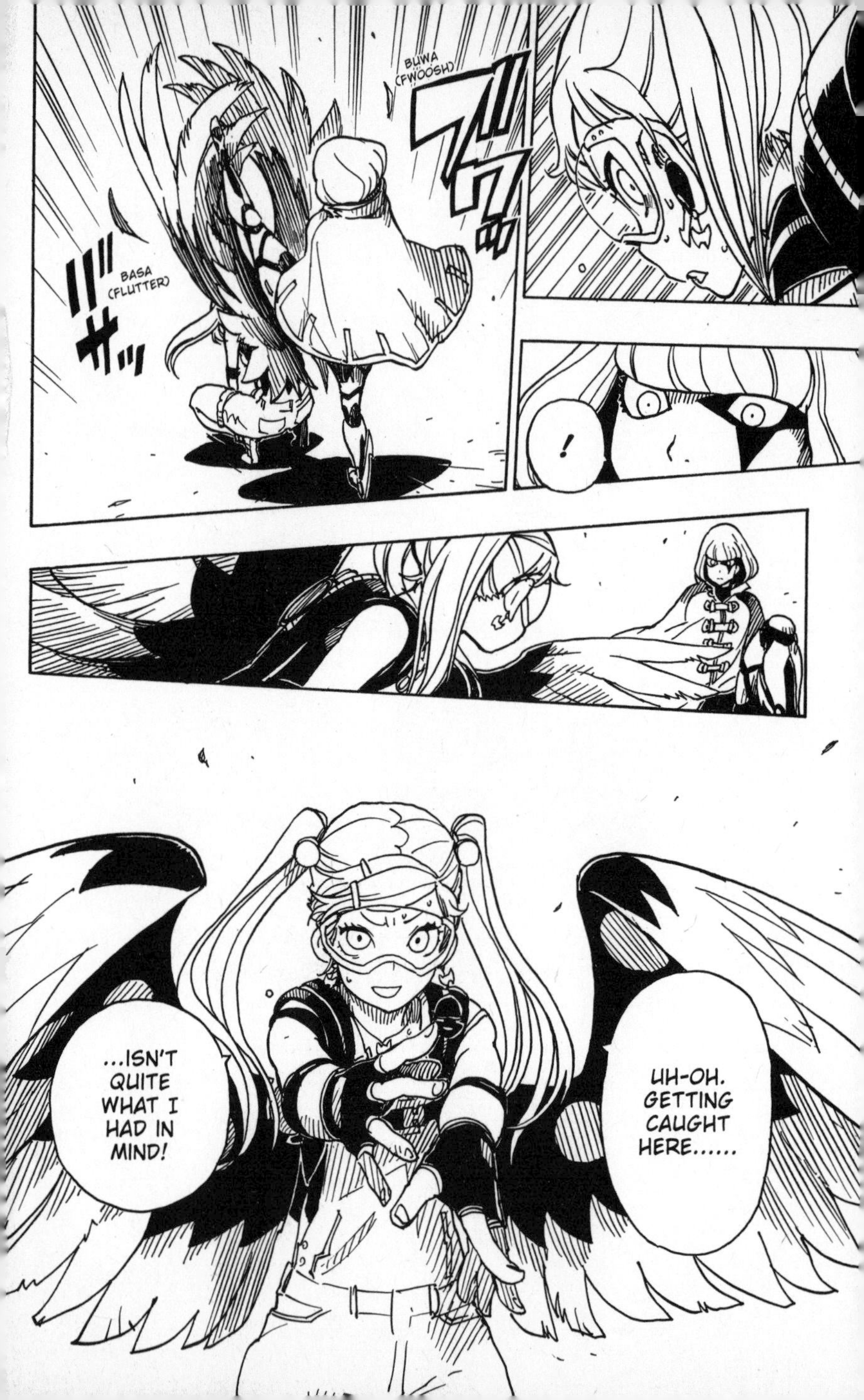
!
BUWA (FWOOSH)
BASA (FLUTTER)
UH-OH. GETTING CAUGHT HERE......
...ISN'T QUITE WHAT I HAD IN MIND!

FILE.83 THE STRONG

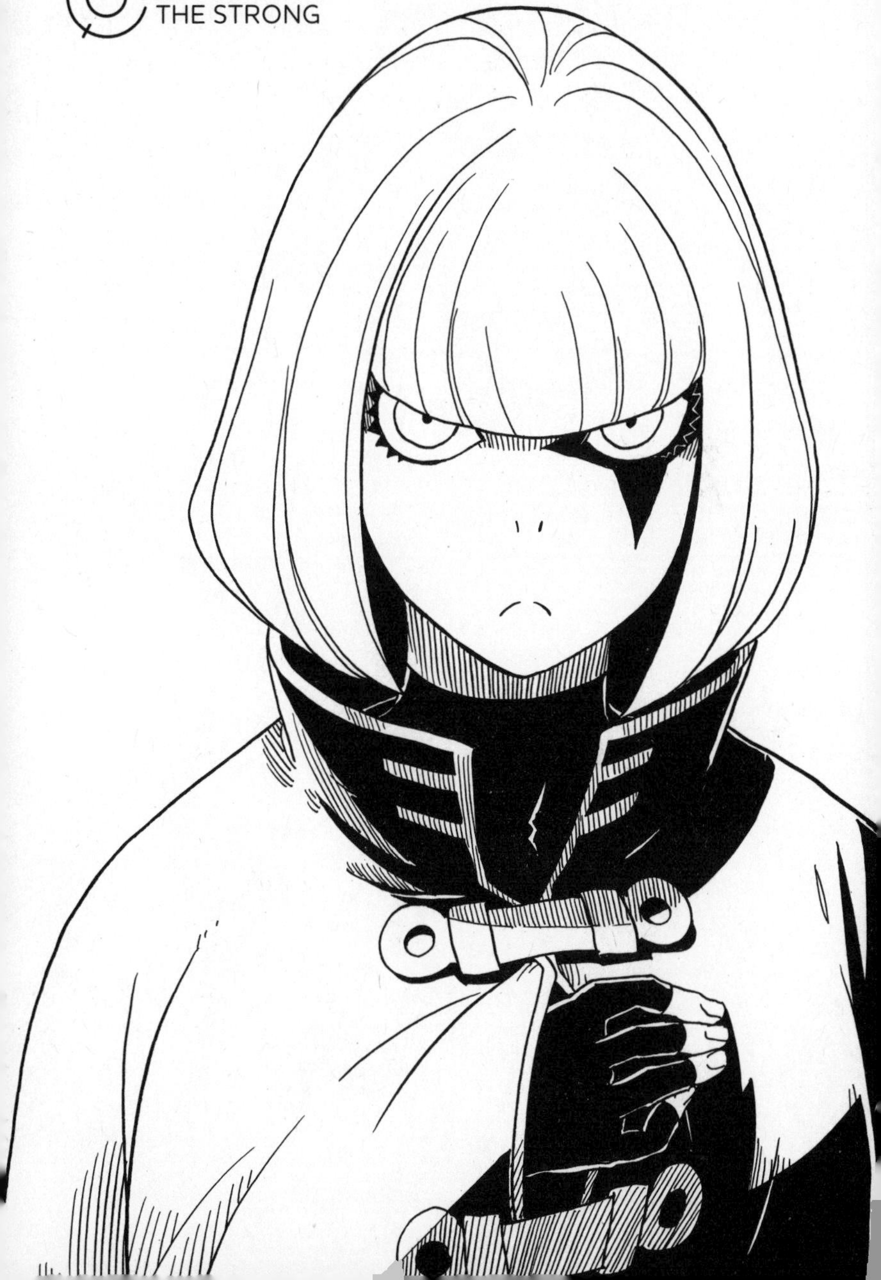

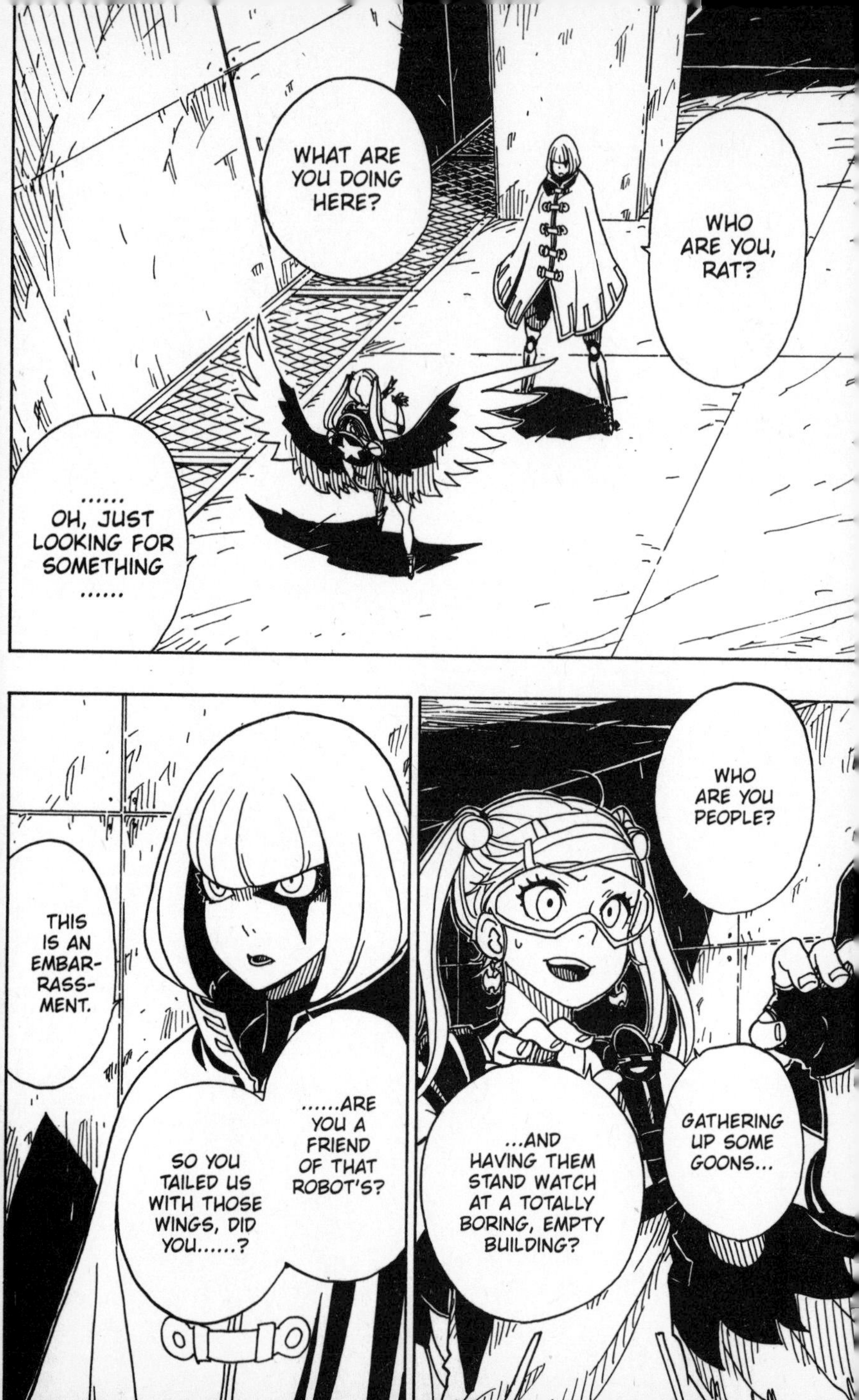
WHO ARE YOU, RAT?
WHAT ARE YOU DOING HERE?
...... OH, JUST LOOKING FOR SOMETHING ......
WHO ARE YOU PEOPLE?
GATHERING UP SOME GOONS...
...AND HAVING THEM STAND WATCH AT A TOTALLY BORING, EMPTY BUILDING?
......ARE YOU A FRIEND OF THAT ROBOT'S?
SO YOU TAILED US WITH THOSE WINGS, DID YOU......?
THIS IS AN EMBARRASSMENT.

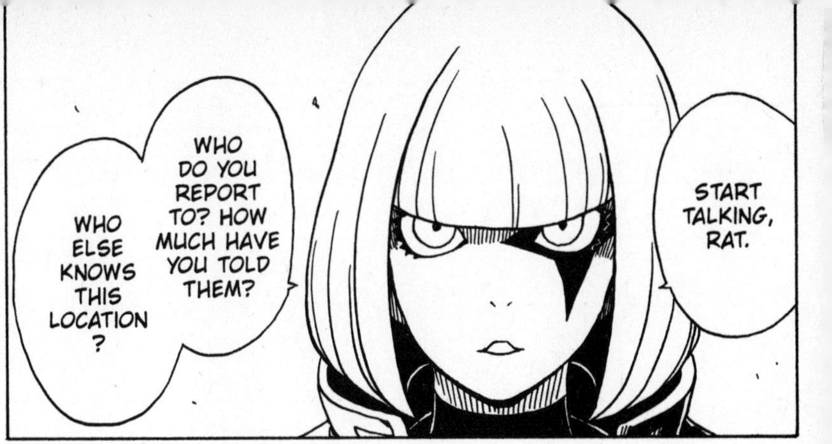
START TALKING, RAT.
WHO DO YOU REPORT TO? HOW MUCH HAVE YOU TOLD THEM?
WHO ELSE KNOWS THIS LOCATION?
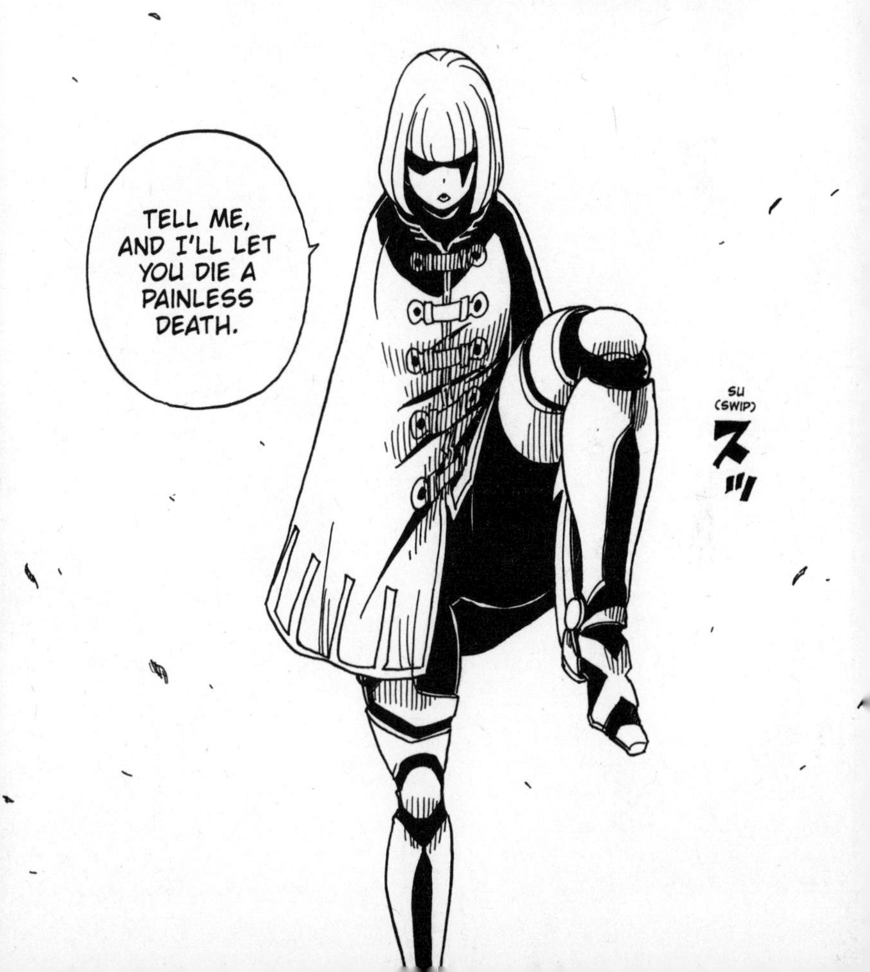
SU (SWIP)
スッ
TELL ME, AND I'LL LET YOU DIE A PAINLESS DEATH.

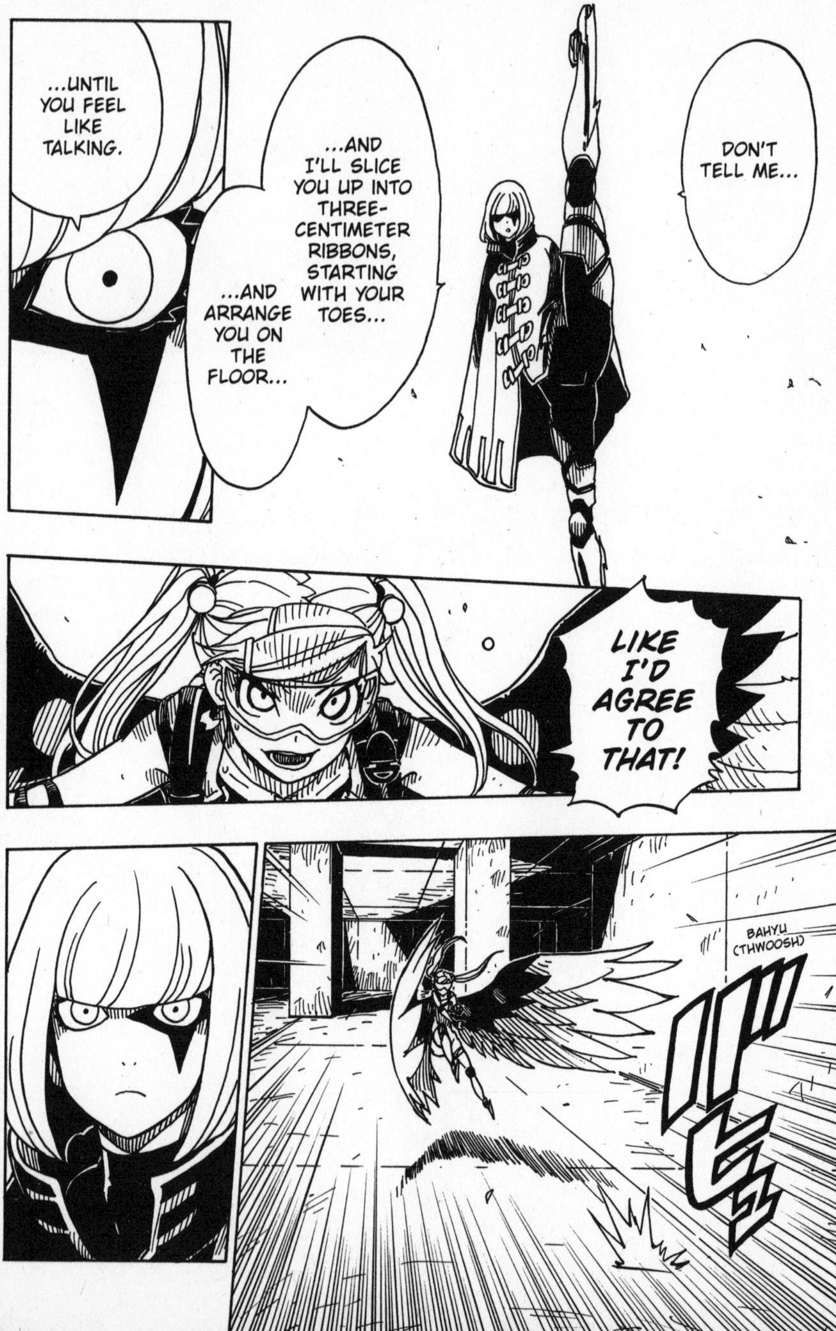
DON'T TELL ME...
...AND I'LL SLICE YOU UP INTO THREE-CENTIMETER RIBBONS, STARTING WITH YOUR TOES...
...AND ARRANGE YOU ON THE FLOOR...
...UNTIL YOU FEEL LIKE TALKING.
LIKE I'D AGREE TO THAT!
BAHYU (THWOOSH)

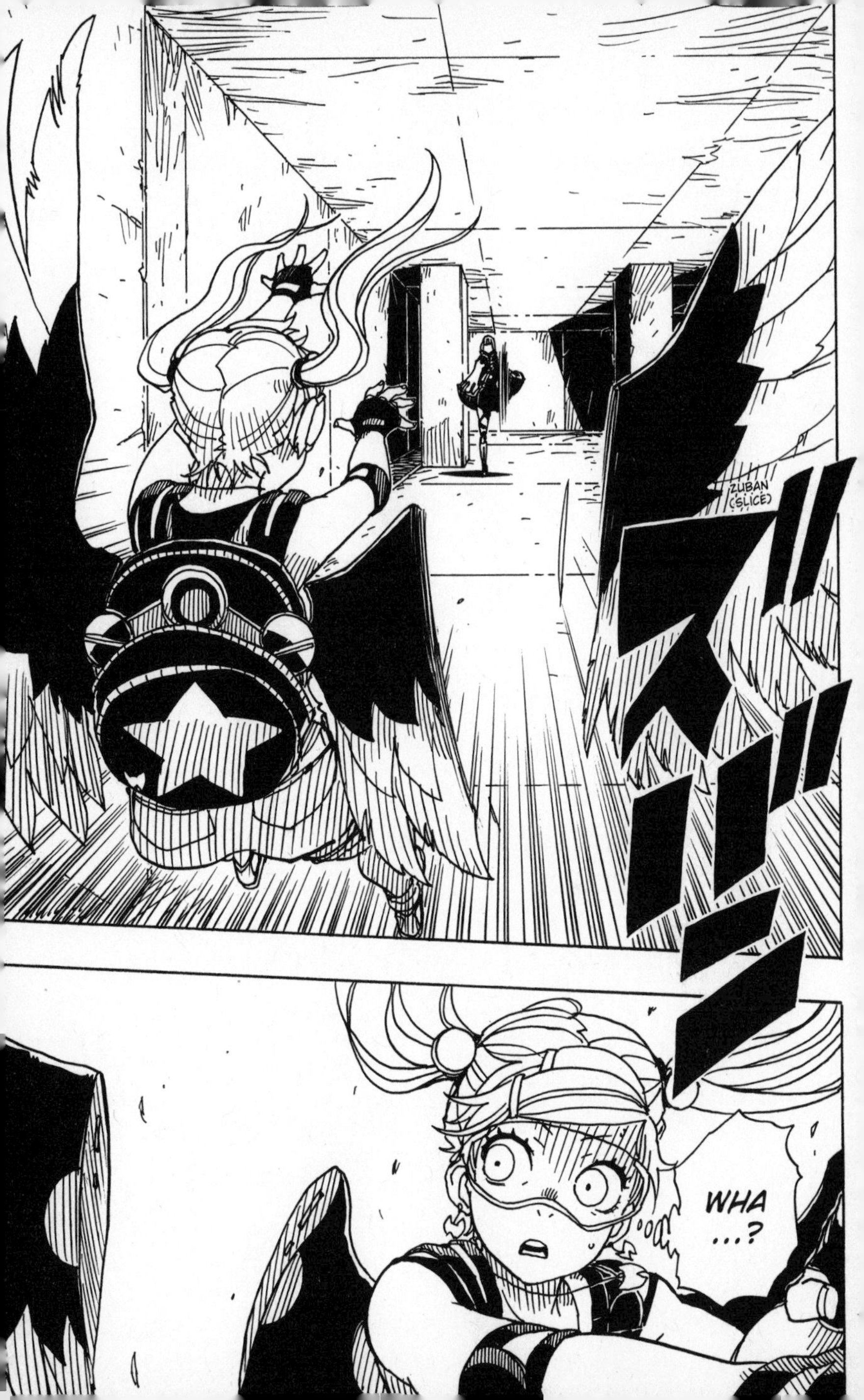
ZUBAN (SLICE)
WHA ...?

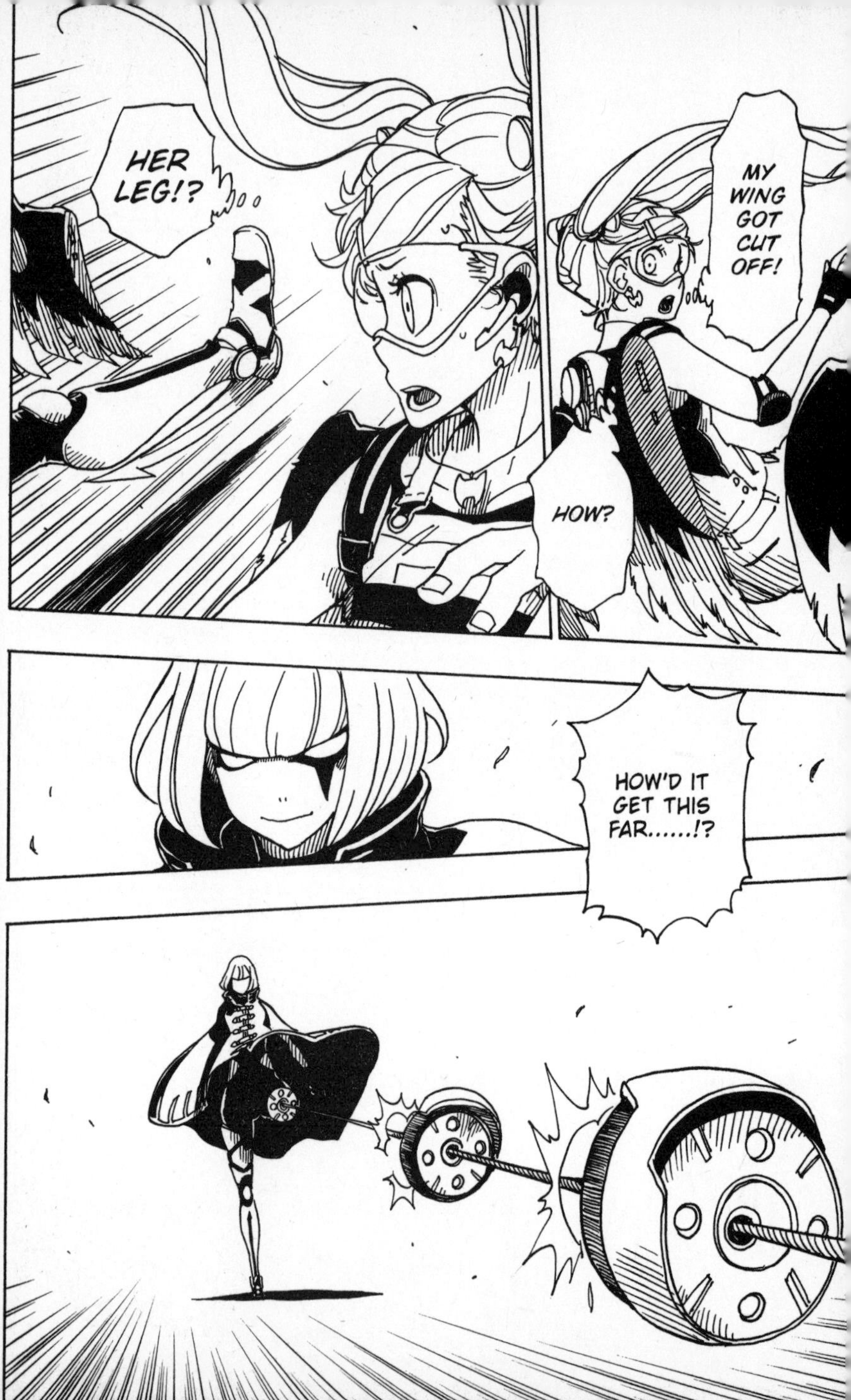
MY WING GOT CUT OFF!
HOW?
HER LEG!?
HOW'D IT GET THIS FAR......!?

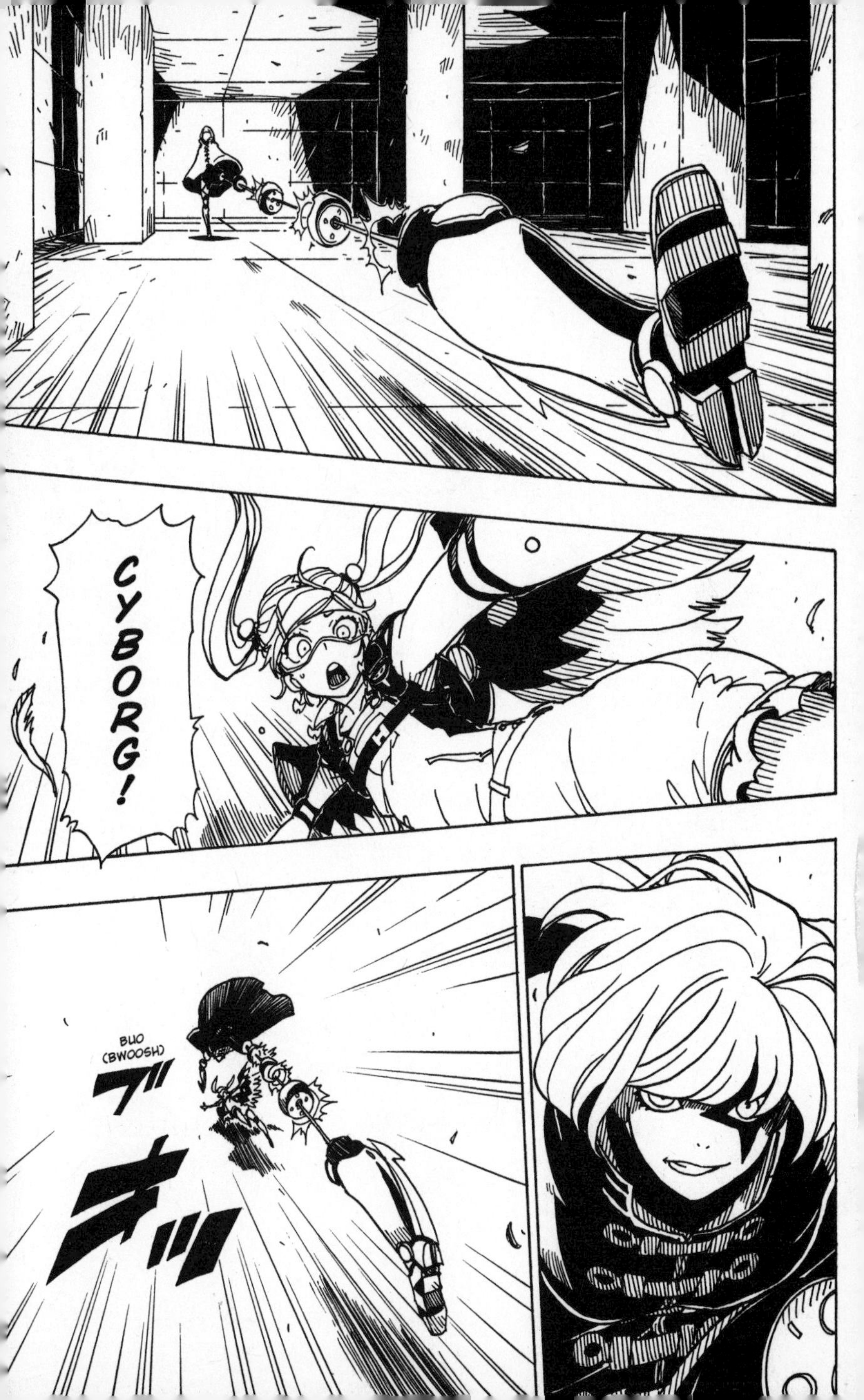
CYBORG!
BUO (BWOOSH)
ブオッ

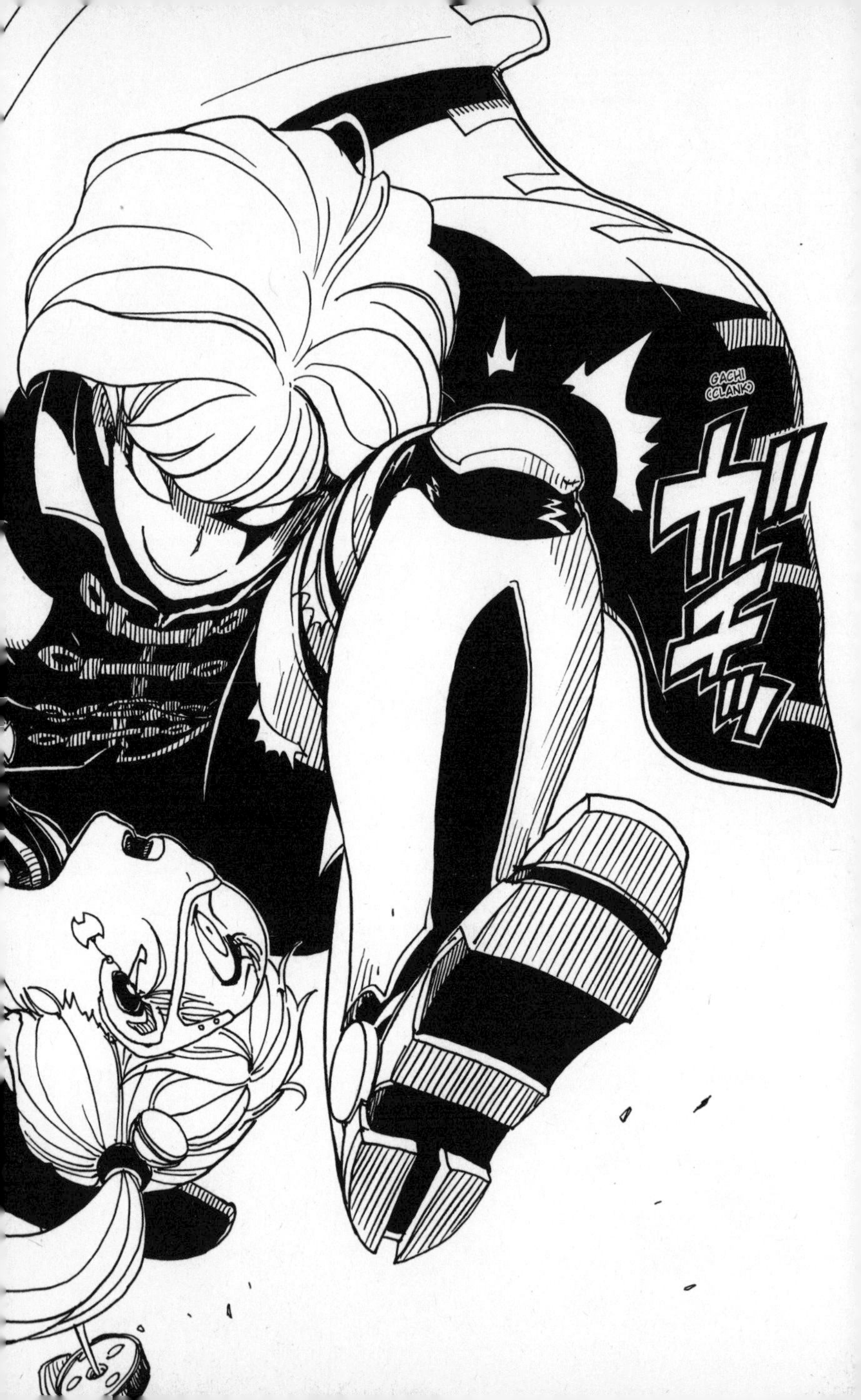
ガチッ
GACHI
(CLANK)

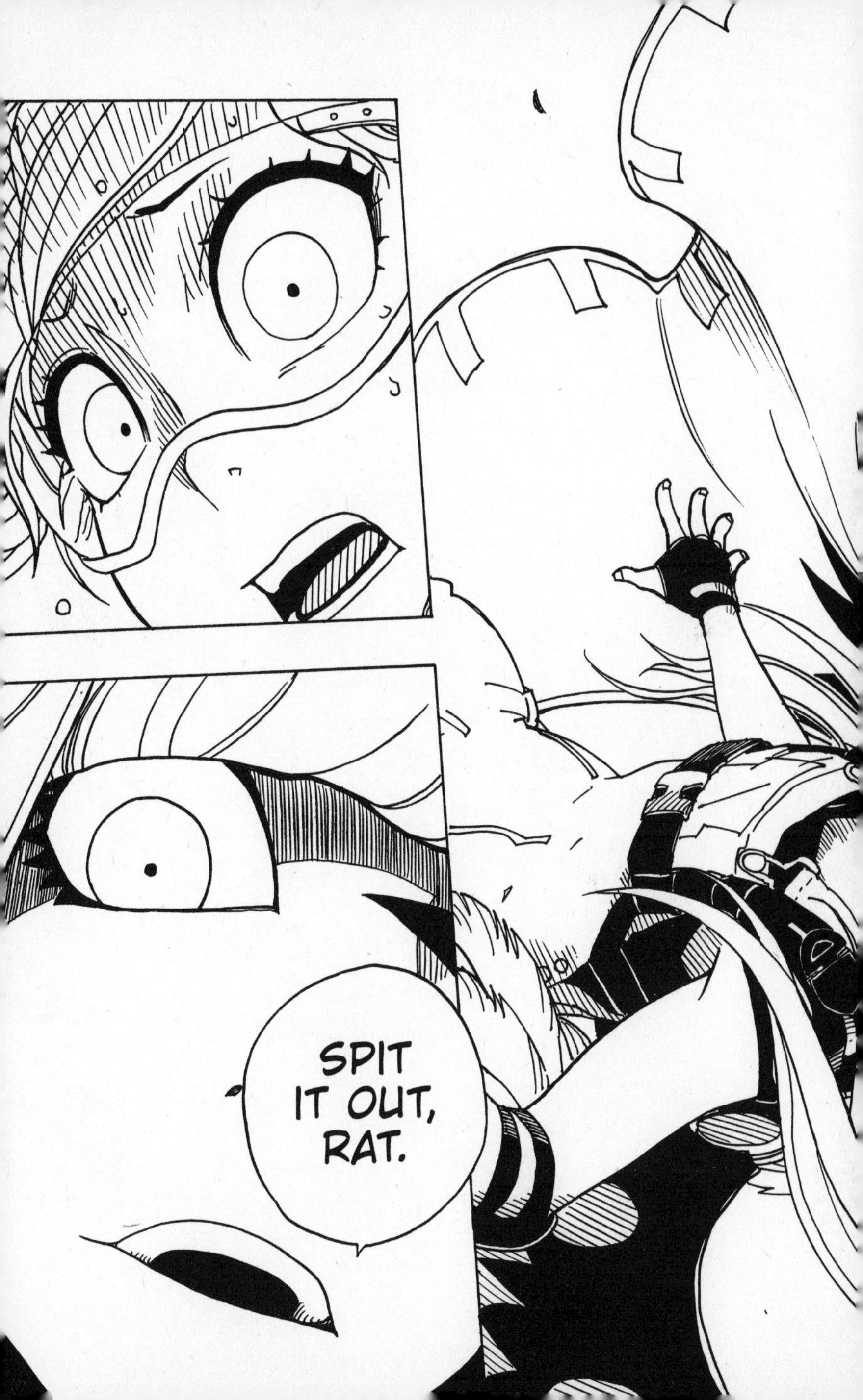
SPIT IT OUT, RAT.

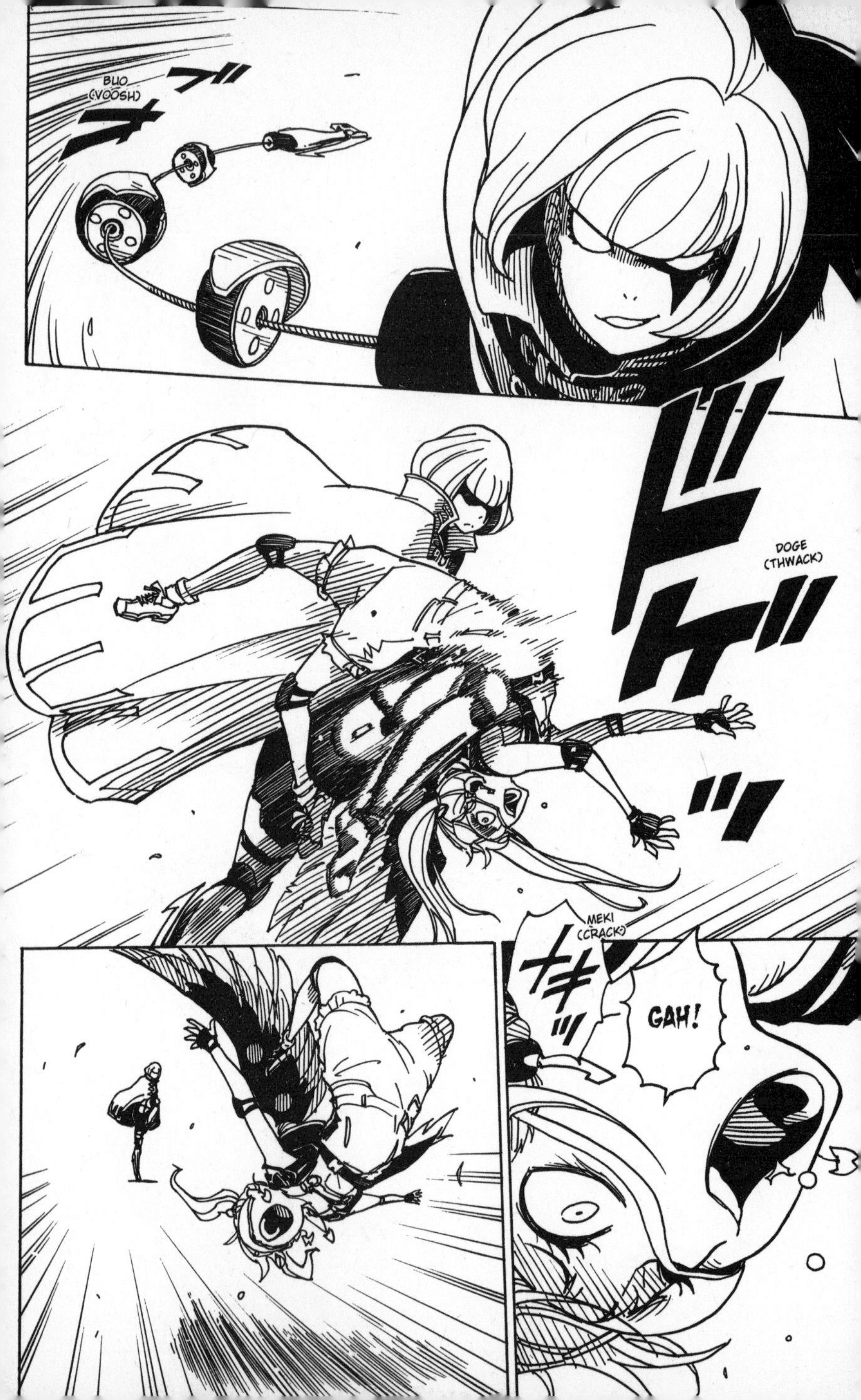
BUO
(VOOSH)
DOGE
(THWACK)
MEKI
(CRACK)
GAH!

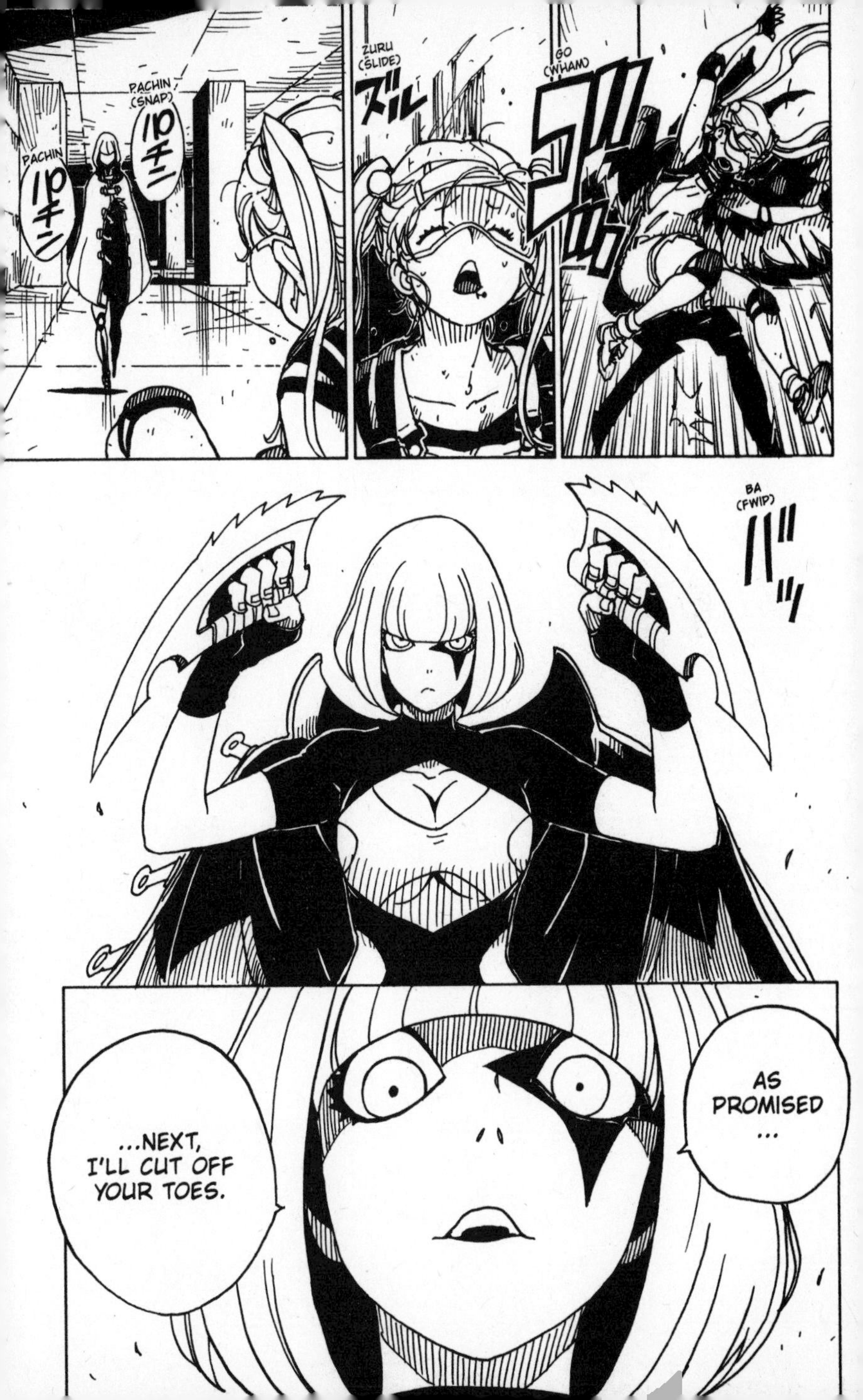
GO (WHAM)
ゴッ
ZURU (SLIDE)
ズル
PACHIN (SNAP)
パチン
PACHIN
パチン
BA (FWIP)
バッ
AS PROMISED...
...NEXT, I'LL CUT OFF YOUR TOES.

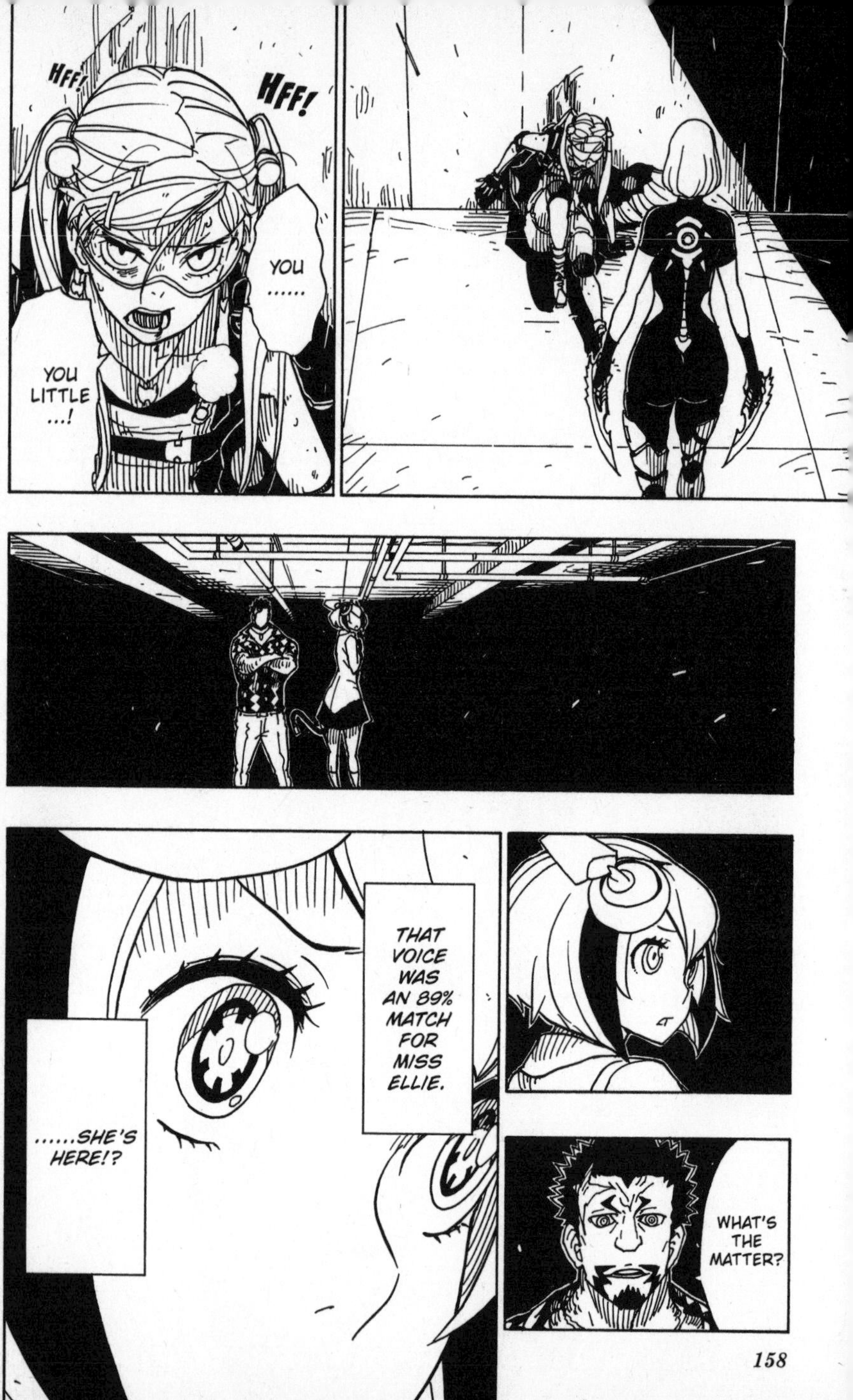
HFF!
HFF!
YOU ......
YOU LITTLE ...!
WHAT'S THE MATTER?
THAT VOICE WAS AN 89% MATCH FOR MISS ELLIE.
......SHE'S HERE!?

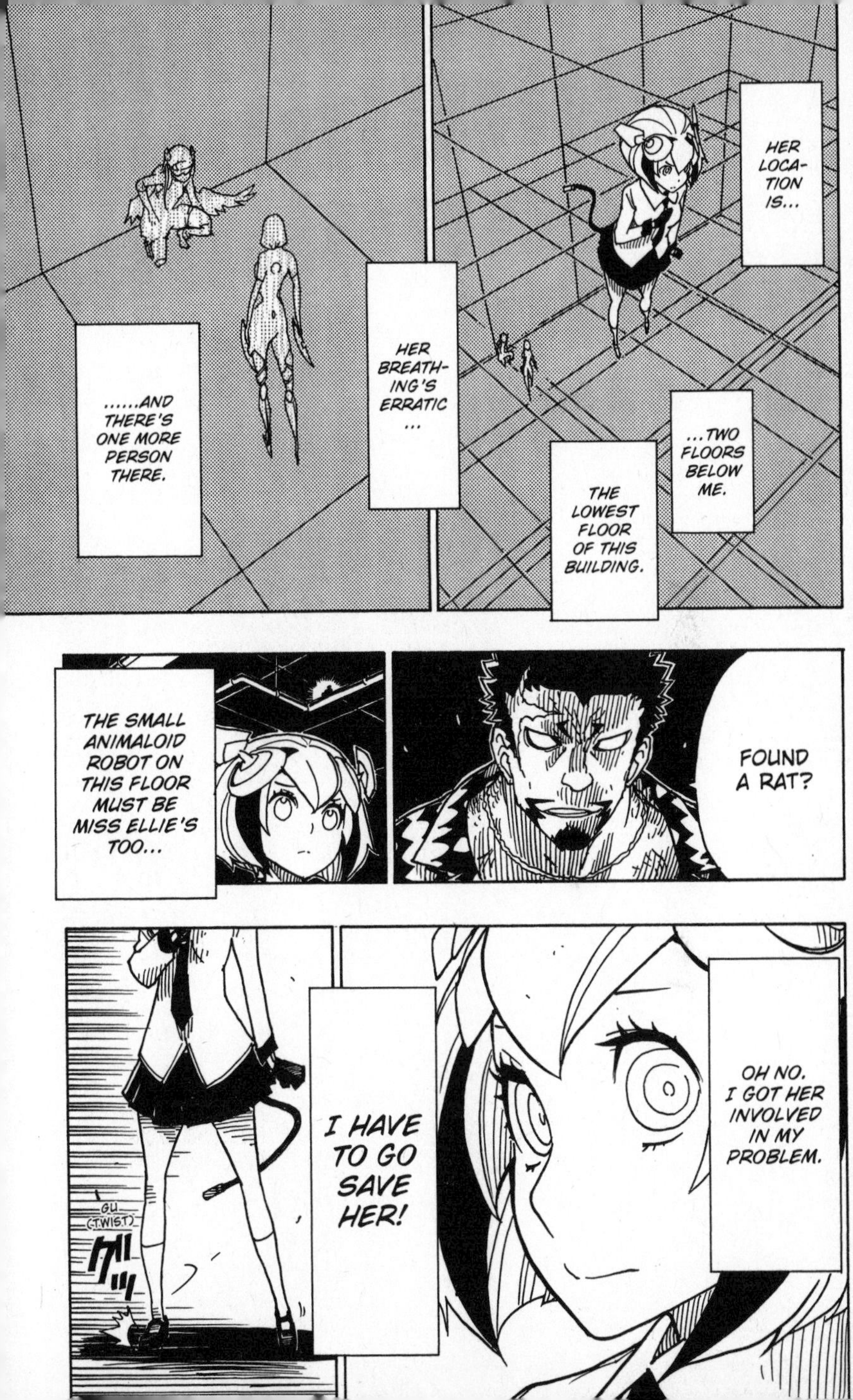
HER LOCATION IS...
...TWO FLOORS BELOW ME.
THE LOWEST FLOOR OF THIS BUILDING.
HER BREATHING'S ERRATIC...
......AND THERE'S ONE MORE PERSON THERE.
FOUND A RAT?
THE SMALL ANIMALOID ROBOT ON THIS FLOOR MUST BE MISS ELLIE'S TOO...
OH NO. I GOT HER INVOLVED IN MY PROBLEM.
I HAVE TO GO SAVE HER!
GU (T.WIST)

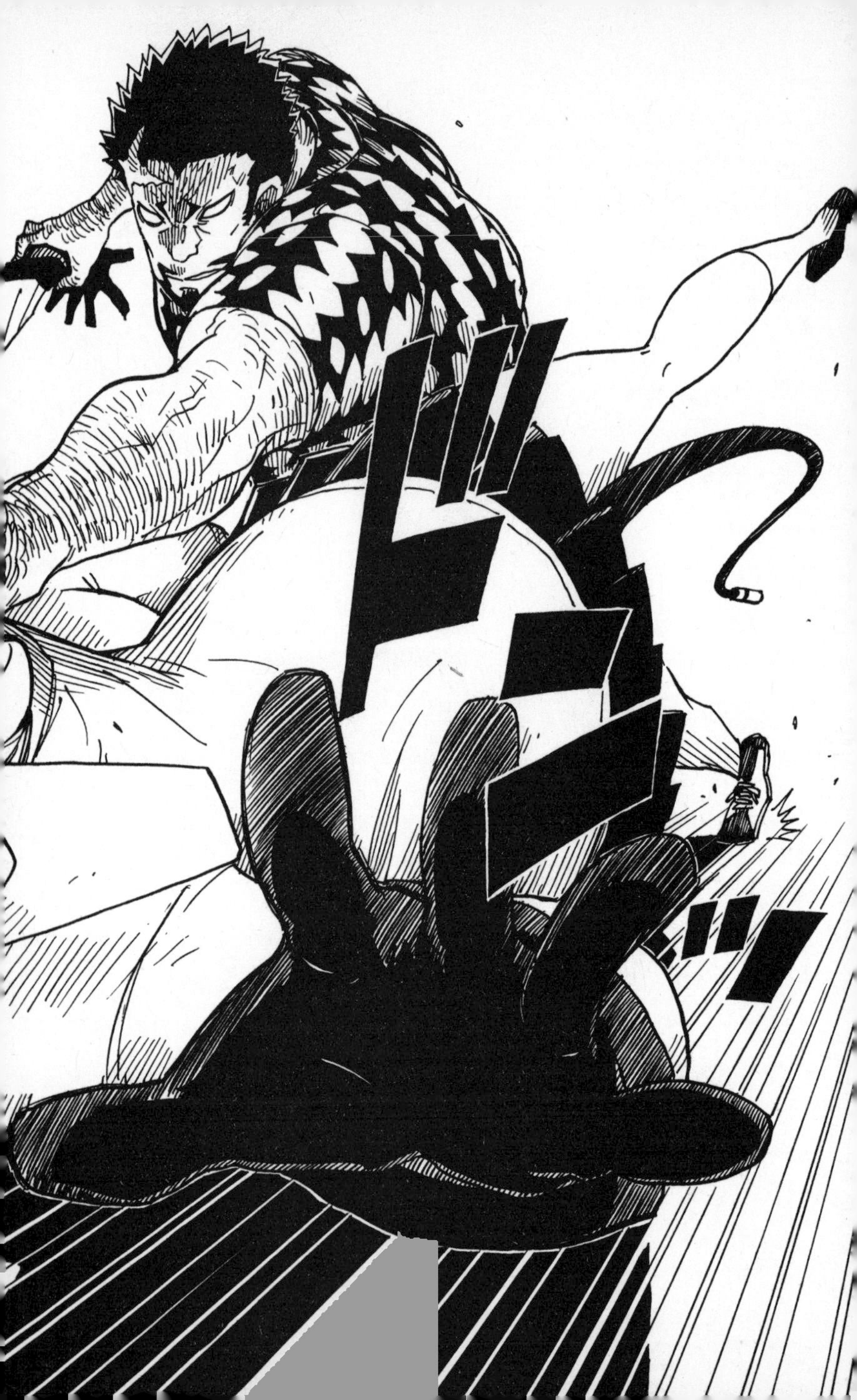

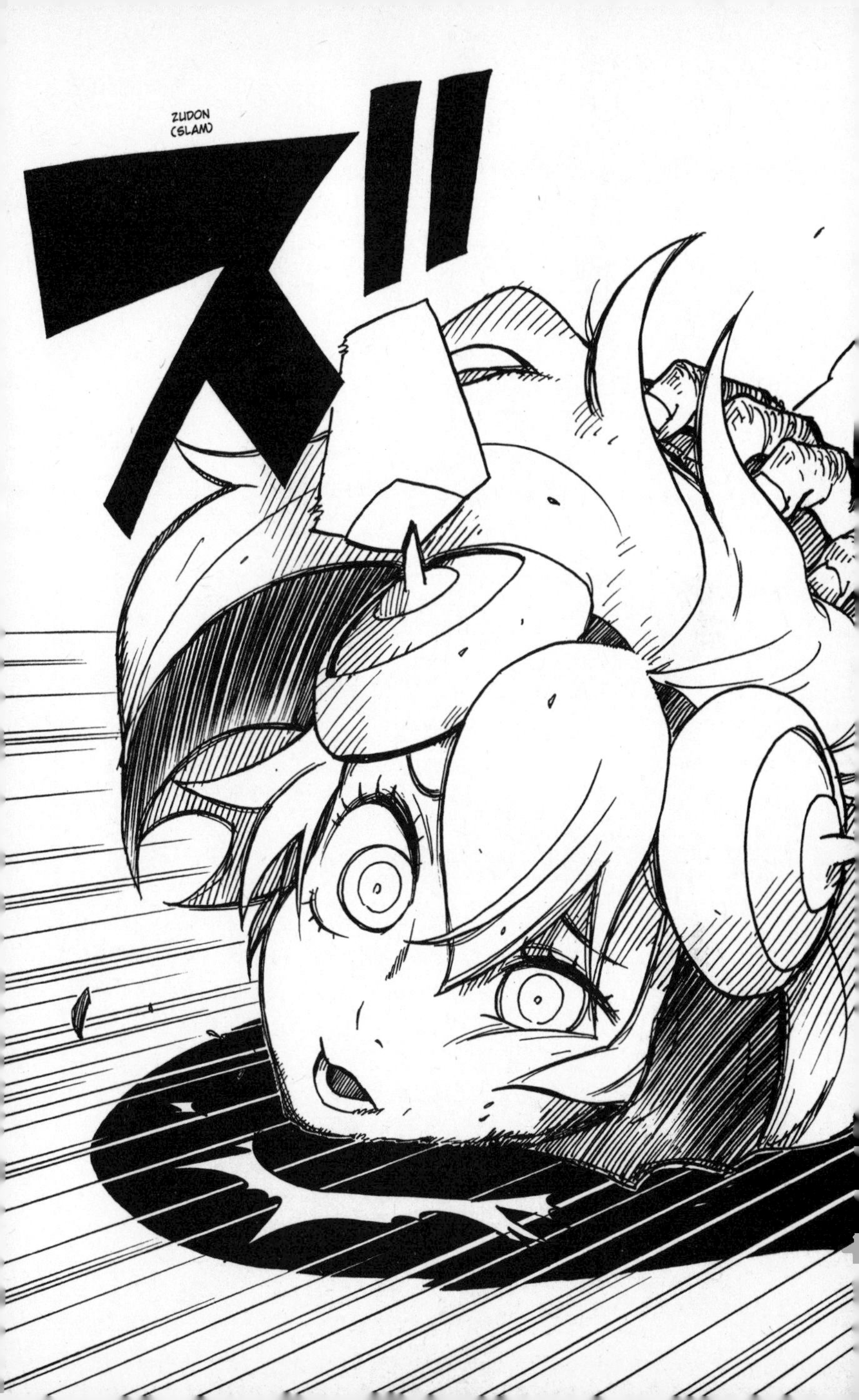
ズ
ZUDON
(SLAM)

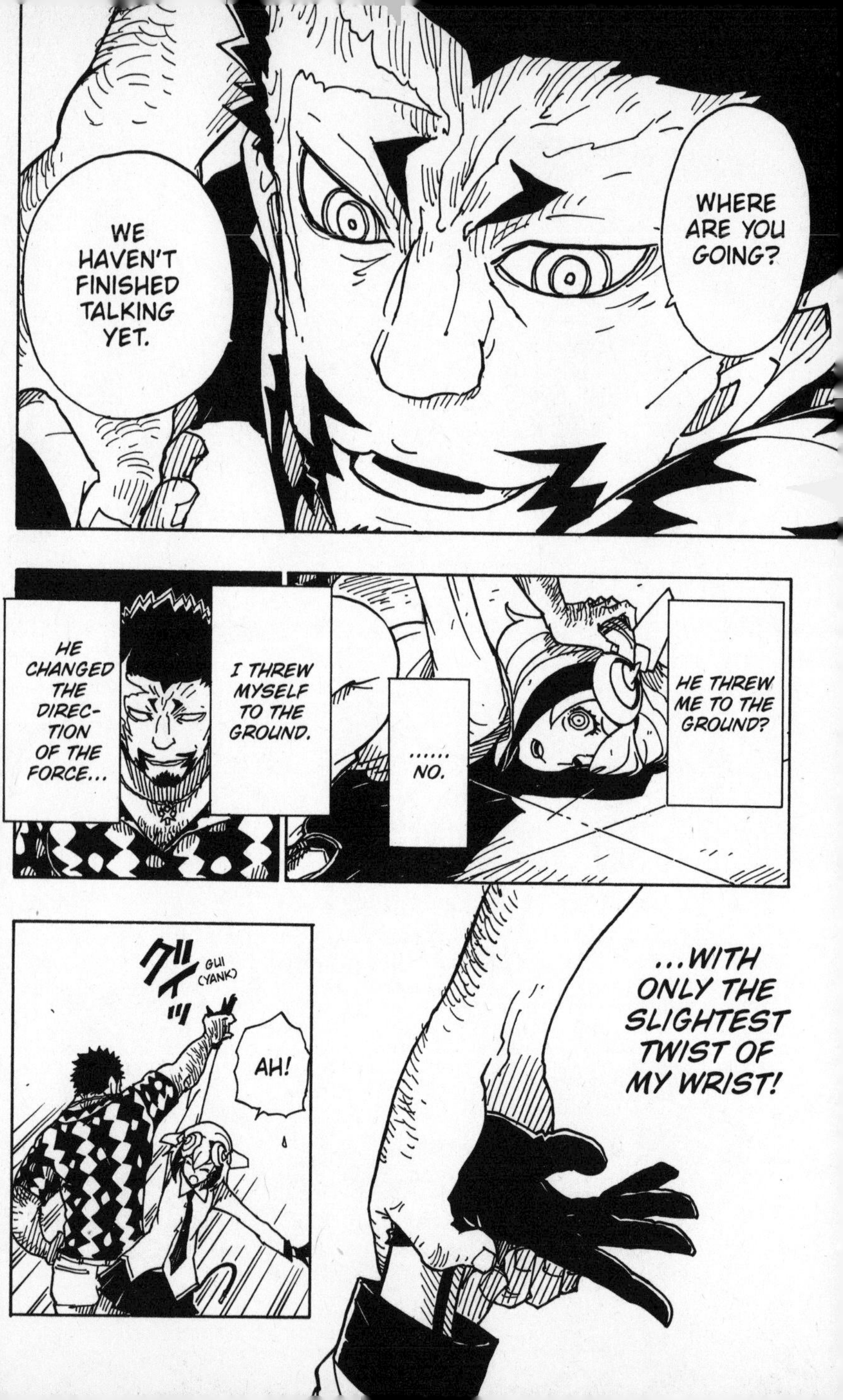
WHERE ARE YOU GOING?
WE HAVEN'T FINISHED TALKING YET.
HE THREW ME TO THE GROUND?
...... NO.
I THREW MYSELF TO THE GROUND.
HE CHANGED THE DIRECTION OF THE FORCE...
...WITH ONLY THE SLIGHTEST TWIST OF MY WRIST!
グイッ
GUI (YANK)
AH!

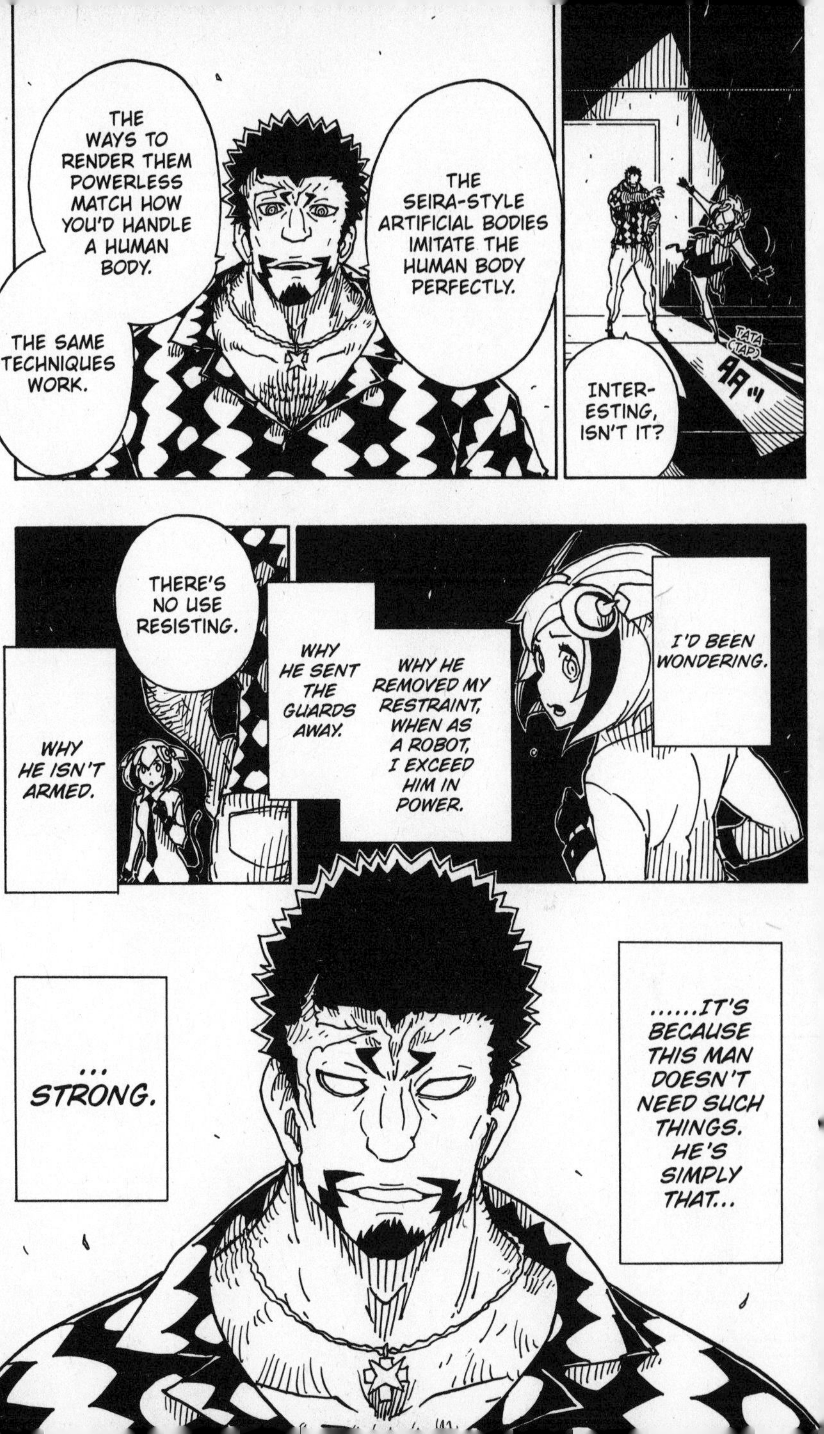
TATA (TAP)
INTER-ESTING, ISN'T IT?
THE SEIRA-STYLE ARTIFICIAL BODIES IMITATE THE HUMAN BODY PERFECTLY.
THE WAYS TO RENDER THEM POWERLESS MATCH HOW YOU'D HANDLE A HUMAN BODY.
THE SAME TECHNIQUES WORK.
I'D BEEN WONDERING.
WHY HE REMOVED MY RESTRAINT, WHEN AS A ROBOT, I EXCEED HIM IN POWER.
WHY HE SENT THE GUARDS AWAY.
THERE'S NO USE RESISTING.
WHY HE ISN'T ARMED.
......IT'S BECAUSE THIS MAN DOESN'T NEED SUCH THINGS. HE'S SIMPLY THAT...
... STRONG.

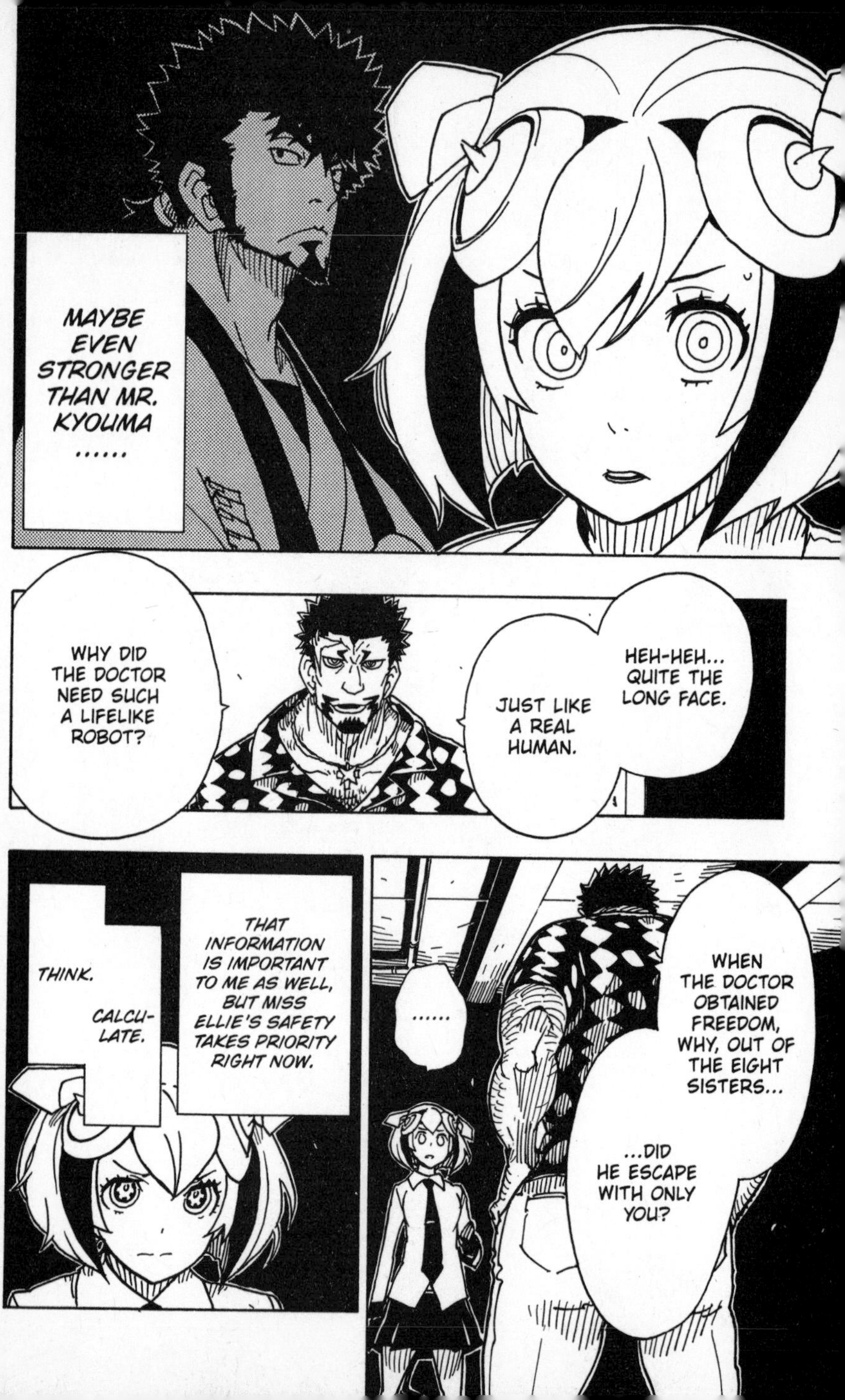
MAYBE EVEN STRONGER THAN MR. KYOUMA ......
HEH-HEH... QUITE THE LONG FACE.
JUST LIKE A REAL HUMAN.
WHY DID THE DOCTOR NEED SUCH A LIFELIKE ROBOT?
WHEN THE DOCTOR OBTAINED FREEDOM, WHY, OUT OF THE EIGHT SISTERS...
......
...DID HE ESCAPE WITH ONLY YOU?
THAT INFORMATION IS IMPORTANT TO ME AS WELL, BUT MISS ELLIE'S SAFETY TAKES PRIORITY RIGHT NOW.
THINK.
CALCU-LATE.

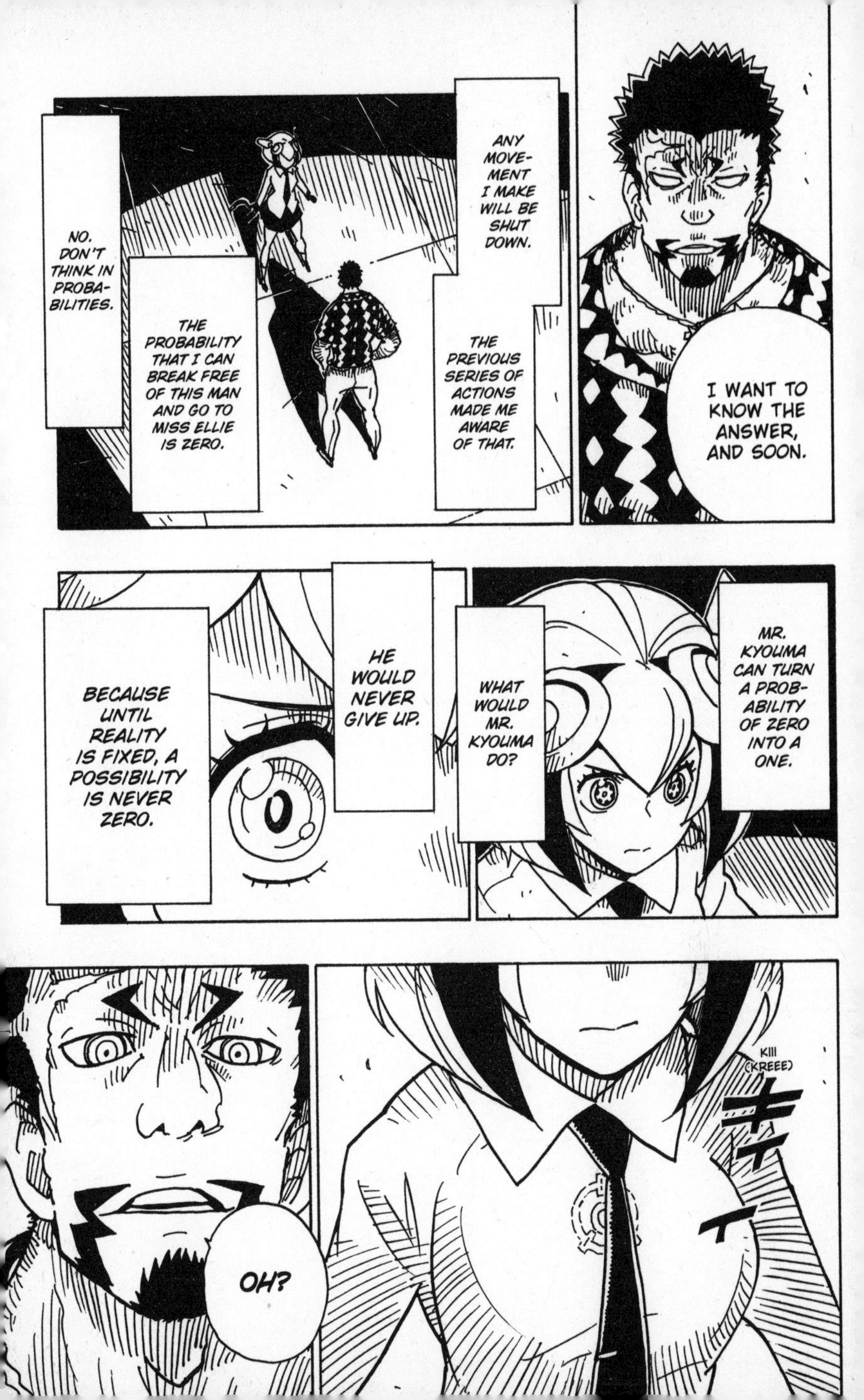
I WANT TO KNOW THE ANSWER, AND SOON.
ANY MOVEMENT I MAKE WILL BE SHUT DOWN.
THE PREVIOUS SERIES OF ACTIONS MADE ME AWARE OF THAT.
THE PROBABILITY THAT I CAN BREAK FREE OF THIS MAN AND GO TO MISS ELLIE IS ZERO.
NO. DON'T THINK IN PROBABILITIES.
MR. KYOUMA CAN TURN A PROBABILITY OF ZERO INTO A ONE.
WHAT WOULD MR. KYOUMA DO?
HE WOULD NEVER GIVE UP.
BECAUSE UNTIL REALITY IS FIXED, A POSSIBILITY IS NEVER ZERO.
KIII (KREEE)
OH?

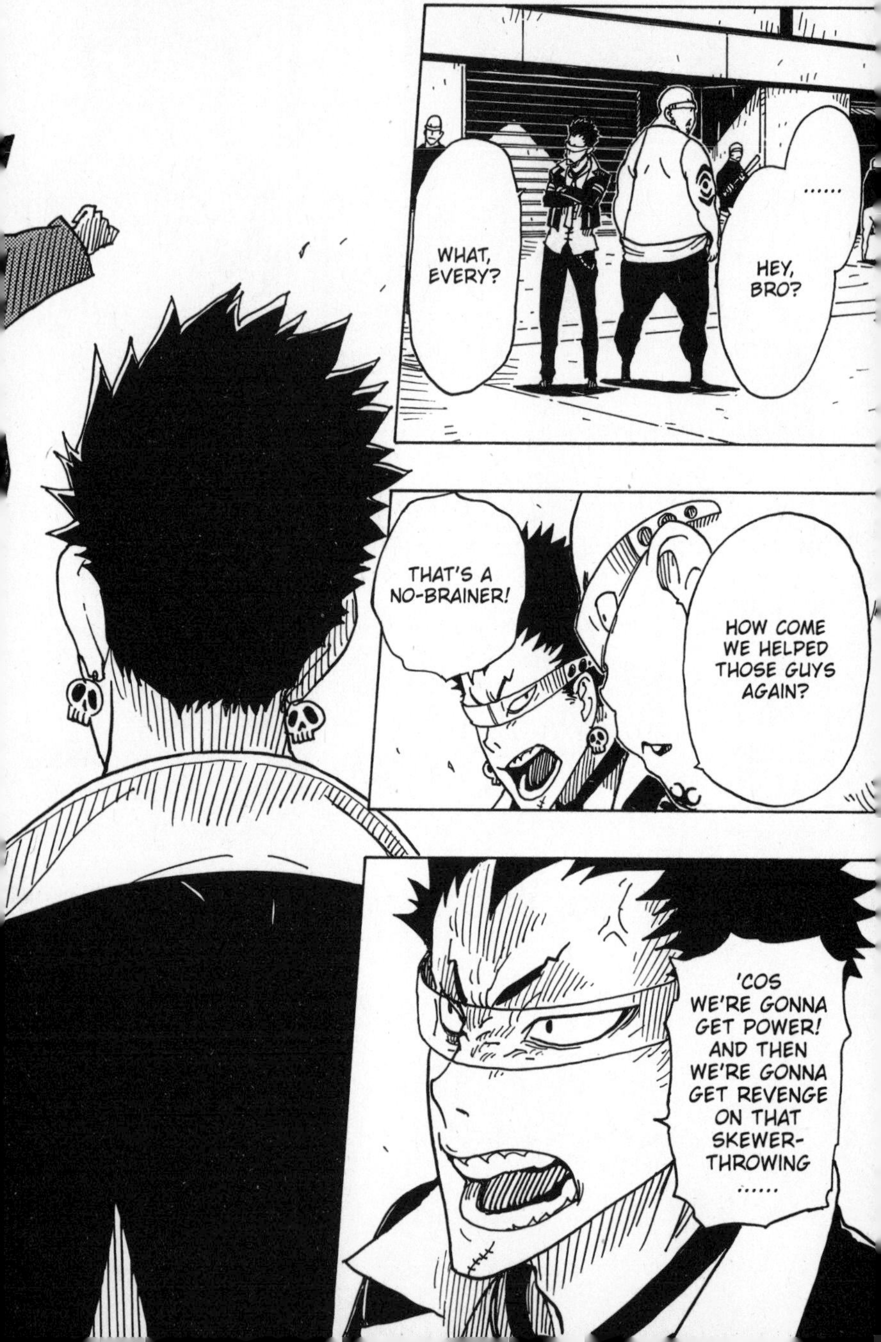
......
HEY, BRO?
WHAT, EVERY?
HOW COME WE HELPED THOSE GUYS AGAIN?
THAT'S A NO-BRAINER!
'COS WE'RE GONNA GET POWER! AND THEN WE'RE GONNA GET REVENGE ON THAT SKEWER-THROWING ......

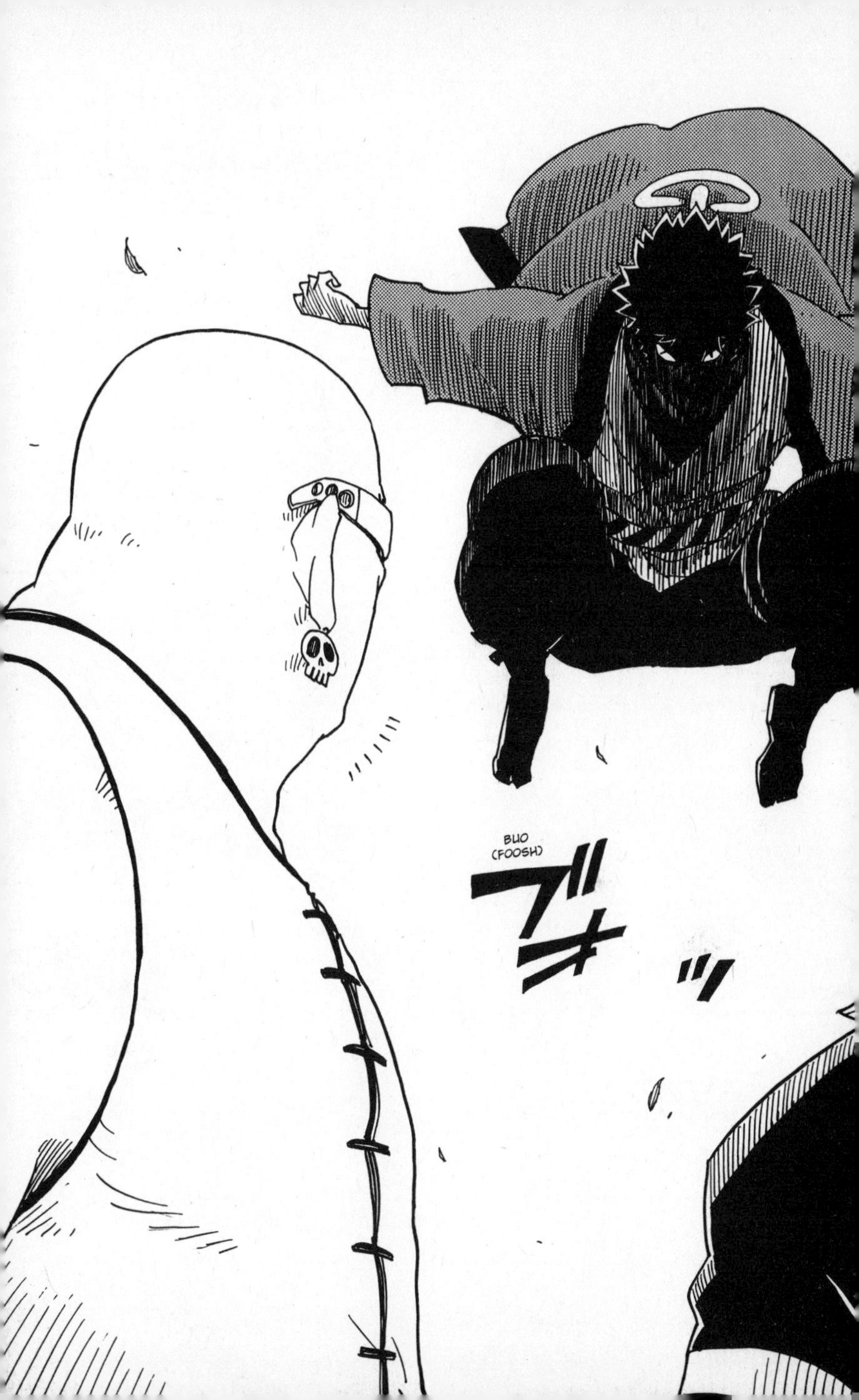
BUO
(FOOSH)
ブオッ

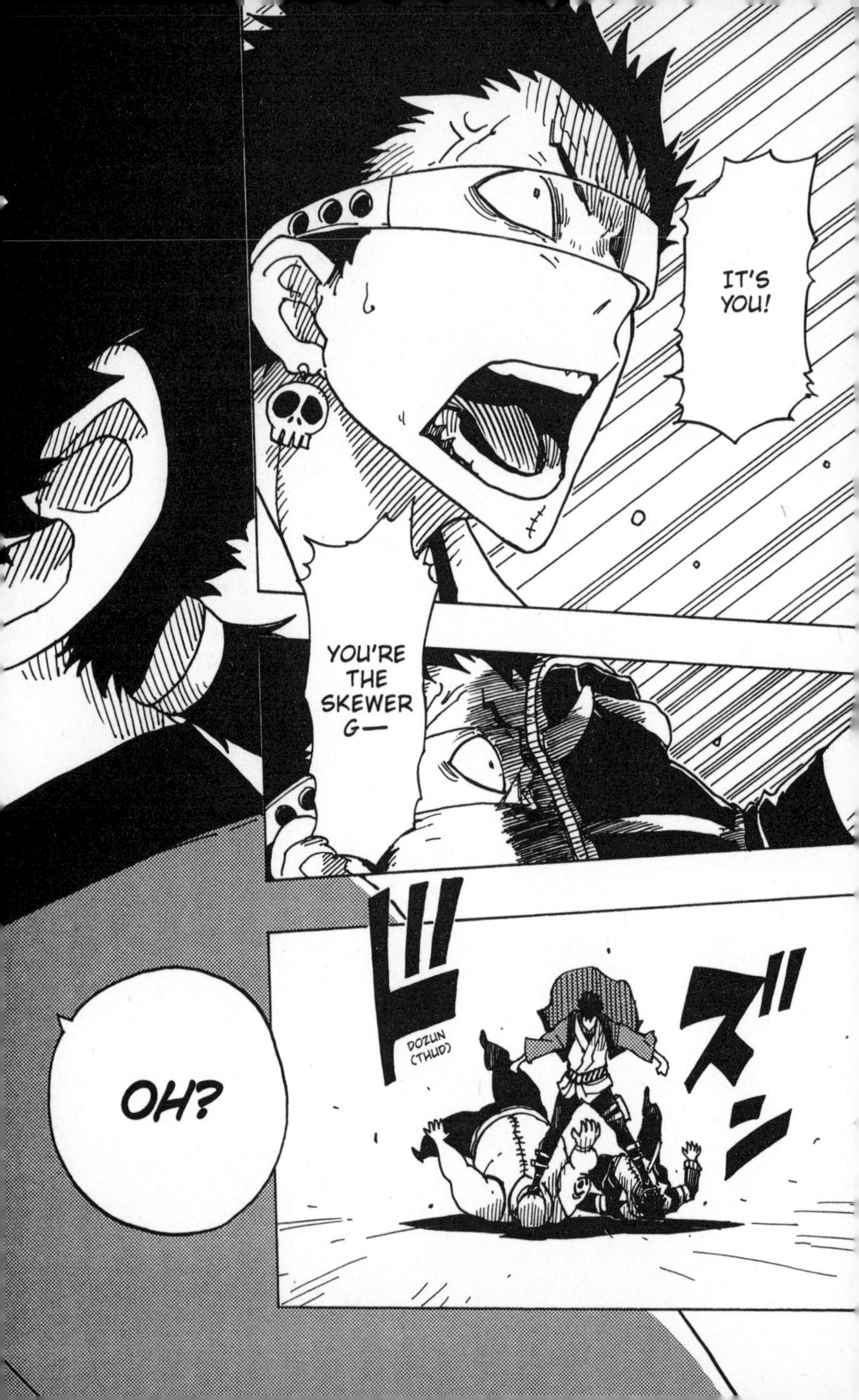
IT'S YOU!
YOU'RE THE SKEWER G—
ドズン
DOZUN (THUD)
OH?

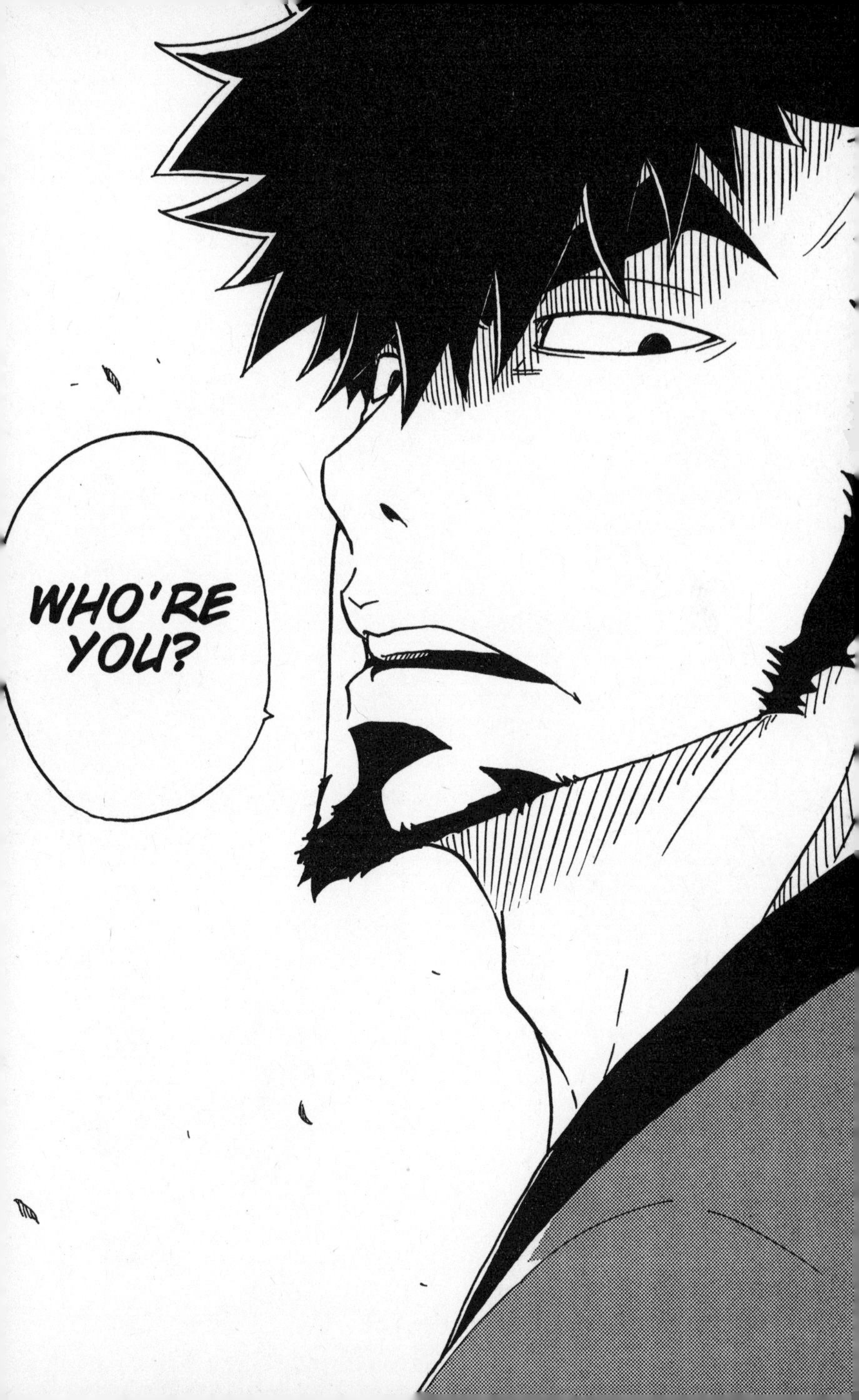
WHO'RE YOU?

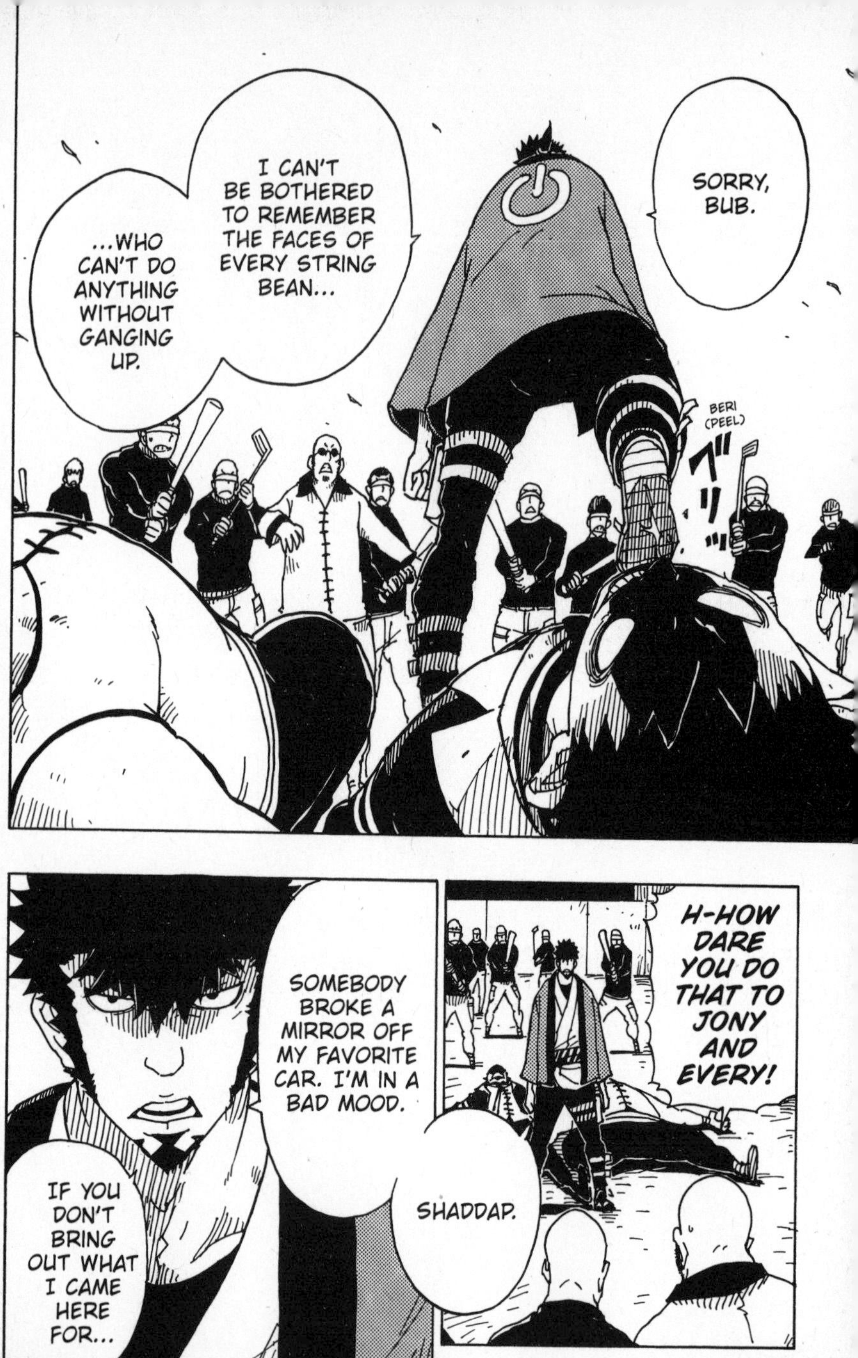
SORRY, BUB.
I CAN'T BE BOTHERED TO REMEMBER THE FACES OF EVERY STRING BEAN...
...WHO CAN'T DO ANYTHING WITHOUT GANGING UP.
BERI (PEEL)
H-HOW DARE YOU DO THAT TO JONY AND EVERY!
SHADDAP.
SOMEBODY BROKE A MIRROR OFF MY FAVORITE CAR. I'M IN A BAD MOOD.
IF YOU DON'T BRING OUT WHAT I CAME HERE FOR...

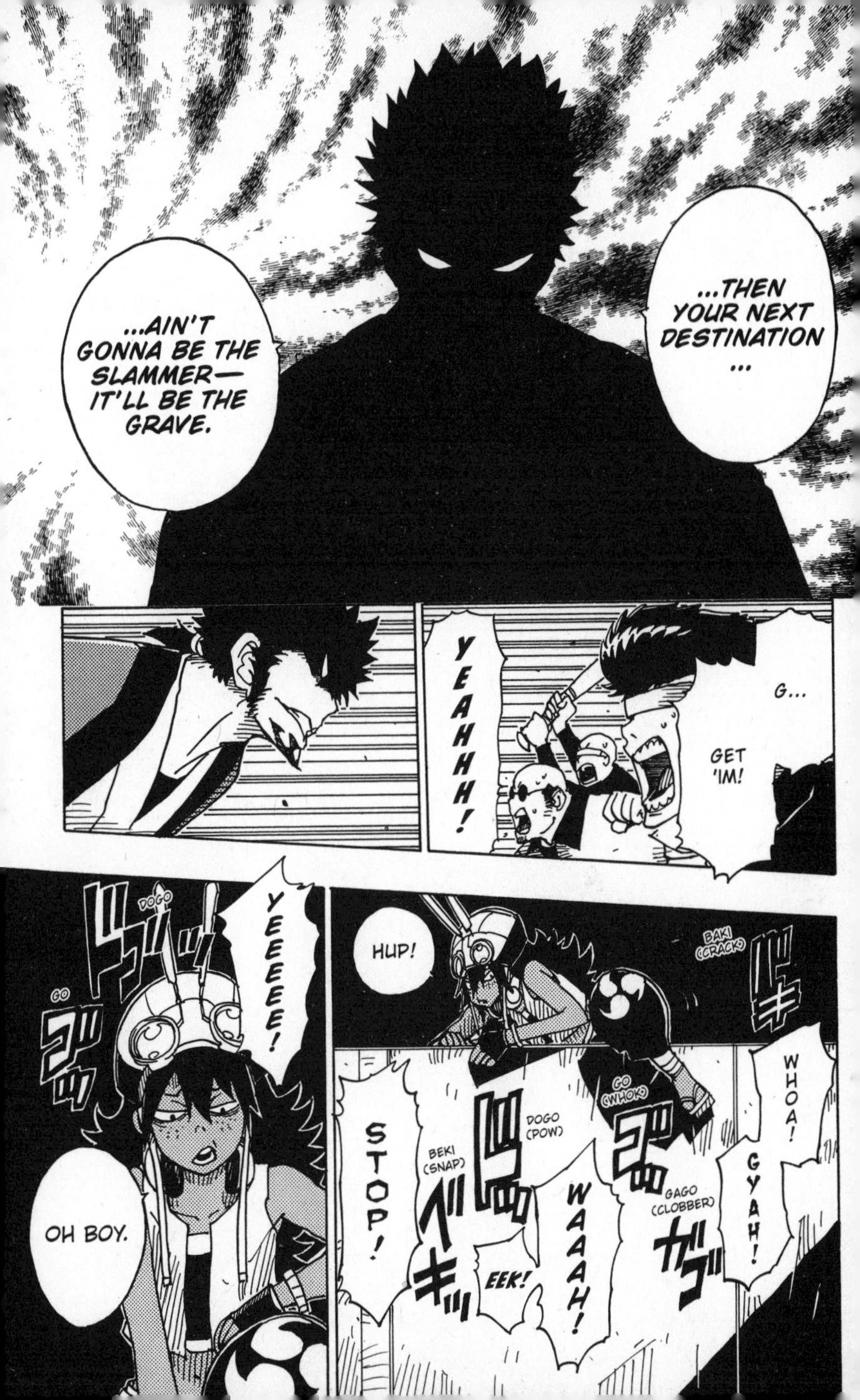
...THEN YOUR NEXT DESTINATION ...
...AIN'T GONNA BE THE SLAMMER— IT'LL BE THE GRAVE.
G...
GET 'IM!
YEAHHHH!
HUP!
BAKI (CRACK)
WHOA!
GYAH!
GO (WHOK)
GAGO (CLOBBER)
WAAAH!
DOGO (POW)
BEKI (SNAP)
STOP!
EEK!
YEEEEEE!
DOGO
GO
OH BOY.

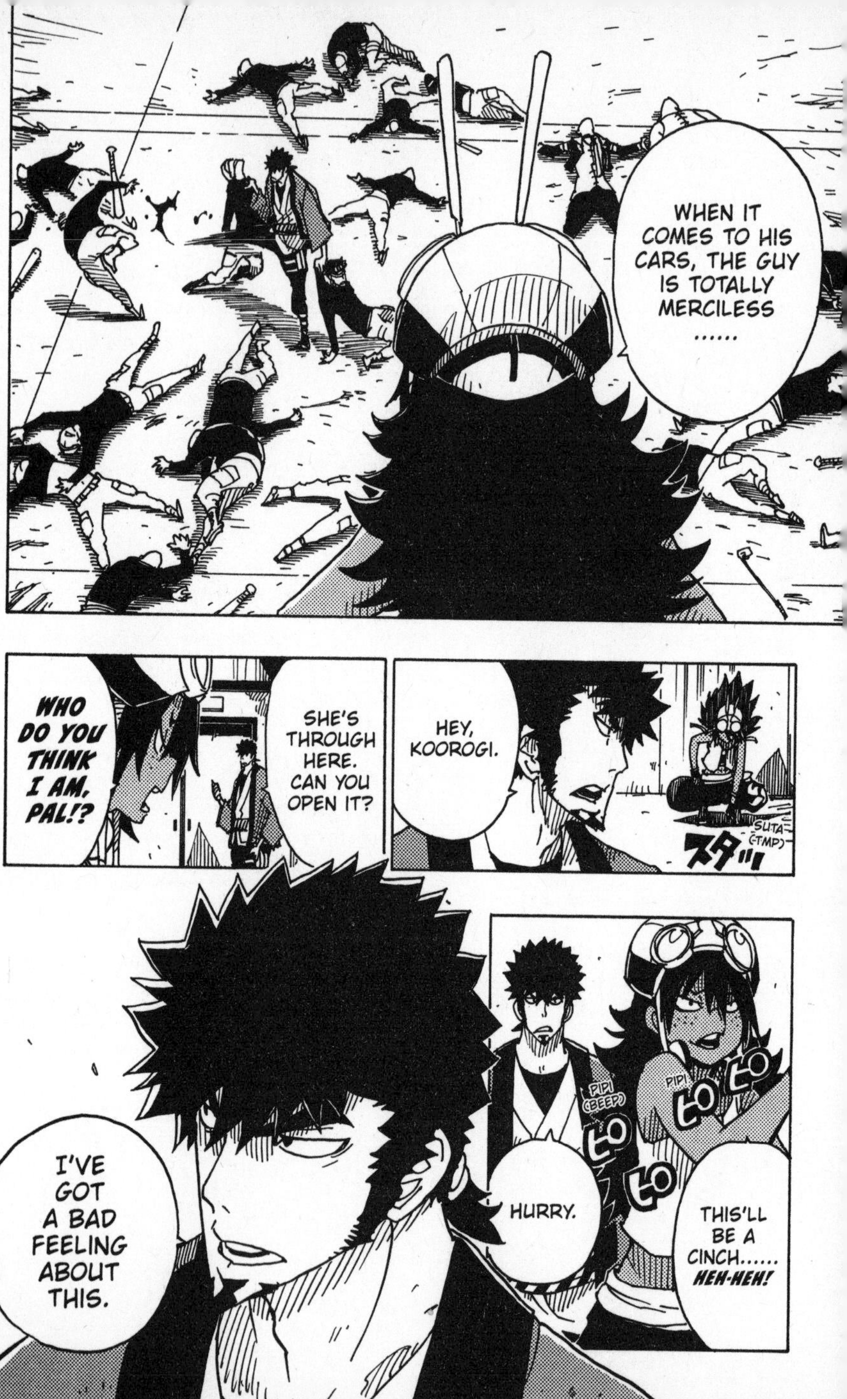
WHEN IT COMES TO HIS CARS, THE GUY IS TOTALLY MERCILESS ......
SUTA (TMP)
HEY, KOOROGI.
SHE'S THROUGH HERE. CAN YOU OPEN IT?
WHO DO YOU THINK I AM, PAL!?
PIPI
PIPI (BEEP)
THIS'LL BE A CINCH...... HEH-HEH!
HURRY.
I'VE GOT A BAD FEELING ABOUT THIS.

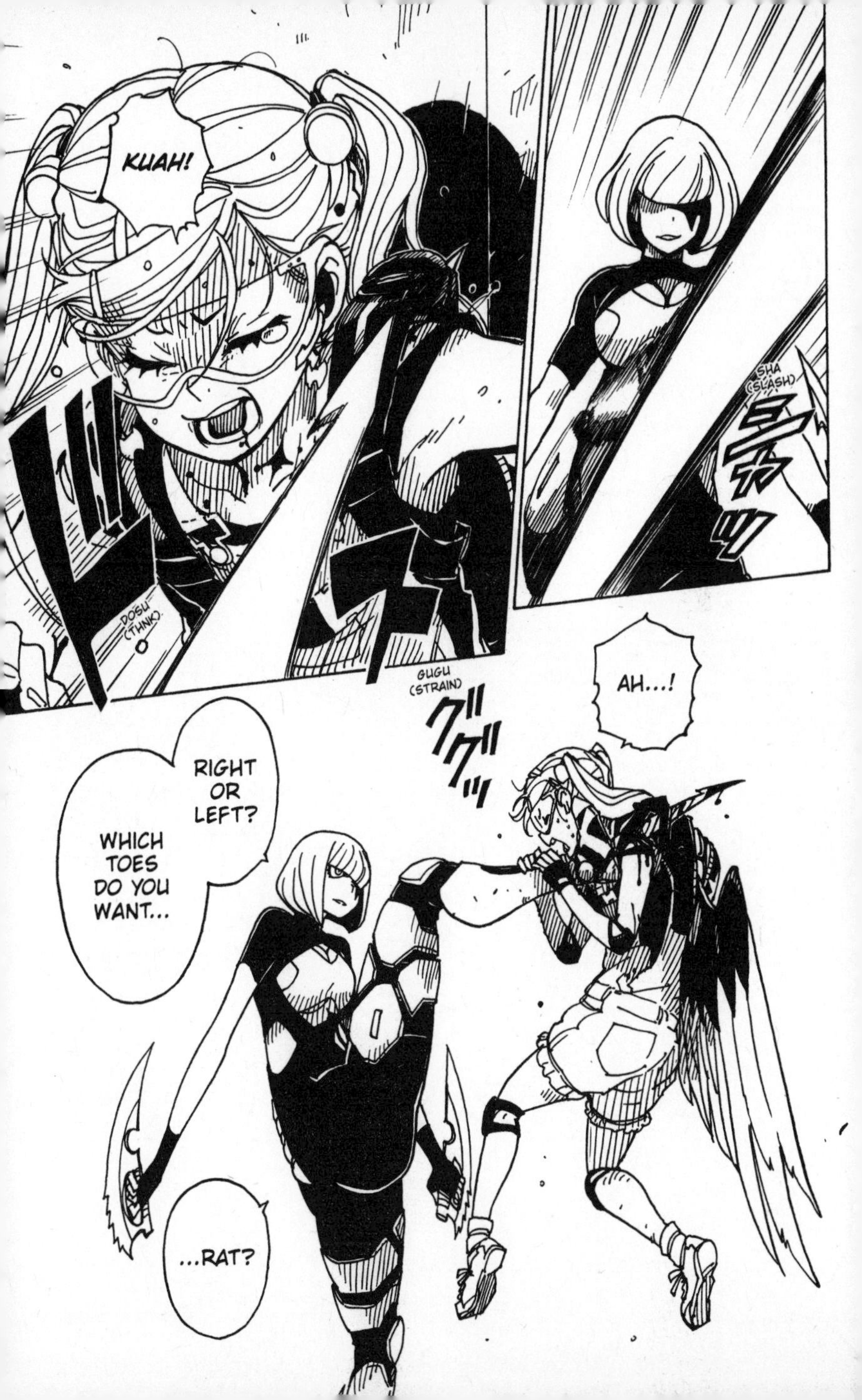

SHA (SLASH)
KUAH!
DOSU (THNK)
AH...!
GUGU (STRAIN)
WHICH TOES DO YOU WANT... RIGHT OR LEFT?
...RAT?

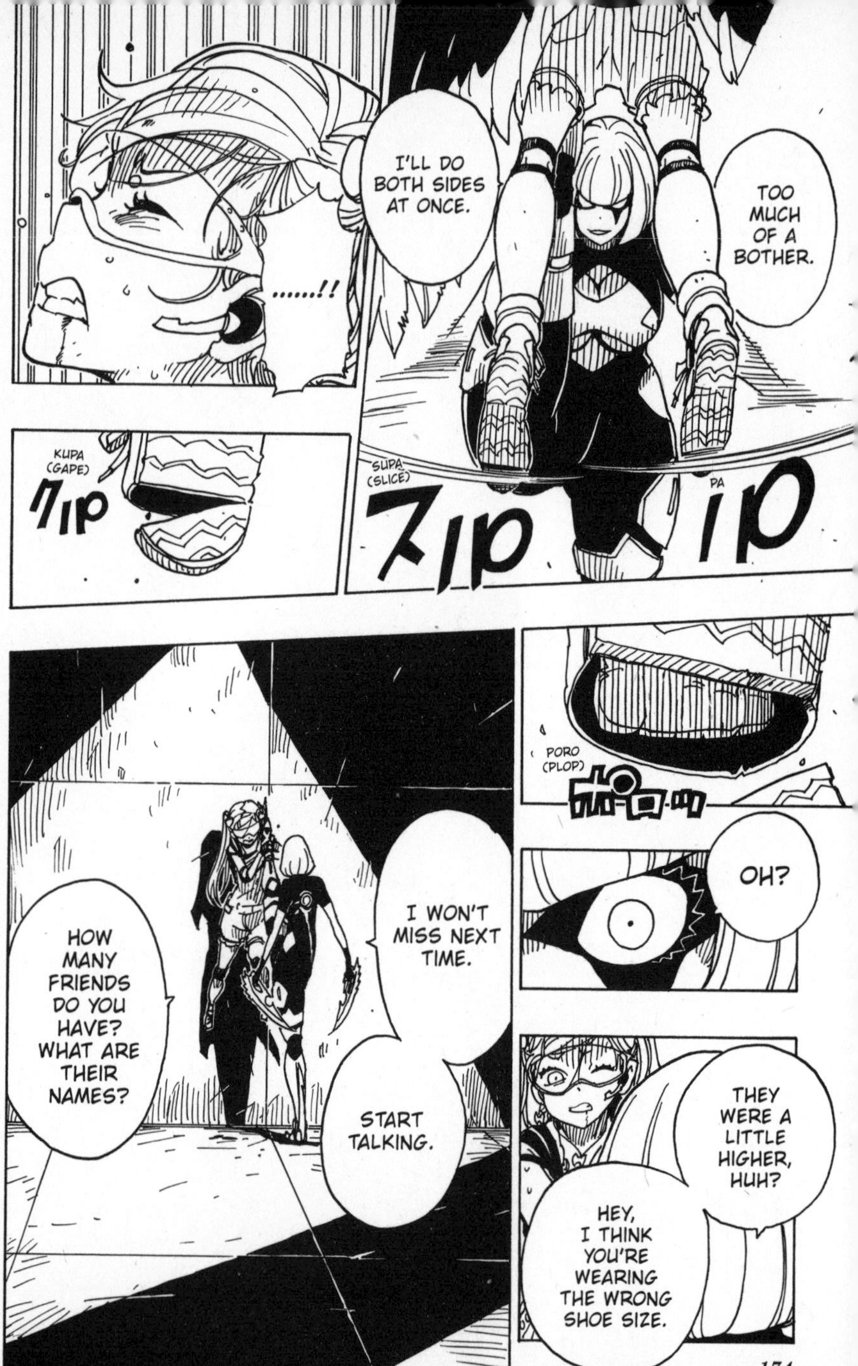
TOO MUCH OF A BOTHER.
I'LL DO BOTH SIDES AT ONCE.
......!!
PA
SUPA (SLICE)
KUPA (GAPE)
PORO (PLOP)
OH?
THEY WERE A LITTLE HIGHER, HUH?
HEY, I THINK YOU'RE WEARING THE WRONG SHOE SIZE.
I WON'T MISS NEXT TIME.
START TALKING.
HOW MANY FRIENDS DO YOU HAVE? WHAT ARE THEIR NAMES?

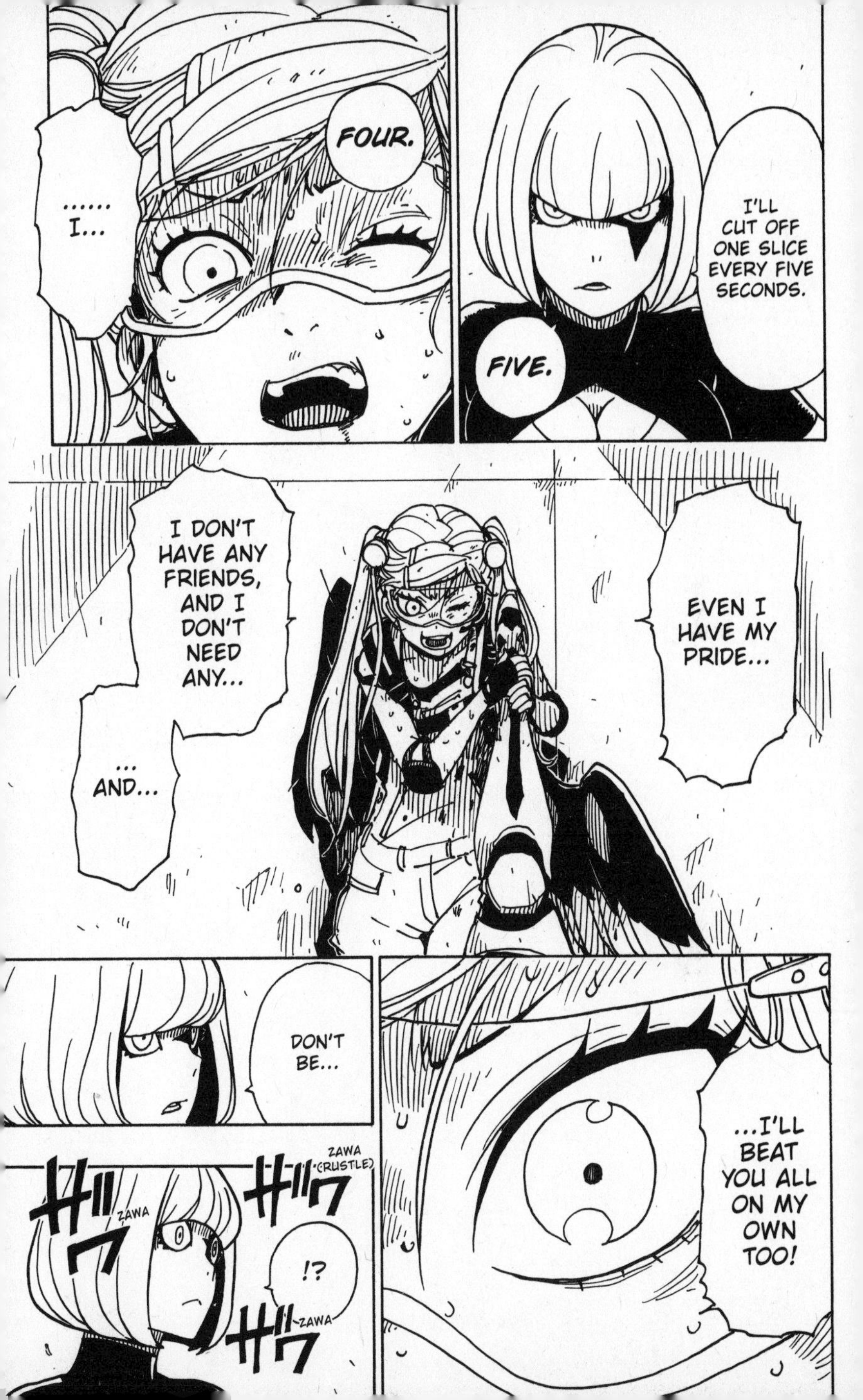

I'LL CUT OFF ONE SLICE EVERY FIVE SECONDS.
FIVE.
FOUR.
...... I...
EVEN I HAVE MY PRIDE...
I DON'T HAVE ANY FRIENDS, AND I DON'T NEED ANY...
... AND...
...I'LL BEAT YOU ALL ON MY OWN TOO!
DON'T BE...
ザワ
ZAWA (RUSTLE)
ザワ
ZAWA
!?
ザワ
ZAWA

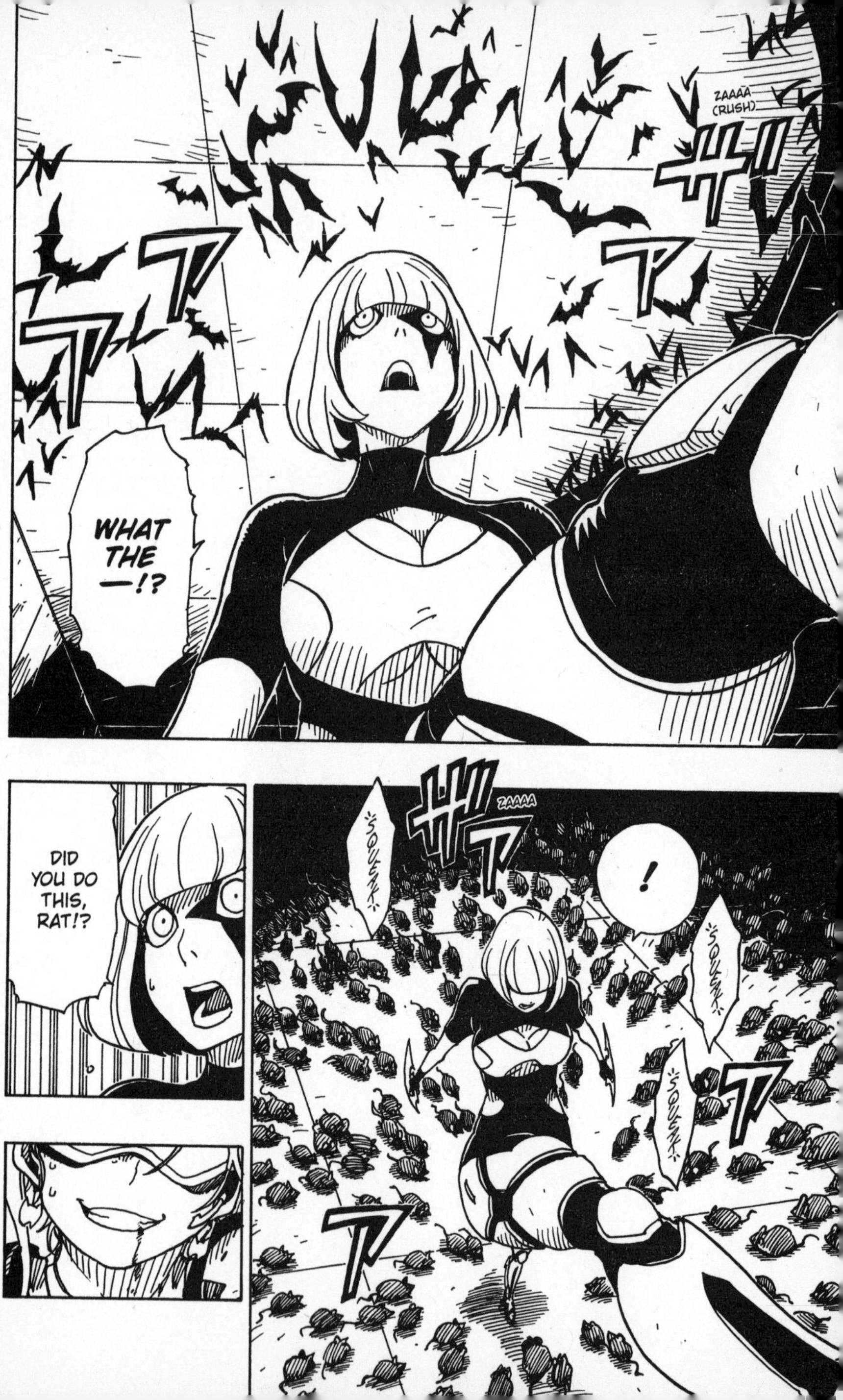
ZAAAA (RUSH)
WHAT THE—!?
ZAAAA
!
SQUEAK
SQUEAK
SQUEAK
DID YOU DO THIS, RAT!?

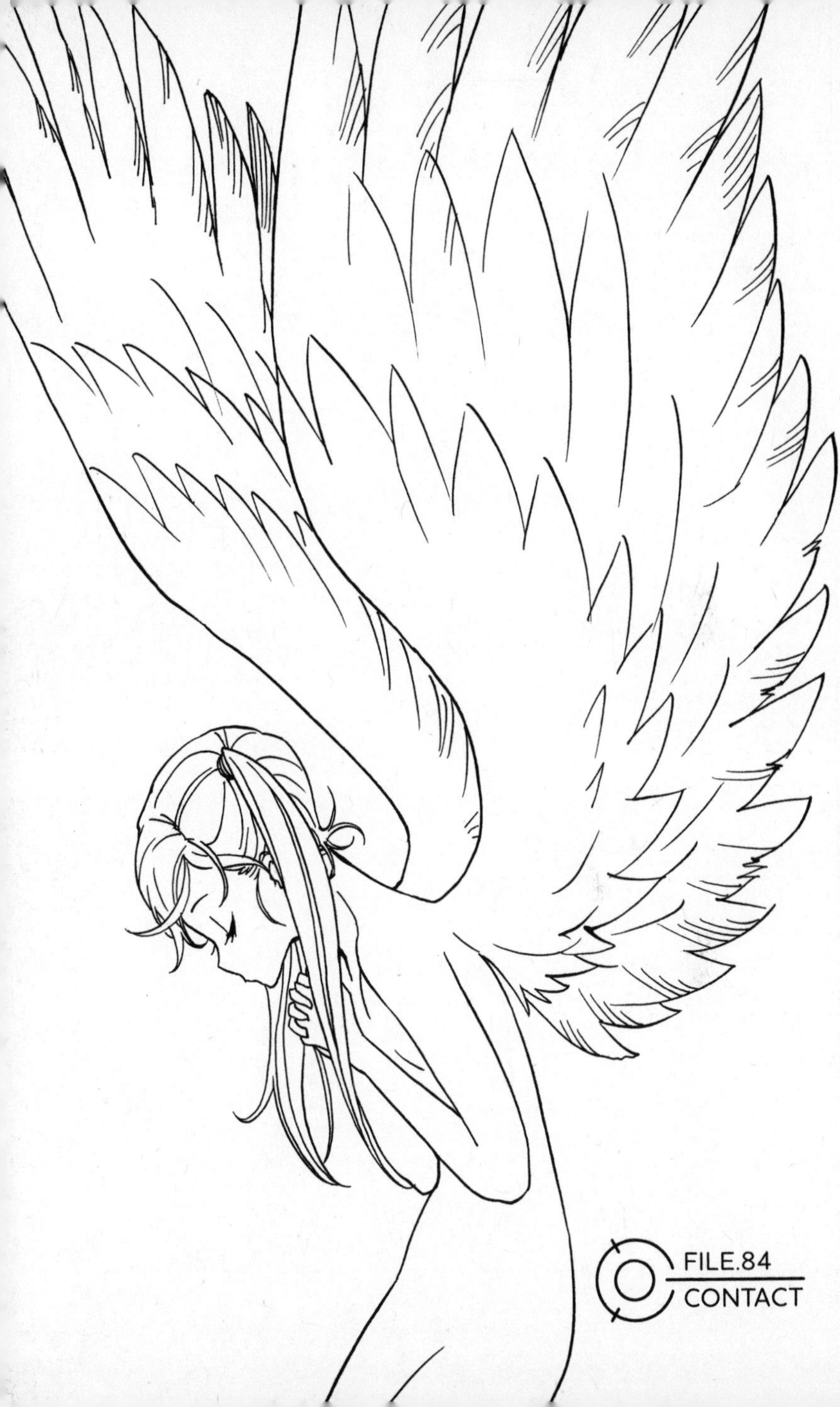

FILE.84
CONTACT

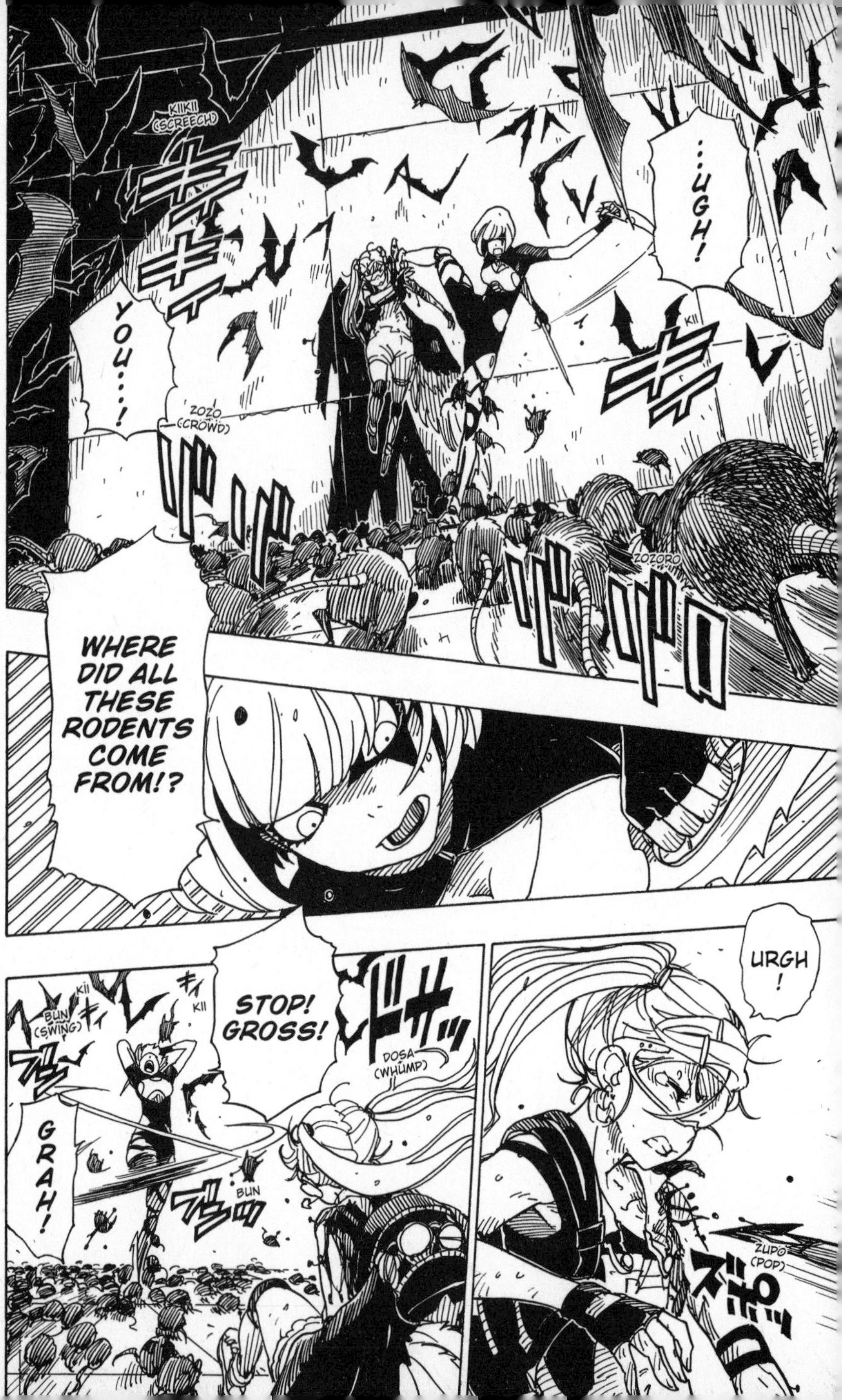
...UGH!
KIIKII (SCREECH)
KII
YOU...!
ZOZO (CROWD)
ZOZORO
WHERE DID ALL THESE RODENTS COME FROM!?
URGH!
ZUPO (POP)
STOP! GROSS!
DOSA (WHUMP)
KII
KII
BUN (SWING)
GRAH!
BUN

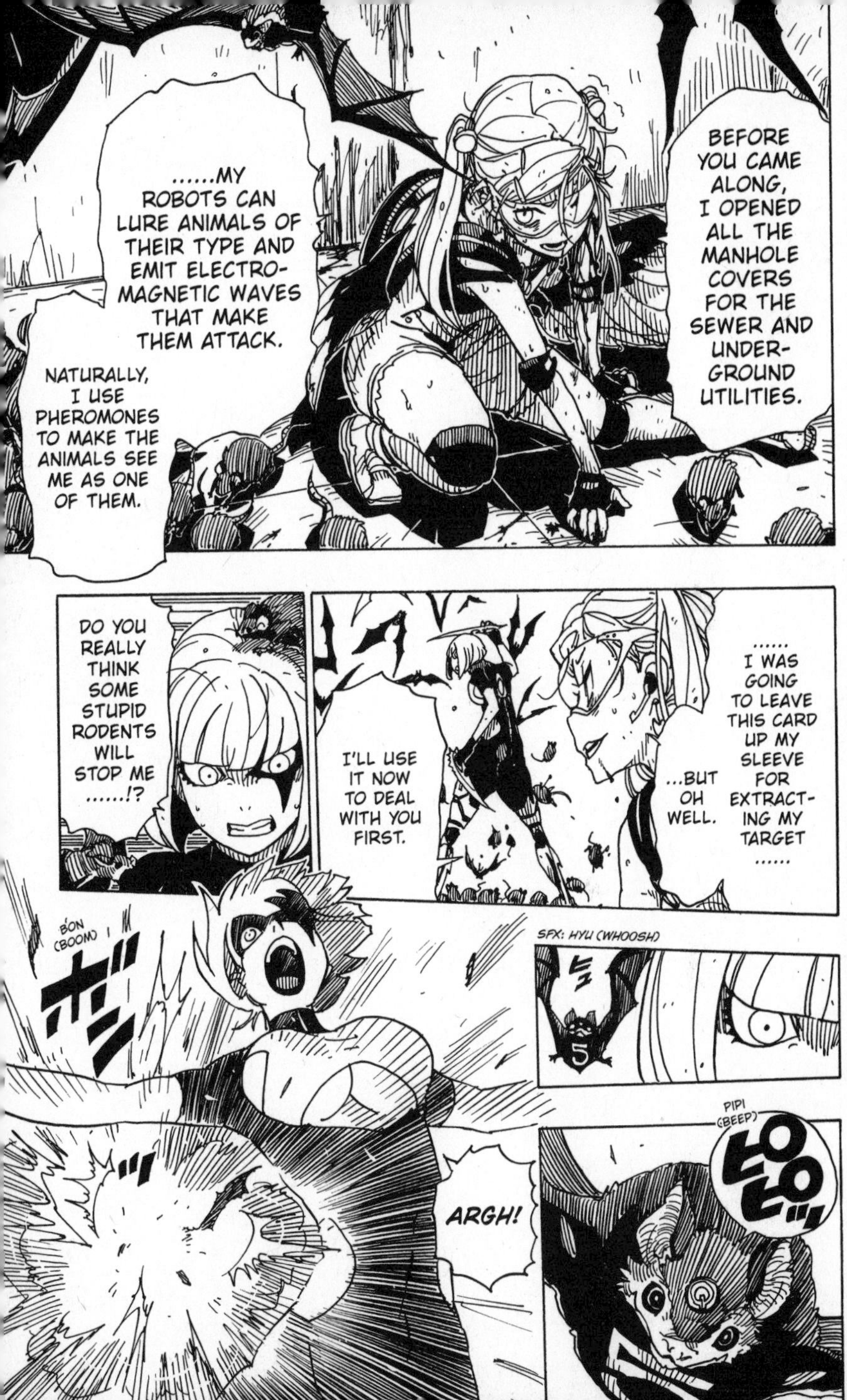
BEFORE YOU CAME ALONG, I OPENED ALL THE MANHOLE COVERS FOR THE SEWER AND UNDER-GROUND UTILITIES.
......MY ROBOTS CAN LURE ANIMALS OF THEIR TYPE AND EMIT ELECTRO-MAGNETIC WAVES THAT MAKE THEM ATTACK.
NATURALLY, I USE PHEROMONES TO MAKE THE ANIMALS SEE ME AS ONE OF THEM.
...... I WAS GOING TO LEAVE THIS CARD UP MY SLEEVE FOR EXTRACT-ING MY TARGET ......
...BUT OH WELL.
I'LL USE IT NOW TO DEAL WITH YOU FIRST.
DO YOU REALLY THINK SOME STUPID RODENTS WILL STOP ME ......!?
SFX: HYU (WHOOSH)
PIPI (BEEP)
BON (BOOM)
ARGH!

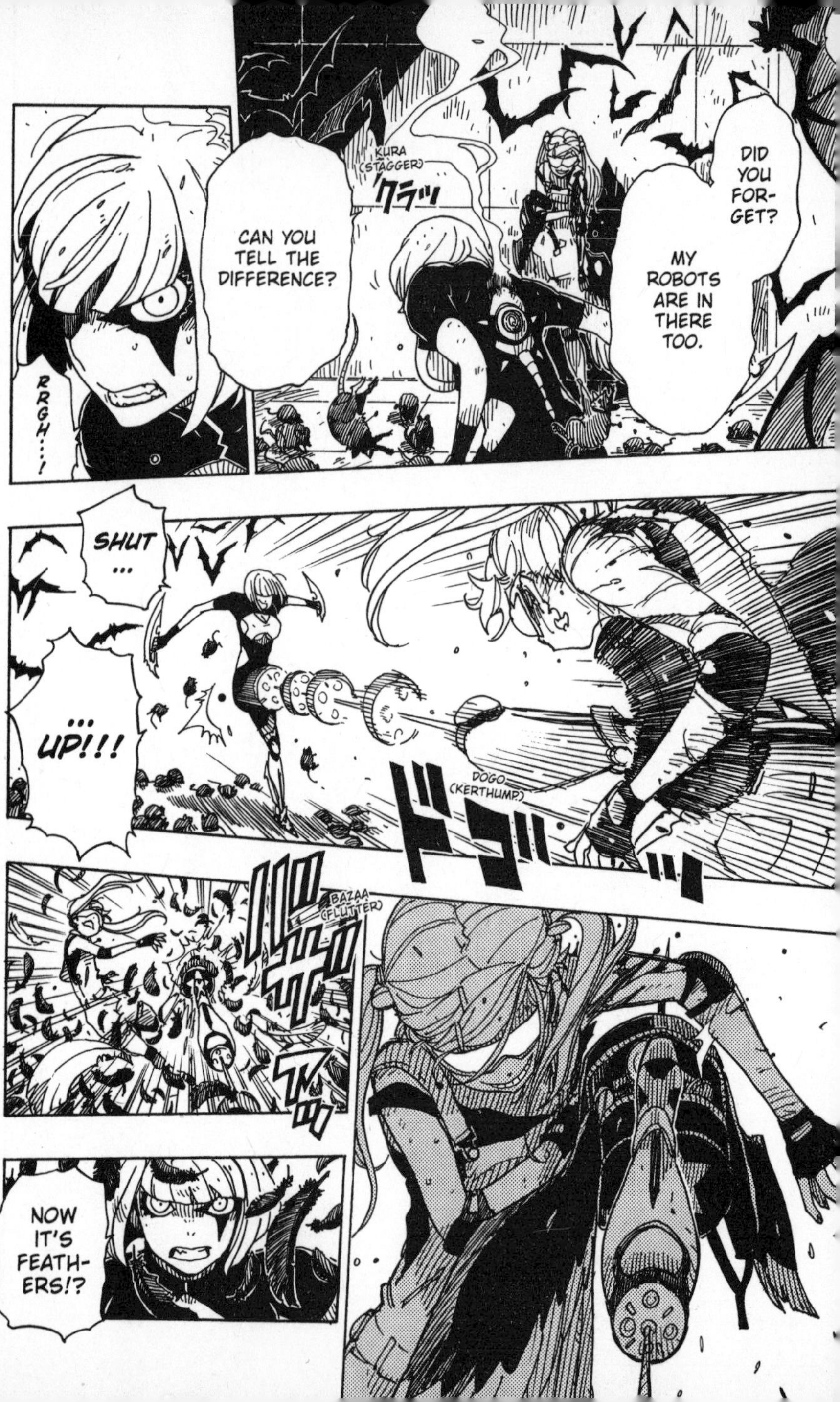
DID YOU FOR-GET?
MY ROBOTS ARE IN THERE TOO.
KURA (STAGGER)
CAN YOU TELL THE DIFFERENCE?
RRGH...!
SHUT...
...UP!!!
DOGO (KERTHUMP)
BAZAA (FLUTTER)
NOW IT'S FEATH-ERS!?

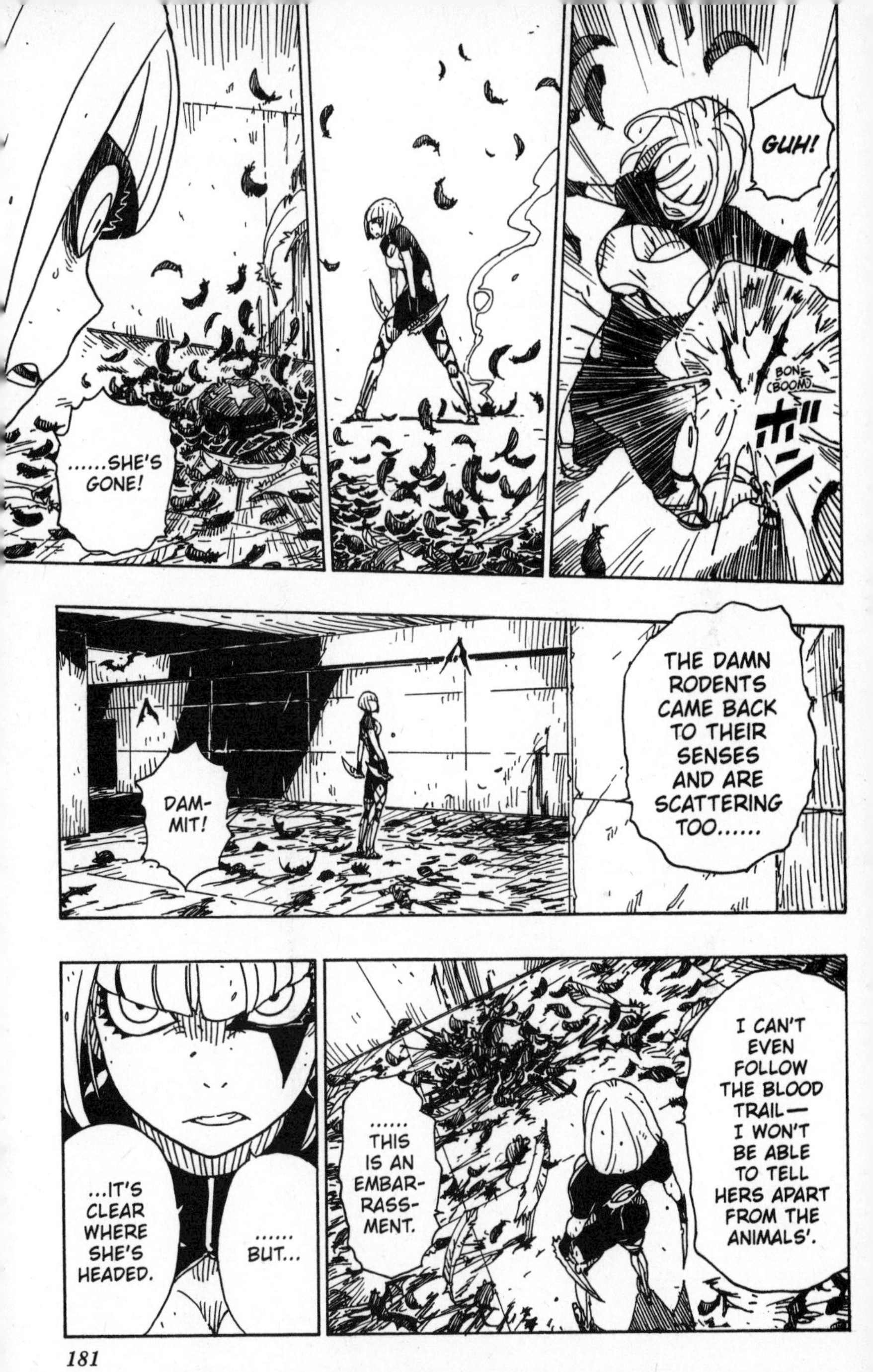
GUH!
BON (BOOM)
ボン
......SHE'S GONE!
THE DAMN RODENTS CAME BACK TO THEIR SENSES AND ARE SCATTERING TOO......
DAM-MIT!
I CAN'T EVEN FOLLOW THE BLOOD TRAIL— I WON'T BE ABLE TO TELL HERS APART FROM THE ANIMALS'.
...... THIS IS AN EMBAR-RASS-MENT.
...... BUT...
...IT'S CLEAR WHERE SHE'S HEADED.

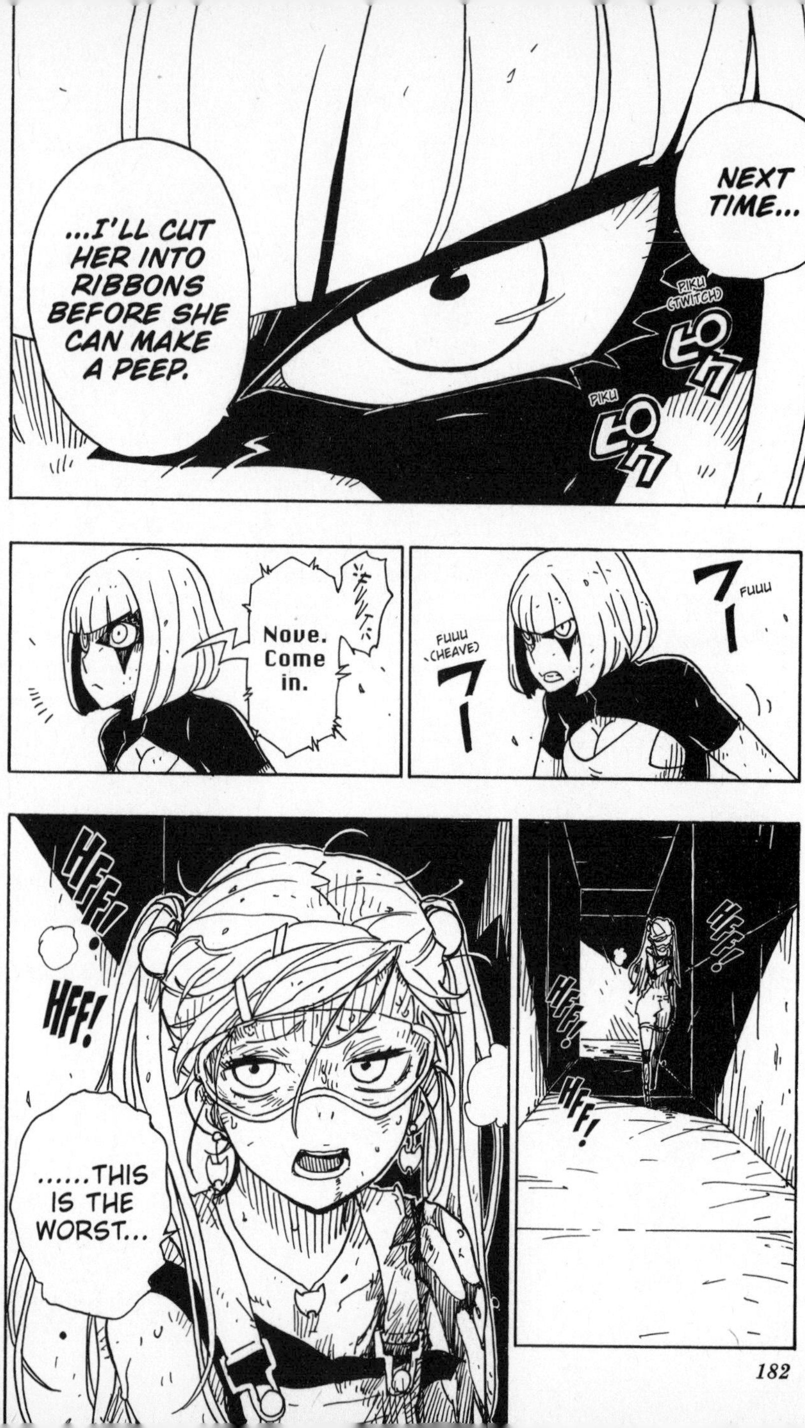
NEXT TIME...
PIKU (TWITCH)
PIKU
...I'LL CUT HER INTO RIBBONS BEFORE SHE CAN MAKE A PEEP.
FUUU
FUUU (HEAVE)
Nove. Come in.
HFF!
HFF!
HFF!
HFF!
HFF!
......THIS IS THE WORST...

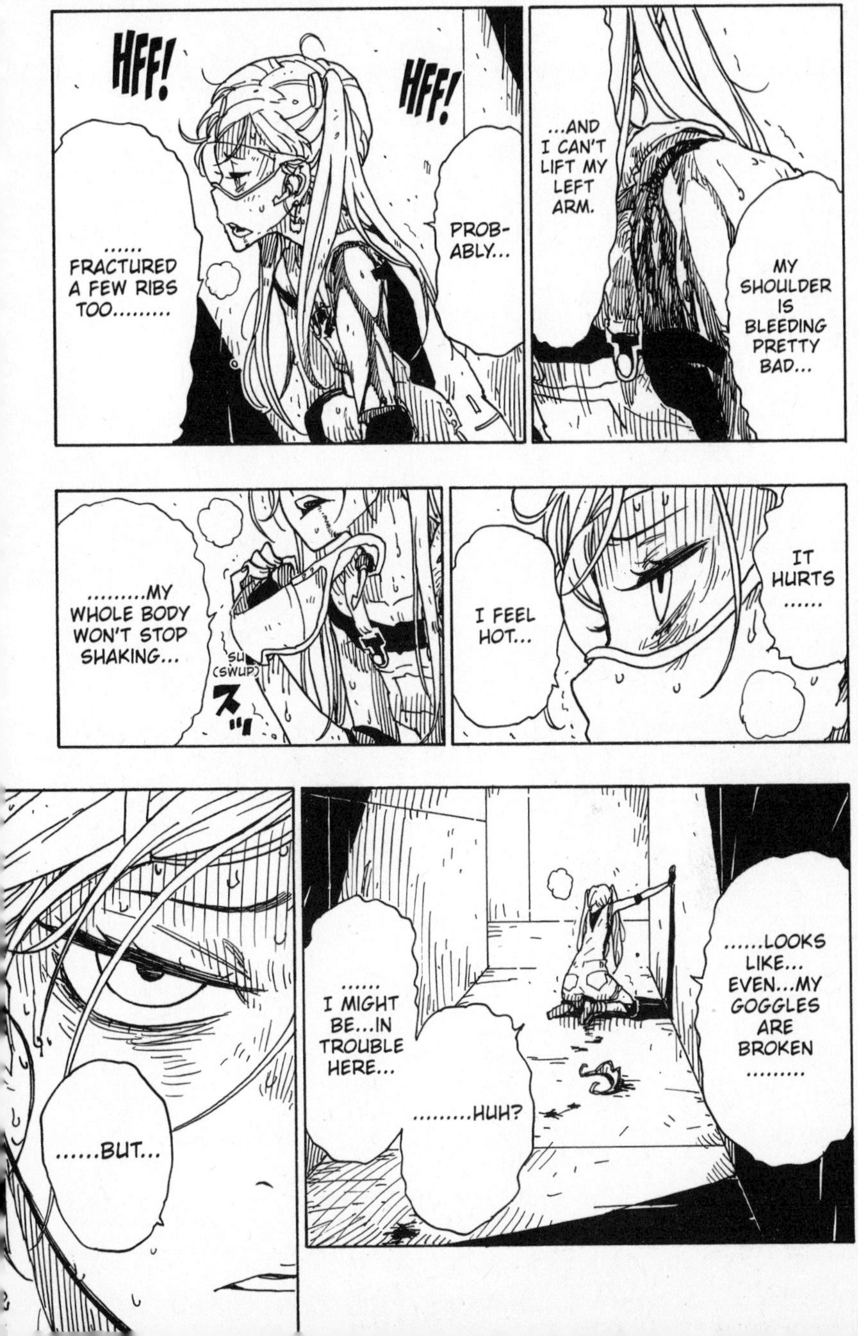
MY SHOULDER IS BLEEDING PRETTY BAD...
...AND I CAN'T LIFT MY LEFT ARM.
HFF!
HFF!
PROB-ABLY...
......FRACTURED A FEW RIBS TOO.........
IT HURTS......
I FEEL HOT...
.........MY WHOLE BODY WON'T STOP SHAKING...
SU (SWUP)
ス"
......LOOKS LIKE... EVEN...MY GOGGLES ARE BROKEN.........
......I MIGHT BE...IN TROUBLE HERE...
.........HUH?
......BUT...

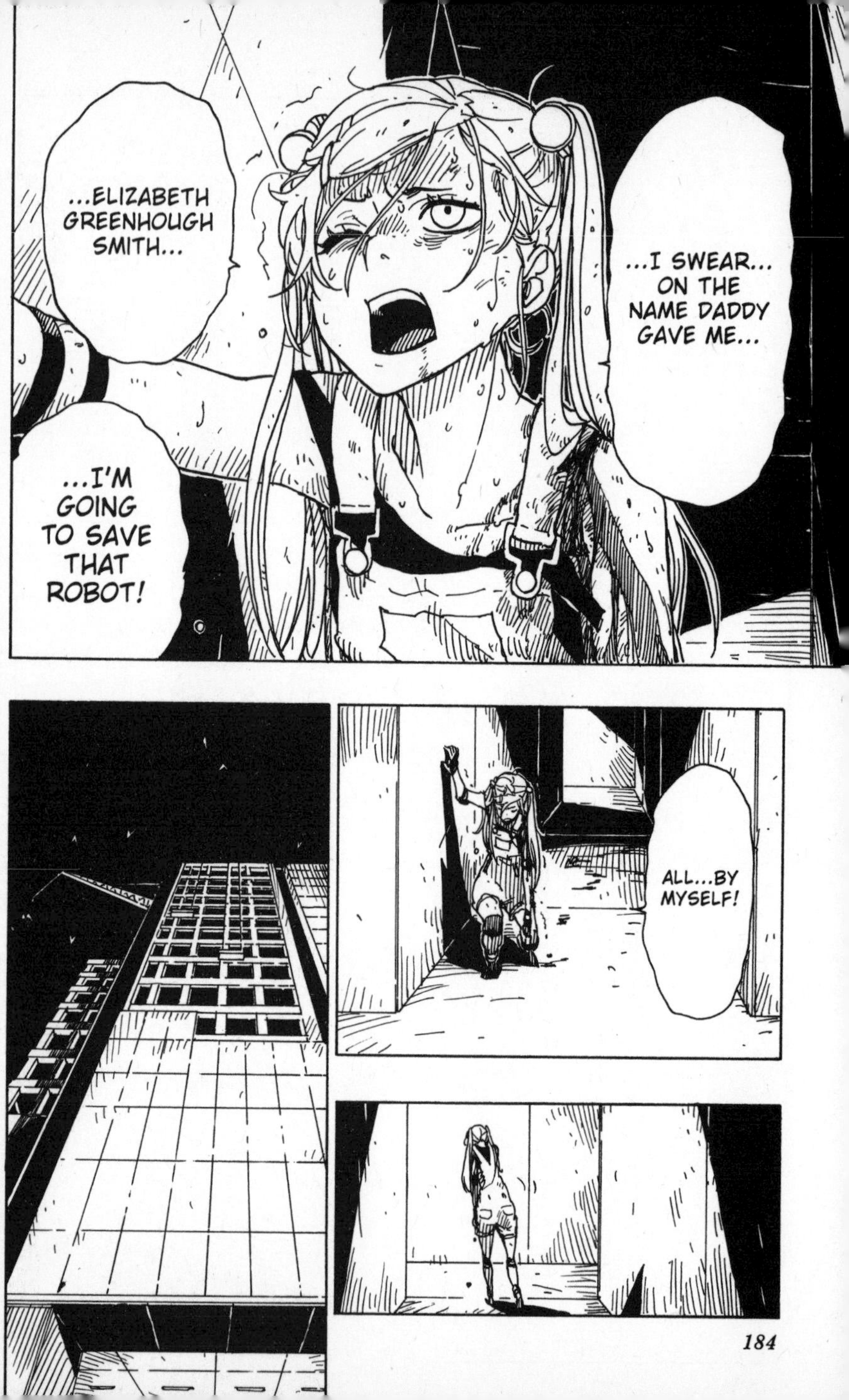
...I SWEAR... ON THE NAME DADDY GAVE ME...
...ELIZABETH GREENHOUGH SMITH...
...I'M GOING TO SAVE THAT ROBOT!
ALL...BY MYSELF!

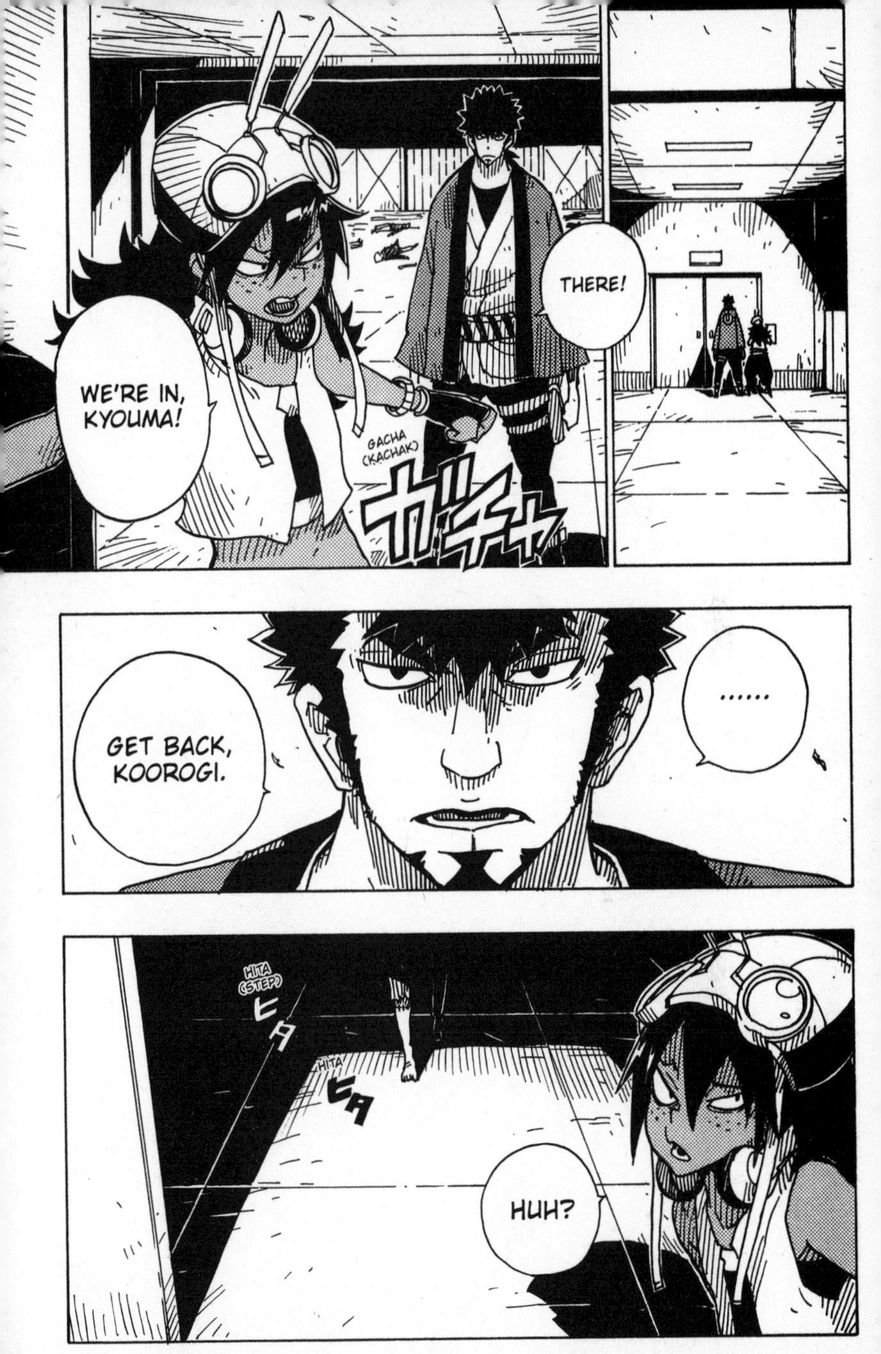
THERE!
WE'RE IN, KYOUMA!
GACHA (KACHAK)
ガチャ
......
GET BACK, KOOROGI.
HITA (STEP)
ヒタ
HITA
ヒタ
HUH?

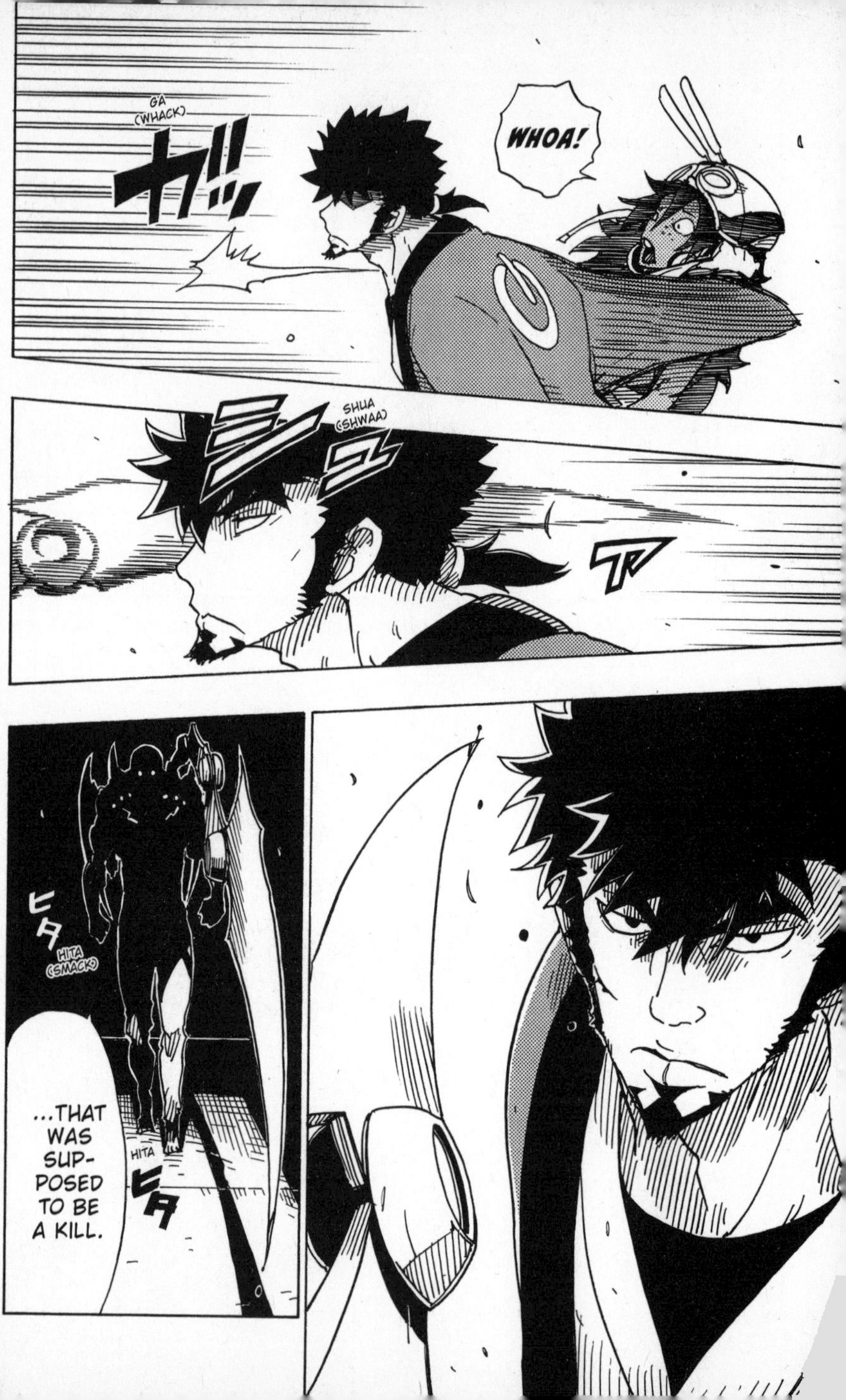
WHOA!
GA (WHACK)
SHUA (SHWAA)
HITA (SMACK)
HITA
...THAT WAS SUP-POSED TO BE A KILL.

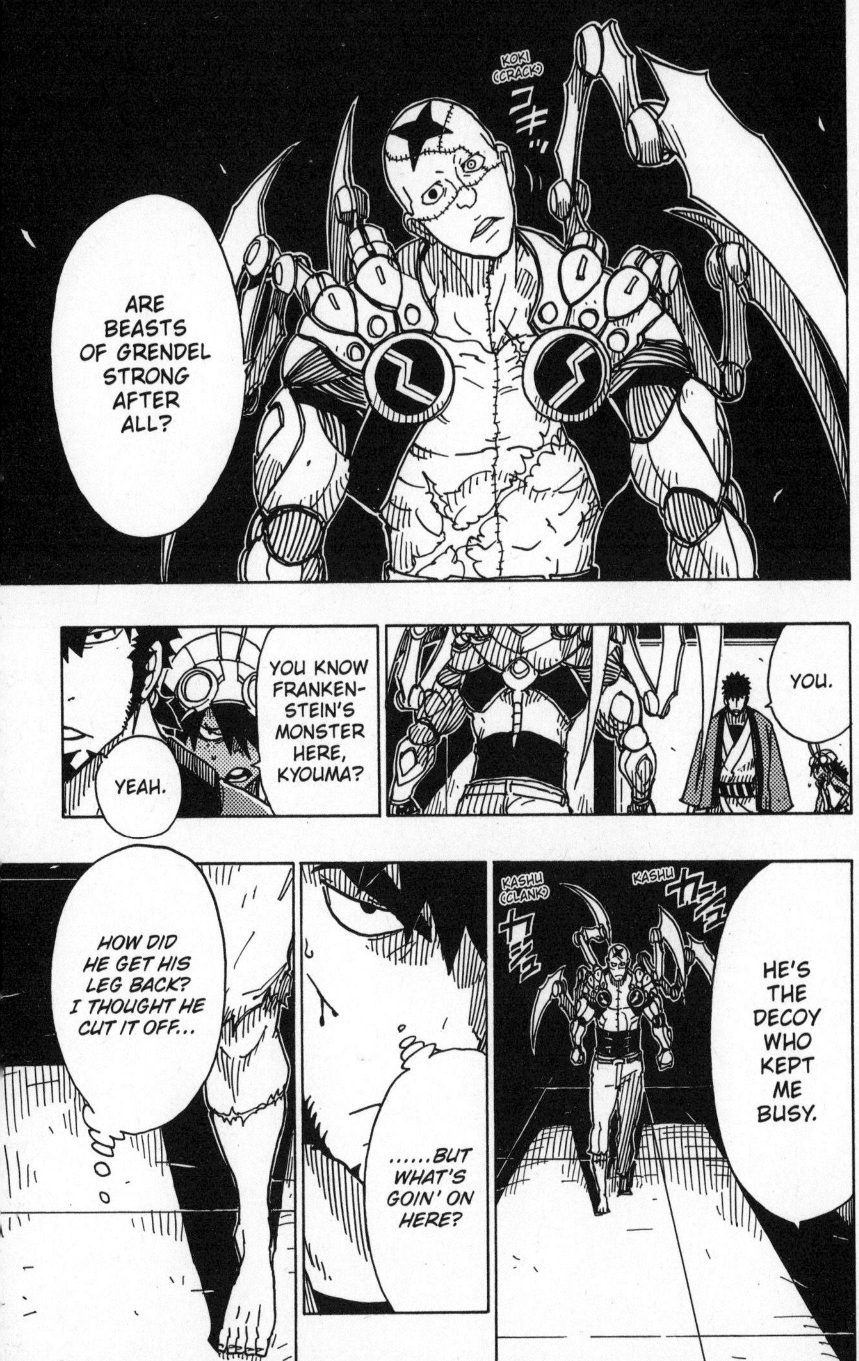
KOKI (CRACK)
ARE BEASTS OF GRENDEL STRONG AFTER ALL?
YOU.
YOU KNOW FRANKEN-STEIN'S MONSTER HERE, KYOUMA?
YEAH.
HE'S THE DECOY WHO KEPT ME BUSY.
KASHU
KASHU (CLANK)
......BUT WHAT'S GOIN' ON HERE?
HOW DID HE GET HIS LEG BACK? I THOUGHT HE CUT IT OFF...

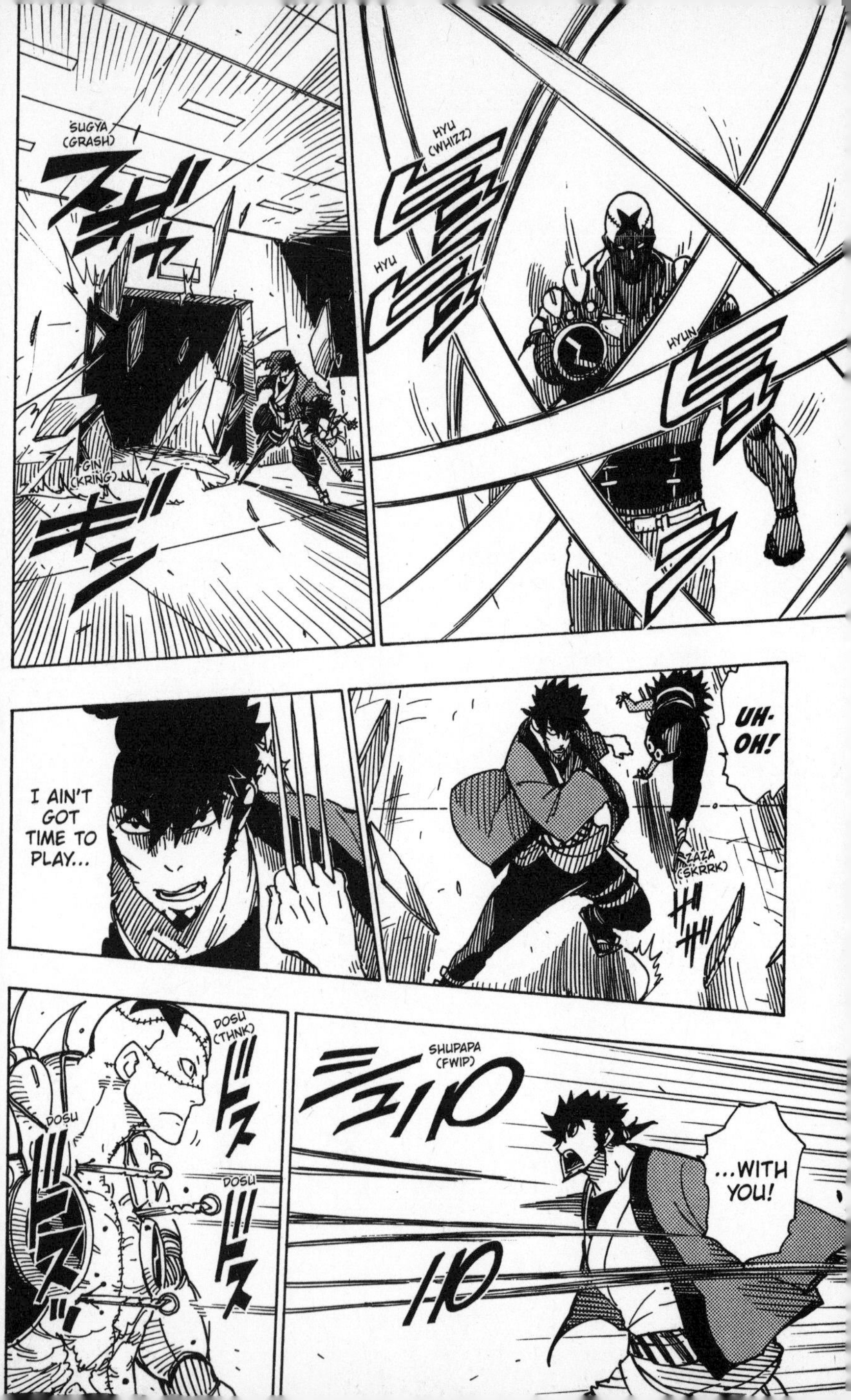
HYU (WHIZZ)
HYU
HYUN
SUGYA (GRASH)
GIN (KRING)
UH-OH!
ZAZA (SKRRK)
I AIN'T GOT TIME TO PLAY...
SHUPAPA (FWIP)
...WITH YOU!
DOSU (THNK)
DOSU
DOSU

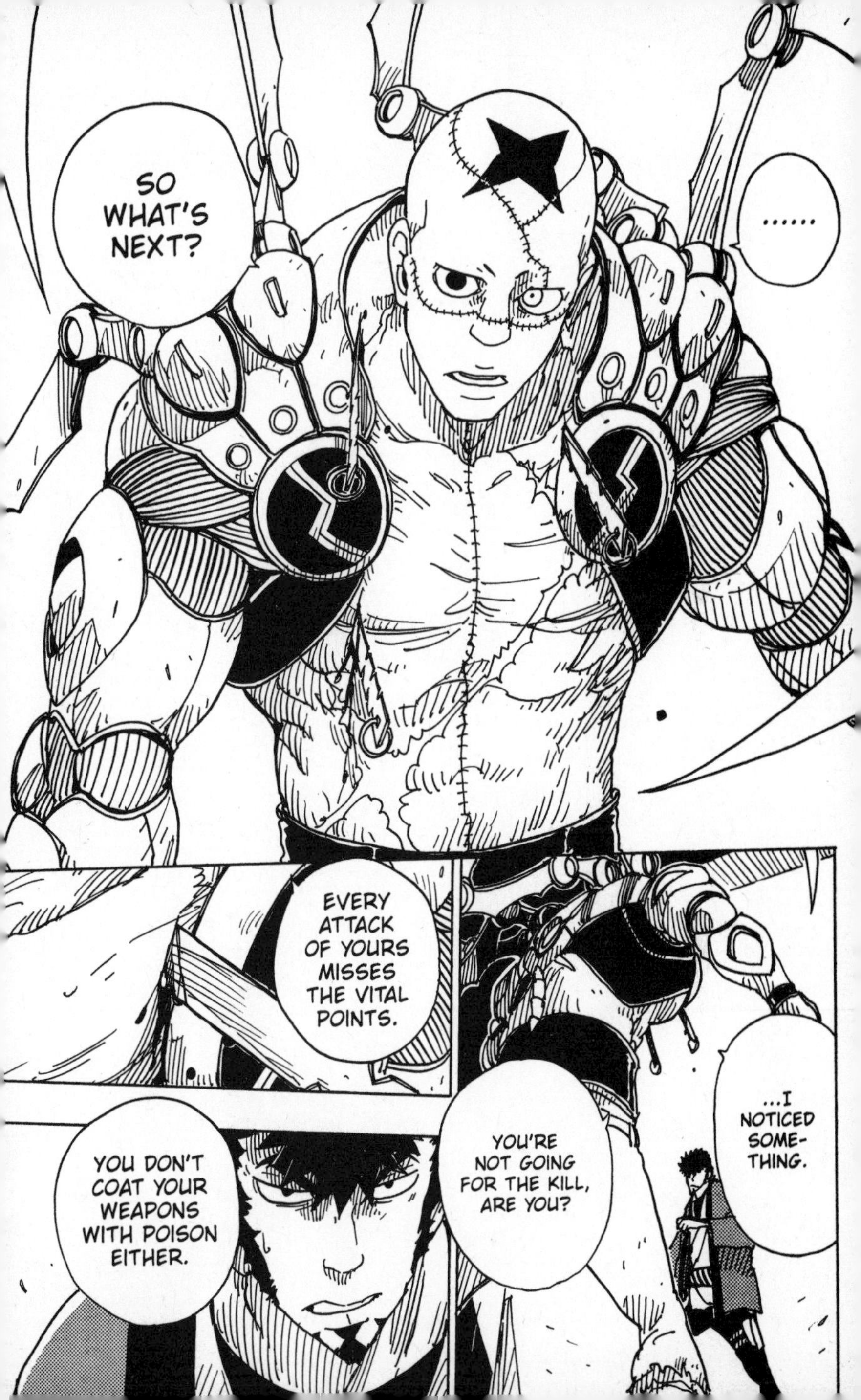
......
SO WHAT'S NEXT?
...I NOTICED SOMETHING.
YOU'RE NOT GOING FOR THE KILL, ARE YOU?
EVERY ATTACK OF YOURS MISSES THE VITAL POINTS.
YOU DON'T COAT YOUR WEAPONS WITH POISON EITHER.

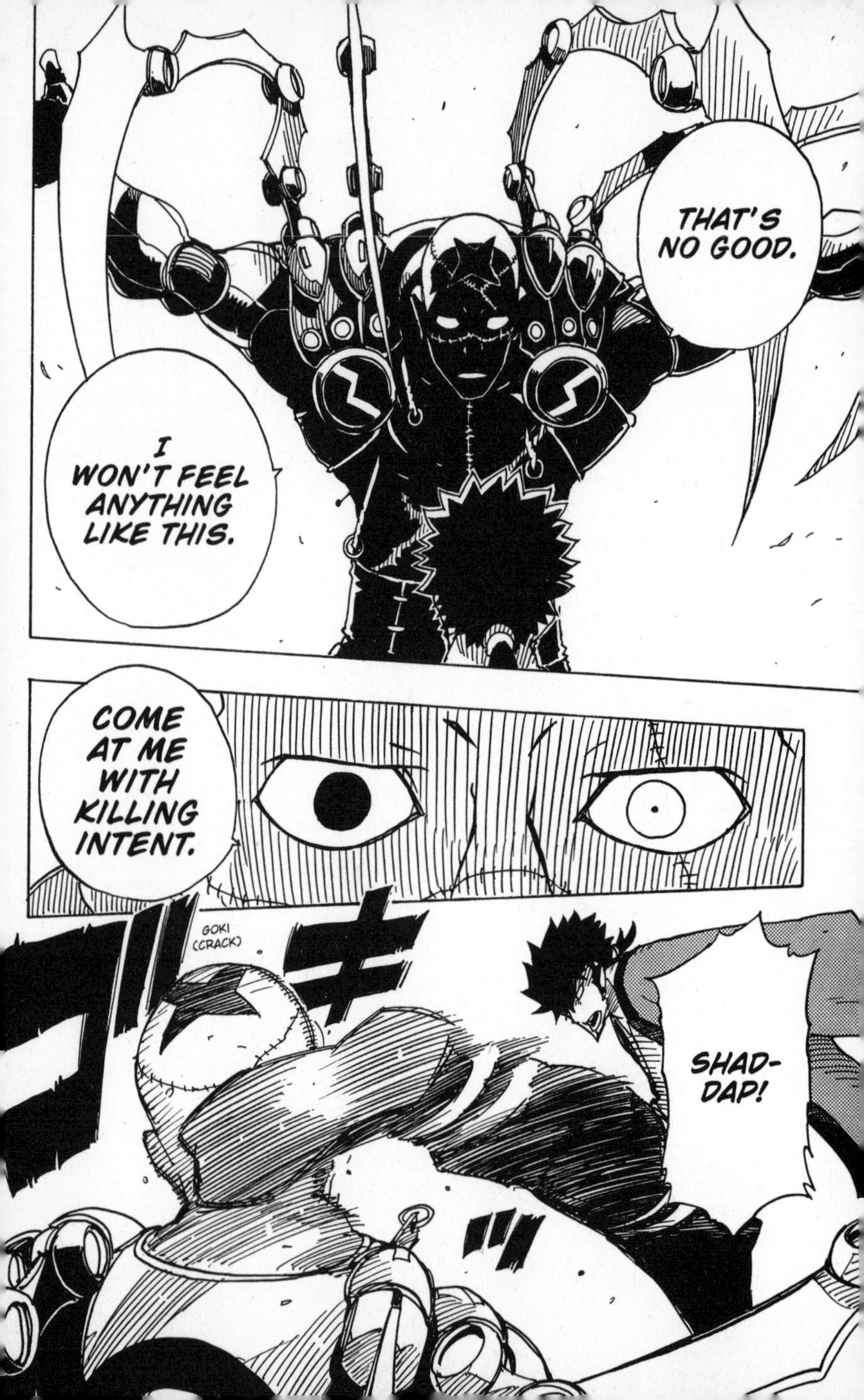
THAT'S NO GOOD.
I WON'T FEEL ANYTHING LIKE THIS.
COME AT ME WITH KILLING INTENT.
GOKI (CRACK)
SHAD-DAP!

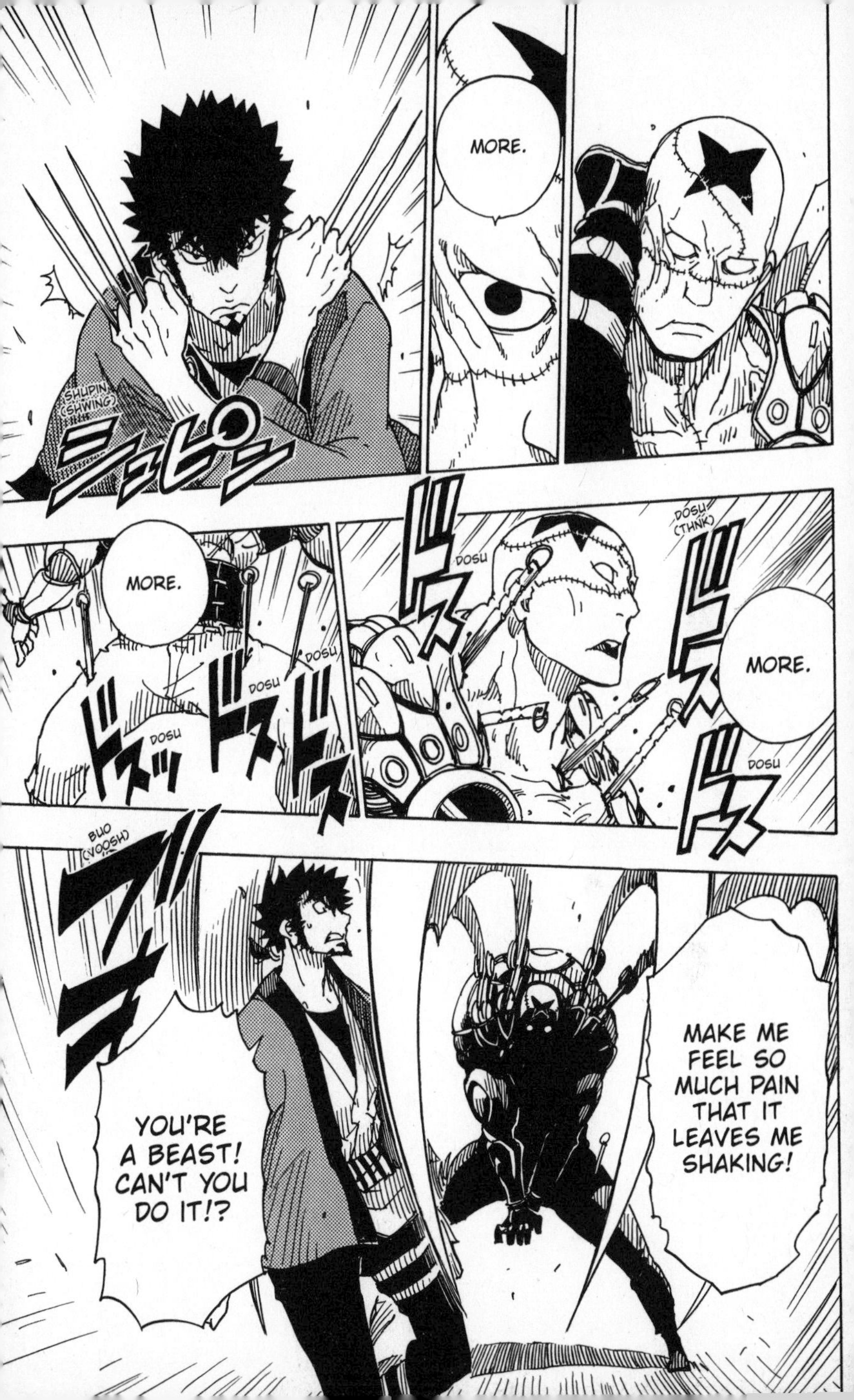
MORE.
SHUPIN (SHWING)
DOSU (THNK)
MORE.
DOSU
DOSU
MORE.
DOSU
DOSU
DOSU
MAKE ME FEEL SO MUCH PAIN THAT IT LEAVES ME SHAKING!
BUO (VOOSH)
YOU'RE A BEAST! CAN'T YOU DO IT!?

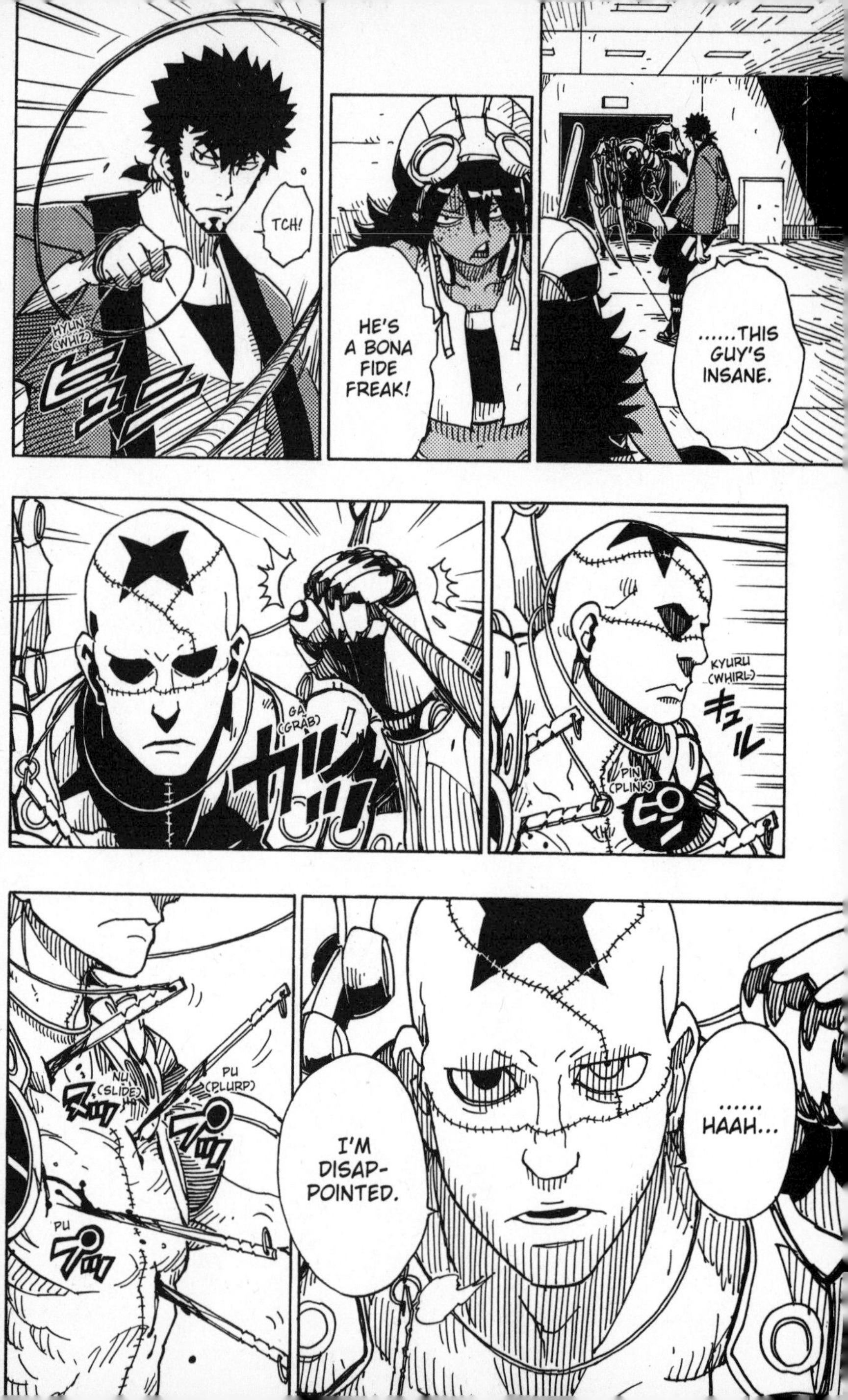
......THIS GUY'S INSANE.
HE'S A BONA FIDE FREAK!
TCH!
HYUN (WHIZ)
KYURU (WHIRL)
PIN (PLINK)
GA (GRAB)
......HAAH...
I'M DISAP-POINTED.
PU (PLURP)
NU (SLIDE)
PU

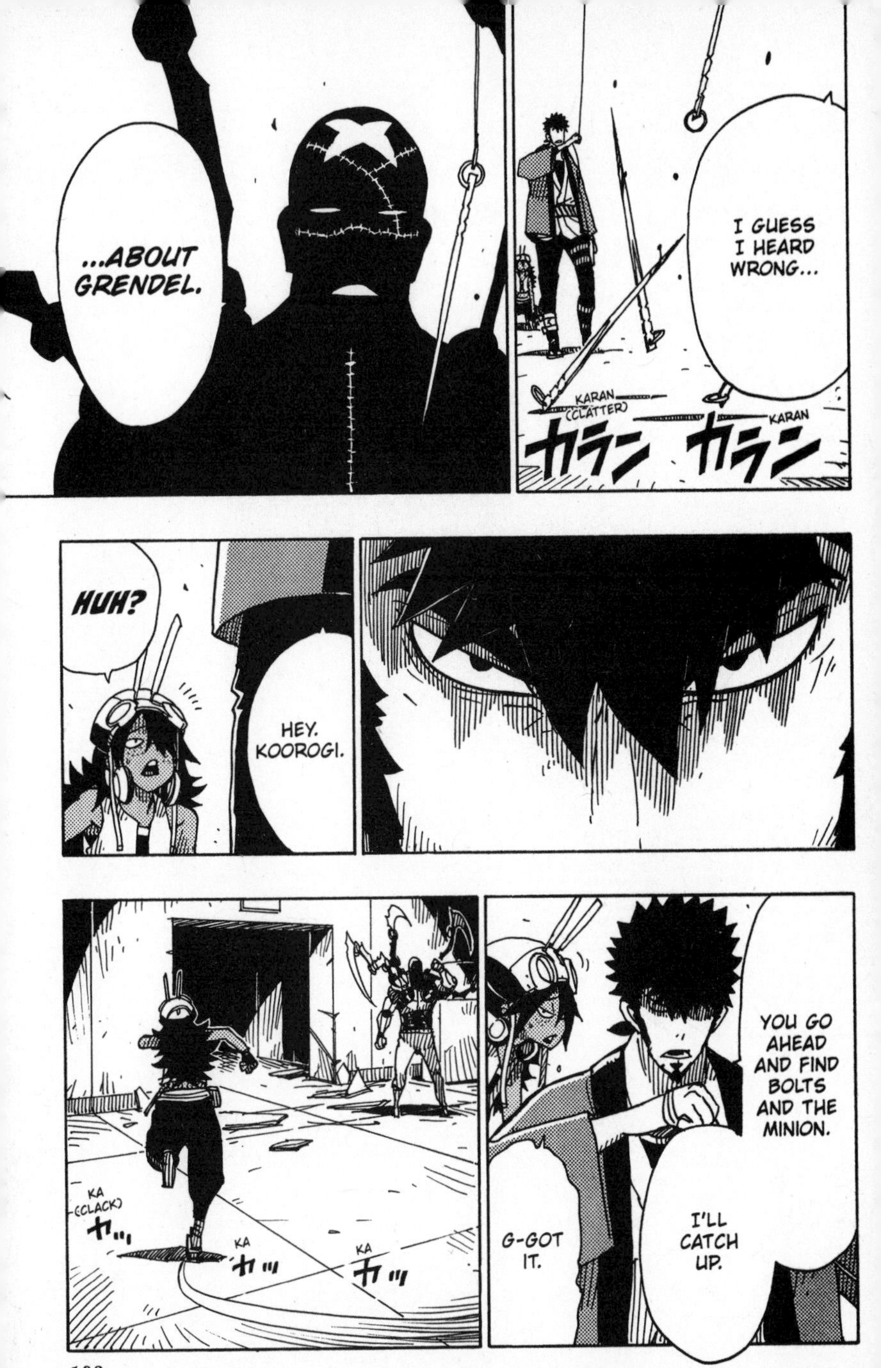
I GUESS I HEARD WRONG...
KARAN (CLATTER)
カラン
KARAN
カラン
...ABOUT GRENDEL.
HEY. KOOROGI.
HUH?
YOU GO AHEAD AND FIND BOLTS AND THE MINION.
I'LL CATCH UP.
G-GOT IT.
KA
KA (CLACK)
カッ
KA
カッ
KA
カッ

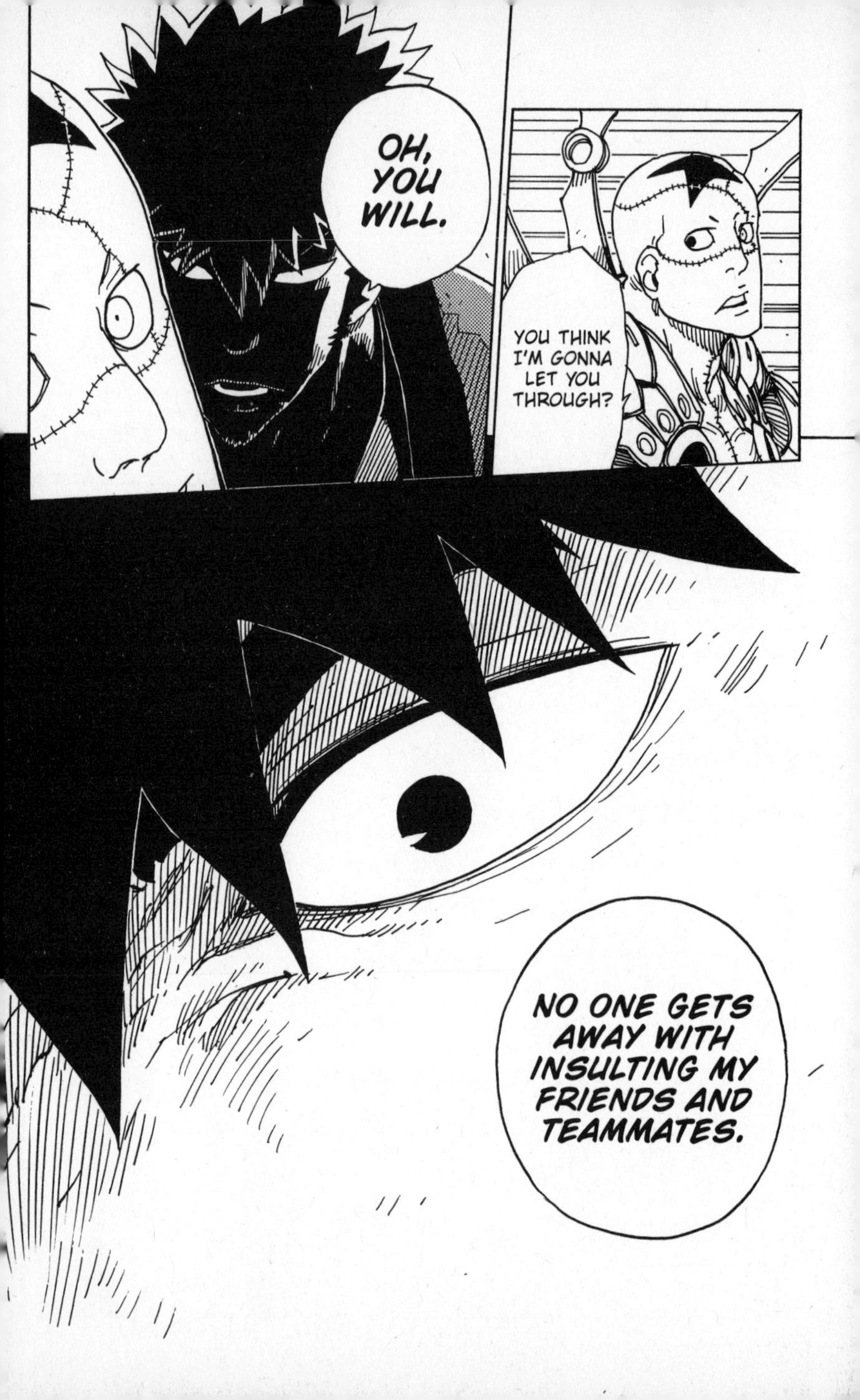
YOU THINK I'M GONNA LET YOU THROUGH?
OH, YOU WILL.
NO ONE GETS AWAY WITH INSULTING MY FRIENDS AND TEAMMATES.

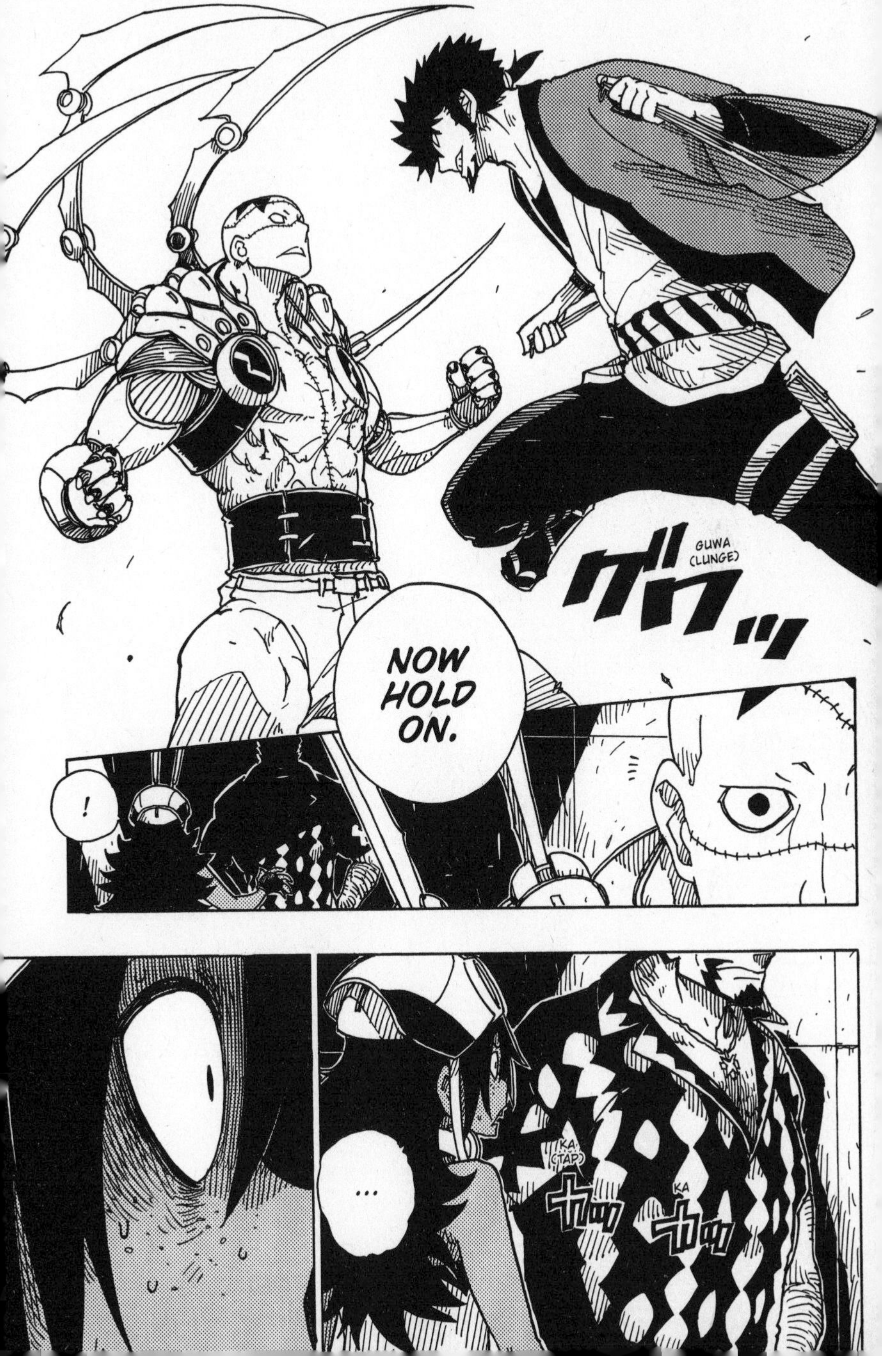
GUWA (LUNGE)
NOW HOLD ON.
!
KA (TAP)
KA
...

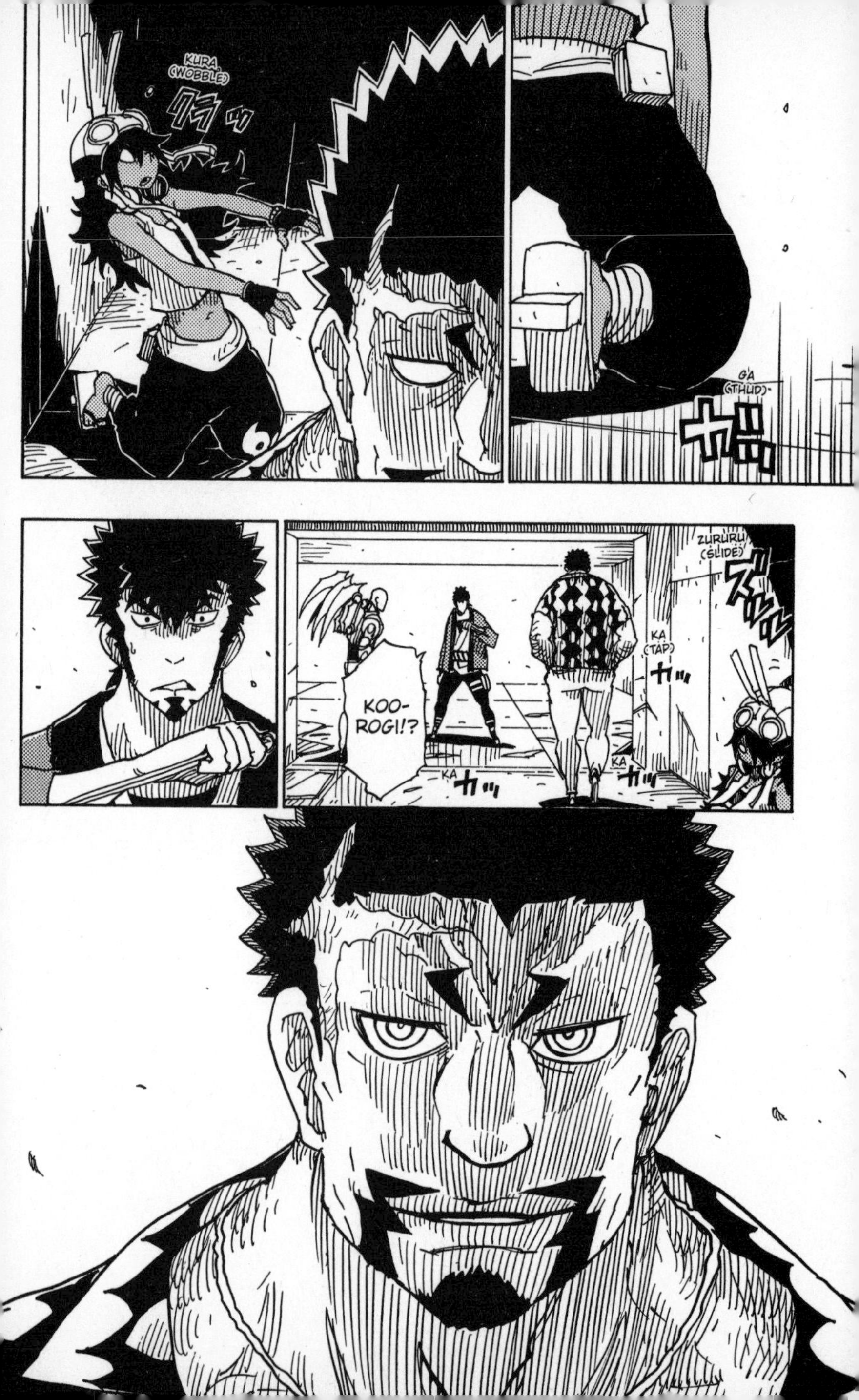

GA (THUD)
KURA (WOBBLE)
ZURURU (SLIDE)
KA (TAP)
KA
KOO-ROGI!?
KA

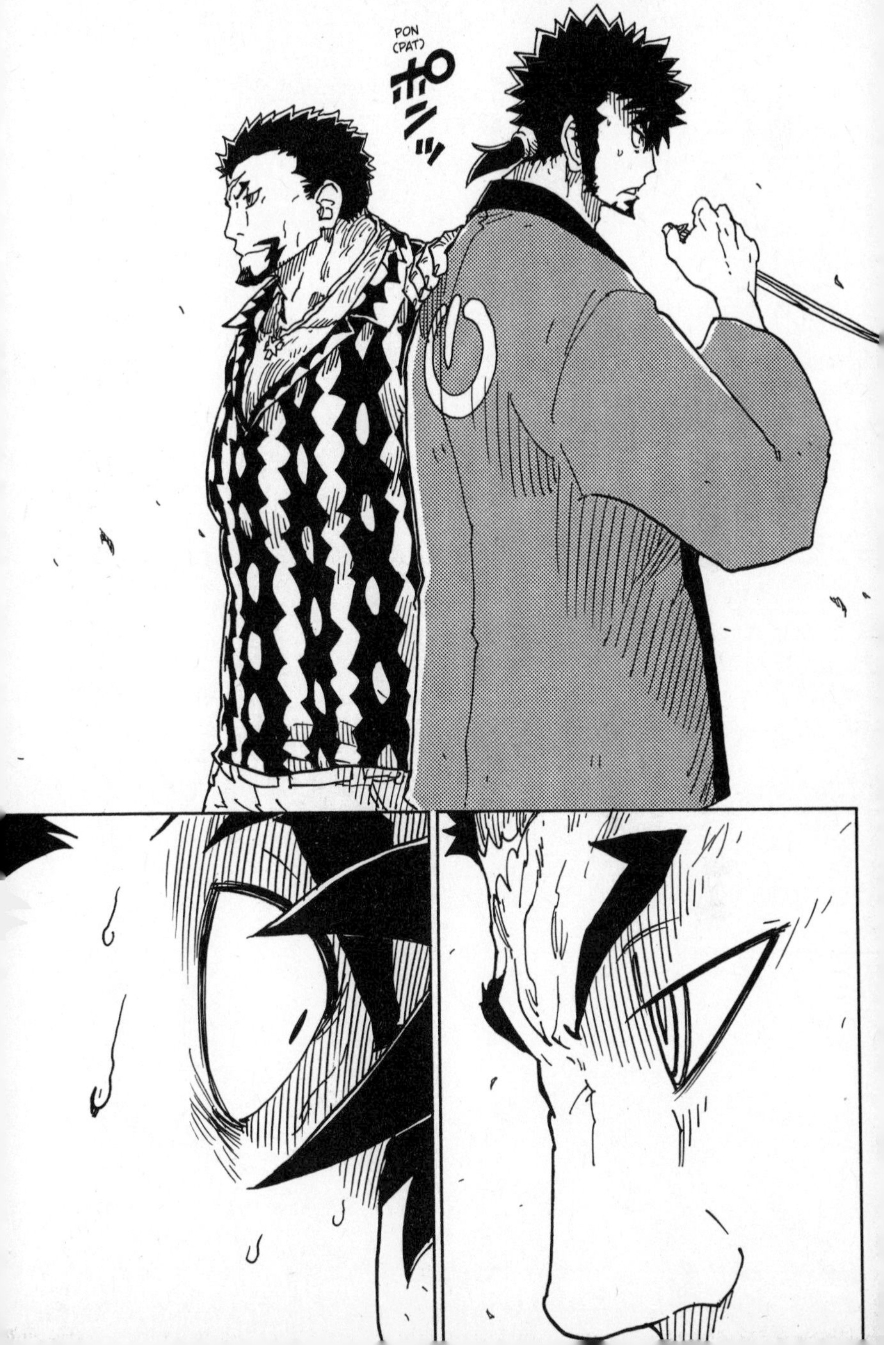
PON
(PAT)
ポンッ

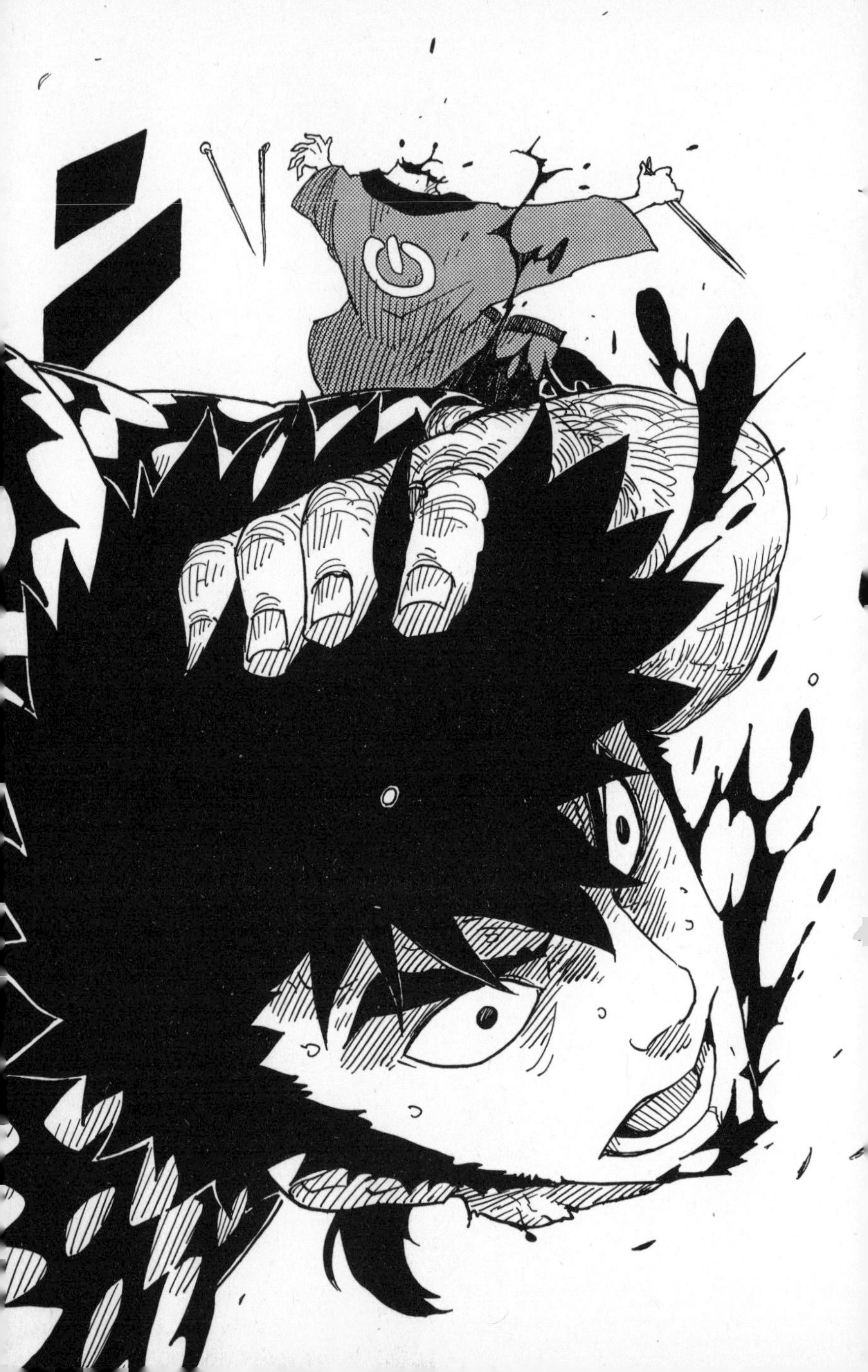

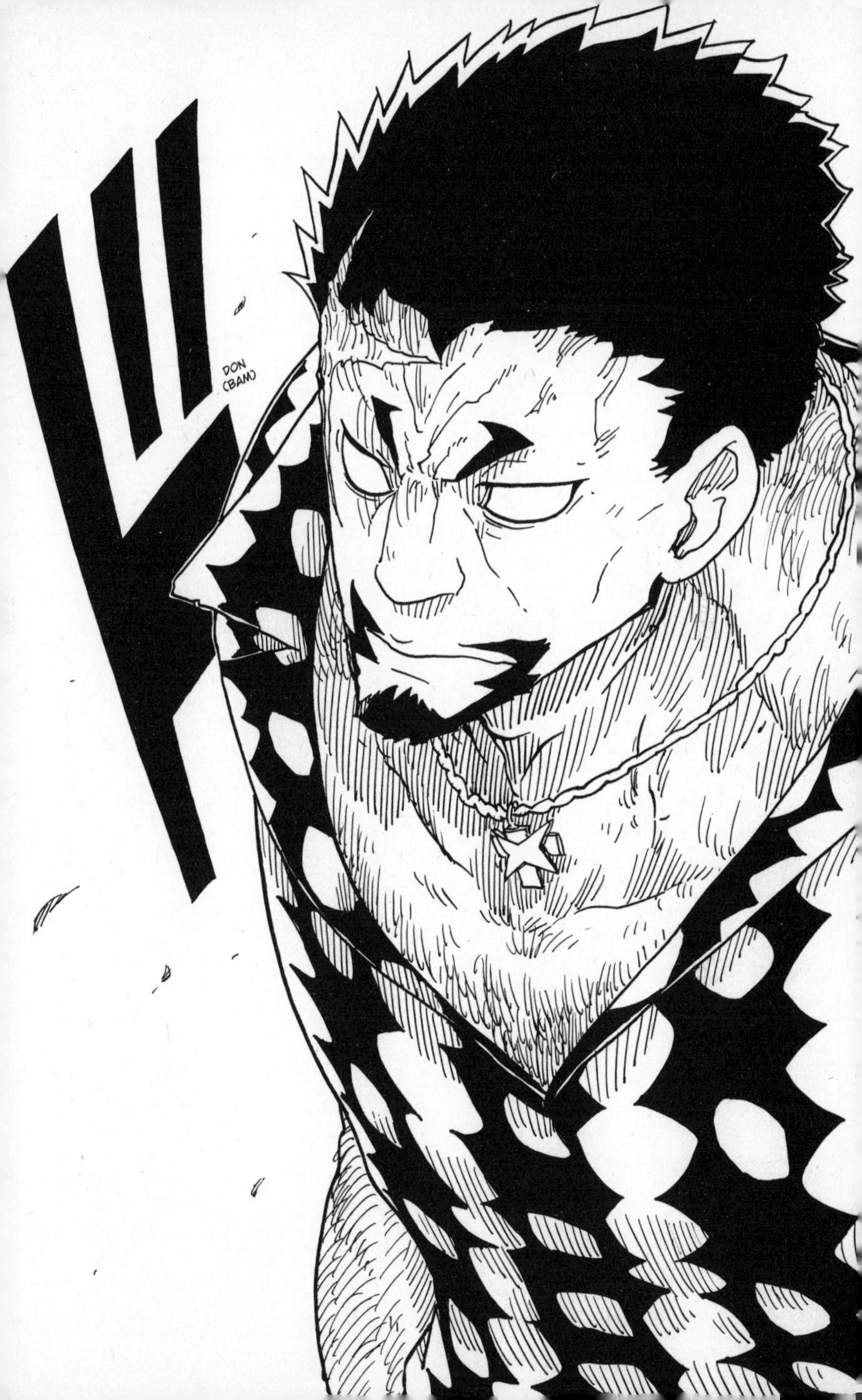
DON
(BAM)

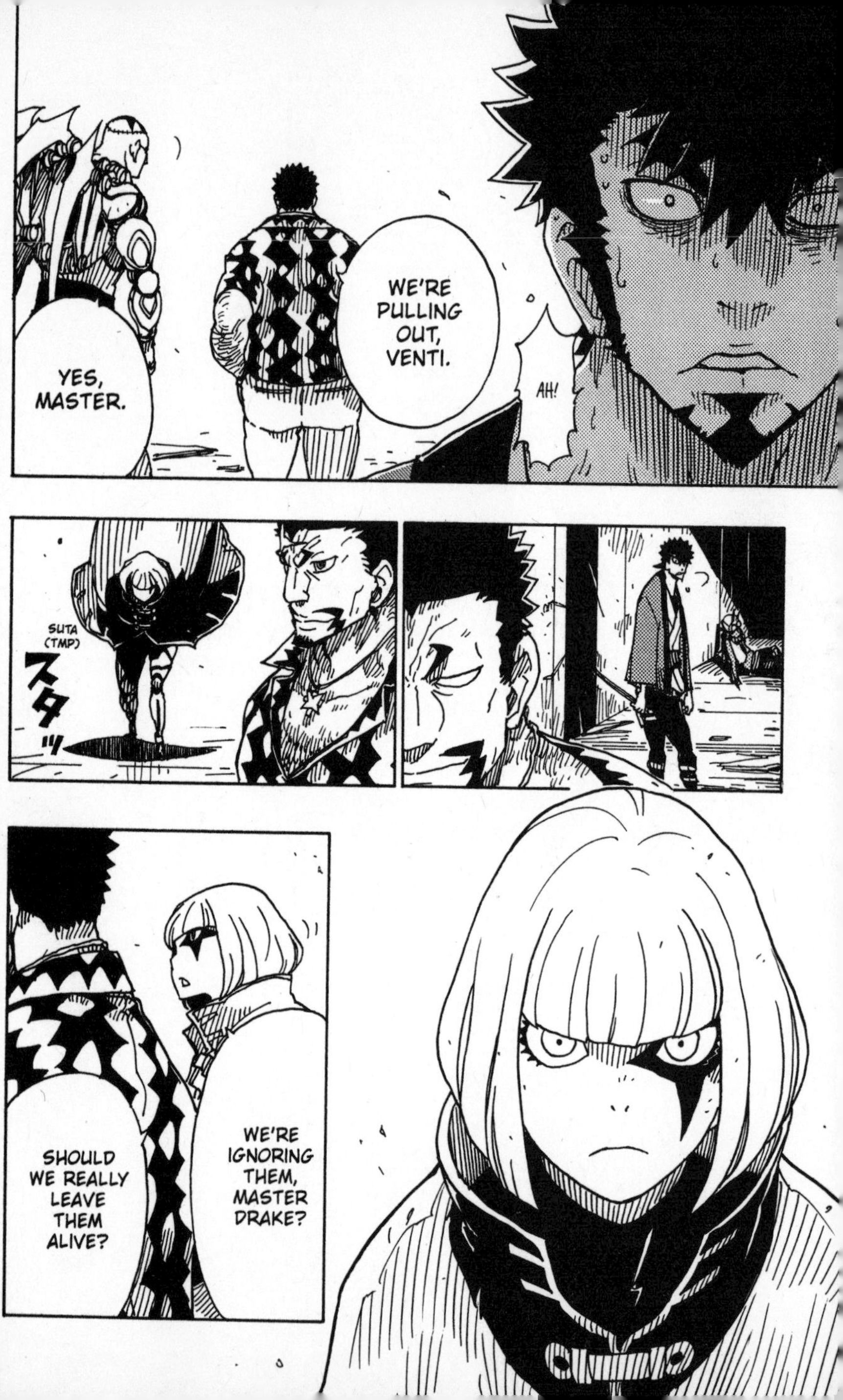
AH!
WE'RE PULLING OUT, VENTI.
YES, MASTER.
SUTA (TMP)
スタッ
WE'RE IGNORING THEM, MASTER DRAKE?
SHOULD WE REALLY LEAVE THEM ALIVE?

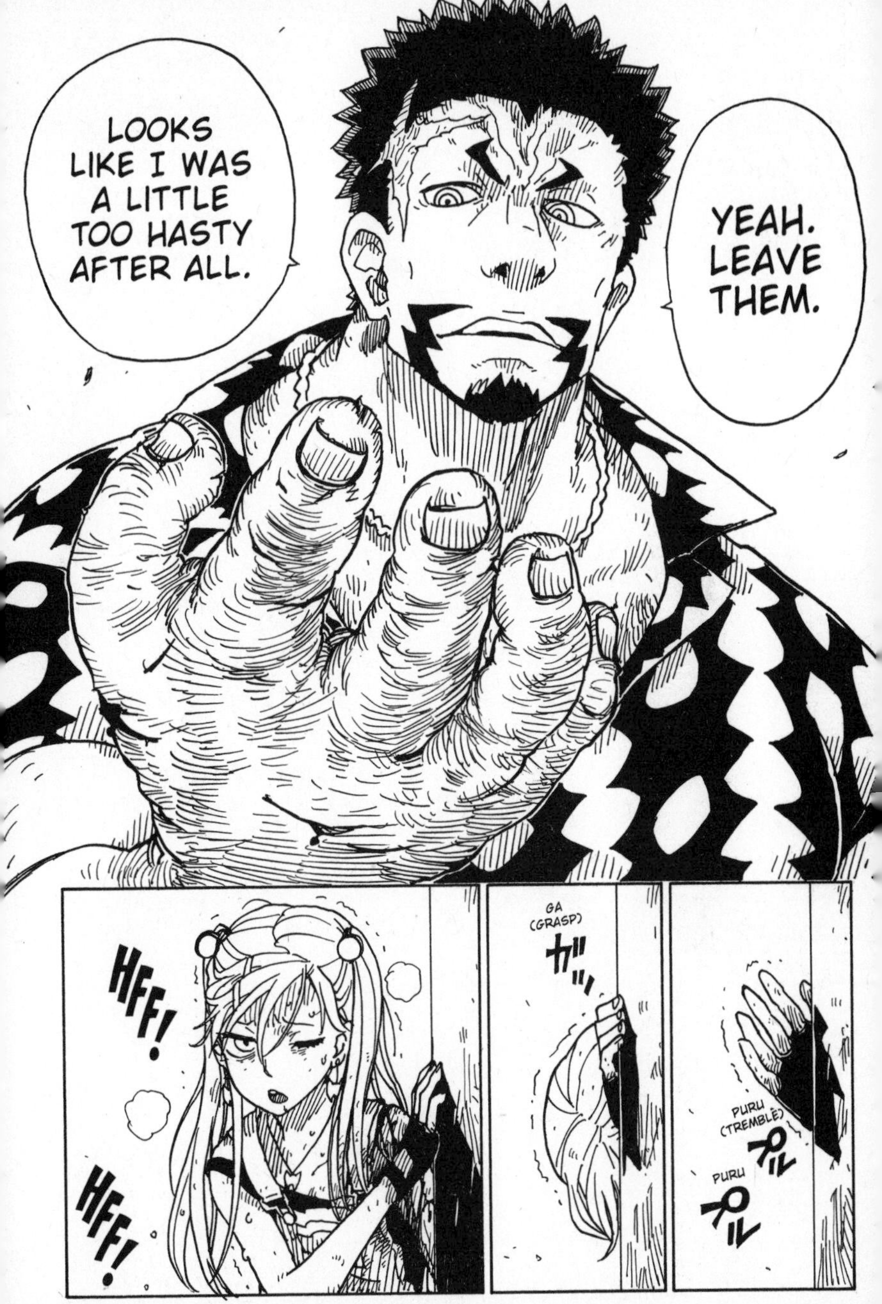
YEAH. LEAVE THEM.
LOOKS LIKE I WAS A LITTLE TOO HASTY AFTER ALL.
PURU (TREMBLE)
PURU
GA (GRASP)
HFF!
HFF!

.........THIS IS THE ROOM...

...WHERE MIRA SHOULD HAVE BEEN......

THERE'S NO ONE HERE.........

I'M TOO LATE ....

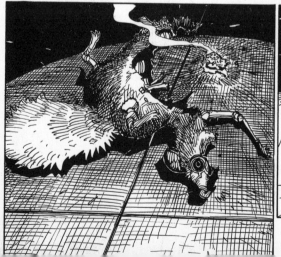

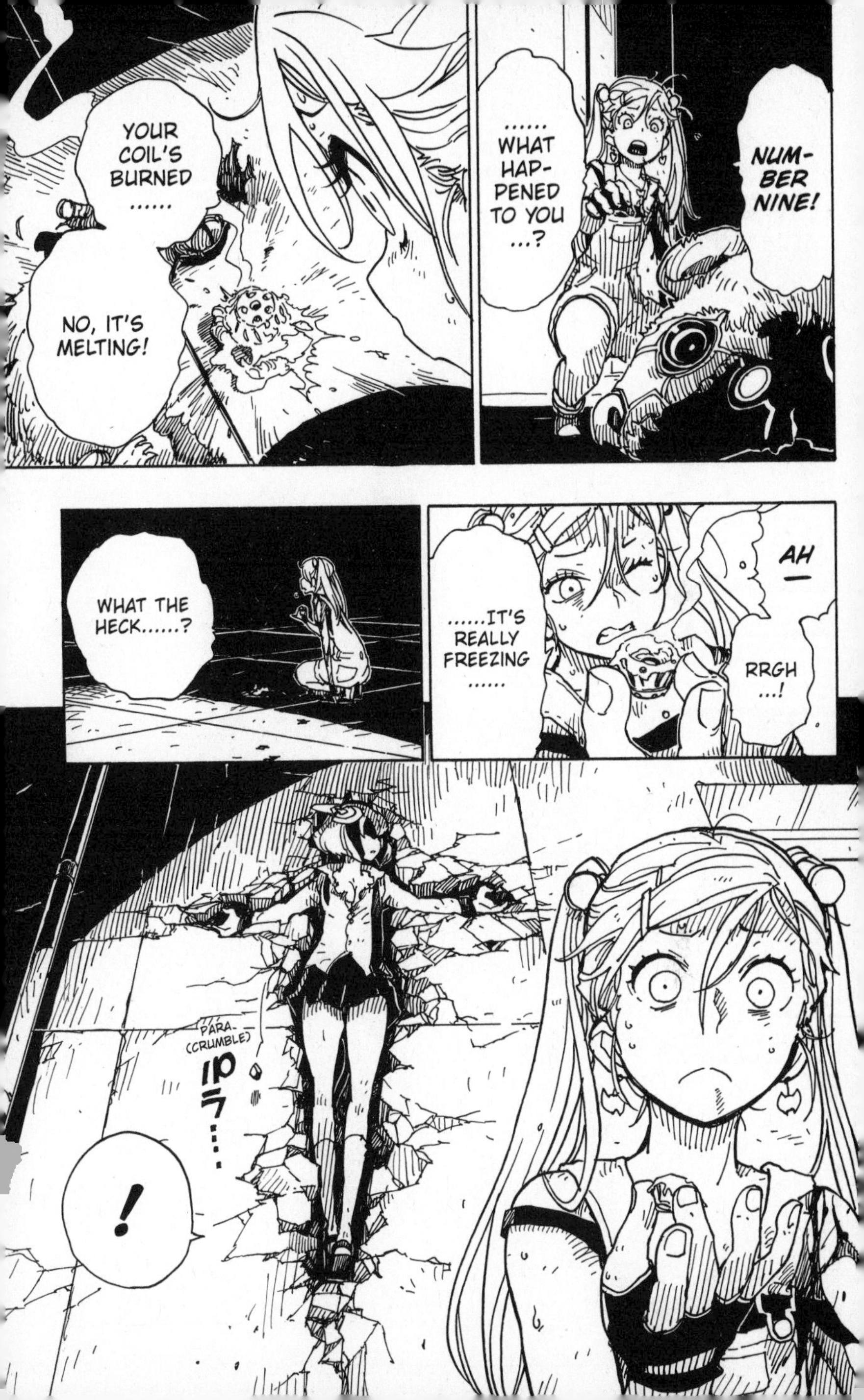
NUM-
BER
NINE!
......
WHAT
HAP-
PENED
TO YOU
...?
YOUR
COIL'S
BURNED
......
NO, IT'S
MELTING!
AH
—
RRGH
...!
......IT'S
REALLY
FREEZING
......
WHAT THE
HECK......?
PARA
(CRUMBLE)
パラ...
!

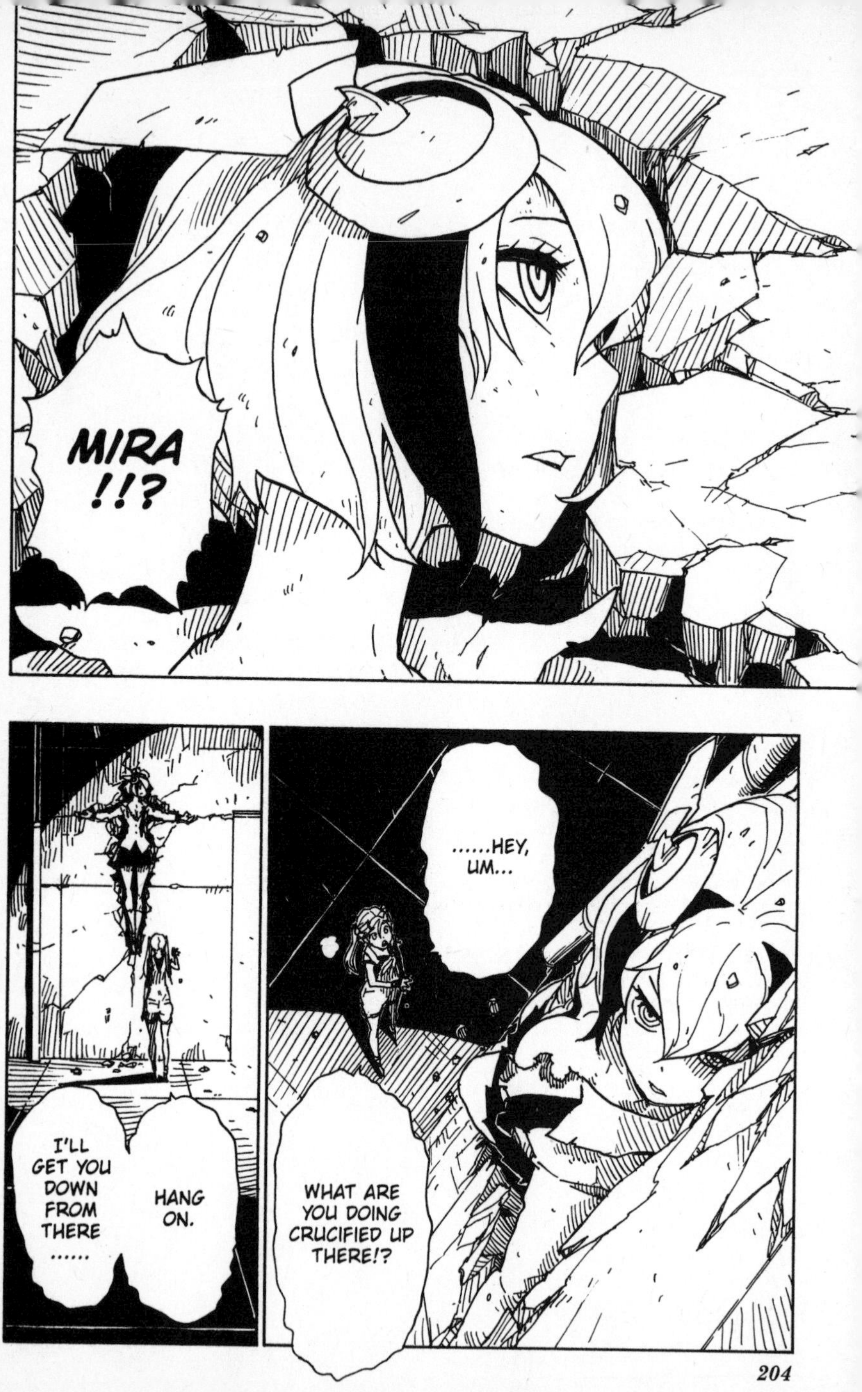
MIRA!!?
......HEY, UM...
WHAT ARE YOU DOING CRUCIFIED UP THERE!?
HANG ON.
I'LL GET YOU DOWN FROM THERE......

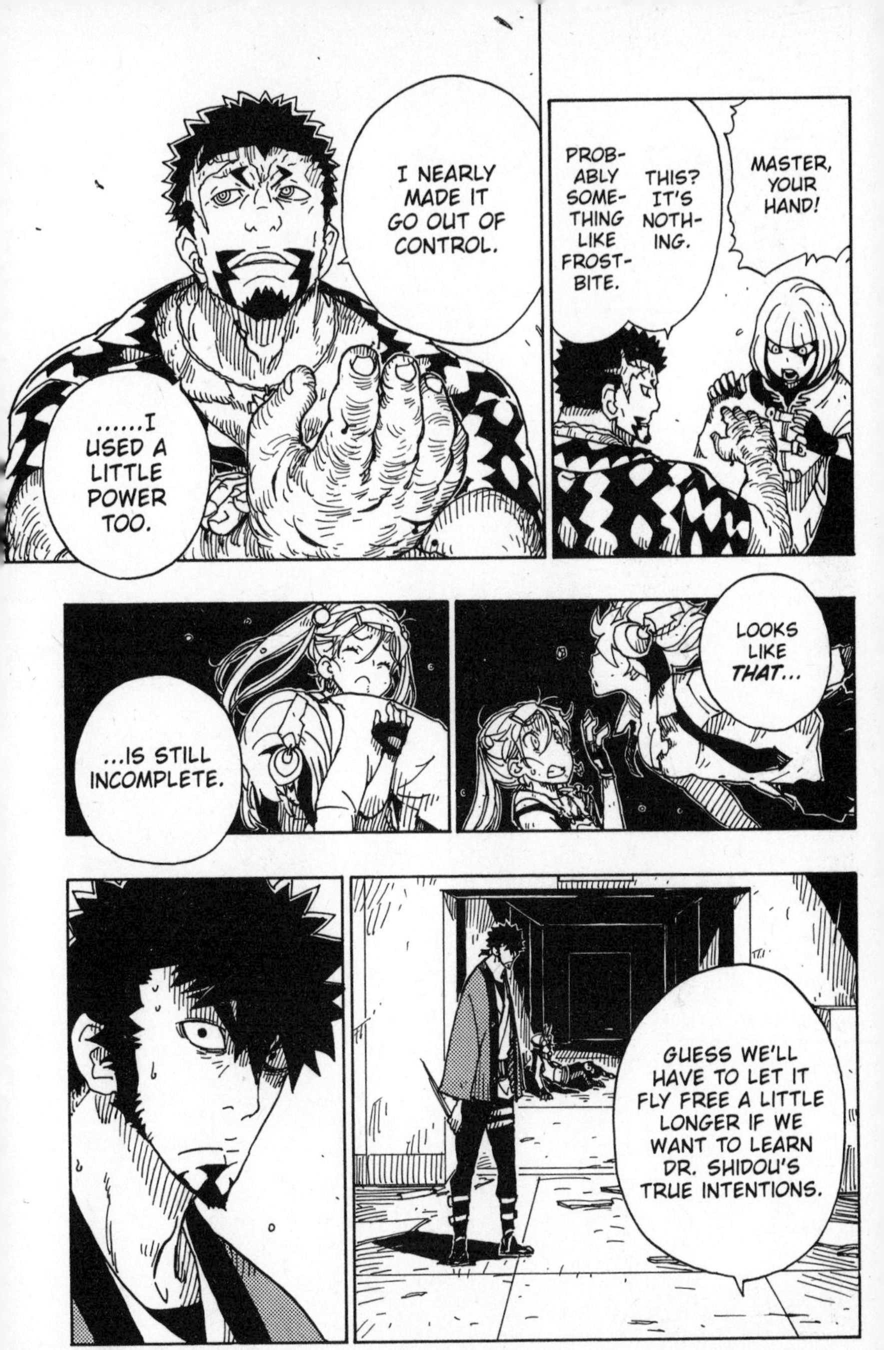
MASTER, YOUR HAND!
THIS? IT'S NOTHING.
PROBABLY SOMETHING LIKE FROSTBITE.
I NEARLY MADE IT GO OUT OF CONTROL.
......I USED A LITTLE POWER TOO.
LOOKS LIKE *THAT*...
...IS STILL INCOMPLETE.
GUESS WE'LL HAVE TO LET IT FLY FREE A LITTLE LONGER IF WE WANT TO LEARN DR. SHIDOU'S TRUE INTENTIONS.

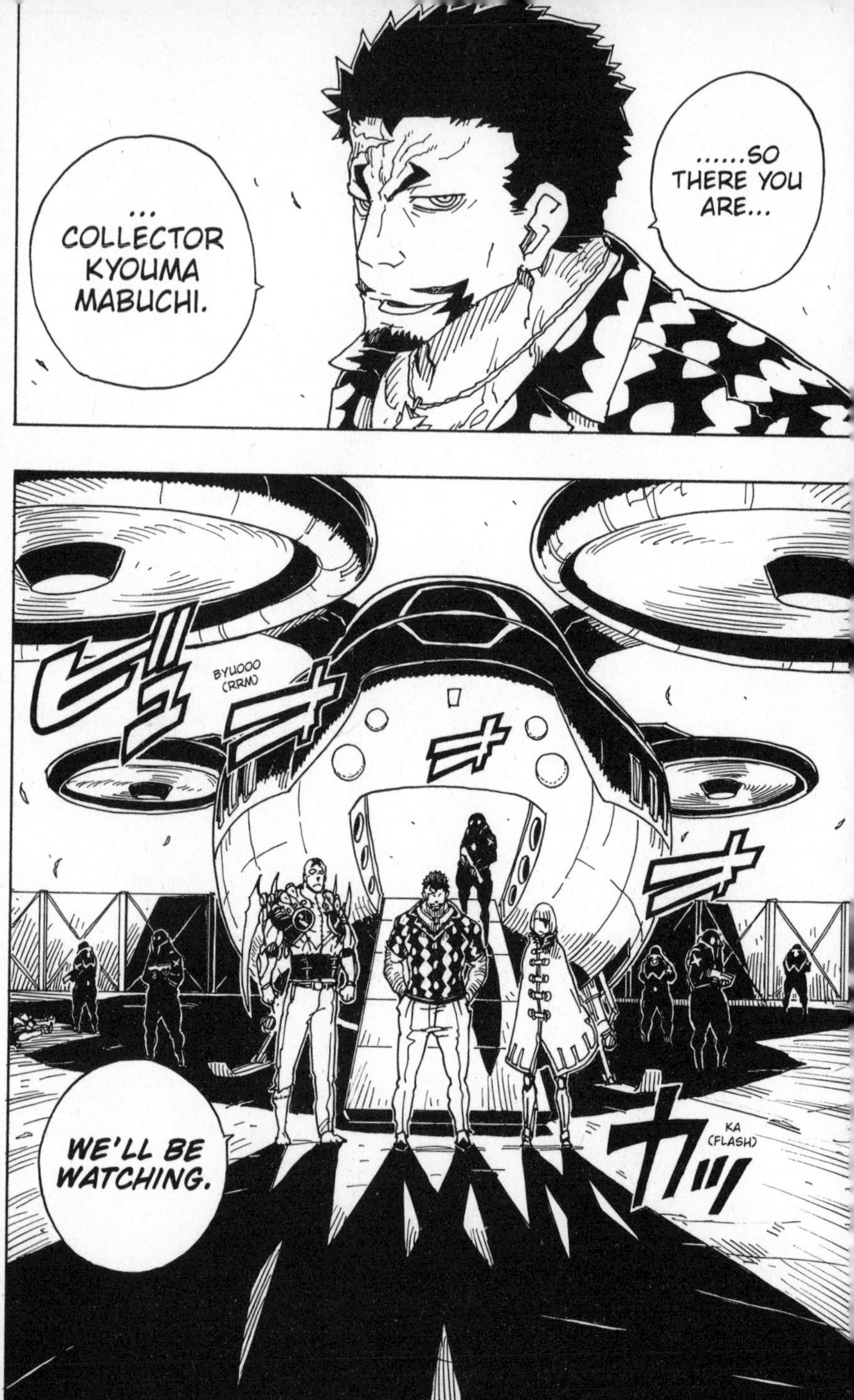
......SO THERE YOU ARE...
... COLLECTOR KYOUMA MABUCHI.
BYUOOO (RRM)
KA (FLASH)
WE'LL BE WATCHING.

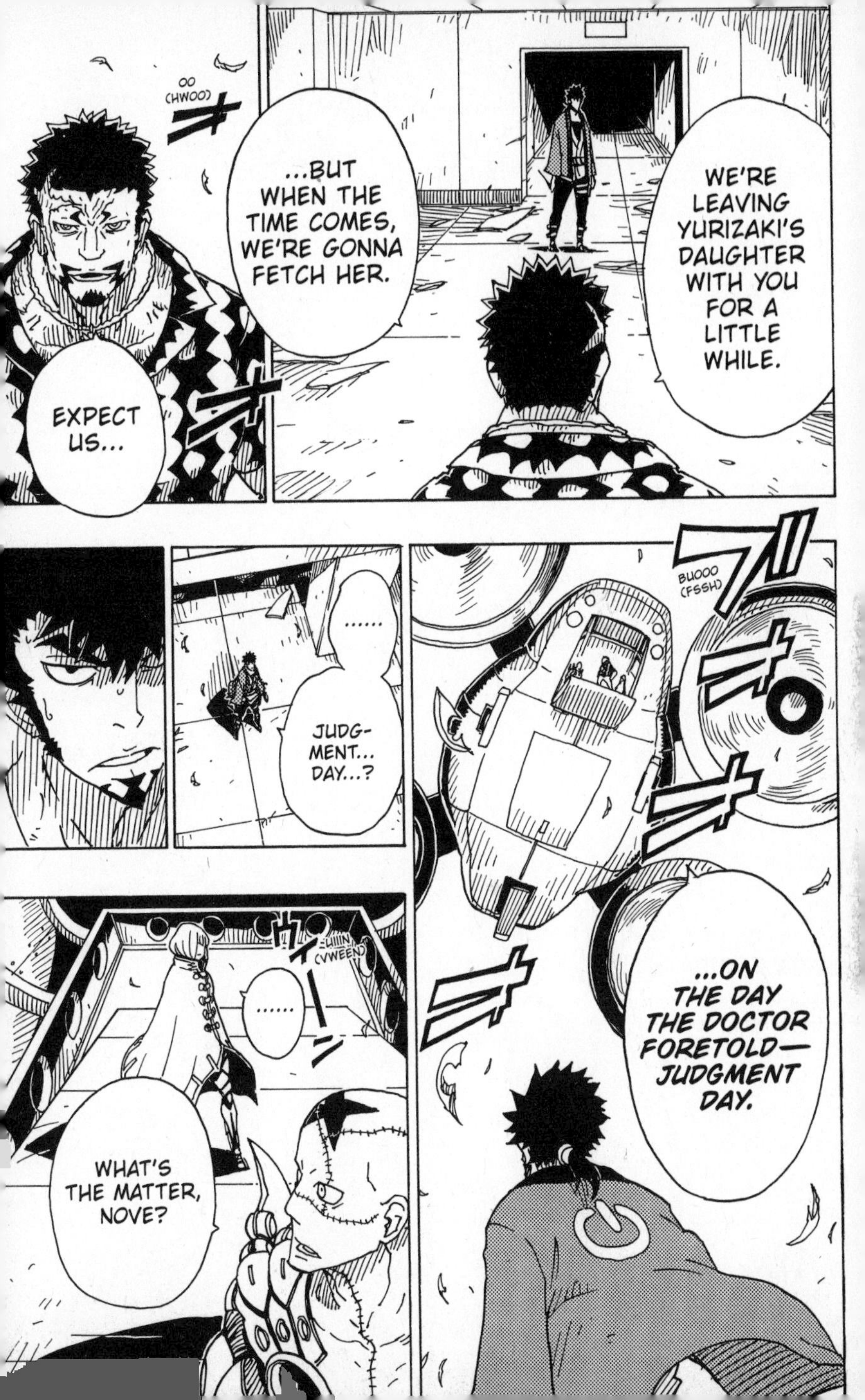
WE'RE LEAVING YURIZAKI'S DAUGHTER WITH YOU FOR A LITTLE WHILE.
...BUT WHEN THE TIME COMES, WE'RE GONNA FETCH HER.
OO (HWOO)
EXPECT US...
BUOOO (FSSH)
...ON THE DAY THE DOCTOR FORETOLD—JUDGMENT DAY.
......
JUDGMENT... DAY...?
UIIIN (VWEEN)
......
WHAT'S THE MATTER, NOVE?

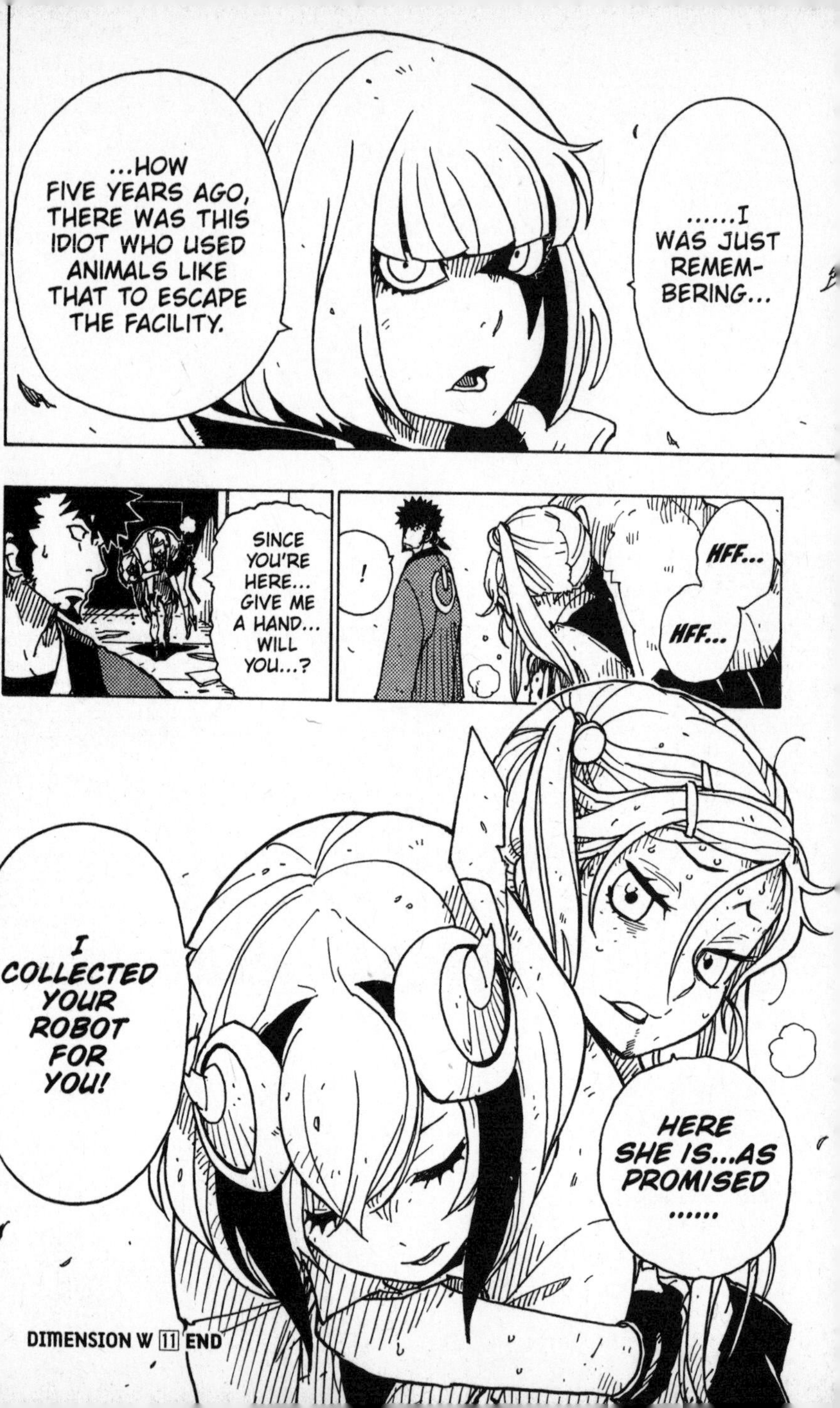
......I WAS JUST REMEMBERING...
...HOW FIVE YEARS AGO, THERE WAS THIS IDIOT WHO USED ANIMALS LIKE THAT TO ESCAPE THE FACILITY.
HFF...
HFF...
!
SINCE YOU'RE HERE... GIVE ME A HAND... WILL YOU...?
HERE SHE IS...AS PROMISED ......
I COLLECTED YOUR ROBOT FOR YOU!
DIMENSION W 11 END

Dimension W

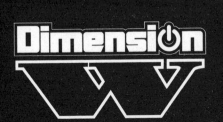

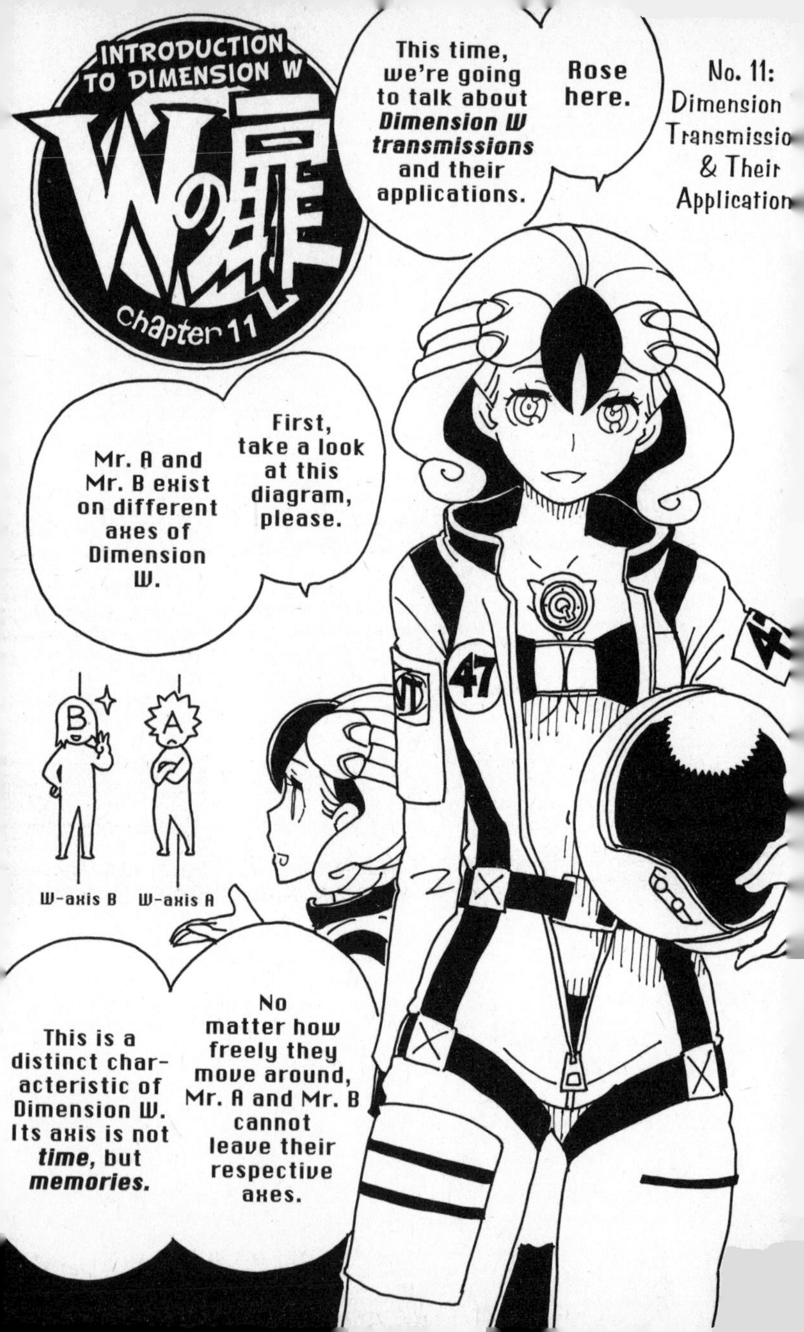

No. 11: Dimension Transmissio & Their Application
Rose here.
This time, we're going to talk about *Dimension W transmissions* and their applications.
INTRODUCTION TO DIMENSION W
Wの扉
chapter 11
First, take a look at this diagram, please.
Mr. A and Mr. B exist on different axes of Dimension W.
A
B
W-axis A
W-axis B
No matter how freely they move around, Mr. A and Mr. B cannot leave their respective axes.
This is a distinct characteristic of Dimension W. Its axis is not *time*, but *memories*.

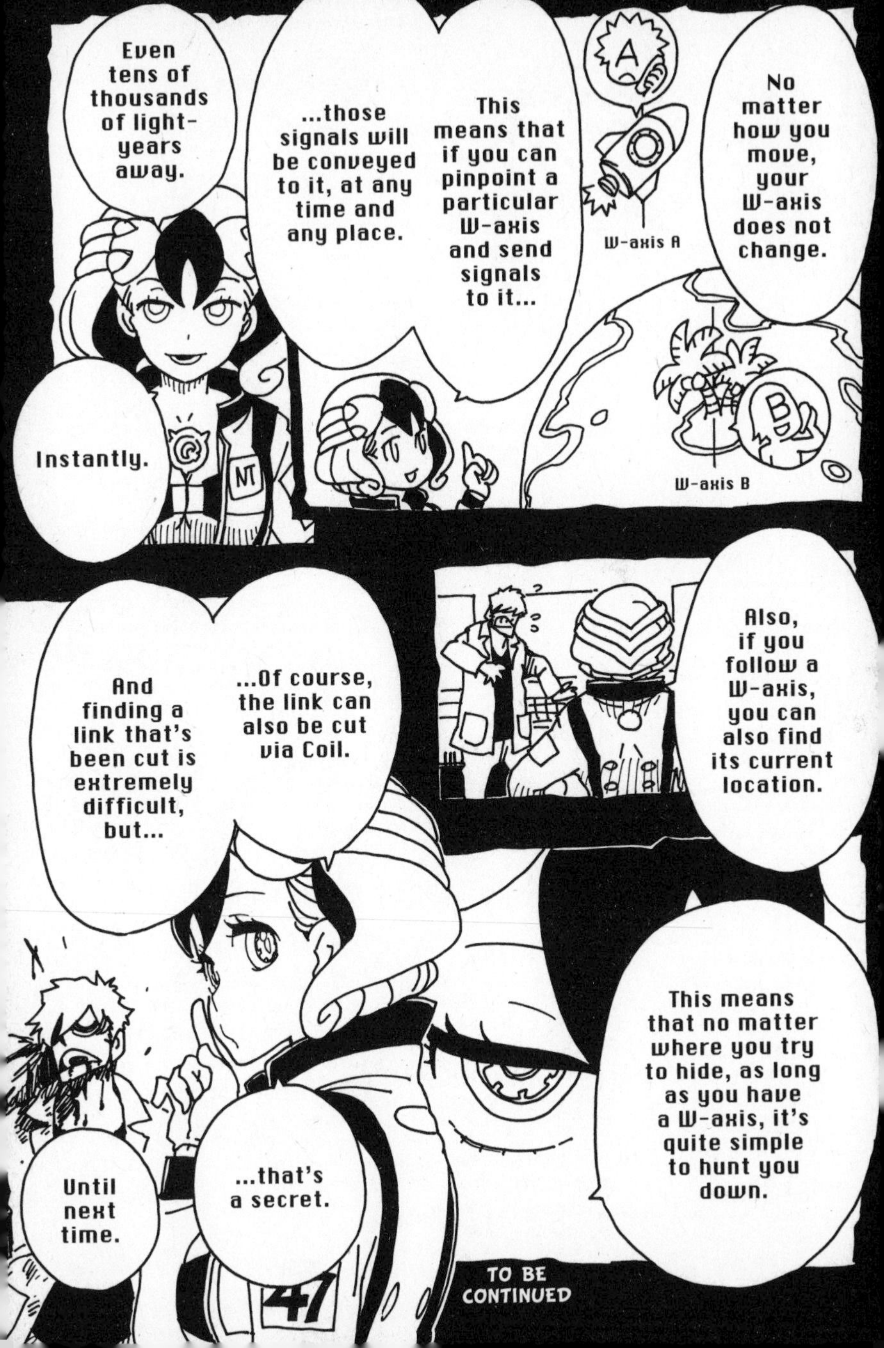
No matter how you move, your W-axis does not change.
A
W-axis A
B
W-axis B
This means that if you can pinpoint a particular W-axis and send signals to it...
...those signals will be conveyed to it, at any time and any place.
Even tens of thousands of light-years away.
Instantly.
Also, if you follow a W-axis, you can also find its current location.
This means that no matter where you try to hide, as long as you have a W-axis, it's quite simple to hunt you down.
...Of course, the link can also be cut via Coil.
And finding a link that's been cut is extremely difficult, but...
...that's a secret.
Until next time.
TO BE CONTINUED

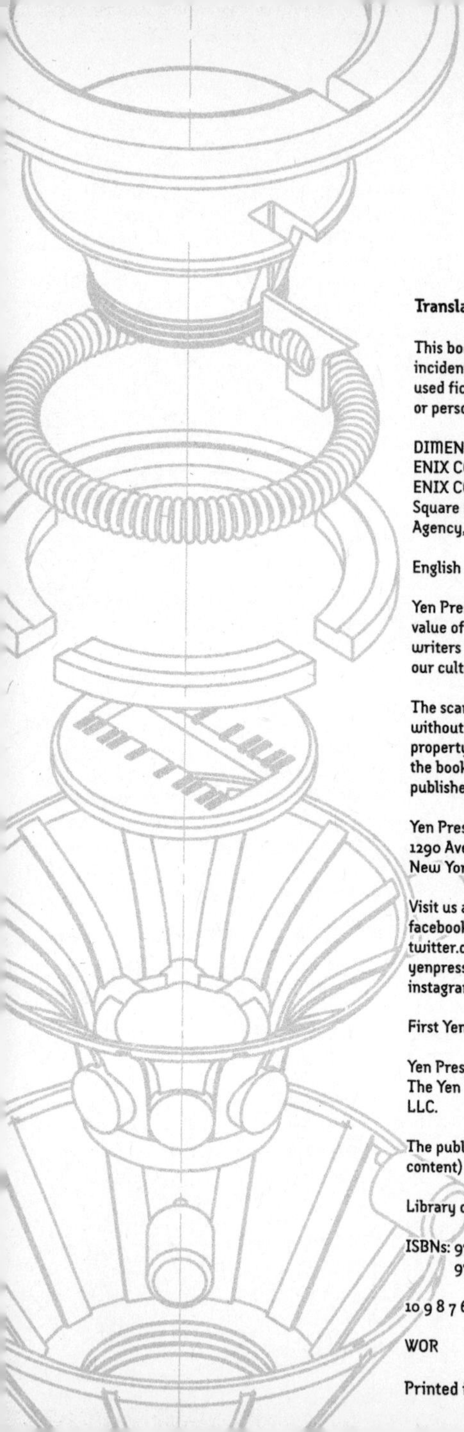

Dimension W

by YUJI IWAHARA

Translation: Amanda Haley • Lettering: Phil Christie

DIMENSION W Volume 11 ©2016 YUJI IWAHARA/SQUARE ENIX CO., LTD. First published in Japan in 2016 by SQUARE ENIX CO., LTD. English translation rights arranged with Square Enix Co., Ltd. and Yen Press, LLC through Tuttle-Mori Agency, Inc.

English translation © 2018 by SQUARE ENIX CO., LTD.

Yen Press
1290 Avenue of the Americas
New York, NY 10104

Visit us at yenpress.com
facebook.com/yenpress
twitter.com/yenpress
yenpress.tumblr.com
instagram.com/yenpress

First Yen Press Edition: August 2018

Yen Press is an imprint of Yen Press, LLC.
The Yen Press name and logo are trademarks of Yen Press, LLC.

Library of Congress Control Number: 2015956889

ISBNs: 978-1-9753-0035-7 (paperback)
       978-1-9753-0036-4 (ebook)

10 9 8 7 6 5 4 3 2 1

WOR

Printed in the United States of America

FILE.78
ELLIE ALL ALONE

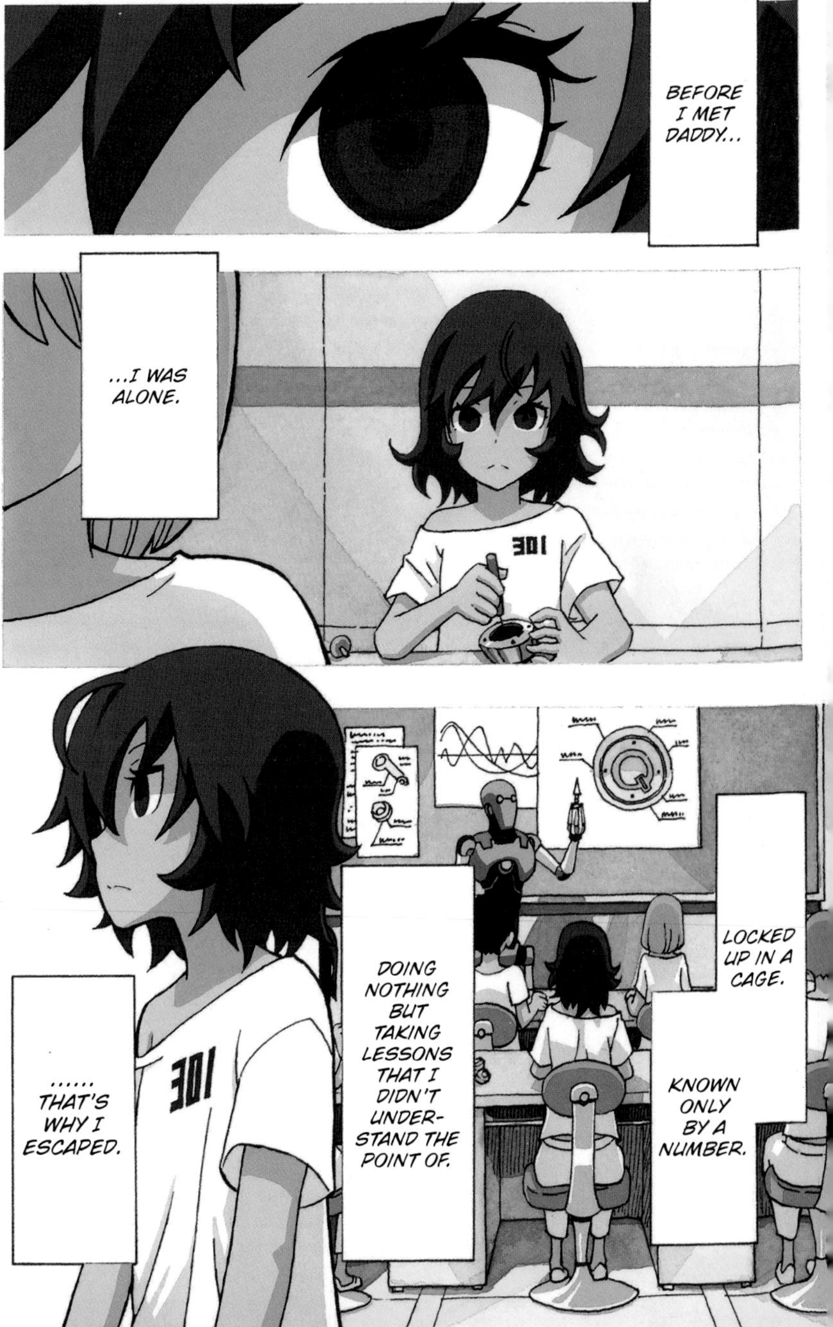
BEFORE I MET DADDY...
...I WAS ALONE.
LOCKED UP IN A CAGE.
KNOWN ONLY BY A NUMBER.
DOING NOTHING BUT TAKING LESSONS THAT I DIDN'T UNDER-STAND THE POINT OF.
...... THAT'S WHY I ESCAPED.

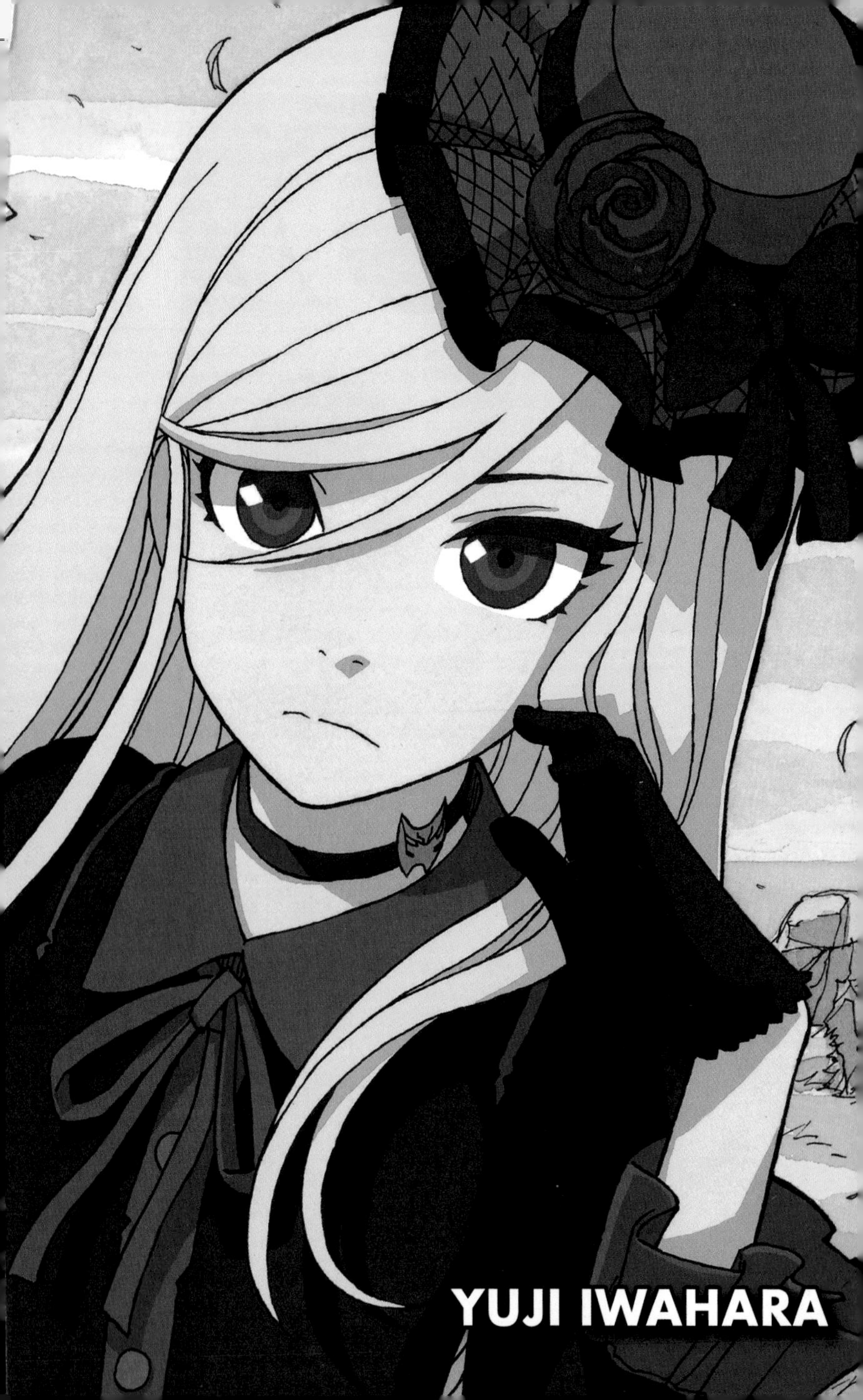
YUJI IWAHARA